YELTSIN'S RUSSIA

Myths and Reality

Lilia Shevtsova

CARNEGIE ENDOWMENT FOR INTERNATIONAL PEACE
WASHINGTON, D.C.

© 1999 by the
Carnegie Endowment for International Peace
1779 Massachusetts Avenue, N.W.
Washington, D.C. 20036
Tel. (202) 483-7600
Fax. (202) 483-1840

Yeltsin's Russia: Myths and Reality
($44.95, cloth, ISBN 0-87003-094-9;
$19.95, paper, ISBN 0-87003-127-9)
may be ordered from Carnegie's distributor:
The Brookings Institution Press
Department 029, Washington, D.C. 20042-0029, USA
Tel: 1-800-275-1447 or 202-797-6258
Fax: 202-797-6004, E-mail: bibooks@brook.edu

Design by Paddy McLaughlin Concepts & Design.
Cover photo: David Burnett/Contact Press Images/PNI.
Printed by Automated Graphic Systems.

Library of Congress Cataloging-in-Publication Data

Shevtsova, Liliia Federovna, 1951–
    Yeltsin's Russia : myths and reality / Lilia Shevtsova.
    p. cm.
"Carnegie Endowment book."
Includes bibliographical references.
ISBN 0-87003-094-9 (cloth)
ISBN 0-87002-127-9 (pbk.)
1. Russia (Federation) — Politics and government — 1991 — I. Title.
DK510.763 .S495 1998
947.086 — dc21   98-49034
                                                                 CIP

Second printing, March 2000

To my parents, Maria and Fyodor

CONTENTS

FOREWORD

No post-cold war leader has played a more central role in shaping the destiny of his country than Boris Yeltsin. This was true during his rise to power as Russia's first elected president and, perversely, during his slow and painful decline into physical debility and political impotence after 1996.

Yeltsin's stubborn refusal to step down from the powerful office he could no longer exercise effectively has since then been the dominant fact of Russian political life. The manner of his ultimate demise could largely shape how Russia's first postcommunist transfer of political power will be conducted.

Yeltsin was indisputably the most important actor in bringing Gorbachev's faltering *perestroika* to an end while heading off a communist restoration, effecting the essentially peaceful dissolution of the Soviet Union, creating Russia's present constitutional system, and launching Russia on the path of liberal economic reform. He was far more successful in dismantling the old system than he was in building a new one.

The Yeltsin era has ended in such monumental failure that the future both of its important positive accomplishments and of its largest mistakes are now in question. Today, the people of Russia, in overwhelming numbers, assess Yeltsin's legacy in sharply negative terms and Yeltsin personally even more harshly. As 1998 ended, 97 percent of Russians polled favored Yeltsin's immediate retirement and many supported efforts in the Russian State Duma to impeach him.

But, as Lilia Shevstova points out in this book, Yeltsin leaves behind as his legacy a Russia that is full of contradictions and paradoxes: a presidential political system akin to an elective monarchy; a market economy dominated by barter; and a gravely weakened state with great-power aspirations. Public opinion polls indicate that while the terms "democrat" and "reformer" now have strongly negative connotations for most Russians, those same Russians continue to remain attached to democratic values, including popular elections and free speech, and to the general principles of market economics (though not to the economic system that actually exists in Russia). Russia's future will depend heavily on how Yeltsin's successors sort out the contradictions and paradoxes of his legacy. The debate is only now beginning in Russia as the Yeltsin succession struggle moves into high gear.

In the West, the provisional verdict on Yeltsin and his legacy is different and less severe. Most regard him as having failed tragically in a noble cause that was derailed by the corruption of greedy oligarchs and the obstruction of a communist-dominated Duma. In this Western perspective, Yeltsin has much in common with his nemesis, Mikhail Gorbachev, who remains highly respected and even revered abroad, even as he is held in low regard at home. In the West, Yeltsin, like Gorbachev, will be best remembered for his role in bringing to an end the cold war, the East-West confrontation, communism, and the Soviet Union itself—Gorbachev more by inadvertence than by design, and Yeltsin more by impulse than by calculation.

Yeltsin's Russia is the first comprehensive account of the Yeltsin era in Russian politics to appear either in English or Russian. Its author, Lilia Shevtsova, is a senior associate in the Carnegie Endowment's Russian and Eurasian Affairs Program, dividing her time between the Endowment's Washington offices and its Carnegie Moscow Center. She is one of Russia's best known and most highly respected political writers and commentators, a master of "inside-the-Ring Road" political analysis, and a frequent participant in international conferences and seminars.

I know of no Russian analyst better able than Lilia Shevtsova to interpret Russian politics for Western readers in a way that makes the distinctive Russian character of those politics accessible without losing the uniquely Russian flavor of Moscow political discourse. The Carnegie Endowment is proud to have afforded Dr. Shevtsova the opportunity to produce this volume. The work of the Endowment's Russian and Eurasian Affairs Program is supported by grants from the Carnegie Corporation of New York, the Mott Foundation, and the Starr Foundation, whose support is gratefully acknowledged.

Arnold L. Horelick
Vice President for Russian and Eurasian Affairs

April 1999
Washington, D.C.

ACKNOWLEDGMENTS

This book would not have been possible without the encouragement, help, and cooperation of many people.

Without the interest and encouragement of the former president of the Carnegie Endowment for International Peace, Morton Abramowitz, and of the former vice president for Russian and Eurasian affairs, Stephen Sestanovich, I might never have undertaken this project. Carnegie vice president Paul Balaran also provided much-appreciated inspiration. I also thank Jessica Mathews, who, after assuming the presidency of the Endowment, offered key support to see my book through to the end.

Arnold Horelick, the Endowment's vice president for Russian and Eurasian affairs, deserves special mention for his contributions and support; he brought much-needed clarity and focus to my ideas and thinking, for which I am grateful.

For help in preparing the manuscript for publication in English, my gratitude goes to Gail Lapidus, Alexander Dallin, Blair Ruble, and Paul Goble, who were the first to read and recommend it for publication. Gail and Alex endured several versions of the manuscript, and their guidance and assistance are greatly appreciated. I also want to thank a number of other colleagues and friends whose input and insights were invaluable to my own thinking: Igor Klyamkin, Anders Åslund, Martha Brill Olcott, Sherman Garnett, Thomas Graham, George Kolt, and Fritz Ermarth. My colleague David Kramer also provided critical support and advice. And to Alan Rousso, director of the Carnegie Moscow Center, and to all my Carnegie colleagues in Moscow and Washington, I extend special thanks for their support and encouragement.

I am greatly indebted to Angela Stent and Daniel Yergin, dear friends and colleagues whose unwavering help during my stays in Washington made it possible for me to finish this project. My special thanks also to Robert Legvold, whose excellent grasp of Russian developments was a major source of inspiration for me.

I also wish to express my gratitude to my friends Martha and John Jones and to Larisa and Frantishek Silnicky, who urged me to produce a book from "my stories" about Russia that I shared with them.

A number of people played instrumental roles in the translating, editing, and rewriting of the manuscript. I especially wish to thank Judith Mandell, who tirelessly and professionally translated much of the book. Michael Kazmarek also provided excellent translating assistance. Teresa Lawson had the very difficult job of putting the book into readable and understandable English; her commitment and dedication to this project is truly appreciated. Deborah Styles expertly copy-edited the manuscript. Special thanks go to Valeriana Kallab for all her editorial contributions and seeing the manuscript through to publication. Thomas W. Skladony, who joined the Carnegie Endowment in the final stages of the project, also contributed valuable editorial suggestions.

I am indebted to Liz Reisch for coordinating the final stages of manuscript completion. I am also grateful to Natalia Udalova, Maria Sherzad, and Sherry Pettie for helping to prepare the manuscript for publication. Other Carnegie staff members who provided invaluable assistance include Stephanie Langenfeld, Denis Maslov, Anna Odintsova, and Rachel Lebenson.

Finally, I express my deepest gratitude to my family: my mother, my husband Igor, and my son Oleg, without all of whose patience and caring this book would not have been possible.

Lilia Shevtsova
Moscow, March 1999

YELTSIN'S RUSSIA

Omnium consensu capax imperii nisi imperasseat.
No one would have doubted his ability to reign
had he never been emperor.

—Tacitus, *Histories*, book I, chapter 1

INTRODUCTION

This book examines the main events of Boris Yeltsin's time in power as president of Russia from the collapse of the Soviet Union and the Communist Party in 1991 to the beginning of 1999, when Russia entered a turbulent election year suffering a severe economic crisis that threatened to undermine its major reform achievements. My aim in this book is not to offer definitive or final answers to the questions of where Russia is heading and what its future will look like. This would be impossible, and any attempt would only over-simplify the true picture. My goal, instead, is to show the contradictions in Russia's political development, the nature of the dramatic challenges facing the country, and some of the trends that will affect its future.

Post-communist Russia is a country of paradoxes. On the one hand, it is a model of endless movement. On the other, there is evidence all around of inertia and continuity. Although the scope and speed of change in Moscow are truly astonishing, little has changed beyond the city limits; the signs of decay deep in the country contrast sharply with the visible new amenities of Moscow. Russia resembles a patchwork quilt. Within the diversity of its social, political, and economic life, there are areas of dynamism and success, areas of crisis and collapse, and, increasingly, areas of stagnation.

Russia's political scene features unrestrained struggle and fierce, open skirmishes. The level of aggression in the confrontations often appears boundless. Constant conflicts—between the executive and the parliament, between the center and the regions, among the "oligarchs" or financial clans, and within the presidential entourage—create an atmosphere of perpetual tension. Those involved in these conflicts battle furiously with one another, but usually no one really wants to rock the boat. Moreover, all political actors watch the rest of Russian society with fear and apprehension that, if their clashes involve major social groups, events may spin out of control. Wages of Russian workers often go unpaid for months and even years, and discontent has become a constant factor in Russian life. The post-communist transformation has been much more painful than expected, and most of those who hoped for a better life feel that they have lost out and have no chance to succeed in the future.

Yet Russia has experienced no social uprisings, and stability has been astonishingly—although sometimes precariously—preserved. Moreover, the current political regime appears ever more entrenched in power, and no one poses a serious challenge to it, at least not in the near future. This calm is deceptive. It is in many ways the consequence of disillusionment, as well as of a perceived lack of alternatives. For the time being, people's efforts just to survive take precedence. Few believe that the most painful economic and social problems will be solved in their lifetimes. This hopelessness breeds frustration, despair, and violence.

How strong can a government be that is built on the disenchantment of the population? There is a group of people who consider themselves fortunate, but they account for only some 5-15 percent of the population. Moreover, most of these "winners" are also unhappy with the government, although for another reason—they fault it for its impotence and failure to guarantee their security. The current regime survives mainly because it is considered the lesser of evils. The question of how long Russia can preserve this "unstable stability" remains open. Who can guarantee that at some moment the desire for violent revenge will not overtake those who feel they have been betrayed? Russia has a long and tragic history of attempts to find justice, and history shows us how they ended.

Another paradox of post-communist Russia is the communist opposition. Despite years of anti-communist reforms, it is still the major organized political force in Russia. The Communist Party seems to have done everything it could to avoid coming to power. The communists are now much more comfortable in the role of the opposition, where they need not bear any real responsibility. Ironically, the communist opposition is the force that helps Yeltsin's regime stay in power. Through its influence over a significant fraction of the dissatisfied population, the Communist Party prevents those people from becoming more radicalized or engaging in open protest against the regime. Meanwhile, it presents a distasteful alternative to the current ruling elite, which helps the latter keep its hold on power.

An even more telling example of Russia's paradoxical nature is Yeltsin himself. With one foot in the grave, he was still able to win the

1996 presidential elections. In March 1997, just as everyone had again begun writing his political obituary, he made a sudden comeback and shook up the government. In March 1998, Yeltsin staged another "revolution," proving that it was still too early to write him off. In August 1998, he executed another "presidential coup," firing his new government. Again and again, the whole country follows Yeltsin's ups and downs. Russia dreads its leader, but it dreads the alternatives to Yeltsin even more.

With all his passions, emotions, and complexes, Yeltsin is the person who has most influenced Russia's development. He is a controversial personality. Many in the West see him as a democrat and reformer. It is true that he helped to bring down the communist system and that, at crucial moments, he has taken the side of reform and tried hard to continue a liberal course. But more often, he has behaved like a demagogue thinking mainly about his own survival. His worst mistake, both for Russia and for himself, has been his failure to establish strong political institutions and stable rules of the game. He has displayed little respect for the law. More often than not, he has obeyed only his sense of political expedience, apparently placing the highest priority on his own political ambitions. Many people, even in Russia, at first hoped that the "superpresidency" that Yeltsin established was only temporary. But this structure, designed to overcome deadlocks and to serve as a major reform force, has now become the main source of political disarray. Thus Russia is involved in a drama as its aging and failing patriarch constantly delays his political exit in the absence of a strong and predictable successor.

Seven years after his meteoric rise to prominence, however, Yeltsin still towers above all others. His leading political role is recognized by all of Russia's political forces. At the beginning of 1999, Yeltsin—in his retreat outside Moscow and seemingly weaker than ever before—still appeared able to influence the balance of forces, or at least defiantly to resist any attempt to force him out. The most crucial test he faces (whether or not he makes it to the end of his presidential term in 2000 or solves some of Russia's most pressing problems) is to guarantee a peaceful transition to the post-Yeltsin period. This task, however, is one that he may not be willing to undertake, and Russia has no structure, apart from Yeltsin and his superpresidency, to manage this transition.

This raises a troubling question: Why were Yeltsin and his team unable to use the opportunities that history gave them to build a solid base for a liberal democracy in Russia? Many of the government's mistakes, failures, and retreats could have been avoided, especially when Russia was first distancing itself from communism. At that time, society was willing to tolerate adversity and hardships, hoping for a better life. Now, however, the possibilities for further reform are slight. Many people are disillusioned with politics and politicians; clan-like ties have formed within the ruling class; the economy is collapsing; members of the ruling elite are busy increasing their own personal wealth; criminal groups have appeared on the scene; and the bureaucracy is demoralized.

One of the most painful issues explored in this book is the sorry fate of reformers in contemporary Russia. To their credit, the reformers were able to disassemble the old political and economic mechanisms and to clear the ground for new ones. But the price that Russia paid for this liberal transformation was disillusion with liberalism itself. The reformers are not national heroes in Russia, and to a great extent they have themselves to blame. They were insensitive to the social consequences of the sudden break with the past. They often displayed a lack of concern with the costs of their decisions, showing the same neglect and contempt for "the masses" as their communist predecessors. Not having considered it necessary to win the support of the public, they have become an isolated group and have increasingly lost power and influence to the conservatives, regional groups, and industrial lobbies that have proven to be more experienced fighters.

The future of Russia's transformation depends on whether its ruling class learns to temper its selfishness and to rectify its moral and political behavior. Is it prepared to make fresh efforts at reform? What will be the price of long-term stagnation and mass discontent? These questions have yet to be answered. Meanwhile Russian society is developing independently and spontaneously, often with disregard for the actions of its government. A new generation of politicians is gradually coming to the fore that will determine Russia's destiny and its development in the new millennium. May they learn from the painful failures of the past and be successful in their attempt to build a more democratic and prosperous Russia.

CHAPTER ONE

THE FAREWELL TO COMMUNISM AND THE FIRST REFORMS: 1989-92

THE NEW RUSSIA AND ITS POST-COMMUNIST REFORMS were immensely influenced not only by the collapse of the Soviet Union, but by the way it occurred. A brief discussion of these events will illuminate the problems and constraints of the first period of post-communist reforms in Russia and the complicated mixture of continuity and change that continues to influence Russia's development.

SOVIET COLLAPSE OR *NOMENKLATURA* REVOLUTION?

The tasks faced by the new Russian state after the Soviet Union collapsed were immeasurably more complex than those in any other post-communist country. The government needed to carry out market reform, continue democratization, overcome a national identity crisis, contend with leftover imperial and messianic attitudes, and define a new role in the post-Soviet space. The most difficult and traumatic problem, however, was that of state building. Even the reformers headed by Russia's first president, Boris Yeltsin, did not anticipate the magnitude and difficulty of the problems they would confront.

When Mikhail Gorbachev came to power, the Soviet system was no longer totalitarian. Indeed, by the mid-1980s this system could have been called a decaying "post-totalitarian" state.[1] The unraveling of a genuinely totalitarian state would have been much more painful and bloody than the dissolution that actually occurred. By 1985, however, Soviet institutions no longer had full control over the lives of ordinary citizens. Observance of communist dogma gradually became little more than symbolic—few people cared about it in any but the most formal and superficial way. A sense of cynicism and pragmatism had begun to dominate the higher echelons of the Soviet political elite. Paying lip service to the ideals of communism while living by a different set of values had, by the mid-1980s, become characteristic of Soviet society, including the Communist Party and its leadership. Underneath the communist lid, a diversity of views had begun to evolve, and, behind the rigid, formal structure, a new, more controversial, and complex reality was slowly emerging. A "shadow economy" or "gray economy" had begun to develop, undercutting the planned economy. Power was slowly diffusing toward the periphery, where the elites in the constituent republics consolidated their hold on it. The old bonds that had kept Soviet society in line, primarily violence and terror, were virtually disappearing. The very weakness of the communist leaders of this period—Leonid Brezhnev, Konstantin Chernenko, Yuri Andropov—helped liberate society from the old fears. The most important developments were taking place within the *nomenklatura* itself, where dissatisfaction with the old regime and its doctrinal harshness was growing. At least part of the establishment was ready for a radical change in the system—eager to become the real owners of the communal property and to get rid of the formal constraints on personal enrichment.

The existence of this shadow political culture accounts for the unbelievable burst of political activity in the late Gorbachev years—the explosion of liberal ideas, the emergence of numerous small parties and movements, and Russian society's ability to adapt so quickly to political freedom. Political hypocrisy had become, in T. H. Rigby's words, "a time-bomb" that accelerated the last stage of communism's decay.[2] For decades democratic rhetoric in the Soviet Union had served as a cover for an authoritarian reality; while it led to double standards in mentality and behavior, it also led people gradually to become accustomed to democratic values. When the moment came, they were ready. "Without democratic rhetoric and pseudo-democratic structures, the processes of the rapid transition to democracy in the USSR and Eastern Europe could scarcely have happened," wrote Rigby.[3] The Soviet Union's particular type of federation was itself a source of conflict and disintegration; it was inevitable that republics, mere imaginary states, would push for autonomy or independence when circumstances were favorable.[4] The inefficiency, technological backwardness, and "bureaucratism" of the communist system also affected the end of the Soviet Union—although these factors alone could not have brought down the entire state so rapidly. Gorbachev acknowledged that he could have presided over this decay for a long time had he played by the old rules of the game.

One of the sparks that ignited the fire leading to the system's implosion was, of course, Gorbachev himself. There is no doubt that with *perestroika*, the Soviet president weakened the communist regime and galvanized the forces of disintegration. However, having loosened the old links that bound society together, especially the Communist Party, Gorbachev could not, would not, or simply did not have time to develop a new consolidating mechanism. It was impossible to hold together the amalgam of cultural, national, and territorial entities that constituted the Soviet Union without a rigid structure or violence and without an effective mechanism for the redistribution of resources.

Yet Gorbachev's actions alone would not have been decisive had they not reflected the interests of powerful social groups and reinforced existing social tendencies. Gorbachev's restructuring policies reflected the interests of a younger and more dynamic generation of Soviet bureaucrats, especially those in the republics and the regions, who wanted to throw off the yoke of the Brezhnev-style gerontocracy that had lingered on in Moscow. This dynamic segment of the *nomenklatura*— the pragmatists—would eventually gravitate to Yeltsin after becoming disappointed with Gorbachev's indecisiveness, lack of vision, and pathetic attempts to preserve his own role, which the pragmatists considered an obstacle to their own long-awaited ascendance. Gorbachev's "socialism with a human face" failed to inspire the pragmatic part of his own political class; this group was ready to go farther and faster toward real capitalism, and it did not cling to the collectivist and socialist principles that Gorbachev still advocated.

The first victors in the great collapse were the Soviet pragmatists, who managed to throw off the fetters that bound them, to create a new political regime, and to preserve a dominant place in it for themselves. The first to fall were the old orthodox communists within the *nomenklatura*, who failed to understand or adapt to the new trends and tried instead to preserve a multinational state. Those who had become too accustomed to depending on the state's help or for various reasons could not adapt to the atmosphere of freedom would also be losers. Ironically, those who initiated the entire reform process, led by Gorbachev himself, would be among the first to fall.

The exit of Soviet communism from the political arena was a drawn-out process that began long before Gorbachev. This process contained elements of adaptation, modification, destruction, revolution, reform, and counterreform. In some areas it was characterized more by destruction; in others, by accommodation or even by a return to the pre-Soviet past (as in some of the former republics in Central Asia). In Russia, the habits and political stereotypes of both the establishment and the Russian population to this day retain many socialist, communist, and even pre-Soviet beliefs and traditions. How the old interconnects with the new is a crucial and recurring issue in Russia's post-communist transformation.

EVENTS THAT DETERMINED THE END
OF THE SOVIET UNION

The most important development influencing the outcome of Gorbachev's *perestroika* and its effects on the new Russian state was the weakening of the Communist Party. The most direct challenge to the Party's leadership came from electoral reform.[5] For the first time in Soviet history, deputies were chosen by popular mandate. In the 1989-90 elections to the new republican legislatures, many senior party officials were defeated at the ballot box. For a party whose power resulted in a guaranteed monopoly, it was the beginning of the end.

Gorbachev, afraid of losing control over events, tried to restore a pivotal element of state authority by introducing the institution of the presidency on March 15, 1990. This came too late in the game, however; it could not halt the defection of the republics, where the consolidation of a new national political class was well under way. Moreover, an attempt to construct a viable presidency without the support of a strong party, of society, or even of the state bureaucracy was doomed to produce only a powerless institution.

The 1990 elections to the new legislatures in the republics provided a strong stimulus to the formation of new ethnic political elites and gave them legitimacy. The newly elected elites, even those that included representatives of the communist establishment, were perceived as nationalist and even as democratic. This fact was a severe blow to the prestige of the all-Union authorities and Gorbachev himself, who lacked the same legitimacy and were unwilling to take the risk of holding a general election: Gorbachev, after all, had been elected president in March 1990 not by the people, but only by the Congress of People's Deputies of the USSR.

Other events accelerated the disintegration. In 1989 the Baltic republics' declarations of independence had served as a powerful example to other republics. Even so, the Union might have continued to exist indefinitely in a stagnant form. A more serious blow was the falling-out between the leaders in the Ukrainian capital of Kiev and the central authorities in Moscow. Without the Baltics and Ukraine, the Soviet Union would no longer be predominantly Slavic but would increasingly have an Asian face.

The fault line between Kiev and Gorbachev's all-Union center had begun to widen after the unprecedented emergence of a political class in Russia itself. This group, united around Boris Yeltsin, acquired considerable legitimacy and support through the process of democratic elections and because it had a genuinely charismatic leader. On June 12, 1990, the new Russian parliament issued a "Declaration of Russia's Sovereignty." The First Congress of People's Deputies of the Russian Federation asserted Russia's "complete authority . . . over all questions relating to state and public life with the exception of those which it voluntarily hands over to USSR jurisdiction."[6] This declaration and the introduction of the Russian presidency on June 1991 clearly dissociated the Russian state from the Soviet Union and stimulated the sovereign aspirations of other Union republics.

The views of the Russian reformers were ambivalent and varied on the issue of the future of the Soviet Union. At first they supported national movements that were trying to form a Union-wide reformist coalition. When it became clear that their partners wanted independence rather than reform, their attitude toward national self-determination began to change. Russian reformers were concerned that this might be directed not only against the USSR but against Russia itself, undermining Russia's territorial integrity as much as that of the USSR.[7]

The rise of Boris Yeltsin as a political personality symbolized the changes taking place in Soviet society. Yeltsin had come to prominence under the communist system and was a part of the old ruling class. Under Gorbachev, he had become the very personification of the anti-establishment forces. Gorbachev himself had pushed his former competitor out of the circle of power, thus turning Yeltsin into an opposition leader. In February 1988 Yeltsin was ousted from the Politburo. In December 1988 he joined the democratic opposition. In March 1989 he was elected a deputy to the new Soviet legislature, the Congress of People's Deputies of the Soviet Union, where he joined the democratic

9

Interregional Group (150 deputies), becoming one of its co-chairmen (with Andrei Sakharov, Gavriil Popov, Victor Palm, and Yuri Afanasyev). In May 1990 he became chairman of the newly elected Russian legislature, the Supreme Soviet of the Russian Federation, and in June 1991 he was elected president of the Russian Federation. Yeltsin's combination of Communist Party background and opposition stance enabled him to achieve what no dissident, even one as influential as Andrei Sakharov, had managed. The fusion of the energies of the democratic movement with the ambitions of the Russian republic elite and the charisma of Yeltsin had a devastating result for the old Soviet center.

Yeltsin, buoyed by the support of an array of social and political groups weary of Gorbachev, began to attack the Soviet president. *"Perestroika's* global strategy had run smack into its inability to make practical reforms, that is, break things down and build them up anew," Yeltsin later wrote. "Gorbachev's reliance on moral leadership and liberal ideologists had not panned out. Despite his expectations, the magic wand didn't work. The system simply would not change, just like that, for the sake of its health."[8] In February 1991 he publicly demanded that Gorbachev resign. Gorbachev's cohorts tried to silence Yeltsin, who responded, as he later said, "You're afraid of Yeltsin? Well, then, you'll get that very Yeltsin you fear!"[9]

Gorbachev had to choose sides, and this was not an easy thing to do. Proceeding with further reforms and liberalization would mean devolution of his own power to the republics and further disintegration of the Soviet Union; for Gorbachev, this was unacceptable. However, attempting to preserve the Soviet Union meant reversing the democratic process and siding with the orthodox communists, which was also unacceptable. Gorbachev could not maneuver endlessly between these choices, and both sides were relentlessly attacking him. The democrats criticized him for his indecisiveness, while the hard-liners accused him of betrayal.

Late in the spring of 1991, therefore, Gorbachev proposed a new Union treaty to be signed by all of the Soviet republics. The arrangement would give the republics unprecedented independence while at the same time preserving the coordinating all-Union bodies. He convened the heads of the republics at a government dacha at Novo-Ogaryovo, outside Moscow, in negotiations that became known as the Novo-Ogaryovo process. The initiative met with a surprisingly positive response from nearly all of the leaders (except those in the Baltics). Even Yeltsin, grudgingly, signed the agreement reached there.

In June and July 1991, Yeltsin's relations with Gorbachev briefly became easier. "Gorbachev and I felt unmistakably that our interests finally coincided," wrote Yeltsin. "Gorbachev preserved his seniority and I preserved my independence. It was an ideal settlement for both of us. We began to meet at length unofficially. Sometimes [Kazakstan's president] Nursultan Nazarbayev also took part in these confidential meetings."[10] The three leaders agreed that, under the new Union treaty, Gorbachev would take the role of mediator as chairman of the coordinating body, Yeltsin would have absolute independence as the leader of the most powerful republic, and Nazarbayev would become prime minister of the new Union.

The signing of the new Union treaty was scheduled for August 20, immediately after Gorbachev's return from his vacation at Foros in Crimea. As Yeltsin wrote, "Much would have been different if what we agreed upon as a threesome could have been put into effect. History would have taken a different course altogether."[11] He said, "I now look back on these meetings without embarrassment and even with regret. What an opportunity was lost! Perhaps it would have been independence for the republics only on paper, not in reality, and Russia's clash with the central Soviet government would have been inevitable in any event. [But] our departure from the USSR would have been far more peaceful and less painful" if the Union treaty had been implemented.[12]

However, as Aristotle said, "Revolutions are not about trifles, but they spring from trifles."[13] During their discussions, the three leaders had decided that Gorbachev's entourage would be replaced after the treaty was signed. Tapes of these conversations, later found in the possession of some of Gorbachev's cohorts, may well have triggered the events of August 1991 that rendered the Novo-Ogaryovo agreements moot.

On August 19, 1991, a group of orthodox communist members of Gorbachev's circle attempted to save the Soviet Union by introducing a state of emergency.[14] Immediately after the failure of the coup, during a session of the Russian parliament on August 23, Yeltsin signed a decree dissolving the Communist Party of the Soviet Union. One may ask how a representative of Russia alone could claim to dissolve the Party for the entire Soviet Union; during this period, legal means seemed inadequate and revolutionary instruments necessary to dismantle the old structures. Unfortunately, Yeltsin seemed quickly to become accustomed to this revolutionary style of rule. On the next day Yeltsin recognized the independence of the three Baltic states, and Ukraine's Supreme Soviet adopted a declaration of independence. The events of August 1991 were the final, crushing blow to the Soviet Union.

The August coup changed relations between Gorbachev and Yeltsin radically, leaving Yeltsin the principal winner. "From August 1991 until the moment of Gorbachev's resignation in December of that year, we had approximately eight meetings," wrote Yeltsin. "I don't know if Gorbachev realized how changed our relations were by then. I had told him that the coup had taught us a bitter lesson, and therefore I had to insist that he not make any personnel decisions without first obtaining my consent. He looked at me intently, with the expression of a person backed into a corner, but I had no other alternative. Everything depended on my taking a position of brutal consistency."[15]

Gorbachev seemed not to understand at first that the failed coup had changed everything. He attempted to proceed with the Union treaty, making concessions that would have been unthinkable before August. He conceded that the future Union could become a confederation of independent states. But in the republics, the ruling elites no longer needed coordinating structures; they reacted immediately with declarations of independence, scheduling their own presidential elections. They all dreamed of elevating their status and joining the United Nations. This was the end of the Novo-Ogaryovo process; nobody wanted to sign a Union treaty.

THE LAST DAYS OF THE USSR

I n a December 1 referendum in Ukraine, people voted nearly unanimously for independence. The painful and protracted process of divorce ended on December 8, 1991, when the heads of the three Slavic republics met at Belovezhskiy Forest, outside Minsk. Boris Yeltsin of Russia, Leonid Kravchuk of Ukraine, and Stanislav Shushkevich of Belarus signed an agreement announcing the end of the USSR and the creation of the Commonwealth of Independent States (CIS).[16] The initiators of the meeting tried to make it absolutely secret; no one was thinking about how to make it more legitimate. Discussing a referendum to approve the dissolution of the USSR was not even on the agenda.

According to Yeltsin, "The Belovezhskiy agreement was necessary to stop centrifugal trends and to stimulate the negotiating process."[17] Yeltsin, fearing the destabilizing consequences of the complete collapse of the Soviet Union, might still have hoped to resurrect Gorbachev's Union treaty, but under his own leadership and with a decisive role for Russia. Yeltsin said after signing the Belovezhskiy agreement, "Cultural, social, economic, and political integration will sooner or later do their work, but these regions will remain in a zone of common cooperation."[18] Yet at the moment of the Belovezhskiy agreement, it is highly unlikely that Yeltsin was really thinking about how to achieve this. Instead, he threw himself in without analyzing the implications. "Perhaps I did not completely fathom the prospects opening up before me, but I felt in my heart that such major decisions must be taken easily," he said about his conduct at Belovezhskiy Forest, and this style of behavior became his trademark.[19] Yeltsin's plan to arrest the centrifugal forces was a complete failure. The way the USSR was liquidated aroused bitter feelings toward and suspicion of the Slavic leaders in the other republics; it was also a shock for many democrats, who were afraid, not unreasonably, that the independence issue would hinder democratic and market reforms.

But the deal was done, and soon afterward the other republics (with the exception of the Baltic republics and Georgia) joined the club. Thus the CIS was formed with eleven independent states on December 21, 1991, in Alma-Aty. The CIS failed, however, to become the model for integration that some of its architects, particularly Yeltsin, had hoped. It helped to manage a more or less civilized split-up of the former Soviet republics, which meant that it did have some positive effects, but in the end it became a club for the presidents of former Soviet republics—a harmless and not very efficient forum.

Communism had undoubtedly prolonged the survival of the empire after the liquidation of czarism. After communism itself had been weakened, the dissolution of the state became a matter of time. However, as Alexander Dallin has pointed out, the collapse of the USSR in 1991 and the form that it took were not inevitable: "Had Gorbachev and his associates not come to power, the Soviet Union would have hobbled along, and might have continued to muddle through without overt instability. It is the only possible conclusion. If we reach that conclusion, based on those premises, then we must give serious weight to the proposition that the much-touted 'collapse of communism' was perhaps not nearly so inevitable and surely not necessarily so imminent as it has been made out to be."[20]

The collapse of the Soviet Union and the manner in which the state disintegrated influenced the further transformation in all of the post-Soviet republics. The fact of the collapse itself made state building a first priority, which complicated democratization and market reforms and in some republics pushed these matters entirely off the agenda. Other goals became dominant instead: securing independence, strengthening the personal rule of those leaders who remained in power, and creating paternalistic networks as a substitute for the old structures. Ethno-nationalism became a more useful ideology of consolidation than democratic values. The way in which the Soviet Union was liquidated—through the decisions of a few people who were not concerned about the legality of their actions—strengthened anti-democratic trends in post-communist Russia. The anti-Soviet coup gave a start to several leaders who succeeded in ousting Gorbachev, but it also forced them to secure their own positions through personal networks and reliance on loyal people. Their success in these endeavors encouraged them to continue to demonstrate disrespect for institutions and rules in their future activities.

The absence of democratic mechanisms in the process of Soviet disintegration helped the former elites to preserve their power. Independence became their main slogan, their weapon, and their instrument of domination. In some cases the tactics of the rivals, starting with Gorbachev and Yeltsin, created the seeds of future conflicts that still influence Russia; this is especially true of their attempts to gain the support of the autonomous republics by elevating the latter's status. No less important was the character of the elite groups that dominated after the Soviet disintegration. More than in most other post-communist states, power in Russia was taken over by a pragmatic segment of the *nomenklatura* whose main goal was simply to grab property. This influenced the process of privatization and the interaction of power and business. In contrast to the elites of the other former Soviet republics, however, the Russian elite demonstrated some tolerance for some democratic procedures.

Finally, the way the dismemberment of the Union had come about caused bitterness and sowed the seeds of future tension and frustration. Most of the population was unprepared for this chain of events. Victory over the "evil empire" ended one of the most dramatic social experiments of this century, but this event was perceived as a tragic development by a huge number of ordinary citizens. The collapse unexpectedly deprived them of their state, their history, their past, and their roots. Life in the new post-Soviet states began, for many people, under a cloud of apprehension and resentment. The price of the dissolution of the Soviet Union was high, and those who closed the Soviet chapter took no time to look for less traumatic and more democratic ways to bring it about.

In Russia, the collapse of the USSR confirmed Yeltsin's primacy on the political scene. The moods of the leader came to mean more than the activities of institutions. From that point on, the style and habits of one person and of those personally connected to him began to shape the formation of the new state.

"THE CADRES DECIDE EVERYTHING"

The new Russian elite—Yeltsin's team and its supporters—had begun to coalesce after the March 1990 election of the first independent Russian parliament, the Congress of People's Deputies. The period preceding the August 1991 putsch had, however, been a confusing and frustrating time for them as they searched for a path to real power. Although Yeltsin won the presidency of the Russian Federation in a popular election in June 1991, the office had been largely ceremonial during Gorbachev's struggle to hold on to the reins of power. The August coup that dealt the fatal blow to Gorbachev and the Union structures was an unexpected gift to Russia's new ruling group: power simply fell into its lap.

Yeltsin first moved to strengthen his political base. He had climbed to the top thanks to his popularity and especially as a result of the support of three major groups: those in the second echelon of the Union bureaucracy who were dissatisfied with Gorbachev; the rank and file of a still powerless Russian political class who hoped for promotion; and, last but not least, the democratic movement.[21] Democratic Russia (DemRossiya), the most influential of the democratic groupings, played a significant role in Yeltsin's political career, at least before August 1991. Its leaders, including such politicians as Lev Ponomaryov, Gavriil Popov, Gleb Yakunin, and Yuri Afanasyev, had helped Yeltsin in his struggle to become leader of the Supreme Soviet of the Russian Federation in

May 1990. DemRossiya had supported him during his June 1991 campaign for election as president of the Russian Federation. During the coup attempt, democrats had rallied Muscovites to come to the aid of the White House in which the Russian government was housed. After August 1991, however, the destinies of both Gorbachev and Yeltsin were decided not in rallies on the city's squares, where democrats were still strong, but behind the scenes, in negotiations among the Russian president's team, the pragmatists from the all-Union institutions, and representatives of the army and other power structures.

After Yeltsin's August victory, the pragmatists from the all-Union structures abandoned Gorbachev and switched their support to Yeltsin, considerably strengthening his position. High-ranking military officials, including Marshal Yevgeny Shaposhnikov and General Pavel Grachev, had already taken Yeltsin's side during the August coup. Some other representatives of Gorbachev's elite, among them the chairman of the All-Russian Union of Industrialists and Entrepreneurs, Arkady Volsky, also backed Yeltsin, although Volsky was among the few who were able to preserve good relations with Gorbachev as well. Yet it appears that the pragmatists decided to support Yeltsin only after receiving his firm assurances that DemRossiya would never get any real power.

Yeltsin's conduct after the August coup surprised and even shocked the democratic supporters who had organized his victory on the streets. It appeared that the president had suddenly forgotten them. A few democrats such as Galina Starovoitova and Sergei Stankevich remained with Yeltsin, but this did not mean much; they were not admitted into the inner circle of the ruling group. Moreover, it became clear that Yeltsin was not inclined to rely on just one political group to support his quest for domination. He undertook the painstaking task of surrounding himself with several groups of persons with different orientations, all competing for influence. Turning his back on popular political movements, Yeltsin began to rely on shadow groups and to introduce behind-the-scenes decision making, which gave enormous power to his team.

In the autumn of 1991 Yeltsin found influential places in the inner circle for some old allies who had proven their loyalty to him during the difficult period when he was out of power. Yeltsin was not interested in their political convictions. He knew how to reward loyalty, and as long as his people did not show excessive ambition and did not try to steal the limelight from him, he never cast them off without rewards.

16

Yeltsin's first team included mainly associates from his days in Sverdlovsk, where he had been the regional party secretary, and those who had orchestrated his victory in the June 1991 electoral campaign for the presidency of the Russian Federation. Members of the Sverdlovsk group who now took senior positions in Yeltsin's entourage included Gennady Burbulis, then known as a democrat but later a supporter of the superpresidential power structure Yeltsin created; pragmatist and former *apparatchik* Viktor Ilyushin; and Oleg Lobov, a conservative representative of the communist *nomenklatura*.

Yeltsin would subsequently add to this group several of his Moscow supporters. Some individuals would drop out and others would be added, but some elements of the Sverdlovsk group would remain part of Yeltsin's inner circle until 1996. The new officials, however, were not always the most effective and professional. It was popular in Moscow then to quote a character in one of George Bernard Shaw's plays: "He knows nothing; and he thinks he knows everything. That points clearly to a political career."[22] Yeltsin's former press secretary, Vyacheslav Kostikov, has recalled, "People who came with Yeltsin to the Kremlin, especially those from Sverdlovsk, understood that they could not win in the intellectual and professional competition with the Gorbachev team. This was one of the reasons for their sharp, even pathological rejection of Gorbachev's associates."[23]

The rise to power of a regional elite was not a novelty in Moscow's political life; under the Soviet regime, powerful regional bosses had always played an important part in the struggle for power at the top. But with Yeltsin's ascent to power, the provincial factor in Russian politics became even more marked. Toward the end of 1991 Yeltsin's entourage comprised not only representatives of the Sverdlovsk and Moscow regional groups but also proponents of various political orientations: radical democrats, liberals, populists, and neoconservatives, as well as bureaucrats typical of the old regime. Yeltsin chose bureaucrat Ivan Silyaev as Russia's prime minister. Andrei Kozyrev, who had not been notable in any political camp, became foreign minister; and one of Yeltsin's close associates, Oleg Lobov, who was well known for his anti-liberal bias, occupied various influential governmental posts. DemRossiya members such as Sergei Stankevich and Galina Starovoitova received advisory positions without real power. Those closest to Yeltsin at the beginning were (with the exception of Burbulis) rather conservative. Therefore, the conclusion that "the democrats came to power in Russia"

17

was a great exaggeration. The Soviet Union had ceased to exist, but a substantial portion of its ruling class, including some former members of its highest echelon, found comfortable places in the new governing institutions.[24]

There were, of course, some changes in the structure and composition of the ruling class. Stratification increased during the stormy events of 1991. Some parts of the old *nomenklatura* suffered defeat and lost control of the administrative and military resources of the state. Their places were taken by more pragmatic people who did not want to endure the lengthy climb to the top typical of Soviet practice and did not care about ideological principles or about what means were necessary to achieve their goals. Thus a regrouping of the communist *nomenklatura* occurred: leadership positions were taken over by energetic representatives of its second generation, who desired to acquire the benefits of access to power and control over state property and changed their ideological positions as frequently as the situation required. But how could it have been otherwise in a country without a counter-elite? There was no one to replace the old elites.

The mix of people around Yeltsin, while disordered, spontaneous, and sometimes altered without rhyme or reason, nevertheless had an internal logic to it. It grew out of Yeltsin's efforts to rely on his trusted old friends regardless of their political orientation and to surround himself with several competing groups. That gave him room to maneuver when he had to make decisions and also when it was necessary to secure his own position. Pluralism at the top impeded the potential consolidation of the bureaucracy as a counterweight to Yeltsin and gave the president a variety of potential scapegoats in case things went badly. Even more important, having representatives of various political persuasions around him enabled the president to appeal to all, or practically all, political forces in the country. It made Yeltsin's political direction unpredictable and often chaotic, however, and internal squabbles at the top were inevitable. Moreover, the fact that Yeltsin rejected the idea of forming his own political party made him more dependent on his entourage and made his politics more byzantine.

Fortunately, none of the emerging groups was able to secure a monopoly on power. For the first time in a long while, the basis of the Russian regime became interest-group pluralism. At first, two apparent centers of gravity formed around Yeltsin: the State Council, an advisory body that in late 1991 was more powerful than the cabinet and was led by Gennady Burbulis, who represented the democratic camp; and the presidential administration (Yeltsin's staff) under the direction of Yuri Petrov, a conservative bureaucrat, former Soviet ambassador to Cuba, and companion from Yeltsin's Sverdlovsk days.

This conglomeration of representatives of different political orientations meant that the presidency inevitably would be the focus of a struggle for influence. Antagonisms first arose between and among individuals, beginning with Burbulis and Petrov, but rapidly evolved into struggles among agencies, factions, individual parties and groups, and institutions. Fragmentation was inevitable within such a heterogeneous group, whose members had little in common. One of the issues that divided the Russian ruling group was the fate of the Union; some favored reforming it, while others argued for its complete dissolution. Those who advocated the preservation of the Union were soon squeezed out of the ruling inner circle. The struggle over the future course of Russia's reforms was not necessarily bad; it showed the existence of a plurality of views, which was a refreshing step forward after so many years of forced Soviet unanimity. However, problems appeared when, at crucial moments of the transformation, the new ruling group was unable to chart a consistent course.

The lack of unity in the government was also due to Yeltsin's inability—and even lack of desire—to forge a cohesive team and to create a sense of mutual obligation and responsibility among the team's individual members. The president himself fostered an atmosphere of competitiveness among his associates. He encouraged mutual antagonism and played the role of judge and conciliator with apparent relish. Yeltsin brought with him to the highest office in the new Russia the mores prevalent in the old *nomenklatura* circles, which had been a formative part of his own political upbringing. There was a crucial difference, however: Yeltsin destroyed the practice of formal unanimity that had existed within the communist establishment and replaced it with the principle of strict personal loyalty to the boss, Yeltsin himself.

YELTSIN CREATES HIS OWN "PYRAMID OF POWER"

The prevailing political mentality of the early period of Russia's new statehood was still, not surprisingly, derived to a large degree from the Soviet past. The assets of the new Russian team did not include skill at debate and dialogue, respect for differing opinions, or self-restraint. One could expect this from those who came to Yeltsin's side from the old Soviet apparatus, but the intellectuals, such as Burbulis, Ruslan Khasbulatov, and Sergei Shakhrai, behaved the same way. The new generation of Russian political actors brought to political life not only dynamism but also a disdain for compromise, and in this they resembled Yeltsin himself.

Divisions among the victorious new ruling group intensified as early as the fall of 1991. Petty struggles among Yeltsin's allies began to distract them from setting priorities and developing a strategy for Russia's economic and political future. As the rivalries among personalities grew into a struggle among different branches of government, some of Yeltsin's supporters began to voice skepticism about him and his team. The intelligentsia was the first to do so, but doubts soon spread to more strata of society. Even the newspaper *Izvestiya*, which was then extremely loyal to Yeltsin, wrote: "Everyone was sure that immediately after the democrats' accession to power there would be a change in the economy. But that did not happen. . . . Currently, everyone is angry about the indifference of the democrats, who are concerned principally with intrigues and the division of Party property. The former all-Union center no longer matters. The democrats no longer have any opponents, which is part of the tragedy. As soon as their opponents disappeared, so did their excuse for helplessness in managing the reform process."[25]

Meanwhile, the Russian economy deteriorated, and the approach of winter threatened desperate problems. After the initial euphoria at the victory over the coup plotters in August 1991, a sense that Russia was at an impasse began to dominate. Now, as the all-Union center lost its power, the infighting within the victors' camp inspired only growing disappointment. The Russian group was running out of time to determine its course and to consolidate its hold on power.

Yeltsin's choice of near-term goals was shaped by the deepening economic crisis and even more by the desire of the new Russian leadership to get rid of the Soviet Union once and for all. By October 1991 the leaders had already resolved to move ahead with Russian independence. This course could have followed several possible paths. It could have involved simultaneous market and political reforms, with an emphasis on the creation of a new, democratic organization of power in Russia—including the holding of elections, the adoption of a new constitution, and the creation of a system of checks and balances. Alternatively, priority could have been given to a new democratic political system, followed by market transformation. A third possibility was eco nomic reform and the redistribution of power in favor of the executive branch. This was the path that Yeltsin chose, rejecting building a system of checks and balances or further democratization. His economic goal was to create a market structure in one bold leap, through the application of fiscal shock therapy. In the political sphere, Yeltsin chose to set up his presidential pyramid (or "presidential vertical," as his advisers called the construct), which meant strong executive power supported by presidential appointments of loyal supporters to leading positions at all levels and rule by presidential decree. This superpresidency did not need any other strong institutions.[26] In fact, it was a new version of the old Soviet transmission belt.

Yeltsin's choice resulted from several circumstances. Despite the fact that he and his team had long thought about squeezing out Gorbachev at the decisive moment, they lacked a definite plan for broad overhaul of the existing system. Moreover, they believed that strong executive power would be the most effective policy tool, especially if Yeltsin's decrees were implemented by his faithful supporters. The emphasis on political leadership rather than on structures and rules and the personification of politics also reflected deep traditions in Russian political life. During the last stage of the Soviet period, attempts had been made to preserve at least an illusion of collectiveness, but Yeltsin did not want any restrictions and limitations on his power.

The choice of fiscal shock therapy was also a result of the economic determinism of Russia's politicians; this was based on a traditional Marxist understanding of social development, according to which economic relations, or the base, determined the evolution of a political system, or the superstructure. There is a certain irony in the fact that Russia's first post-communist political elite tried to get rid of the communist system by following a Marxist formula. The deepening economic crisis also pushed them to tackle the economic tasks first.

The new ruling group believed that any counterweight to its authority would only impede reforms and that all power should be held in one fist. It was not just the conservatives in Yeltsin's entourage (including former *apparatchiki*) who opposed creating strong political institutions and implementing the rule of law. The majority of liberals and even those who considered themselves democrats and who still had some influence with the president also supported the new pyramid of power. This apparently stemmed not only from their belief in the unlimited possibilities of the leadership, but also from uncertainty over the outcome of the democratic process, as well as from a fear of losing the power they had miraculously acquired. Thus they lost the chance to reinforce the legitimacy of the new political structures by adopting a new constitution and holding direct elections, and thereby to establish new, non-Soviet rules of the game at a time when most of society still supported Yeltsin's team and democratic evolution. As Juan Linz and Alfred Stepan have concluded, "Yeltsin's choice to privilege economic restructuring over democratic state restructuring weakened the state, weakened democracy, and weakened the economy."[27]

Thus in the fall of 1991 the Russian political system was a mix that included the presidency and a legislature made up of the Congress of People's Deputies elected in 1990 and its permanent organ, the Supreme Soviet. According to the existing constitution, the Congress was the highest organ of power in the Russian Federation. The superpresidency that Yeltsin was building would inevitably become a permanent source of conflict between the two branches of power. At first, however, the legislature supported Yeltsin's attempts to strengthen his rule. This support became the decisive instrument in the liquidation of Gorbachev's center of power.

In response to the president's requests, the Congress adopted two major decisions. The first, "On Organization of Executive Power During the Period of Economic Reforms" (valid until December 1992), gave Yeltsin the power to appoint heads of the local executive bodies in oblasts,[28] although not in the former autonomous republics, which had the right to elect their presidents. The second gave the president the right to issue decrees that could contradict and override existing laws and to reorganize the government without asking the consent of the parliament. The mood at that moment was favorable to Yeltsin, and the Congress approved the resolution giving him these additional powers for one year and deferring local elections for a year. Thus Yeltsin achieved his goal of unchallenged power—his presidential pyramid—for the coming year.

GAIDAR APPEARS ON THE SCENE

The next goal on Yeltsin's agenda was to create a new government. The first Russian government, headed by Ivan Silyaev, had fulfilled its role as a transitional mechanism. It had quickly taken control of the major administrative, economic, and financial resources of Russia but could not move further with reforms; Silyaev, a typical Soviet *apparatchik*, was too cautious, lacked vision, and was too involved in the old networks.

Discussions about the new government began immediately after August, but it was not until October that the question of the reform team was resolved and Yegor Gaidar was appointed to lead the team.[29] Two factors may account for the choice of Gaidar to head the economy at that crucial moment. First was his acquaintance with Burbulis, who at the time was very close to Yeltsin and was in control of the decision-making process in Russia. In September, Burbulis had asked Gaidar to create a working group to prepare scenarios for economic reform; the group also included Andrei Nechayev, Aleksei Golovkov, and Konstantin Kagalovsky. Second, Gaidar's political goal of complete independence for Russia fully corresponded with Yeltsin's basic political aim of getting rid of the Gorbachev center.[30] Other circumstances, mainly of a political or psychological nature, also contributed to Gaidar's selection. Yeltsin needed people who were energetic, courageous, ready to take risks, and not bound by stereotypes. He also required associates who had not been too involved with Gorbachev. This was a shortcoming for Grigory Yavlinsky, for example, although his candidacy for the post of prime minister was considered. Yavlinsky had another more substantial drawback: he opposed the dissolution of the Soviet Union. Gaidar, aside from his readiness to implement an independent course for Russia, had several other advantages: he had a working team in place and good contacts with the West. He also was a grandson of the famous writer Arkady Gaidar, and his family name apparently had a mesmerizing effect on Yeltsin. Sometimes such irrational factors can be decisive. Yeltsin himself explained his choice: "Gaidar impressed me most of all with his confidence. . . . He was simply an independent man with an enormous but not ostentatious sense of his own worth. . . . Gaidar had a knack for speaking simply."[31] Sometime later, Yeltsin made another interesting confession: "I never believed that Yegor Gaidar was a physician who could cure our sick economy, but I didn't think he was a quack who would finish the patient off, either."[32]

Gaidar and his team were young and were not integrated into the existing bureaucratic networks. Many believed that they would be able to find a new approach to Russia's problems. It would be a mistake, however, to consider Gaidar an outsider. He was raised in a *nomenklatura* family that had enjoyed many privileges and was himself a member of the *nomenklatura*—as a department head for *Kommunist,* the leading journal of the Communist Party. That a member of the former political establishment became one of the leaders of the market breakthrough and the liquidation of the previous system in Russia is yet more evidence of how complicated the interconnections between past and present are in Russia's political and social transformation.

Yeltsin's first declaration on economic reform came in a speech before the Fifth Congress of Russian People's Deputies on October 28, 1991, at which Yeltsin's loyal cohort and future enemy, Ruslan Khasbulatov, was elected speaker of the parliament. Yeltsin also expressed readiness to head a new government himself as a way of trying to shield his young government from attacks. This was an act of personal courage, as the implementation of liberal decisions would hardly add to his popularity. On November 6, 1991, Yeltsin signed a decree on the formation of a new government and assumed the responsibilities of prime minister. He designated Yegor Gaidar, Gennady Burbulis, and Aleksandr Shokhin as vice premiers. Gaidar started with the portfolio of minister for economics and minister for finance. (He would be appointed acting head of the Council of Ministers of the Russian Federation on June 12, 1992.) It took another month and a half to complete the full reform team, but the core had already been constructed.[33] Yeltsin professed himself satisfied with the new team. In November he declared, "I have confidence in the government. This is a unified team, made up of intelligent and fairly young people. The main thing is that they worked together to prepare a program and they are eager to implement it. There will be no disorder here as there was in the Silyaev government."[34] The president did not expect the new government to remain in place for very long. "During the period of reform," he predicted, "the government will change two or three times in two years."[35] Thus, from the very beginning, Yeltsin considered the Gaidar government a kamikaze team.

The market marathon really began on November 15, with the publication of ten presidential decrees that delivered the final knockout to the structures of the Soviet Union. Russia took over control of all of the financial institutions on its territory, including the State Reserve Depository and the State Printing Bureau. It also dissolved the Union ministries. All strategic metals were transferred to the control of the Russian government. Thus, with a single stroke, Yeltsin took over all economic power in Russia.

Yeltsin's decision to appoint a radical-liberal government made up of unknown people with little practical management experience ("junior researchers," as they were maliciously dubbed in Moscow) and to shield them with his authority says much about his intentions at the time. He was evidently sincere in his determination to make a complete break with the communist past. He was even ready to sacrifice his own popularity to that end: the expected decision to raise prices in 1992 would certainly not bring him any public support. However, Yeltsin's actions also reflected a certain lack of caution. The president, armed only with his experience as a provincial party leader, had no understanding of the complexities of macroeconomic stabilization; nor could he predict its consequences. He acted in accordance with the old Leninist principle: "First get into the fray, and then we'll see what's what."

This behavior was partially justified because the economic situation was becoming worse every passing day. By the fall of 1991 it was evident that the country was in a severe economic crisis. The real economy was shrinking at an unprecedented rate, and the consumer sector was being hit particularly hard. Of the 130 food and consumption items necessary for everyday life, fewer than twelve were available with any regularity. Store shelves usually stood empty. The food situation was especially catastrophic, and fear of famine in the coming winter was widespread. Rationing systems for distribution of goods were introduced. Barter became the norm in economic transactions. Inflation had reached about 20 percent a month by the end of the year. The situation was aggravated by the collapse of the ruble.

Government inaction could have resulted in economic disaster. "There was, however, no real plan of action, no detailed program in December 1991," wrote Richard Ericson. "There were just vague ideas, objectives, and slogans, the poorly understood example of Poland in 1989, and a small group of enthusiastic, radical economists determined to do something in the face of impending disaster. Yeltsin placed the development of reform in the hands of these largely self-taught economists."[36] From the very beginning, "it was more [of an] *ad hoc*, albeit market-oriented, response to [an] on-going crisis." It was "a plunge taken with optimism, in ignorance of the depth of the problems to be overcome and with hope that the situation could not get much worse than it already was at the end of 1991."[37]

As soon as the reformers began their new course, alarms were sounded even by economists who were close to the democrats. One

25

such warning was an open statement to the press by the liberal economist Semyon Kordonsky, who expressed widespread fears in Russian economic circles about Gaidar's plan. Kordonsky entitled his article "Planning the Catastrophe: The Third Wave of Reform Will Kill Russia." He wrote caustically about Gaidar's team: "Ph.D. candidates represent the last reserves of Marxist thought, with its characteristic views of the limitless flexibility of the social fabric and of the dominance of economics over politics and culture."[38] Kordonsky's judgments were harsh, but they were not without truth.

Others too, not just economists, were worried by the fact that no one had actually seen either the conceptual framework for the proposed reforms or the analysis of the expected consequences. Only a short summary of the plan ("Memorandum on the Economic Policy of the Russian Federation," February 27, 1992), written by Gaidar, was ever made public, and that was prepared hurriedly, for the benefit of the International Monetary Fund. The economic reform plan was not discussed among experts, and everything was kept in strict secrecy. Alternative reform plans were not considered, although this had been done even in Gorbachev's time. Liberal-minded academics Stanislav Shatalin, Oleg Bogomolov, Nikolai Petrakov, and Pavel Bunich affirmed bitterly that the "Gaidarites" simply avoided them and, if they saw them at a reception or conference, would hardly listen to their comments and criticism. This behavior did not help improve the reform plan, which, as later became clear, existed only as a package of diffuse ideas.[39] Yeltsin himself was very vague and inconsistent when he spoke about liberalization.[40]

Among ordinary people, shock therapy was accepted unenthusiastically, but with patience. Prices were freed on January 2, 1992. Journalists rushed to the shops to film the expected crowds of furious Muscovites, but, to their disappointment, found no dramatic scenes. People stood quietly in line; there was no social explosion. But as prices continued to climb, patience gave way to resentment. Gaidar had promised merely a two-fold increase in prices, but in January–February 1992, prices rose ten- to twelve-fold. The fall in industrial production was also much sharper than anticipated. The most serious problem was that the drop affected essential goods and products. Summing up the results of the first weeks of liberalization, the experts concluded: "The positive effect is hardly noticeable. The measures taken to stabilize the ruble resulted in turning the ruble into nothing more than a joke. . . . The most significant condition [of the economy] has become the shortage of cash, which, in conditions of spiraling hyperinflation, is threatening to become chronic."[41]

STRUGGLE AS A MEANS OF SURVIVAL

The beginning of 1992 demonstrated that conflicts would surface much faster than in the Gorbachev period. Deepening rifts within Yeltsin's entourage and open warfare among rival factions became increasingly distracting. More serious, the first signs of public dissatisfaction with the president appeared. The formation of an anti-Yeltsin opposition was a harbinger of trouble to come. Signs of a split within the democratic movement also began to surface. Tensions increased between the legislature and the executive.

The start of the new year witnessed an intensification of the struggle between the two groups around Yeltsin headed by Burbulis and Petrov. This was not just a conflict between individuals, each of whom desired a monopoly on influencing the president; it was also a conflict between political philosophies—the radical-liberal view personified by Burbulis on the one hand, and Petrov's neoconservatism on the other. The Burbulis group was in favor of radical steps in every field, concentrating first on economic transformation, and without much concern for political and social constraints. It openly supported strong presidential power and rule by decrees. Petrov and the neoconservatives preserved close ties to the former Soviet bureaucracy—in fact they themselves sprang from its ranks—and were dreaming, evidently, of a new paternalistic state that resembled the former Soviet system, only without both the orthodox communists and radical reformers. Practically all members of the Yeltsin team were eventually drawn into the conflict and forced to choose sides.

Yeltsin continued to play the role of arbiter, paying attention first to one party, then to the other, and not coming down definitively on either side. During this period, if the issue was one of strategy, Yeltsin listened more often to Burbulis, who was practically the only one in his entourage with any expertise in complicated political maneuvering. Until the end of 1992, Burbulis, formerly an obscure professor of Marxism in Sverdlovsk, was de facto number two after Yeltsin on Russia's political Olympus and the leading architect of his reformist policies, including the dissolution of the USSR and the destruction of communism. He exercised decisive influence on the political process in Russia—especially in those moments when Yeltsin disappeared from the scene, leaving his audience to wonder where their president was and what he was doing.[42]

The growing antagonism within Yeltsin's entourage was not the only division in the executive branch. In 1992 the "Rutskoi phenomenon" materialized: a serving vice-president, Aleksandr Rutskoi, publicly and vocally opposed the policies of the nation's leader but refused to resign. A veteran of the war in Afghanistan, a fighter pilot, and a general, Rutskoi had thrust himself impetuously into politics during the run-up to the Russian parliamentary elections of March 1990. He was not close to the Yeltsin group, but Yeltsin had nevertheless taken the advice of some of his assistants and proposed that the two of them join together for the first presidential election in June 1991.[43] Yeltsin's strategists calculated that, as a military man and a patriot, Rutskoi could draw votes from the conservative part of the population and help win the support of the army for Yeltsin's candidacy. As Yeltsin described Rutskoi at that time: "He had the look of an accomplished actor, he was a combat pilot, a recipient of the Hero of the Soviet Union Award, and he spoke firmly and eloquently. A real tiger! Middle-aged matrons would swoon with delight at the sight of such a vice president!"[44] The liberal intelligentsia, suspicious of Rutskoi, was puzzled by Yeltsin's motives, questioning both Rutskoi's intelligence and his suitability for the vice presidency. Yeltsin's advisors asked in reply: "Is the vice presidency a real job?"

After the elections, Rutskoi, too, felt that the vice presidency was not a real job. He had gotten into the Kremlin, but he was not admitted into the decision-making circle. Moreover, when he tried to break in, he was firmly pushed out. Rutskoi finally acknowledged that he had been brought into power for merely ceremonial purposes. Yeltsin made this quite clear, saying: "Rutskoi's main error—or, rather, not mistake but an inherent feature in him—was his stubborn refusal to understand and accept his own status. From the very first day he believed that the vice president was, to put it simply, the president's first deputy. As even a high-school student knows, however, a vice president is a ceremonial figure."[45] Others in Rutskoi's place might have contented themselves with that role. The vain pilot decided instead to join Yeltsin's attackers. Rutskoi's first assaults were directed against Gaidar's cabinet; at first he avoided attacking the president himself. Perhaps if Yeltsin's closest advisers had been more flexible and had found some niche for the ambitious vice president, the Rutskoi phenomenon might never have occurred. But Rutskoi was never given any serious functions, and he began to pour out his emotions publicly. "They don't let me in anywhere!" he proclaimed pathetically, and declared that he was not prepared to be the president's "Chinese dummy" ("yes-man"). The appearance of a such a high-level dissident in Yeltsin's circle immediately attracted the attention of the communist and nationalist forces, which saw in Rutskoi a potential leader.

In January 1992 Rutskoi began an all-out attack on the government and its political course. His personal dissatisfaction with his position had gradually turned into active political opposition to both Yeltsin and his course of action. Finally, on the advice of his aides, Yeltsin tried to neutralize his vice president, designating Rutskoi as the person "responsible for agriculture," although Rutskoi knew nothing about agriculture. Anyone familiar with Soviet history knows that those assigned the agriculture portfolio were generally marked for political death, given that resolving the country's agricultural problems was an impossible task. Moscow chuckled when it heard about the ambitious general's new duties.

Rutskoi, however, was still a charismatic figure who appealed to a substantial part of the general public, especially in the provinces. Even though he had no clear principles or convictions and was rude and aggressive, he learned quickly and could attract people to his side. His demagoguery impressed certain groups, and he was frequently able to present himself as an upright and honest man. Soon Rutskoi's public approval rating was second only to Yeltsin's. Whereas he had previously appeared to be merely an annoyance, he gradually became a liability for the president. In fact, Rutskoi's behavior seemed to repeat in many ways Yeltsin's own conduct under Gorbachev. A potential rival was slowly emerging.

CHAPTER TWO

THE NEW POLITICAL SPECTER: 1992

BY 1992 THE RUSSIAN DEMOCRATIC MOVEMENT had begun to languish. The fate of the Democratic Russia movement (DemRossiya), which had become an amorphous umbrella organization of many smaller groups and associations, illustrated this trend. The movement had originally been organized to combat communists in the first Russian parliament in 1990. It remained combative for some time afterward, mounting demonstrations and processions. Its activism and its unity thrived in an environment of continuous struggle and polarization. It was not effective when constructive action was needed, however, and it began to fall apart after the revolutionary stage of Russian reform was completed.

POST-COMMUNIST PLURALISM

The Russian democratic movement differed fundamentally from the anti-communist movements of Eastern Europe—such as Solidarity in Poland, the Union of Democratic Forces in Bulgaria, and Civic Forum in Czechoslovakia—with which it has been compared. The principal difference was that DemRossiya never gained real access to power. The social makeup of the majority of democratic groups in Russia was also different. While analogous organizations in Eastern Europe arose from outside the political system and the Communist Party, the democratic movement in Russia was formed around people who were part of the Soviet system and even the Communist Party elite. This largely explains the character of Russian democrats, their style of thinking and conduct, their occasional lack of consistency in following democratic principles, and their attempts to rely mainly on leaders and clientelistic networks rather than on the support of the society at large.

The leadership of DemRossiya tried at first to present an ultimatum to the president: unless Yeltsin gave the democrats real power and allowed them to participate in actual decision making, DemRossiya would abandon him and go into opposition. "The conflict between Yeltsin and the movement which brought him to power is imminent," said one of the leaders of DemRossiya, Lev Ponomaryov, at the end of 1991. "We have been trying for months to get a meeting with Boris Nikolayevich. He has become inaccessible." Yuri Afanasyev, a member of the movement's brain trust, was even more explicit: "We need some procedure for reaching agreement between ourselves and the president on personnel selected to senior positions in the government."[1] At the beginning of 1992, Yeltsin finally signed an agreement to coordinate his policy decisions with the democratic groups, but he never took this obligation seriously. He had decided not to tie himself to any one party or movement, democratic or otherwise, but instead to be the president of "all Russians."

Yeltsin's troubled relationship with the democrats was partly the result of his personality. He evidently could not forgive the democratic leaders, especially the refined Moscow intellectuals, for their lack of deference, as well as their previous attempts to use him for their own purposes.[2] Moreover, he concluded, probably correctly, that the democrats' views were not representative of the political beliefs of a majority of Russia's population. Their followers were mainly in big cities, and the rest of the country was rather suspicious of them. Once Yeltsin achieved power, he wanted to be absolutely independent. Moreover, he himself was beginning to demonstrate a lack of strong democratic convictions; the autocratic habits he had cultivated during his long life in the *nomenklatura* began again to dominate his behavior.

Thus the leaders of DemRossiya were confronted with a dilemma: should they continue to support Yeltsin, despite the fact that he had excluded them from real power, or should they go into opposition to his regime? In January 1992 divergence on this question provoked a crisis within the DemRossiya leadership. A large group of intellectuals—including the first wave of democrats such as Yuri Afanasyev, Yuri Burtin, and Leonid Batkin, the main theoreticians of the democratic movement—decided that they should have nothing to do with the new power structure and walked out of DemRossiya. The conflict between the ideologues and the bureaucrats pitted those who were outside the governing political structures against those who, in one way or another, had managed to gain a foothold within the power structures.

The conflicts within DemRossiya touched on still another fault line: personal relationships and attitudes toward Yeltsin led to a split between independents and loyalists. The independents, comprising the ideologues and theoreticians of the democratic movement, took a fairly critical view of the president. Afanasyev expressed their attitude: "The confrontational character of the relations between the government and the society has changed little since communism's collapse. The president's team is trying to reconcile reform with counterreform . . . [while] Russian society is excluded from the decision-making process."[3]

By the spring of 1992, the split between democrats who were not in power and those who were, in even a minor way, became public. The differences were not merely a product of the frustrations and thwarted ambitions of those who were excluded. They reflected a struggle between those who continued to advocate a democratic form of government and those who either preferred a strong personal rule or were increasingly drawn to a bureaucratic and clannish style of politics. The latter continued to call themselves democrats, but they were forging a new political group that advocated liberal authoritarianism.

Despite their dissatisfaction with Yeltsin, the first generation of democrats did not join the ranks of the opposition. They confined their critical statements about the new Russian government to cases of "constructive opposition." The democrats were caught in a trap: while they could not endorse the bureaucratic style of government that the Yeltsin group adopted, they also did not want to be in the same camp as communist and nationalist-patriotic groups. For that reason, even Dem-Rossiya dissenters supported Yeltsin at crucial moments, albeit reluctantly. By the beginning of 1992, however, the gap between the small group of real democrats in Russia and those around Yeltsin was widening.

Pessimists might argue that the democrats in Russia never had a chance to gain power. Structural, historic, and other constraints accounted for their failure to dominate the political scene and to proceed with democratic reform. The most important factor was that the democrats were not ready for victory. They lacked a program of action, and they failed to unite and to create a powerful nationwide organization. They had their chance during the precipitous decline of the Soviet center, when Yeltsin was dependent on them and all of the other forces were in disarray. They could have tried to create a strong party, to adopt a new constitution, and to build a new system. But they missed this chance. As Alexander Dallin has written, "Their failure to oust the incumbents and to launch meaningful reforms in the economy, the judicial system, the dismantling of the military-industrial sector—in brief, to complete the revolution—foreshadowed their subsequent disintegration and general failure as a political force."[4] The democrats chose to rely not on rules and institutions, but on a strong personality, that is, on Yeltsin. They hoped to control and manipulate him. But Yeltsin was a man who would owe his success to no one. The democrats lost, and they wasted this opportunity for Russia.

Meanwhile, the communists and nationalist-patriotic groups on the right moved to consolidate their strength. The preeminent nationalist newspaper *Den* (The Day) began to disseminate propaganda slogans, as it had done before the August 1991 attempted coup d'état. These inflammatory slogans—"The democrats have ruined everything"; "The Gaidar government is experimenting on the people"; "Down with Yeltsin's occupation regime"—would soon become the rallying points around which an anti-Yeltsin movement would rise. In January–February 1992 the red-nationalist opposition took to the streets for the first time. It did not draw big crowds, for the coalition of reds and browns was not a very inspiring one. Even so, by various accounts, it managed to gather 10,000–40,000 people for demonstrations in February. The democrats soon organized a counterdemonstration, attended by 50,000–100,000 people. As these numbers suggest, the willingness of Muscovites to come out into the streets had fallen sharply in comparison with the first euphoric days of freedom, when hundreds of thousands had taken part in rallies. Nonetheless, the government was worried and could not decide which tactics to use against the street demonstrations. Meanwhile, the opposition did not stop at organizing rallies; they gradually began to unite in the parliament, particularly around the Russian Unity faction led by Sergei Baburin, a deputy from Novosibirsk originally elected to parliament with support from DemRossiya. Members of the democratic movement were beginning to defect.

In February, the red-nationalist opposition made an attempt to unite its diverse groups into a single movement called the Congress of Civil and Patriotic Forces. It included both patriots of the new wave, formed after the dissolution of the Soviet Union, and communists ready to cooperate with the anti-communist nationalists. They were joined

by a few former democrats who had switched to a nationalist orientation
and who now advocated restoration of a unitary state and a strong
imperialist policy. These new nationalists included former Yeltsin supporters Viktor Aksiuchits and Mikhail Astafyev, who quickly became
some of the most vocal parliamentary critics of Yeltsin's government.
The opposition became more active: a new communist or nationalist
party or movement was announced almost every week. The Workers
of Moscow and Workers of Russia united communists under the leadership of Viktor Anpilov, a former journalist and admirer of Fidel Castro.
The Commune movement, filled with red patriots, was headed by the
former commander of the Urals Military District, General Albert Makashov. The Russian National Assembly brought together nationalist deputies from the parliament. The Russian National Union, headed by Sergei
Baburin, and the Russian Sobor (Assembly), headed by former KGB
general Nikolai Sterligov, were also part of a long list of new left and
nationalist groups.

None of these groups was large in number, but all were vocal and
visible. In September the representatives of these groups made one more
attempt to unite the red and the anti-communist oppositions, forming
the Front for National Salvation. In its leadership (the political council),
representatives of former Yeltsin allies, communists, and nationalists—
Mikhail Astafyev, Sergei Baburin, Gennady Zyuganov, Viktor Isakov,
and Albert Makashov—all sat together for the first time. Yeltsin demonstrated his concern over the formation of a united opposition on the
right, speaking on a number of occasions about the red-brown threat.
Yet it soon became clear that this threat had been greatly exaggerated.
The opposition movement failed to become a powerful force. The crisis
of ideas and leaders was not limited to the ranks of the democrats.
Nonetheless, there are several indications that in the winter of 1992, in
response to the opposition's activism, the president's supporters began
to discuss a plan for the imposition of a state of emergency in Russia.

Soon it became clear that it was not only the right wing that had
became more active. The industrialists, headed by Arkady Volsky, an
old *apparatchik* with ties to the military-industrial complex and a long-
time chairman of the Russian Union of Industrialists and Entrepreneurs,
undertook to fill the empty place in the middle of the political spectrum,
creating a centrist party to defend the industrialists' interests against
Gaidar's reforms.

THE CLAY IS NOT EASILY MOLDED

Developments in the Russian political arena kept Yeltsin from relaxing. Beginning in 1992, a series of scandals rocked the Russian government. Some of Yeltsin's appointees, including those close to him, began to abuse their power, lining their own pockets from the state treasury. When Gaidar was asked in February 1992 to name the greatest obstacle he faced, he replied that it was corruption among governing authorities. The central and provincial bureaucrats openly put their own enrichment first. Their abuses of government power in the first months of post-communist reforms sent the message that anything was allowed and that no one would be punished. From then on, corruption spread rapidly in the new Russian political class.

Yeltsin slowly acknowledged that society was resistant to reform and that a rapid break with the past would be far more difficult than anticipated. The old *apparatchiki* who had remained in place after the fall of the Soviet system firmly opposed Gaidar's reforms; they dragged their feet and sabotaged his efforts. So did the factory managers and local officials. At the same time, the political opposition was strengthening its influence in the parliament and crowding out the democrats. Constant internal fighting over policy issues, participation in the decision-making process, and influence with the president occupied Yeltsin's entourage. Rumblings of dissatisfaction grew louder as the population became discouraged by the lack of improvement in the economic situation.[5]

The most serious obstacles to radical economic transformation were the weak institutionalization of political life, the confused relations between political institutions, the lack of support for the reform team, and the absence of a clear reform strategy.[6] The reformers found themselves in a trap: having no institutional and social influence of their own, they were forced to rely on the president. Meanwhile, by the beginning of 1992 Yeltsin was already beginning to distance himself from the team; he became less and less accessible, isolating Gaidar and his people. One reason for this behavior was that he had apparently lost confidence in his young team. More important, as Yeltsin became increasingly engaged in the political struggle, he was forced to think about his own position. Tying himself to just one tiny group was not the best way to survive in a conservative environment.

As time passed, Yeltsin began to lose his sense of direction. His style of leadership grew more erratic and began to trouble even his supporters. His actions and statements were becoming more unpredictable and impulsive. He could not or would not weigh the consequences of his decisions, and it was difficult to avoid the impression that he was growing more obstinate and autocratic. He was not ready to discuss problems and to analyze options. His inclination to rule by decree was becoming more evident. He was increasingly less accessible, even to his closest associates, while his circle of advisors narrowed significantly. Those who did remain close to him, however, received enormous power and were able to act in his name. This happened more than once, for Yeltsin chose to vanish at the most inopportune moments.

Yeltsin's abrupt reversals of political decisions, as well as his many contradictory statements, also reflected disagreements among the members of his own team and the lack of a well thought out conceptual framework for Russian political and economic development. This became increasingly awkward, causing considerable embarrassment for the president on more than one occasion. The excessive ambitions of the new inhabitants of the Kremlin added little that was positive to the developing structure of the new authority. To his credit, Yeltsin was still shrewd enough to occasionally correct mistakes that he made. This was the case, for example, with his decision to unite in one organization the functions of state security (formerly the KGB) and internal affairs (the Interior Ministry and similar institutions). This would have created a superagency even more forbidding than the KGB. Yeltsin did not oppose the Constitutional Court's decision declaring his decree unconstitutional, even though he could probably have succeeded in ignoring it. Yeltsin still exercised a moderating influence on his associates and kept them from going too far with their struggles among themselves. Although he restrained their appetites, he did not try to put an end to the infighting within his entourage.

PARLIAMENT BECOMES THE ENEMY

In early 1992 the crisis in relations between the president and the legislative branch escalated gradually. Yeltsin had struck the first blow at the parliament when he began to create his presidential pyramid. At the time of the 1991 coup, he had already appointed his first representatives to the regions and had named heads of local administrations. By the fall of 1991, presidential representatives had been appointed to all major constituents of the federation, and by the end of

1991, Yeltsin had his own representatives in sixty-two regions. Not surprisingly, Yeltsin's attempts to build parallel power structures aroused resistance on the part of the parliament and of the local legislatures (the soviets).

In February 1992, the Supreme Soviet, led by former Yeltsin associate Ruslan Khasbulatov, adopted a resolution declaring that the local soviets were not subordinate to Yeltsin's provincial representatives. This was the beginning of the parliament's attempt to construct its own pyramid of power to counter that of the president. Personal animosity between Yeltsin and Khasbulatov, who had until recently been allies, grew stronger, for each of the two leaders considered himself the fundamental center of power. The executive and the legislative branches gradually turned into the focal points of opposing interests. The president was becoming the chief spokesman for the liberal-technocratic segment of the elite, while the parliament increasingly came to represent the nationalist and populist segments. Another reason for the growing discord between the two branches was the struggle over state property. The president's group and the parliamentary bureaucracy had begun a frenzied scramble for control of the process of divestiture of Soviet state assets, a struggle the executive branch had a better chance of winning.

The growing animosity between the executive and legislative branches gave rise to a number of political myths. First, with encouragement from the Yeltsin group, the mass media tended to portray the parliament as the main obstacle to reform. This approach oversimplified reality and apparently resulted from the media's emotional bias regarding the key participants in Russian political life: Yeltsin, whatever else might be said about him, had a far more attractive personality than his competitor Khasbulatov. Khasbulatov's gloomy character and acerbic manner inspired a strong dislike for him in many people, and he was generally regarded as the evil genius of Russian politics. His team of unappealing *apparatchiki* generally compared unfavorably with the dynamic, polished, and articulate people around Yeltsin.

Yet the reality of political life in Russia was much more complicated and subtle than the media's portrayal of it. There were many democratically minded people in the Russian parliament. This was the same parliament that had, by large majorities, supported Russian sovereignty, launched economic reforms, and given Yeltsin the additional authority he had requested to see those reforms through. Many of the regional legislatures or soviets that were elected in March 1990 cooperated con structively with the corresponding local executive authorities. In most cases the opposition of the local legislatures to Gaidar's reforms was prompted by a desire to soften the social consequences of reform rather than by a desire to return to the past. The Russian parliament and the local soviets could not be labeled strongholds of the *nomenklatura*, since the executive branch, at both the local and the national levels, was where most members of the old *apparat* had found comfortable places for themselves. The local soviets represented a wide range of political orientations, and a considerable number of newcomers to political life had joined them after the March 1990 elections. All of this, of course, does not mean that the parliament and the soviets were engaged in constructive and reformist activities. The prevalence of populist and provincial mentalities impeded reforms, and often the legislatures blocked new policies. But calling them the main obstacle to Russia's transition to a market economy would be an exaggeration. The legislatures were more in the nature of debating societies; real power, at both the national and the local levels, belonged to the executive branch.

Gradually, however, even those regional soviets loyal to Yeltsin began to show their dissatisfaction with him. The principal reason for this was the new national authorities' neglect of their local counterparts and the interests of the regions. The attempt by the central government to place responsibility for solving social problems on the shoulders of the regional authorities—an impossible burden—also played a part in their alienation. Sensing popular dissatisfaction with Yeltsin's reform policies, the federal parliament openly declared war on the government. On March 15, 1992, Speaker Khasbulatov demanded the resignation of the Gaidar team. Forces in the parliament began to regroup; democratic forces in the parliament were weakened and in disarray, and a number of former democrats began to oppose Yeltsin openly. Other democrats and centrists moved from the legislative into the executive branch. This migration was prompted by a desire to avoid serving under Khasbulatov, a lack of faith in the future of Russian parliamentarianism, or simply the desire to move closer to the real source of power.

With the departure of democrats from the legislature, the opposition there was predominantly communist and nationalist. The president's team, having rejected political dialogue with the deputies, lost the opportunity to win over those who were wavering. Yeltsin's people were no longer trying to persuade their opponents and had decided to ignore the parliament altogether. The president ceased to visit the White House, where the Supreme Soviet and the Congress of People's Deputies met. Government ministers came before these bodies only reluctantly, when they were called to account for themselves, and then they generally behaved in a supercilious manner. The term corps of deputies began to sound odious to the ears of liberals and democrats. Among the deputies, aggressive, extremist, irrational, and even psychologically unstable demagogues began to come to the fore. Ironically, the most vocal of the president's opponents were his formerly ardent supporters, among them Viktor Aksiuchits, Mikhail Astafyev, Mikhail Chelnokov, and Sergei Baburin. The defection of Yeltsin's former supporters and their change of political orientation was due not just to their personal ambitions or their refusal to accept the policy of executive power, but also to the political community's lack of stable principles and deep convictions and to the continuing fluidity of social interests. Moreover, at least part of the blame for turning the parliament into a center of anti-Yeltsin opposition rested with Yeltsin's own team, which obstinately refused to cooperate with the legislative branch.

THE CONGRESS AS POLITICAL THEATER

Before the "September 1993 revolution," when Yeltsin dissolved the parliament, sessions of the Congress of People's Deputies were important milestones in the development of Russian political life, as the entire Russian political establishment, including its regional representatives, gathered together. The power struggles that had gone on behind closed doors burst into the open. These periodic explosions of passions and emotions could hardly be expected to resolve problems productively, but, given Russia's political circumstances and the weakness of its institutions, such public reaction at least served to express society's interests and orientations, to refine or change the balance of power, and to force major political actors to look for ways to resolve their conflicts.

By the time of the Sixth Congress in April 1992, the Supreme Soviet was increasing its pressure on the government, hinting at a possible vote of no confidence in the Gaidar cabinet. Gaidar was forced to defend himself, repeating, "We shall not resign." Mutual enmity reached such a level that members of the government tried not to appear in the halls of the Supreme Soviet at all. The executive and legislative branches had become irreconcilable, polarized camps, and there was less and less political space for moderate, centrist forces. Meanwhile, leaders of the parliament, especially Khasbulatov, sensing that the deputies' support for Yeltsin was declining, began to search for a way to weaken the president further. The opposition loudly demanded revocation of the additional powers that had been granted Yeltsin at the Fifth Congress. Reviving the Bolshevik slogan "All power to the soviets," the Supreme Soviet passed a resolution giving local councils the right to ignore decisions made by the executive branch. Vice President Rutskoi, who was beginning to think of himself as a political successor to Yeltsin, stepped up his attacks on the government.

Meanwhile, the former autonomous republics tried to take advantage of the infighting in Moscow. They had long called for sovereignty, and now they began to act to acquire it. In 1989-90, the attempts of the Soviet republics to achieve more independence from a weakened center had accelerated the collapse of the Soviet Union; now, Russia's autonomous republics followed suit, threatening Russia with disintegration. The first to set out on this path was the Republic of Tatarstan, whose March 21, 1992, referendum on independence was supported by the majority of those voting (61.4 percent). In November 1992 Tatarstan adopted a new constitution, which asserted Tatarstan's sovereignty and declared that, as a subject of international law, it might associate with Russia through a bilateral treaty.[7] Soon the republics of Tuva and Yakutia-Sakha, as well as Krasnoyarskiy Krai, each declared that its own legislation took priority over the constitution of the Russian Federation. An attempt to proclaim an autonomous Yenisei Republic in Russia's Far East indicated that Russia's regions were also beginning to move in this direction. The primary source of this centrifugal trend was the inequality in the status of the Russian Federation's many constituent parts.

The relations between the center and some subjects of the federation were based on formal agreements, and the subjects had a lot of leverage. Those whose relations with the center were based on the constitution were not in as strong a position, but they wanted rights equal to those of the others. To many Russians, the rights the autonomous republics had acquired seemed unfair. Why, they asked, should Tuva, with its small electorate of 174,000, have more representation in the parliament than Moscow, with its 7 million voters? Why did Tatarstan have the right to keep and spend a portion of the taxes it collected, while the Russian regions were obliged to send all their taxes to the center? These sentiments were expressed with growing intensity during 1992 and 1993 in the Russian-dominated regions.[8] This tension could only be mitigated by a new formula to regulate relations between the federal center and the Federation's subjects. However, the Russian central authorities did not even try to find such a formula. They continued to govern according to the divide-and-conquer principle, buying off some subjects and threatening others, thereby producing alienation, distrust, and conflict.

The beginning of the Sixth Congress of People's Deputies of Russia on April 6, 1992, coincided with the very moment when the conflict between the executive and legislative branches became openly polarized. Both sides were seeking to alter the balance of power that had been established after the events of August 1991. The attacking side this time was the parliament, headed by the ambitious Khasbulatov. Ironically, he was a former Yeltsin ally. He had acquired the nickname "Faithful Ruslan" for his loyalty to Yeltsin, who had supported him as a candidate for speaker; now Khasbulatov was the leader of the anti-Yeltsin opposition. He embodied the proverb: "To have a good enemy, choose a friend; he knows where to strike."

Khasbulatov's efforts to transform the parliament into Russia's dominant power center undoubtedly helped escalate the conflict between the two branches. Thanks in some degree to Khasbulatov, however, Russia had for the first time developed an independent legislature. Khasbulatov had fought against the executive branch's efforts to rule by decree and had encouraged deputies to exercise control over the actions of the government. Yet the way he established parliament's independence frequently provoked fierce reactions from Yeltsin's team. The drama of 1992-93 was caused by ignorance on each side of how to be a civilized counterweight to the other. Instead of attempting to resolve the crisis of power, most of the political actors involved were trying to use the political struggle to advance their own interests.[9]

On the very eve of the Congress, Yeltsin made a number of important concessions to appease the deputies. Gaidar still remained vice prime minister, but on April 2 Yeltsin took away his finance ministry portfolio, which narrowed Gaidar's sphere of influence. The president removed Burbulis, who was the main target of the deputies' animus, from his position as the "political" vice premier. Burbulis retained the official title of state secretary, but the title suddenly began to be written in small letters. For Burbulis, this was the beginning of a downward slide; everyone sensed that his moment of glory and power as Yeltsin's right-hand man was coming to an end.

Yeltsin's concessions did not, however, appease the deputies. They demanded more sacrifices, specifically the resignation of Gaidar and his team. Suddenly Gaidar himself announced that he and his team were ready to resign; to make the point, they walked out of the hall of assembly in the middle of a session. Many observers thought that this was a brilliant ploy devised by the subtle Burbulis. Yeltsin, however, subsequently wrote: "Gaidar had made a major political decision completely independent of Burbulis. No one expected it, although it was outwardly so logical, simple, and normal." The president admitted that he "had not expected the whole government's resignation. . . . This was like a punch in the face."[10]

Those in the parliament who had fiercely attacked Gaidar and his associates did not seem to know how to react. They had not considered the possibility that the entire cabinet would voluntarily resign, and the opposition had not agreed on a course of action to cover this eventuality. Worried that Yeltsin might use harsh measures to save his government and that he might try to dissolve the parliament, the Congress withdrew its resolution calling for the resignation of the reform ministers. The deputies left Gaidar in place, but they demanded that the government be reorganized within three months. The most important outcome, however, was not the survival of Gaidar. The intrigues had distracted the deputies from the more serious issue of the additional powers that the president had managed to retain.

YELTSIN PREPARES HIS CONCESSIONS

The early results of economic reform were contradictory. The first year of transformation had halted the chaos that had characterized the last months of the Soviet Union. The reformers had succeeded in establishing control over state expenditures and increasing revenues, although the situation was improving very slowly. The biggest change had taken place in the sphere of the quasi-private and private sectors. By the end of 1992, about one-third of all enterprises in trade and services had already been privatized. The total number of privatized businesses exceeded 950,000. A new stage of privatization began on October 1, 1992, when vouchers that could be used to purchase shares of state enterprises were issued to Russian citizens. It was a significant step toward a qualitatively new economic system.

The government's main economic goals, however, had not been reached. The liberalization of the market was far from what had been planned. Retail prices were still set not by the enterprises engaged in trade, but by state institutions. Many regions retained state control over prices of basic goods and a quota system for distribution. At the local level, the authorities had set up their own system of state orders. Street markets, which created the appearance of a nascent market system, were merely buying up goods from the state system and reselling them for higher prices. The large number of intermediaries involved in this process substantially increased the price of goods. Limits on foreign trade continued in the form of quotas and licenses. Financial stabilization had not been achieved. The cash crisis became endemic, and wage arrears became the norm. The huge leap in prices devalued everyone's savings. Problems with tax collection remained, and local governments began to conceal the taxes they collected from Moscow.

According to official data, in January 1992 inflation was more than 350 percent; in February it increased by an additional 24 percent; and in March, by another 21 percent. Independent experts suggested that the real level of inflation was 150–200 percent higher than the official figures. Industrial production continued to fall; in January–March 1992 it dropped to 87 percent of the 1991 level.[11] Thus depression in the real economy continued. Throughout 1992 the growth of non-state economic activity, although substantial, remained essentially extensive and parasitic rather than intensive and self sustaining.[12]

Privatization also aroused widespread popular dissatisfaction. The liberal economist Nikolai Shmelyov said of the privatization program: "For me, it was simply a comedy. Judge for yourself: at first people were robbed of 98-99 percent of their savings. Then, so that they would not complain too loudly, they were given a piece of paper [a voucher] whose face value was just one-fifteenth of what had been taken from them, and that was supposed to solve the problem. . . . How harshly [the reformers] implement their program!"[13] Several years later Burbulis acknowledged: "Our reform program appeared to be dangerously, even criminally, insensitive to the social needs."[14]

Grzegorz Kolodko, deputy prime minister and finance minister of Poland from 1994 to 1997, compared Russian and Polish economic reform as follows:

As a former Polish finance minister, I believe that if Poland had continued the policies pursued up until 1992 (the infamous "shock therapy") we would now be where Russia is today— that is, in a seemingly permanent financial crisis. "Shock without therapy," as we called it, was Poland's attempt to privatize without a social welfare net. The idea was to liberalize and privatize as quickly as possible. This led to growing poverty and unemployment as well as social and political tension. [The Polish government was forced to look for another strategy.] We finally discovered how to manage our economic affairs by establishing a "Strategy for Poland"—a way to introduce a market economy without hurting the people. Poland privatized companies gradually (while ensuring true competition), controlled trade and opened financial markets. As a result, inflation fell and unemployment and domestic debt declined, as did foreign debt. Output and consumption soared.[15]

Gaidar's reforms met with a wave of criticism in Russia and abroad. On the one hand, the reformers were accused of lacking sufficient radicalism and of inconsistency; on the other, they were criticized for extremism and for misunderstanding Russia's real needs. Neoliberal critics of Gaidar such as Larisa Piyasheva, Andrei Illarionov, and Vitaly Naishul were convinced that the problems of Russian liberalization were due to the ruling team's lack of courage. The first Russian reformers were too slow and cautious in making their market breakthrough, they said, which made it more painful for the population: "Better to cut a cat's tail with one stroke." According to this view, the reformers made too many political concessions, moving one step forward and two steps back; as a result, the necessary decisions were delayed until circumstances were even more unfavorable.

This view was also supported by some observers in the West. Richard Ericson, evaluating the Gaidar reforms, said that they "are so far rather shallow and fragile. . . . Truly new operations are only loosely anchored in the economy, without fixed and lasting structures."[16] In his opinion, the main reason the economic situation remained critical was that, "despite the substantial price liberalization of January 2, 1992, no comprehensive shock therapy was seriously attempted." Ericson thinks that "neither stabilization nor liberalization policies were sufficiently thorough, even if to some they appeared shocking. Moreover, after the first quarter, government fiscal irresponsibility grew, driven by political pressures from parliament and state industrial and defense lobbies."[17]

Anders Åslund also argued that Gaidar's reform was not shock therapy at all. It was "gradual liberalization." The main cause of its gradualism was, in his view, "the power of the old establishment interests."[18] Åslund has emphasized the political obstacles to radical economic reform in Russia: "Yeltsin hesitated and did not know what he really wanted. Gaidar failed and compromised rather than taking a firm stand on principles. . . . Liberalization and stabilization were understood by Gaidar but few others; understanding among the elite, much less among the people, was completely absent."[19]

The majority of Russian economists, however, doubted the validity of the liberal-monetarist doctrine underlying Gaidar's effort. In the views of economists such as Oleg Bogomolov, Nikolai Petrakov, Stanislav Shatalin, and Yuri Yaromenko, this doctrine assumed the existence of at least a rudimentary market mechanism, which was absent in Russia. They advocated an even more gradual approach to economic transformation, preserving substantial state regulation of prices and deliveries during the transitional period.

Russian economist Aleksandr Nekipelov expressed a widespread attitude toward Gaidar's reforms when he wrote, "I fully agree with Gaidar's thesis about the necessity of price liberalization in 1992, which was an urgently needed measure. This liberalization, however, brought with it a powerful structural shock . . . which should have been anticipated, and an adequate policy should have been prepared in advance."[20] The reformers apparently were not thinking about the consequences of the price liberalization and had no strategy to reduce its social costs. They had not expected their fiscal policy to cause non-payment of debts and wages. According to Nekipelov, the reformers made a mistake in refusing to maintain at least partial state control where it was appropriate for preserving stability. In response, Gaidar and his supporters pointed out that the preservation of state regulation would have both promoted permanent monopolies and led to more corruption.

The privatization policy implemented by Anatoly Chubais also encountered serious criticism. According to many Russian analysts, it was based on the assumption that the only solution for Russia was to turn state property over to the *nomenklatura* that had controlled it before. The reformers apparently hoped that this would force the former political establishment to give up its power and concentrate on business. But this never happened, and Russian privatization resulted in a new concentration of power and property mainly in the hands of representatives of the old ruling class.[21] An additional problem with privatization was that it could not be effective unless "ownership" was a clearly defined legal term.

Meanwhile, the attacks of the opposition and the gloomy mood of the populace forced Yeltsin to think about how to protect himself and his cabinet. He decided to implement the Congress's decision and to reorganize the cabinet, bringing in the pragmatists, if only to ensure the support of the enterprise managers' group. New faces were added to the government line-up: Georgi Khizha was appointed a vice premier on May 20, Viktor Chernomyrdin on May 30, and Vladimir Shumeiko on June 2.[22] All of them were typical industrialists who had become successful under the Soviet regime.

The new appointments prompted a variety of reactions in the liberal press, but the most common conclusion was that the Gaidar team was finished. "These appointments signify the end of the reform," commented Russian television. "This is very dangerous," concluded *Izvestiya*.[23] Everyone from the International Monetary Fund to the average Russian was worried, but the apprehensions were not borne out. Pressure from various directions had already begun softening Gaidar's shock therapy in the spring of 1992. The new vice premiers, contrary to expectations, did not demand a sharp change from the course taken. Shumeiko even joined the liberals and soon became one of Yeltsin's closest allies.

Another important development during this period was the president's June 3 decree creating the Security Council; Yuri Skokov, a person close to the military-industrial complex, was named the executive secretary of the council. Formerly the director of the Kvant industrial association, he had defeated a democrat in the March 1990 elections to the Russian parliament and had soon begun to play a significant role in Russian politics. The newly created Security Council was given substantially greater powers than State Secretary Burbulis ever had; it was dubbed "the new Politburo." The appearance of this new structure was another example of Yeltsin's efforts to rely on his own institutions, even if they did not have total legitimacy.

THE HOT SUMMER OF 1992

During the first five months of the year, 300 protest demonstrations had taken place in Moscow—nearly 200 of them without official sanction. Throughout the summer, the communist extremists and the nationalist-fundamentalists became increasingly active. They were few in number, but conspicuous and vociferous. Some of the more aggressive elements in these groups came up with a plan to express their dissatisfaction with the regime through an attack on a well-known symbol of the new Russian government. The Moscow television center Ostankino, which had long annoyed the opposition with its liberal programming, made an ideal target. On June 22, 1992, the united opposition began a siege of the television tower. As clashes between the anti-Yeltsin forces and the militia began, the authorities appeared confused and ambivalent, incapable of dealing with these events.

Tensions in Moscow rose throughout the summer of 1992. Many envisioned a repeat of the summer of 1991, as countless warnings of an impending coup d'état began to circulate. Valery Zorkin, the chairman of the Constitutional Court, warned, "Our Constitutional system of government is being threatened. The confrontation between various political forces is approaching extreme limits. There is a danger that the army will be drawn into resolving our internal conflicts."[24] Such bluntness was unprecedented, but Zorkin was not alone. Sergei Shakhrai, an influential member of the president's team, added his own warnings, and Minister of Foreign Affairs Andrei Kozyrev said in a speech: "The threats to the government are real."[25] Thus several influential political figures were suddenly hinting at the possibility of a new attempt to overthrow the established regime, but while Zorkin was suggesting that the threat emanated from the presidential team and from Yeltsin himself, people in the executive branch were pointing their fingers at the opposition.

How serious was the danger of a coup? The president's entourage was trying to create the impression that the activities of the communist-nationalist opposition were a threat. It was no secret that plans for introducing presidential rule had been under consideration within the narrow circle close to Yeltsin. The warnings by Yeltsin's associates about the possibility of a coup were probably motivated either by a desire to justify the introduction of direct rule by Yeltsin himself or as a means to calm the opposition.

The communist-nationalist opposition mobilized during this period, but it still remained an uncoordinated and clamorous mass that could hardly present a real threat to the regime. Much more dangerous for the government was the growing disenchantment with the government's policy among ordinary citizens. According to polls, even in Moscow, where the population was most favorable to reform, 43 percent "did not trust any political force." In August, 55 percent of the people who had supported Yeltsin in 1991 said that the new team did not fulfill their expectations.[26] The leaders of the regime, not knowing how to address this popular discontent, felt threatened. For the first time since 1991, Russia faced the possibility of rule by force.

On June 1 another leap in prices engendered broad and open dissatisfaction. Yeltsin feared that public agitation would burst into the open. Rumors circulated that he was strongly dissatisfied with his liberal cabinet and was demanding a stabilization of prices. Meanwhile, the powerful industrialists' lobby increased its pressure, demanding that Yeltsin fire the government and change its liberal course. Gaidar was clearly at a loss, and, without firm political support, he retreated. The government decided to forgive millions in enterprise debt—an enormous boon to the industrialists. This decision meant the end of Gaidar's monetarist policy.

During the summer, while divisions deepened, a more complicated political mosaic was being created. The opposition, consisting of various nationalist and leftist groups, was further galvanized, but there was much more rhetoric than real action. The various opposition groups (both within and outside the parliament) were unable to put aside their differences and unite. The extremists of the communist-nationalist camp frequently turned their criticism against Khasbulatov, who spoke as the representative of the interests of the former Soviet bureaucracy and groups connected to it, such as the agrarian lobby and some of the industrialists. Khasbulatov's compromises were too moderate for their tastes. Soon it became clear that the oppositionists of leftist and nationalist persuasions, like their democratic counterparts, could not live long under one roof. These divisions gave the president's team room to maneuver.

Frustration was also mounting in the army. The commanders of armies and military districts were dissatisfied with Yeltsin's course and especially with the government's disregard for the deteriorating status of the military. The most outspoken representative of military anger was Aleksandr Lebed, the commander of the 14th Army located in the self-proclaimed Trans-Dniester Republic. He interfered in politics and issued a virtual ultimatum to both the government and his commander-in-chief. "It's time to stop fooling around in the swamp of little-understood politics," stated the general. "It is time to get to work; the interests of the state must be defended."[27] It was not always clear what exactly the general was demanding; he often used harsh words without explaining what he really meant. But Lebed's message was not difficult to read: he was attacking the government from a nationalist and populist position. Soon Lebed began to threaten Moscow openly, warning that "the army is a serious and powerful force."[28] Such pronouncements from a military man would previously have been unthinkable, but with the army increasingly restive, nobody was especially surprised by Lebed's conduct.

Forces claiming to represent the political center also began to assert themselves. On May 21 the Civic Union coalition was formed by three prominent political leaders: Arkady Volsky, an industrialist; Nikolai Travkin, a democrat-populist who had been a well-known figure during the Gorbachev period; and General Aleksandr Rutskoi, the vice president. At first glance this appeared to be an unlikely troika. Yet these politicians seemed to need each other. Volsky was looking for a social base, which the Travkinites had, and for links to the military, which he evidently hoped could be provided by Rutskoi. The vice president needed closer ties to the provinces and to the industrialists, which Volsky could offer. Travkin, who had found himself alone on the political spectrum, needed high-profile allies. Despite the fact that Rutskoi was then out of favor, Volsky and Travkin probably calculated he was currently Russia's only charismatic political figure besides Yeltsin as well as the president's legitimate heir.

Theoretically, the idea of forming a centrist movement in Russia was a productive one. The time had long been ripe for expanding beyond the tense polarization of reformers versus communists. Civic Union's ideology, however, was very eclectic, and it did not always fit the centrist criteria. Its constituent groups opposed the Gaidar government's liberalism and favored a socially oriented economy with a greater level of government regulation. In the political sphere, Civic Union pronounced itself to be pragmatic and a supporter of moderate patriotism and of a strong, centralized Russian state with elements of strict federalism (statism). The new movement tried to attract the industrialists and those within the federal and regional bureaucracy who were dissatisfied with the liberal course. Even if its criticism of Gaidar's reform program was justified, however, this movement represented the groups that had failed to adapt to the new reality; they were trying to preserve or reestablish the old accustomed paternalistic relations under the state umbrella, which made them potential allies of the communists. When the leaders of Civic Union attempted to mobilize social pressure to force Yeltsin to share power with them, it became clear that they had little real influence.

More and more people were leaving democratic organizations and groups. DemRossiya continued to lose support: in less than a year, from May 1991 to April 1992, the number of its adherents in the parliament dropped from 205 to 73. Those who left joined other groups or became independent deputies. The situation in the democratic camp was aggravated by the growing distance between its leaders and Yeltsin's team, which felt no need to cooperate with democratic groups, whose loyalty it had begun to take for granted.

The country as a whole barely reacted to the political maneuvering at the top. Public disappointment and apathy grew stronger as the weeks and months wore on. For example, only 30 percent of eligible voters turned out in the elections for chief executive of the local administration in the provincial city of Dmitrov in the summer of 1992. Russia was tired of constant political struggle. Polls began to show declines in Yeltsin's popularity. In July 1992 only 24 percent of those questioned had full faith in the president; another 33 percent had some faith; and 32 percent had none. For the first time, Rutskoi's favorable rating surpassed Yeltsin's: 28 percent had full faith in Rutskoi; 36 percent had some faith; and only 19 percent said they had no faith in him.[29]

The president's team had neither a unified vision of its objectives nor a sense of how to address the growing social tensions. Morale within the executive structure was low. Shakhrai provided this curious and rather alarming assessment: "If one speaks of power on the scale of the entire Russian government, then it is no longer being directed, but is drifting aimlessly."[30] These words came from one of Yeltsin's closest allies, who was himself partially responsible for this "drifting" of power. Another Yeltsin associate, Press Secretary Vyacheslav Kostikov, complained: "While the opposition escalated its attacks on the Kremlin, Yeltsin remained lethargic, neither responding nor trying to organize a defense."[31] Yeltsin's increasing passivity led his close associates Burbulis, Mikhail Poltoranin, Chubais, and Kozyrev to hold a press conference for foreign journalists on October 16, 1992, at which they warned again of the threat of a communist coup d'état. Their hope was that they could prompt Western leaders to wake up Yeltsin and force him to act decisively. Meanwhile, leaks from the presidential entourage revealed new plans to dissolve the parliament, and soon the discussion of ways to get rid of the parliament would become the daily occupation of the president's advisers.

THE LIBERALS SENSE THEIR ISOLATION

Gradually Yeltsin grew more aware of the divergence between reality and his expectations. The usually self-confident president seemed increasingly uncertain. While liberal radicalism still prevailed in the rhetoric of the presidential team, the group's actions appeared to zigzag in various directions. The Burbulis-Gaidar government seemed to have lost its bearings and was merely being dragged along by events without responding. In the autumn Gaidar and his associates briefly came to life and began traveling to the provinces, meeting with industrialists and local officials to explain their goals, but by then it was too late, and the regions greeted the reformers with suspicion and hostility.

By the end of the summer, Gaidar's government was being criticized from all sides. Radical liberals accused him of abandoning a decisive push for a market economy. The opposition called the cabinet "an occupation government." Within the cabinet itself, the split between the radicals and moderates widened with the introduction of the privatization program developed by Chubais, one of the most active liberals in the government. The program was opposed by the ministers who represented the industrialists' group, especially the military-industrial complex, and it also was opposed by many radical democrats, who saw it as an opportunity for the bureaucracy and the emerging financial clans to reap most of the benefits of the redistribution of state property at the expense of Russia as a whole.

Russia's political and economic life was turning into an unruly and spiteful struggle among lobby groups. The key interest groups that would come to play a significant role in Russian politics were beginning to take shape: the financial capital interests (increasingly associated with commercial interests); the raw materials and natural resources lobby; the agrarian groups; the manufacturers; the military-industrial complex; and regional elites. The financial lobbies, which from the beginning established close contacts with the government bureaucracy, were especially active. All interest groups tried to influence the government's policy. More than eighty decrees issued by the Burbulis-Gaidar government between January and August 1992 contained concessions and exceptions that benefited particular groups, enterprises, or regions.[32] Almost every chief of every Russian administrative agency bowed to pressure and approved concessions for at least one of these interest groups—and presumably was rewarded for his generosity.

The primary drawbacks of such practices were that economic and political actors became accustomed to putting pressure on the government. Such pressures had, of course, existed even under the communist regime, but there had been unwritten rules of conduct by which interest groups were expected to behave. Under Yeltsin, the old norms and taboos were broken, and the authorities became more susceptible and more accommodating to the pressures of powerful interest groups and even criminal clans. The growing influence of special-interest lobbies on the process of government decision making hastened the spread of corruption at all levels of power.[33]

The popularity ratings of leading Russian politicians were dropping significantly. When asked, "Do you trust the following political leaders?" in a September 1992 poll, 33 percent did not trust Yeltsin; 26 percent did not trust Rutskoi; 55 percent did not trust Khasbulatov; and 52 percent did not trust Gaidar.[34] This was a serious warning for all Russian politicians, including the reformers, who had done little to build on the trust they had won from the people in August 1991.

Meanwhile, another critical juncture was approaching. At the Seventh Congress of People's Deputies, scheduled for December 1, 1992, the extension of Yeltsin's extraordinary powers would be considered, and it was unlikely that the delegates would agree to renew them. This finally forced Yeltsin to emerge from his apathetic state and take steps to counter the opposition's attacks. What he did, however, shocked his closest liberal advisers: he named his old crony Oleg Lobov, a Communist Party associate who had worked with Yeltsin in Sverdlovsk and had never been known for reformist thinking, as chairman of a new experts' council to advise the president. Given Lobov's orthodox views, this step was clearly intended as a conciliatory gesture to the old guard. The new appointment rounded out the ranks of the conservative group that now surrounded Yeltsin. Yuri Petrov, Skokov, and Lobov headed extraconstitutional bodies—the presidential administration, the Security Council, and the expert council—that were now much more influential than the constitutionally established structures, including the cabinet.

The president's turn to pragmatists and neoconservatives was meant to strengthen his position, and soon he began a series of new maneuvers. In September he tried for the first time to mend fences with the local soviets. He urged an end to calling the activities of deputies "useless"—a sin that he himself had most energetically committed.

Yeltsin also conciliated his appointed representatives in the local executive and legislative branches by proposing to "work things out" for two and a half years without calling new elections. (The existing moratorium on elections of local administrative heads, which had been approved at the president's request by the Fifth Congress of People's Deputies in October 1991, was set to expire in December 1992.) The proposal to defer elections was intended to temper the dissatisfaction of the local soviets with the president and also to preserve his control over the local administrative chiefs that he had appointed. Not all regional administrators, however, liked the second rationale. Their position was already strong enough, and they did not fear the results of an election. Indeed, some of them even wanted to hold elections—to establish their own legitimacy and to free themselves from their dependency on Yeltsin and the central authorities.

CHAPTER THREE

A BREWING CONFLICT WITH PARLIAMENT: 1992-93

IN A SPEECH TO THE SUPREME SOVIET on October 6, 1992, Yeltsin publicly criticized Yegor Gaidar, acknowledging for the first time the mistakes of the "starting year" of Russian reforms[1]:

> The policy relied too much on macroeconomic theory at the expense of resolving concrete human and economic problems. . . . The problem of monetary supply was allowed to become extremely serious. The issue of nonpayment of debts and wages has also become most troubling. Despite predictions, the fall in production was not just sectoral but general, and has affected the enterprises that supply consumer goods, services, and manufactured products.[2]

YELTSIN PREPARES FOR THE MOMENT OF TRUTH

The president also extended a hand to the parliament and proposed a cease-fire: "I am ready for a patient dialogue with the opposition, for constructive debate. It is not on the basis of confrontation, but only on the basis of civil agreement, that we can make the painful transition to a civilized and democratic society."[3] Yeltsin had expressed in an unambiguous way the desire to be reconciled with his opponents, and it took supporters in the democratic camp by surprise.

The parliamentary leadership, headed by Ruslan Khasbulatov, paid no attention to Yeltsin's conciliatory gestures. Instead it launched a series of corridor intrigues aimed at consolidating all opposition to the government, although for the time being it tried to avoid excessively sharp attacks on Yeltsin himself. The extreme opposition, represented in the parliament by Russian Unity and outside it by the National Salvation Front, demanded the resignation of Gaidar's entire group and the repeal of Yeltsin's extraordinary powers. The democrats were in disarray and could not offer Yeltsin any real support. In these circumstances much depended on the position of the centrist Civic Union, which during the summer had begun to assume more influence. Although not long before its leaders had only dreamed about getting their people into the government, they now reached for a chance to form a new cabinet.

The tug-of-war between the parliament and the executive intensified the competition among these groups for influence in the Russian republics and regions, strengthening centrifugal tendencies. Representatives of the regional political forces were generally more conservative than their Moscow counterparts and were usually more strongly influenced by the Supreme Soviet than by the president and his government, whose actions were often incomprehensible to them. Yet it was the executive branch that gave the regions their subsidies, thus holding a powerful source of control over them. These factors motivated the regional authorities to stay out of the Moscow fights. Most local ruling groups that sympathized with the position of the parliament also tried to preserve good relations with the government, but some regional groups, notably in Tatarstan, Bashkortostan, and other former autonomous republics, took advantage of the fights in Moscow to establish greater independence from the center.

In October Yeltsin continued his complicated game of concessions. Rumors leaked from the president's entourage that Yeltsin was ready to agree to a broad compromise with the deputies, but only on condition that they agree to defer the next Congress of People's Deputies until 1993. Yeltsin understood that at the Congress he would have to account for the results of the past year's reforms—an unwelcome prospect. He probably hoped that by 1993 the economic situation would have improved, as Gaidar constantly assured him it would.

The president also engaged in dialogue with Civic Union. This gave the impression that he was almost ready to replace his reform cabinet. Observers began to predict new policies of state regulation. Such speculation was reinforced by Gaidar's cabinet, which prepared a new action program, the "Federal Program for Structural Reform of the Economy." This program reflected the lobbying interests of the economic sectors, especially those of the energy and raw materials sectors. As a result, people asked what good the sacrifices of the reform's previous stage had been if the only winners were the representatives of a few interest groups. Regardless of the government's substantial modifications to its economic course, however, various forces (now even including some democratic groups) continued to demand the resignation of Gaidar and his team.

To soften the approaching blow and to pacify the opposition, Yeltsin decided to sacrifice some of his associates in advance. He dismissed three ministers: Aleksandr Titkin (industry), Andrei Nechayev (economy), and Pyotr Aven (foreign trade), the latter a close associate of Gaidar. He did not dismiss Foreign Minister Andrei Kozyrev, although the opposition specifically demanded it. Yeltsin did not want to risk destroying the liberal foreign policy that Kozyrev symbolized. At the end of November, just before the Congress, Yeltsin reluctantly fired his two closest associates, Gennady Burbulis and Mikhail Poltoranin (who was then vice premier and minister for information), and Yegor Yakovlev, a democrat who was the head of state television.

The efforts of the president's team to persuade parliament and the Constitutional Court to postpone the meeting of the Congress of People's Deputies were in vain. The session was scheduled to open on December 1, 1992. There was growing nervousness within the presidential entourage, as public opinion polls indicated another drop in the president's popularity rating: only 19 percent supported Yeltsin, while 27 percent were against him, and 15 percent supported him only because there was no alternative. Another poll indicated that only 19 percent thought that the government could end the crisis, while 58 percent saw no hope in any direction. About 70 percent of those surveyed were dissatisfied with their lives, and 58 percent did not believe that the government's current economic reforms could be successful, but only 11 percent believed that market reforms should be reversed. This meant that the majority of those questioned hoped for another, less painful path to reform.[4]

The October 29 publication of the government's annual report increased the bleak mood in the capital. According to the report, one-third of Russia's 148 million people lived below the poverty line, earning less than 2,000 rubles (or five dollars) a month. Independent sources indicated that an even greater number were below the poverty line. Prices had grown in the preceding ten months by 1,300 percent, and production had fallen 18 percent compared with 1991. According to a poll taken in largely pro-reform Moscow, 40 percent advocated the resignation of Gaidar's cabinet. Gaidar himself was forced to admit that he could not rule out the possibility of personnel changes in the government before the Congress, but he hoped that they would not be radical.

In the meantime, Yeltsin tried to demonstrate that everything was going according to plan. On October 26, meeting with a group of American businessmen, he affirmed that the major difficulties in the reform program were in the past. He again promised that crucial economic issues would be solved in the near future. By now, however, everyone had become accustomed to the president's promises and treated them with skepticism. Despite their confident statements, the members of Yeltsin's team were increasingly uneasy over prospects for the coming weeks.

November became even more turbulent. Yeltsin continued to defend the government as it came under more and more vicious attacks from the opposition. Using one of Gorbachev's tactics, Yeltsin tried to win over the former autonomous republics and regions of Russia. At the eleventh hour, he offered to create two new organs, a council of republic heads and a council of governors. Yeltsin's campaign to mobilize allies did not end there. A train full of miners from the Kuzbass region was organized into a demonstration of public approval for the president's policies.

CHERNOMYRDIN APPEARS ON THE SCENE

Not long before the opening of the Seventh Congress of People's Deputies, the Supreme Soviet had approved a law on government that put the cabinet under the direct control of the legislative branch. Either the president and his government would have to agree to a sharp curtailing of their authority, or they would have to battle with the parliament in circumstances that were less favorable to the executive branch than ever before.

The Congress opened on December 1, 1992, as scheduled, but it was a disillusioning experience. It was clear that many who had been considered powerful were not; this was especially true of Civic Union, which had managed to create the myth that it was one of Russia's most powerful political forces. The Congress also demonstrated that none of the extremist groups was influential either. For the first time, the decisive role of the wavering delegates—the swing vote—became apparent. This was the so-called swamp, which at critical moments in the past had usually taken the side of the president. This time, however, it supported the opposition, reflecting the changing balance of forces in the parliament and in the country as a whole.

Yeltsin tried to find political accommodation with the deputies while preserving his control over the government. He also made a half-hearted attempt to keep Gaidar. Nevertheless, the deputies adopted constitutional amendments that increased the legislature's control over the executive branch. The Congress got the right to approve not only the prime minister but also nearly all heads of the most important ministries. In addition, the deputies restored the right of legislative initiative to the government and made the government responsible not only to the president but also to the Congress and the Supreme Soviet. The right to reorganize the government was transferred to the Supreme Soviet. A procedure for the impeachment of the president was established. As a result, Yeltsin effectively lost most of the additional prerogatives he had gained at the Fifth Congress.

Yeltsin was forced to retreat. He offered the Congress a new deal. In exchange for confirming Gaidar as prime minister, he would submit the nominees for the power ministries (the defense and interior ministries and the security service) and the foreign affairs ministry to the Supreme Soviet for approval. However, the Congress saw these concessions as too little, too late. It rejected Gaidar's confirmation for the office of prime minister.

After that defeat, Yeltsin could, in principle, have again designated Gaidar as acting prime minister, or proposed a compromise figure for the position. Instead, he decided to pursue confrontation, apparently assuming that the Congress would get cold feet (as it had the last time) and retreat. On December 10 he appealed to the nation, demanding that the dispute be resolved by a referendum. In a passionate address to the Congress, Yeltsin declared: "We cannot work with this parliament. The only solution to this fundamental crisis of power is a nationwide referendum to give the people a way to demonstrate which side they trust more—the president or the parliament."[5] He then called on his supporters to leave the hall. This, however, was a mistake. The democrats were so disorganized that most of them stayed, and only a small group of people followed Yeltsin. The country witnessed this pathetic spectacle on television. This time, the Congress did not retreat, as it had done in the spring. Moreover, after the president's speech, the prosecutor-general and the power ministers went to the podium and one after another declared their support for the constitution. In the convoluted language of this confrontation, this meant the betrayal of the president. The situation became extremely tense. The opposing camps began to prepare demonstrations of support, which threatened to erupt into street clashes.

At the very moment when further confrontation appeared inevitable, Valery Zorkin, chairman of the Constitutional Court, took on the role of mediator. He organized a meeting between the antagonists and helped them find a compromise solution. Neither side, apparently, was then prepared to aggravate the already tense situation. The antagonists—Yeltsin and Ruslan Khasbulatov—signed the document, "About Stabilization of the Constitutional System." They agreed to hold a national referendum on a new Russian constitution on April 11, 1993. They also agreed to freeze amendments to the existing constitution adopted by the Congress. The Supreme Soviet would draft the proposed new constitution, but the president had the right to make changes to it before its publication. If the parliament and the president could not agree on a joint draft of a new constitution (not unlikely, given the incompatible goals of the two branches), then the competing drafts would be presented for public approval. The third element of the compromise was an agreement between the two sides to choose a new prime minister. The president would select five people from a list of candidates nominated by parliamentary factions and would present those five names to the Congress for a non-binding vote. From the top three who won a simple majority of votes, Yeltsin would select one and offer this candidate to the Congress for approval.

These results meant a victory for Yeltsin, but this time he paid a price for it: being forced to sacrifice Gaidar.[6] He most likely understood that it would have been too dangerous to risk his own position over the issue of Gaidar's unpopularity. As a result, the president gave up his chief reformer in exchange for an extension of his own extraordinary powers.[7]

The various factions of deputies proposed about twenty candidates for the prime minister's position, including Gaidar, Yuri Skokov, Viktor Chernomyrdin, Vladimir Kadannikov, and Vladimir Shumeiko.[8] From this range of candidates Yeltsin selected five: Skokov, Chernomyrdin, Gaidar, Kadannikov, and Shumeiko. Skokov and Chernomyrdin polled 637 and 621 votes respectively, with Gaidar third, receiving 400 votes. "I could have proposed Gaidar as a candidate to the Congress," Yeltsin later said. "But I didn't do that. My reasoning was as follows: if Gaidar's share was twenty to thirty votes more, that is, if he'd had a solid third place among the three preferred candidates, there would have been no question. I would have nominated him . . . although as I now see it, we would have been likely to fail."[9]

Before the final decision, Yeltsin summoned the three candidates to the Kremlin for a private conversation. First he spoke with Gaidar, who understood Yeltsin's dilemma and supported Chernomyrdin's candidacy. However, there was a note of bitterness, Yeltsin later recalled. Gaidar strongly objected to the appointment of Skokov, whom the reformers considered to be a representative of the military-industrial complex. The most difficult for Yeltsin was a conversation with Skokov, to whom he had offered the post of prime minister a long time ago. "You oppose the democrats in the government," said Yeltsin. "Your name is linked with the military-industrial complex. In short, I cannot do it."[10]

In the end Yeltsin selected Chernomyrdin, who was approved by the Congress with a vote of 721–172. Skokov had received more "yes" votes than the less well-known Chernomyrdin, but Yeltsin's desire was apparently to have a prime minister who would be more manageable, without too much influence of his own. "Chernomyrdin seemed to be a compromise figure, a candidate with whom everyone could be happy," said Yeltsin. "The choice was dictated—let's face it—by regrettable necessity." Yeltsin took into account the fact that Chernomyrdin "had worked for a time in the Gaidar government [and] saw the magnitude of what was going on." Chernomyrdin "knew all too well that there couldn't be mistakes, that he would have to answer for every step he took."[11] In Yeltsin's view, Chernomyrdin had some advantages over Gaidar. "Gaidar never fully understood what industry was all about, and in particular the steel, petroleum and gas, defense, and consumer industries. All of his knowledge was rather theoretical in nature, which was potentially quite dangerous," Yeltsin complained. "Chernomyrdin knew industry."[12] At least in one respect Yeltsin's intuition appeared to be perfect: Chernomyrdin would show himself to be solid and reliable, as the president had expected. "I was impressed with his taciturnity and reserve, his very sober thinking, and his tough masculinity," Yeltsin later said.[13]

The deputies supported Chernomyrdin's candidacy. The opposition leaders apparently viewed the new prime minister, with his solid *nomenklatura* background, as a future partner and even ally, and the reformers expected him to begin a reversal of reforms. As events would demonstrate, both sides were wrong: the new prime minister was able both to adapt to the new reality and to pursue his own interests.

With Chernomyrdin as the new prime minister, the liberal-radical period of Russian political development came to an end, and the stage of consolidation began. Chernomyrdin's ascent meant a fundamental change at the top. The new premier belonged to the generation of pragmatic managers. He came from the group of gas industry enterprise directors and had begun his political career under Gorbachev as the minister of the gas industry and a member of the Central Committee of the Communist Party. It was hard to suspect Chernomyrdin of any liberal sympathies. But in reality he was an example of those members of the former ruling class who, thanks to their pragmatism, were able to find good places for themselves in the new market structure. Chernomyrdin could be viewed as the representative of a new class of director-entrepreneurs, straddling two epochs and groups and adjusting his method of operation accordingly. Depending on the external circumstances, he could favor first one side, then the other. He was thus able to become the nucleus for a consolidation of centrist and neoconservative forces interested in both stability and gradual market reforms. Thanks to his roots and his ties to industrialist circles, and also to his moderation and lack of charisma, he could play the part that Yeltsin wanted him to play—the role of loyal manager without political ambitions. It would also become clear that Chernomyrdin was not very decisive. It may have been precisely this quality that Yeltsin liked so much in his new prime minister. In any case, Yeltsin deliberately placed his bet on Chernomyrdin, and it was a good bet.

Yeltsin would not have been Yeltsin if he had not tried to appoint a counterweight to the new prime minister. For this, the president brought a liberal, Boris Fyodorov, into the cabinet as the new minister of finance and vice premier. Fyodorov was an even more avid market advocate than Gaidar. Yeltsin also appointed as head of the presidential administration Sergei Filatov, the former deputy chairman of the Supreme Soviet, a man known for his close ties to the democratic camp and his active dislike of Khasbulatov. Filatov was the diametric opposite of his predecessor, Yuri Petrov, an outspoken conservative. Yeltsin refused, however, to dismiss his foreign minister, Andrei Kozyrev, despite pressure to do so. Kozyrev would long remain the "candidate for replacement," and he showed remarkable endurance in that role.

Yeltsin parted with Gaidar without any particular regret. In his memoirs, the president commented: "The Gaidar government, which was rapidly making one decision after another, was in complete isolation. Gaidar and his people never traveled around the country to take the pulse of the nation. From the outset, these ministers perceived the Khasbulatov parliament as an instrument of pressure on them, as a symbol of everything that was reactionary, everything that had to be fought. . . . It was a kind of childish infantile division of people into 'ours' and 'theirs.'"[14] In fact, all these accusations could be directed equally at Yeltsin himself. This was Yeltsin's public farewell to his chief reformer, who had taken the blame for liberalization's flaws and failures, even though they were not always his own, and had thereby allowed Yeltsin to restore his political fortunes and public support. Away from public view, Yeltsin could show gratitude to those who had been loyal to him or helped him; he assisted Gaidar in setting up a research institute to study the transitional economy. But the Gaidar period of the Russian transformation was over.

Debate over the results of Russian economic transformation continues. There is not enough evidence to indicate for certain whether radicalism or slow liberalization, monetary illusions, lack of structural policy, or mistakes in its implementation were the main obstacles to healthy economic change. Could the pain of the economic reform have been less, and could the reformers have done better? It is true that the most essential preconditions for a market were missing in Russia: it lacked the necessary institutional framework (such as a banking system, legal structure, or stock market) and the traditions of honest competition. There were, however, also serious problems with the government itself and its policy. Gaidar himself later acknowledged that his cabinet had failed to realize the immense complexity of its tasks. "The biggest failures awaited us in the process of strengthening the ruble. We hoped that tough financial stabilization would help us to lower inflation. . . . Unfortunately, starting in June [1992], a substantial weakening of financial policies took place. . . . In October we had 25 percent monthly inflation. This was close to the threshold of hyperinflation, when global collapse of the monetary system would have been possible."[15]

This recognition, however, came much later. At the beginning, the self-assurance of the reformers and their refusal to admit to any mistakes produced negative reactions even among their supporters. One could get the impression that the Russian reformers were defending their errors as if they were defending their inheritance. Yavlinsky summed up the results of Gaidar's activity: "October 1991—inflation 6 percent per month, production decline 15 percent per year, exchange rate 60 rubles to the dollar. October 1992—inflation 28 percent per month, production decline 25 percent per year, exchange rate 308 rubles to the dollar. A lot of people had the feeling that they had been cheated."[16] Another evaluation of this period was made by a member of the Gaidar government, Aleksandr Shokhin: "One of our mistakes was neglect of people's savings. . . . If we had understood that inflation would be so great, we would have done our privatization program in such a way that it would be perceived by the population as a compensation for the decline of living standards. . . . But unfortunately privatization took another form."[17]

The primary weaknesses of the Gaidar team resulted not just from the lack of a clear economic strategy—about which they simply did not have enough time to think. The members of the government were often out of touch, and they did not know the lives of ordinary people and could not predict their reactions. Even more important, they were insensitive to social issues and to the price of their economic decisions; and they were even proud of their kamikaze role. This quickly resulted in public hostility toward the reformers. The harshness with which the young reformers carried out their program was evident in Gaidar's own pronouncements. When he was asked if he knew that prices had risen much faster than the reformers had at first predicted, not by two or three times but by twenty or thirty times, Gaidar answered, "Yes, we expected that. But imagine what would have happened if we had announced that prices would increase twentyfold!"[18] Gaidar may have had a point, but perhaps the truth, at a time when people still had faith in the reformers and were prepared to sacrifice, would have been better than a soothing lie. Sergei Vasilyev, who had been an advisor to the Gaidar government, was even more candid: "The reform team had no ethical or social-cultural reflexes."[19] With their technocratic approach, the reformers alienated large segments of the population. "And yet," Alexander Dallin has written, "with creativity it should have been possible to anticipate and minimize, if not totally to avoid, the personal costs to the Russian population."[20]

Another weakness stemmed from the fact that the first Russian reformers were liberals without strong democratic convictions; they did not think much about creating a more civilized regime or democratic procedures. In fact, they were quite happy with strong presidential power. This turned against them; in the end, they lost the support of the proponents of democracy, and they themselves helped the former bureaucracy to regain its position. Their lack of a political and social base became one of the major obstacles to a market breakthrough.

The reformers, in their neoliberal claims about the self-sufficiency of the market, ignored the role of the state and state regulation. As Robert Dahl has underscored, "Although it is true that a market economy exists in all democratic countries, it is also true that what exists in every democratic country is a market economy modified by government regulation."[21] One could not escape an impression that the philosophy of the Gaidar team too much resembled Friedrich von Hayek's conception of "spontaneous order" that at different times influenced other neoliberal teams. According to Hayek's theory, market institutions arise as the unplanned outcomes of human actions. Hayek's analysis of market institutions was based on the English experience, in which markets arose through the development over centuries of the common law. As John Grey has observed,

> If a policy of legislative quietism is pursued, inspired by Hayekian ideas of spontaneous order, then we may expect a replication in most of the post-communist societies of the Russian experience to date—namely, an outbreak of "wild," "spontaneous," or "Hayekian" privatization, that is in fact merely the latest episode in nomenklaturist rent-seeking, in the context of an economic order best characterized as an anarchy-capitalism of the mafia. Such a development is very unlikely to be politically stable. It will reinforce popular suspicion—well founded in terms of actual experience of nomenklatura-controlled markets—that market exchanges are typically exploitative, zero-sum transactions, and it will evoke a political backlash to market return that is syndicalist, dirigiste or autarchic in character.[22]

The reformers also failed to address the existing economic problems consistently. This inconsistency was partly the result of their underestimation of the strength of the Soviet legacy and partly the consequence of pressure by numerous lobbies and popular demand. Indeed, the Gaidar government did attain its primary short-term goal: it destroyed the state-run economy and made it impossible for Russia to return to the old system of state planning. Many observers both within and outside Russia, however, consider the social price of that achievement to have been too high.

THE CEASE-FIRE IS BROKEN

The cease-fire did not last long. A gradual move away from the compromises of the Seventh Congress soon began. One of the instigators was the chairman of the Constitutional Court, Valery Zorkin, who called for the cancellation of the proposed constitutional referendum in April and for simultaneous early elections for both the legislative and executive branches. Zorkin also proposed a moratorium on all changes to the constitution, except for an amendment dissolving the Congress, which he suggested should be replaced by a bicameral legislature. Zorkin believed that a new constitution should be adopted only after stabilization of the situation in the country.

Zorkin was not the only one for whom the prospect of a referendum posed serious concerns. Both before and after the Seventh Congress, the idea of a referendum was resoundingly criticized by various political forces. Many expressed concern that the referendum would be held at a time when fundamental questions about Russia's state structure were still unresolved and answering them with a simple "yes" or "no" was not possible. There was growing anxiety that holding the referendum might deepen the polarization of forces and accelerate the disintegration of the Russian Federation. The latter concerns were not without basis: some of the Russian republics indicated that they might add questions about their independence to the referendum (just as had been done at the time of Gorbachev's referendum on the fate of the Soviet Union on March 17, 1991). Any attempt to draw the nation into these political debates, many feared, presented a real danger of causing a split in Russian society itself.

The inability of the political leaders to reach a working compromise and their mutual intolerance made the prospect of early elections for all offices a reasonable solution, since it would have created a new balance of forces. No serious analyst in Russia doubted that Yeltsin would have every chance of being reelected president. A strong argument for new elections was that both branches had been elected during the communist period, and elections would give them new legitimacy. If he had agreed to new elections, Yeltsin could have created conditions for a peaceful transformation and the selection of a new parliament.

There were those, however, who were against early elections. Many deputies feared becoming political nonentities. More significantly, many members of the president's team were opposed to new elections. Their reluctance to hold early elections, despite Yeltsin's excellent prospects for winning, can be explained by one thing only: the president did not want to reorganize the government under a compromise that might have led to the creation of a new system of counterweights just when he intended to turn the parliament into a purely decorative fixture that could not obstruct his actions.

Meanwhile the number of political forces advocating a revision of the December agreement and cancellation of the constitutional referendum continued to grow. Many local administrative heads and centrist forces, and even the majority of members of the Presidential Council, who were generally close to Yeltsin, came out against the referendum. On February 5, 1993, the first round-table discussion was held; it included Rutskoi, Khasbulatov, Chernomyrdin, and representatives of trade unions and various political movements (even including Democratic Choice, in the role of observer). The participants called on Yeltsin to cancel the April referendum. Finally, on February 9, 1993, Yeltsin said that the referendum was not a goal in itself and that he would agree to parliamentary elections in 1994 and presidential elections in 1995. He opposed holding the elections simultaneously, however, asserting that this would be extremely destabilizing. Yeltsin's proposal predictably failed to satisfy his opponents, who demanded simultaneous elections. The political situation in Russia was thus at an impasse, as the existing state of affairs was no less unstable than holding simultaneous elections, which Yeltsin refused to sanction.

Trying to find an exit from this dead end, Yeltsin proposed a new constitutional agreement on the division of powers between the parliament and the executive branch and called for an extraordinary session of the Congress of People's Deputies to ratify it. If this received approval, he would agree to cancel the referendum. At a press conference on February 17, Shakhrai said that the president was ready to give up his right to initiate legislation, withdraw from the day-to-day management of the economy, and seek the Supreme Soviet's approval of his appointments to the executive branch. If the Congress refused to approve this agreement, however, Yeltsin would go ahead with the referendum.[23] There were hints at the time from Yeltsin's entourage that the president might cede to the parliament some of his prerogatives in the areas of foreign policy, national security, and defense. Such concessions on Yeltsin's part would have been an unprecedented and risky experiment that would have demonstrated the weakness of his position. On February 27, during a meeting of Civic Union, Yeltsin also proposed adoption of a "Law on Power" that would create a framework for the activities of all political institutions for a transition period. Despite these proposals, his team continued to prepare for the referendum. Yeltsin apparently did not expect to reach a compromise with the parliament, and he may not have tried hard to do so. It is likely that he was merely trying to buy time for his next move.

While making conciliatory moves, Yeltsin simultaneously set out to strengthen his support in Russia's regions. He issued a decree reestablishing the system of presidential representatives in the provinces, which had been abolished by the Seventh Congress, and he created a new organ, the Administration for Territorial Affairs, which gave him another mechanism to control the regions. This was a signal that, while offering parliament a compromise, Yeltsin was actually trying to regain what he had lost in his previous battles with the parliament. He wanted to restore his presidential pyramid of power and to rejoin the battle.

The Supreme Soviet rejected Yeltsin's February 19th proposal for a constitutional agreement, interpreting it as an attempt by the president to sign the legislative branch's death warrant. Its leaders believed that, since Yeltsin was in retreat, it would take only one more blow to knock him out completely. Therefore, the leaders of the opposition decided to convene the Eighth Extraordinary Congress. Reason and restraint clearly were absent in the legislative branch, while all moderate forces recognized that a new confrontation was becoming inevitable, and the situation was threatening to spin out of control.

On March 9, meeting for a round-table discussion, the representatives of political parties and groups—including Democratic Choice, Civic Union, the Congress of Left Democratic Forces, the Communist Party of the Russian Federation, and independent unions—called on Yeltsin and the deputies to show "good sense and maximum responsibility." Many understood that the leading political figures, stirred by their mutual animosity, might do something that would lead to irreversible damage. In an effort to allay public concern, Defense Minister Pavel Grachev issued an official statement that the army would remain neutral. The leaders of Russia's republics and regions, alarmed that a referendum would only aggravate tensions in the country, also began to call for the cancellation of the referendum. On March 9, under growing pressure, Yeltsin declared at a meeting of the Council of Heads of Republics (which was revived for this occasion) that he was ready to cancel the referendum if the Congress of People's Deputies would adopt the new constitutional agreement about power sharing.

The Eighth Extraordinary Congress of People's Deputies, convened on March 10, 1993, only deepened the crisis. At the opening session, Yeltsin again tried to take a conciliatory tone, proposing that the president and the parliament each surrender some authority to the Chernomyrdin government. The deputies rejected this. Yeltsin's draft resolution was also defeated, with 382 votes in favor (less than the required majority) and 329 against. Khasbulatov repudiated the agreement of December 12 that he had signed with Yeltsin.

After its offer of truce was rejected, the president's team renewed attempts to force a dissolution of the legislative branch. Plans for such a radical scenario had long been in preparation by Yeltsin's associates. Its discussion dated back to the beginning of 1992, and it had been a real threat as early as December 1992, even though it was not then implemented. This time, the president's team had prepared more carefully for a scenario involving the use of force, and there were numerous rumors of such a plan. The Western press reported what most political observers in Moscow had already suspected for some time—that Yeltsin had polled Western leaders to see whether or not they would support him if he took extraordinary measures, particularly the dissolution of the pro-communist parliament.[24] Judging by the president's next steps, he believed that he had the approval of Western leaders for such an action.

YELTSIN LOSES—AND RESPONDS

March 12, 1993, was a decisive and troubling day in the Eighth Congress of People's Deputies, and the threat of violence was in the air. Leaders of the Federation of Independent Trade Unions prepared a statement to be issued in case a state of emergency were declared. Many Muscovites looked out their windows expecting to see soldiers and tanks in the streets.

On that day Congress terminated all the extraordinary powers that had been accorded to Yeltsin by the Fifth Congress in October 1991. This deprived him of the powers to issue decrees with the force of law, to appoint local administrative chiefs, and to name ministers without the approval of the parliament. These extraordinary powers should have ended in December 1992, but they had been extended by the compromise reached at the Seventh Congress. The March Congress, in other words, reversed the decisions of the previous Congress. At the same time, it substantially strengthened the government's powers. It also elevated the positions of head of the Central Bank and head of the Pension Fund to cabinet level, as Yeltsin wished. Contrary to the president's wishes, however, the parliament went further and gave the cabinet the right to propose legislation, thus strengthening the government at the president's expense. No less important, the Congress activated certain dormant amendments to the constitution; among these was an article prohibiting the president from dissolving constitutionally established bodies.

It was not in Yeltsin's nature to wait passively for events to unfold. He took the floor and tried to fight back, calling on the Congress not to destroy the compromise reached in December. It was too late; the compromise no longer satisfied anyone except the radical democrats and the presidential team. Yeltsin objected to giving the government greater independence, apparently forgetting that he himself had called for such power sharing. The deputies stood their ground. Finally, the president warned that he had few resources left to maintain the stability of the situation. He had already taken soundings in the West on how it would react to the imposition of a state of emergency in Russia. There was nothing left for Yeltsin to do except, conspicuously, leave the Congress hall. His supporters stated that they, along with the president, would never return to it.

The emboldened deputies, however, did not stop. On the following day, they firmly rejected Yeltsin's proposal to hold a referendum on April 25 on the delineation of power and private land ownership. The Congress put a spotlight on Speaker Khasbulatov. In the past, although Khasbulatov had maneuvered to weaken the president, he nevertheless had tried to meet him halfway at decisive moments; now he came out unequivocally against Yeltsin.

Yeltsin's defeat was the most remarkable result of the Eighth Congress. It was brought about not by the mobilization of the opposition, but by the centrists' rejection of the president's policies. Yeltsin suddenly lost the role of omnipotent leader to which he had become accustomed. Still, it would not be accurate to conclude that Yeltsin had lost everything; he still had many ways to manipulate the situation.

Following the conclusion of the Eighth Congress, the tension in Russia was palpable. The pause lasted only until Yeltsin's television address to the nation on March 20, 1993, when he announced that he was instituting a special regime of rule and would hold the referendum on April 25. Any decisions of the parliament that purported to alter presidential decrees would no longer have juridical force. Thus what many had expected and others had feared came to pass: Yeltsin decided to deliver a fatal blow to parliament and to eliminate all obstacles to his personal rule. The parliament's intensely negative reaction to Yeltsin's move was predictable, and so was Vice President Rutskoi's immediate opposition to the special regime. No one, however, had expected Constitutional Court Chairman Zorkin and Prosecutor General Valentin Stepankov to come out as forcefully against the president as they did on March 21.[25] Even more surprising, the president's move was not backed by some who were usually his loyal supporters, including Yuri Skokov, chief of the Security Council.

Without even waiting for a copy of the written text, the Constitutional Court began hearings on the constitutionality of Yeltsin's decree. The Supreme Soviet scheduled the Ninth Extraordinary Congress of People's Deputies for the end of March. Prime Minister Chernomyrdin, meanwhile, managed to avoid stating his position on the decree, and the noncommittal power ministers, urgently summoned to appear before the parliament, managed to talk about everything except whether they supported the president's decision. Several of them emphasized their loyalty to the constitution, which had to mean that they were against Yeltsin's decree, as their statements put the emphasis on the fundamental law rather than on the action of the chief executive. Only after extreme pressure from the president did the prime minister appear on national television, where, surrounded by his key ministers, he gloomily read out a statement of support. It was clear that the government was far from enthusiastic about the president's maneuver.

Meanwhile, no one outside the close presidential circle had seen the notorious decree, and questions about its actual text, and even its existence, were raised more and more persistently. Yeltsin's associates assured everyone that the decree would soon be produced for public scrutiny. In the meantime, they offered awkward, disingenuous, even absurd explanations, such as that the staff responsible for duplicating and disseminating documents did not work on Saturdays and Sundays. It soon became clear that either the president's team, insufficiently prepared for the imposition of the special regime and for resistance to it, was completely preoccupied with damage control, or that the announcement of the decree, which no one outside the Kremlin had seen in writing, was a kind of trial balloon intended to gauge reactions. This time, even taking into consideration the usual impulsiveness of Yeltsin's policy-making style, the lack of basic coordination in the president's move was stunning. His most serious tactical flaw was the failure to line up support from the power ministries and the regions. Under the circumstances, Yeltsin's associates apparently decided not to produce the actual decree in order to retain their freedom of maneuver. Instead, they sat back and watched the behavior of various forces in response to the announcement of the special regime, and they bided their time.

The Constitutional Court, having reviewed the president's oral presentation, ruled that Yeltsin's proposal was unconstitutional. This gave Khasbulatov grounds for issuing a statement in which he noted that new elections for the executive and legislative branches were now more timely than ever. Khasbulatov did not rule out the possibility of a move to impeach Yeltsin and to transfer presidential powers temporarily to the vice president. He appeared certain that Yeltsin was defeated for good, and it really did seem that Yeltsin and his supporters were likely to lose their grip on power. Never before had Rutskoi been so close to receiving the presidential post. Suddenly, Yeltsin seemed to lose his resolve. When it became clear that even his closest allies were not prepared to support the use of force, Yeltsin retreated. He let it be known that he had misspoken when he mentioned the "special regime."

Meanwhile, on March 26, the Ninth Extraordinary Congress of People's Deputies was gathering in Moscow, although it was no longer clear what its objective was. As soon as Yeltsin retreated, the problem of the special regime became moot, but the assembled deputies soon managed to find a new reason for dissatisfaction. The president and the speaker, however, took a short recess and came to a truce. They negotiated and presented the deputies with a new draft agreement: Yeltsin agreed to give up the referendum and to hold early elections for both branches of government; Khasbulatov, in turn, agreed to dismiss the Congress and to support the formation of a two-chamber parliament.

This was the optimal solution for the country. It opened the door for a peaceful way out of the impasse in which the entire Russian government had found itself for months. To the deputies, however, this was the last straw. Both the democrats and the anti-reformists were upset that the two leaders had made a deal behind their backs.[26] The Congress stood up against both Yeltsin and Khasbulatov, and the deputies put to simultaneous votes the questions of confidence in the president and in the speaker. Yeltsin just barely managed to avoid impeachment, with the motion falling seventy-two votes short of the required two-thirds majority; 617 deputies voted against the president, and only 218 supported him. Never before had Yeltsin come so close to losing power completely. Yet no one believed that he was ready to give up his post voluntarily.[27] Khasbulatov did better, receiving 339 no-confidence votes and 558 votes of support. Evidently the deputies, despite their dissatisfaction, decided that no one was better able to defend their interests than Khasbulatov.

Having rejected the compromise worked out by the president and the speaker, the Congress promptly set out on a path to a new impasse. It appeared that all possibilities of breaking out of the situation within the existing political alignment were exhausted, but everybody understood that Yeltsin was not going to give up easily and that the only way out for him was to use force and dissolve the parliament. The deputies finally understood that trapping the president was simply too dangerous. In the end, the Ninth Congress was compelled to step back and to adopt a resolution approving the April referendum. For a humiliated Yeltsin it was a breath of fresh air. At the same time, the deputies tried to phrase the referendum questions in such a way as to avert a victory for the president in April. The referendum was to have four questions: (1) Do you have confidence in the president? (2) Do you support the economic and social policies of the government? (3) Do you favor early elections for the presidency? (4) Do you favor early elections for the parliament? The deputies hoped that the referendum would be the beginning of the end for Yeltsin and his policies.

THE PRESIDENT WINS

Before the Ninth Congress, Yeltsin had seemed to be on the verge of falling, but he once again miraculously managed to survive. Now he hoped that the nation would support him. The referendum was scheduled for April 25, 1993. While it could not bring the country out of its constitutional and political crisis, it did allow Yeltsin to buy time and mobilize his resources for continued political struggle. The results of the referendum were a surprise to many. Given the

73

deepening economic crisis in the country, few people had expected to see such a high level of political activism by the public and such a resounding endorsement of the government's social and economic course. About 69.2 million of the 107.3 million eligible voters took part in the referendum. Of that number, 58.7 percent expressed confidence in the president, and 53 percent supported his social and economic policies. Only 31.7 percent of the voters favored early presidential elections, while 43.1 percent of voters favored early parliamentary elections.

Yeltsin had clearly won both a moral and a political victory. Nevertheless, it would be a mistake to view the results of the referendum as a mandate for the president to take any action he pleased. The 38 million voters who did not take part in the referendum could be said to have demonstrated their dissatisfaction with the situation and their distrust toward all political institutions. Notably, the president's policies were not supported by a majority in Russia's republics. The referendum was not even held in two of them, and in twelve of nineteen others, the president did not receive majority support; nor did he receive majority support in a number of Russia's regions.[28] On the whole, Yeltsin received 7 million fewer votes of support in the 1993 referendum than he had in the presidential elections of 1991. Many supported the president as simply the lesser of two evils, given the absence of any real democratic alternative. Notwithstanding popular dissatisfaction with Yeltsin, public attitudes toward the parliament were even more negative; many people viewed it as merely an assembly of ambitious clowns.

The results of the referendum did not have the force of law and had to be turned into something more concrete and specific. According to the law on referendums then current, the president had the right to make substantive changes in his course only if his position was supported by a majority of all listed voters, which meant that he would have had to gain the votes of 75 percent of those who took part in the April 25 referendum. The president's team thus had no grounds for excessive optimism. On the contrary, moderate observers interpreted the results of the referendum not as a victory for the president but as evidence that a substantial majority of Russians opposed any kind of sharp turn. The results could also be interpreted as a vote for the preservation of a balance of power between the legislative and executive branches.[29]

After the referendum, Yeltsin had to decide how best to use the support he had received. His activities were directed toward the preparation of a new draft constitution. Yeltsin also had several tactical objectives, notably the need to strengthen his own position and to neutralize his competitors, especially Vice President Rutskoi. Rutskoi's popularity had continued to grow, and he had become, arguably, Yeltsin's chief rival. The radicals in Yeltsin's circle expected that the president would take advantage of his success in the referendum to name an unambiguously liberal cabinet—one without conservatives or representatives of the old industrial-sector interests. The resignation in May of the representative of the industrialists, Vice Premier Georgi Khizha, and the departure of Yuri Skokov, whom the liberals had disliked, seemed to confirm this expectation. Gaidar supporters hoped for the return of the "chief reformer" to the cabinet.

Once again, however, events demonstrated that Yeltsin would always go his own way. The president unexpectedly named the decidedly conservative Oleg Lobov as first vice premier, with responsibility for the key economics ministry. The president also appointed Oleg Soskovets, a former Soviet-era minister of metallurgy, as another first deputy prime minister. Soskovets was a typical *apparatchik*, far from the reformist camp.[30] The result of these appointments was a shift in the balance within the new cabinet in favor of sectoral representatives who did not support liberal ideas. Lobov, a long-time enemy of the radicals, made an attempt to reestablish the traditional Soviet pattern of governing and even to reintroduce elements of state planning. Yeltsin had thus used his success in the referendum to strengthen the ranks of traditionalists and representatives of the old guard in the government.

In the summer of 1993, Vice President Rutskoi was the only politician who received a favorable rating from all of Russia's different social groups. Although Yeltsin's popularity ratings surpassed Rutskoi's in Moscow, St. Petersburg, and other large cities, the president trailed Rutskoi considerably in the provinces. A national poll conducted in June asked, "Who is the most authoritative political figure in Russia?" and 22 percent of the respondents named Yeltsin, while 16 percent named Rutskoi.[31] In polls taken in rural areas in July, 85 percent of the respondents expressed a negative attitude toward Yeltsin. When asked who was capable of leading the country out of the crisis, 26 percent of these respondents named Rutskoi.[32] This could only encourage Yeltsin's team to seek a way to get rid of the vice president. The possibility of an early presidential succession was not imaginary: Yeltsin was growing physically weaker. The regime's fear of Rutskoi was a significant stimulus to drafting a new constitution that would eliminate the post of vice president.

In the summer of 1993 the president's team quickly organized the Constitutional Conference, which set out to create a new Russian constitution. Participants were chosen to ensure that Yeltsin supporters predominated. After the successful April referendum, the president was content to play the role of peacemaker. He even made concessions to his opponents, agreeing to consider not only the presidential draft constitution, which incorporated a strong central government, but also the draft on which the parliament had long been at work. It was important for Yeltsin to get the new constitution at any price, not because he was attached to constitutionalism, but because the new constitution would be a vehicle for legitimately strengthening his own power. Yeltsin appeared to believe sincerely that his personal rule was the most important prerequisite for stability, and perhaps the only one. At this stage, in the summer of 1993, Yeltsin was trying to use legitimate means to strengthen his power.

The Constitutional Conference quickly set about reconciling the presidential and parliamentary drafts. The result was a combined text that diluted the authoritarian tone of the presidential draft. The work of synthesizing the two versions had proceeded surprisingly peacefully. The Constitutional Conference was not only the first successful political round table in Russia but also a school of real political dialogue.

A new source of conflict, however, soon emerged between the Russian regions and the non-Russian republics organized on ethnic lines (such as Tatarstan, Bashkortostan, and others) that were desperately trying to preserve their hard-won sovereign status. The latter insisted on regarding Russia's federal system as a treaty matter rather than a constitutional arrangement. In response, the Russian territorial-administrative regions renewed their attempt to raise their status to that of the autonomous republics. All of these tendencies had existed in latent form before the conference, and the elaboration of the new draft constitution focused interests and brought conflicts to the surface.[33]

Another surprise—one that might easily have been anticipated—was that many regional bosses were not inclined to support the proposed strong presidential system of government. The structure outlined in the parliamentary draft was more to their liking. The president and his advisers found themselves caught in a craftily structured trap. If the representation of the local leaders were increased, they might support Yeltsin and approve the preeminence of the executive branch in the new state structure proposed by the president's draft. Yet the governors would agree to this only in exchange for a guarantee of greater independence from the center. That would transform Yeltsin, or any other president, into a largely ceremonial figure and lead to further erosion of the powers of the federal center.

To acquire the same status and rights as the autonomous republics, Russia's regions advanced a proposal that had been widely discussed earlier: returning to a territorial division of Russia based on districts, or *gubernias*, as in the times of the Russian empire. When this failed to gain support, some regions began a grassroots struggle for equal status with the republics. This fight began while the Constitutional Conference was still in session. The Yekaterinburg (Sverdlovsk) regional government in Yeltsin's birthplace voted to establish the Urals Republic. Eduard Rossel, governor of Yekaterinburg, explained: "All regions and republics are equally independent in economic matters. But where is the equality when a region transfers more taxes to the federal budget than the republics do, republics whose inhabitants have greater social benefits than those who live in the Russian regions?"[34]

The federal center's preferential economic policies toward some republics were a constant issue in the disputes among Russia's regions. The center closed its eyes to the inequality between the regions and the republics so as to placate influential republic bosses and win them over to Yeltsin's side. Such a policy, however, inevitably aroused protests from the Russian regions, which were strictly required to transfer all of their taxes to the center. Other Russian regions, especially in Siberia, began to raise their heads. In Irkutsk, in a remarkable display of unity, the leaders of both the legislative and the executive branches of the regional government declared that they were going to form a unified East Siberian or Central Siberian Republic. This was an open challenge to the power of the center. Some regions, such as Tomsk, even began to write their own constitutions. The regions began to treat the central authorities as if they were their equals.

The leaders of the regions found a number of specific features of the new draft constitution unacceptable. They spoke out categorically against the designation of the republics as "sovereign states." "If that formula is retained in the new draft, we will also declare ourselves sovereign," they said. They also spoke out sharply against incorporating treaties between individual republics and the center in the draft constitution, a proposal intended to pacify Tatarstan and Bashkortostan. That move, regional leaders argued, would increase the apparent inequality

77

of the federation subjects and would become a source of constant tension in the future.[35]

Thus the Constitutional Conference stimulated centrifugal tendencies in the country. By involving the representatives of the people in drafting a new federal constitution, the president strengthened the role of the subjects of the Russian Federation and involved them in the battles of the top echelons of federal power. He thereby inadvertently encouraged their ambitions and allowed the long-concealed dissatisfactions of the regional elites to rise to the surface. Unwittingly and unwillingly, he had invigorated the efforts of the former autonomous republics to gain independence and, more important, had risked the Russian Federation's spinning out of control. The conference facilitated the transition of local ruling teams to a new stage in the struggle for self-determination. One result was the reconciliation of the local legislative soviets and local executive administrators. Conditions were fertile for an even more serious conflict between the federal center and the constituent parts of the federation.

Khasbulatov had thus far remained in the shadows, maintaining that the constitutional meeting made no difference to the opposition forces in the parliament. A shrewd politician, he understood that once a constitution was drafted, the crucial question would be how to adopt it. In this process, Yeltsin could not circumvent the parliament without creating a new crisis. The parliament began a new offensive: It delivered an unexpected blow to the president by adopting a draft law, "On Procedures for Adopting the Constitution," which gave it unilateral control over the elaboration of the draft and called for its submission to a Congress of People's Deputies by November 1993. It became ever more evident that neither the April referendum nor the Constitutional Conference had resolved the fundamental impasse between the branches.

CHAPTER FOUR

YELTSIN'S SEPTEMBER "REVOLUTION" AND THE ELECTIONS: 1993-94

BY THE END OF SUMMER 1993, THE POLITICAL STRUGGLE in Moscow had reached a new level of intensity. The opposing sides made ever graver accusations of corruption against each other, and many influential politicians were implicated. Aleksandr Rutskoi on one side, and Yeltsin's close associates Vladimir Shumeiko and Mikhail Poltoranin on the other, were among the primary targets as well as the most spirited accusers.[1] Neither members of parliament nor officials of the executive branch were left unscathed. Everybody in Moscow felt that the moment of truth was approaching.

THE STRUGGLE REACHES A NEW LEVEL

Meanwhile, Russia was buzzing with rumors that Yeltsin was seriously ill and incapable of fulfilling his presidential duties. In August 1991 no one had believed that President Gorbachev was ill, but in August 1993 few believed that President Yeltsin was healthy. At the beginning of August several prominent Western publications discussed the health of the Russian president, with one claiming that, "over the past three weeks Yeltsin's health has worsened to such a degree that he is no longer in control of the situation."[2] Such stories became so widespread that the president's representatives were compelled to issue an official statement asserting that he was in good health. This failed to reassure people. *Sovietskaya Rossiya*, an anti-Yeltsin newspaper, provoked a new scandal in early August by publishing an anonymous "analytical memorandum," or plan of action, allegedly prepared by Yeltsin's entourage. The memorandum, which was obviously forged by the opposition, suggested that Yeltsin "was not able to act" and was completely under the control of his associates. It said that the time had come to prepare for a coup in order to prevent the transfer of power to Rutskoi.[3] The memorandum prescribed actions "to polarize the situation and cause an explosion . . . to publicize material on the Rutskoi-Khasbulatov plot; to go to any lengths in misinformation to create the necessary intensity of public antipathy; to begin to prepare public opinion for the possibility of a communist coup; to issue a decree in Yeltsin's name setting a date for parliamentary elections in autumn 1993; [and] to provoke a sharp reaction by the Supreme Soviet and respond with punitive measures." The events of the end of September showed that, although the analytical memorandum was a fabrication, it may well have been based on some actual facts and leaks from the top.

The president, meanwhile, continued his vacation away from Moscow, increasing suspicions that he was incapacitated. Journalists began to call him "Mr. Nowhere," hinting that he could not be found when he was needed. A list of his most notorious disappearances was published: after the failure of the August coup, in September 1991; during the visit to Russia of Japanese Foreign Affairs Minister Koji Watanabe in January 1992; during the scandals surrounding the Black Sea Fleet in May 1992; and when deputies had attacked Yegor Gaidar in December 1992. Most ridiculous and inexplicable was the time President Clinton had been unable to reach Yeltsin for several days and had been told that Yeltsin "is someplace where there is no phone."[4]

Talk of possible successors to Yeltsin was constant. The only official heir to Yeltsin was still Rutskoi, and, indeed, Rutskoi had no other role, for Yeltsin had taken away his other duties. Signs that Yeltsin's team had decided to break the stalemate by using force multiplied. Khasbulatov, feeling that the moment of reckoning was near, called back all the deputies who had left Moscow.

Yeltsin returned to Moscow at the beginning of August looking a bit infirm, but certainly not deathly ill. New speculation arose that the president might be feigning illness as part of some subtle game. But Yeltsin began his assault on the opposition in earnest. The entire democratic elite gathered for a conference of the leaders of the Russian state television and radio companies on August 12 at the House of the Russian Press. The real objective of the meeting was to consolidate the heterogeneous democratic groups and to sanction decisive action by the president against the opposition. The tone of the conference was set by the most radical democrats—those from the first revolutionary generation who had fought Gorbachev—and the conference participants were in an uncompromising mood. They demanded that the president put an end to both the parliament and the opposition. Yeltsin responded with the words that his comrades wanted to hear: "This autumn there must be elections for a new parliament," declared the president. "If the parliament itself does not take this decision, then I will."[5]

Yeltsin now attempted to secure military support. He increased his contacts with the power ministries, especially with Defense Minister Pavel Grachev, who now joined Yeltsin's entourage. The president also made a point of visiting elite military units in the Moscow region, and he donned military gear in front of television cameras for the first time.

Before making his final decisions, however, the president tried once more to neutralize the parliament by peaceful means. On August 14, 1993, in Petrozavodsk, capital of the Republic of Karelia, Yeltsin met with the republic's leaders and proposed the creation of a new organ, the Council of Heads of Republics. His idea was to position this new council to replace the Supreme Soviet and the Congress.[6] Gorbachev, too, had dreamed of forming a counterweight to the Congress of People's Deputies of the USSR, but neither Gorbachev nor Yeltsin succeeded in this. In August 1993, the idea of the Council of Heads of Republics went nowhere.[7]

THE DENOUEMENT APPROACHES

Moscow political circles were frantic by the beginning of September 1993. The president's loyal press unleashed a wave of articles arguing that Russia was not ready for broad-based democracy, much less for "extreme parliamentarism." References to the successes of General Charles De Gaulle's Fifth Republic in overcoming France's internal political crisis became especially popular. There was no doubt that preparations were under way for what the president called an impending "hot September."[8]

The presidential camp was far from consolidated. The pragmatists, grouped around Viktor Chernomyrdin, represented the interests of the bureaucracy from different branches of the economy and the governmental apparatus who were in favor of modernization through slow and cautious market reform. The radicals reflected the interests of Russia's new *nomenklatura*, dynamic technocrats who pushed for radical reform. They were represented by Yegor Gaidar, Sergei Filatov, Gennady

Burbulis (who was now receding in importance), and those of their supporters from the liberal camp who had succeeded in getting a foothold inside the government structures. Representatives of the orthodox bureaucracy—those conservatives who retained tenuous positions in the executive branch—also tried to influence the president, often successfully. Typical of these players was Yeltsin's old friend Oleg Lobov. As a result of these conflicts, Russian politics did not resemble a purely bipolar model of confrontation between the president and parliament; instead, the battle was waged on several different political levels. The struggles of these various groups within the executive branch may explain Yeltsin's contradictory behavior during this period. Although he chose a policy of using force against the parliament, supported and encouraged by the radicals, he also made a number of concessions to the conservatives within his own circle.

At the end of August, Lobov began an attempt at counterreform. He offered a plan to reorganize the Ministry of Economics that would have meant a return to a state-directed economy. The president, who had little understanding of economic questions, initially supported the Lobov project. He later rejected it only under coordinated pressure from both the radicals and the pragmatists, who managed to unite on this issue. Had Lobov succeeded, Russia would have had a mini-coup within the government: the cabinet would have started carrying out the very policies that the parliament was demanding.

Soon, however, Yeltsin made a new sharp turn. The radicals were heartened by his proposal to bring Gaidar back into the government, and the first reformer accepted the invitation. From this some observers concluded that Yeltsin had unequivocally returned to radical market reform. The rejoicing radicals hoped that the period of the president's wavering was over, and with it the era of Chernomyrdin, his *apparatchik* bureaucrats, and conservatives like Lobov. Given Gaidar's views and his hostile attitude toward the parliament, his return to the cabinet increased the likelihood that the political crisis would be resolved by force.

At the beginning of September, Yeltsin has recalled in his memoirs, "I made the decision [to end the stalemate with parliament]. No one knew about it. Such a parliament in Russia would no longer exist."[9] Aware of what was approaching, the leaders of most of the factions in the Congress of People's Deputies made a final appeal to the president, proposing to discuss the crisis together. At this moment the major factions might have been prepared to sacrifice Khasbulatov in exchange for a peaceful dialogue with the executive authorities. Even the most staunch opposition factions—Industrial Union, Agrarian Union, and Communists of Russia—were inclined toward reaching some kind of accommodation with the executive branch. Their turnaround had its basis in a number of factors, including the factions' instinct for self-preservation. Representatives of various sectors of the economy, the regional groups, the enterprise directors, and the agrarian bureaucracy applied pressure. They did not want a clash between the parliament and the president that might give Yeltsin and the radicals a pretext to establish an authoritarian regime, which could harm their own interests. The present shifting balances of power gave them more room to maneuver.

Thus the possibility of a compromise arose. It might have meant holding elections for the parliament and the presidency in early 1994. Considering that after the most recent referendum the president had not succeeded in his struggle with the parliament, and that all his major policy initiatives aimed at the legislative branch (such as the new constitution and formation of the Council of the Heads of Republics) had been frustrated, a compromise with the parliament probably would have been the optimal nonconfrontational solution for the executive branch. Yet the president did not respond to the increasingly conciliatory mood in the legislature. It became evident that this time Yeltsin and his team wanted a clear victory and a free hand in implementing their own agenda.

Near the end of September the signs of crisis increased. Khasbulatov gave a television interview on September 18 in which he attacked the president. A pretext for initiating the open confrontation could have been found at any other moment as well, however. The plan for getting rid of parliament had been prepared in December 1992, when Yeltsin was threatened with impeachment, and had been on Yeltsin's desk frequently since then.[10] He rejected any possibility of a peaceful exit from the crisis. The clash between the branches of power became inevitable, and both sides were to blame for the outcome.

YELTSIN AVENGED

On September 21, 1993, Yeltsin struck, issuing Presidential Decree No. 1400, "On the Stages of Constitutional Reform in the Russian Federation." By this decree, Yeltsin dissolved the parliament and de facto introduced presidential rule. To slow down the response of the opposition, all government-controlled lines of communication to the White House, where the parliament was housed, were cut. In a nationwide television address, Yeltsin claimed an urgent need to overcome the paralysis of authority that he blamed on the Supreme Soviet and its leadership. He announced that elections for new representative organs and a referendum on a new draft constitution would be held December 11-12, 1993.

Two hours after the announcement of Decree No. 1400, Vice President Aleksandr Rutskoi was sworn in by the parliament as president of the Russian Federation. The next day, the parliament's leaders handed out arms to civilians willing to guard the parliament, and one day after that, on September 23, an emergency Tenth Congress of People's Deputies was hastily called at the White House. The parliament had decided to fight back.

To try to co-opt the deputies, Yeltsin signed a decree guaranteeing benefits for the deputies of the 1990-95 term; this was in effect a bribe, or an open invitation for those meeting in the White House to disperse peacefully. The majority of the deputies, however, decided to stay in the building and resist the president's actions. On September 25, by decree of the president, the White House was blockaded by militia and interior ministry troops, who allowed people to leave but not to enter.[11] Attempts at negotiation did not yield any positive results. Both sides appeared incapable of compromise.[12] While the presidential team evidently counted on a complete and quick victory and no longer wished to make any concessions, Rutskoi and Khasbulatov apparently believed that the country and the army would support them. Indecisiveness on the part of certain military leaders and regional bosses (some of whom had probably promised their support to the opposition) also contributed to the deputies' decision to resist Yeltsin. They believed that they were five minutes away from toppling him, and so they decided to fight all the way to the victorious end that they believed could not be very far off. This was an enormous mistake.

According to Defense Minister Pavel Grachev, on October 2 Yeltsin insisted that army troops be brought to Moscow to augment the forces already there.[13] The first clash between the parliament's allies and forces of the Interior Ministry occurred on October 2 in Moscow's Smolensk Square. On October 3, in response to the inflammatory summons of

Rutskoi and Khasbulatov, thousands of parliament supporters stormed the Moscow mayor's office, just opposite the White House. The first blood was spilled. That evening, prompted by their leaders, the opposition forces tried to take over the Ostankino television station. The attempt was stopped by government troops only after midnight on October 4, with many casualties among the civilians.

While the opposition's mobs were flowing through the streets of central Moscow, television showed a distressed and agitated Gaidar calling on people to defend the government. One can only imagine what might have happened if Yeltsin's supporters had also gone to the streets and had clashed with the opposition crowds; Gaidar's summons could have unleashed a real civil war. However, many members of the intelligentsia, as well as many ordinary Muscovites, including those who had gone into the streets to support Yeltsin at the White House during the August coup of 1991, remained at home. To them, what was happening was simply a feud between two opposing cliques. Hearing Gaidar's urgent call to arms, a number of well-known journalists quickly took to the radio and objected. They argued that Gaidar had no moral right to call citizens into street confrontations and that military detachments, not unarmed civilians, should be defending the government.

The regions and the republics for the most part simply watched the rows from a distance. Republic and regional leaders generally adopted a wait-and-see attitude, as their Soviet counterparts had done during the August 1991 coup attempt. Representatives of some regions called on both sides to stop the confrontation and demanded that the president lift the siege of the White House. The regional elites preferred simultaneous early elections of both the president and the parliament as the way out of the crisis, yet they had neither the will nor the means to insist on this option.[14]

Early on October 4, the president declared a state of emergency in the city of Moscow. Tanks attacked and started firing on the White House at 6:45 in the morning to try to force the deputies out. By 5:00 p.m., the White House had been captured by forces loyal to the president. Speaker Khasbulatov and other leaders of the "parliamentary sit-in" along with "president" Rutskoi found themselves in prison. Yeltsin had scored a crushing victory over his opponents, and he quickly set a date for the new parliamentary elections and a national vote on the draft constitution.

There have been various interpretations of these dramatic events. According to one, Yeltsin and his team were on the edge of defeat and almost lost control over the situation: during the events of October 3 and 4, Moscow was on the brink of a civil war. The president had to force the army and its leadership to act because the military did not want to settle politicians' scores, and many military personnel, including some at the highest level of command, were sympathetic to the parliament. Some in the Defense Ministry, most notably General Boris Gromov, a deputy minister, were constantly in contact with Rutskoi and his associates.[15] Yeltsin conceded that the army was reluctant to get involved: "I saw that the army, notwithstanding all the assurances of the Minister of Defense, for some reason was not in condition to quickly come to the defense of Moscow." Even more eloquent was the refusal by the Alpha and Vympel elite presidential guard units to participate in the attack on the parliament. "Are you prepared to fulfill the president's order?" Yeltsin asked them at the decisive moment. In response, as he himself wrote after the events, he heard "silence, a terrible, inexplicable silence from such an elite presidential military unit."[16]

Yeltsin spent a considerable part of the day and night of October 3 calling Defense Minister Pavel Grachev, who kept saying that army units were already on their way to Moscow, when in fact they were not. Grachev simply defied Yeltsin and lied to him, not wishing to take responsibility for any of the bloodshed. Yeltsin was forced to humble himself, going personally to the generals to beg for help. At an emergency meeting of the Collegium of the Ministry of Defense, the generals were morosely silent and avoided looking Yeltsin in the eye. Minister of Defense Grachev finally asked for a written order to use tanks against the parliament. "Yes, and you must shoot, Pavel Sergeyevich," Yeltsin admonished as he signed the order.[17] During the crisis that day, Yeltsin's faithful bodyguard Aleksandr Korzhakov did most of the work of organizing the armed suppression of the opposition.[18]

There is also another, more conspiratorial interpretation of the events of September and October 1993. Some people believe that the seeming lack of preparation, confusion, and chaos among Yeltsin's allies were a premeditated show aimed at disorienting the opposition—to induce it to believe that victory was both easy and near. If the parliament were provoked to initiate violence, the government would have a pretext for harsh treatment. According to this version of events, Yeltsin's people had lured the "squatters" from the White House and created conditions for their march through Moscow, by removing the police barriers and even leaving police cars and military trucks standing in the streets with their keys in the ignition. In other words, the confusion of the interior ministry's forces and their failure to challenge the crowds moving on the mayoral building and Ostankino were stage directions enunciated by the director himself, Yeltsin. The adherents of this view think that the government provoked the opposition to bloodshed in order to avoid the need to make any kind of compromise.

Yeltsin's team certainly made provocative moves during the "September revolution." The president himself, once he had decided to dissolve the parliament, was no longer interested in a peaceful resolution of the conflict. Thus the destructive actions of the supporters of Rutskoi and Khasbulatov worked to Yeltsin's advantage. However, when the deputies refused to leave the parliament building and the population of Moscow got involved, things began to spin out of control. The president's advisors underestimated how much the military and Defense Minister Grachev would resist taking part in the action and overestimated their readiness to support the president. During the disorder, some people close to the president and in the government rushed to send their families and property to safe places, showing that they were not fully confident that they would win. The conspiratorial interpretation of these events is thus rather dubious.

There are, however, several indisputable and crucial lessons of this dramatic period. First, Yeltsin was ready to use force, and virtually nothing could stop him. Only through force, not negotiations, could he achieve his goal to get rid of the institutions that were limiting his authority. Peaceful resolution of the conflict would have undermined his plan to adopt a new constitution and to form a new governing structure.

Second, the irresponsible conduct and even recklessness of the opposition leaders—most of all Rutskoi, who imagined himself the victor and goaded the crowds around the White House to storm government buildings—played into Yeltsin's hands. Both Rutskoi and Khasbulatov evidently got caught up in the logic of the fight and lost interest in any peaceful solution. All of Valery Zorkin's attempts to persuade Rutskoi and Khasbulatov to agree to negotiations with Yeltsin failed; Rutskoi vowed to fight "until the last bullet," and Khasbulatov said, "Compromise is impossible."[19] The conduct of Rutskoi, who sent civilians to attack guarded targets while he stayed safely behind, surrounded by bodyguards, was especially repugnant.

Third, some of Yeltsin's closest associates, including Filatov and Chernomyrdin, were against the use of force, fearing its destructive consequences. Even the power ministries asked for postponement of the edict to dissolve parliament because they were unprepared for the struggle and wanted to avoid violence. This demonstrated that a significant part of the Russian establishment had become weary of confrontation.

Fourth, the increasingly furious opposition they faced helped to create some solidarity among the diverse groups within the presidential entourage and the government and forced its members, even those who hated one another, to hold together at crucial moments. Afterward, however, the suppression of the opposition deepened the schism within the presidential team.

The leaders of the communists and their allies, the agrarians, did their best not to get involved in the direct clash. At the moment of conflict, Gennady Zyuganov was on vacation and stayed there, trying to remain safely out of the way until the conflict was over. The leader of Agrarian Union, Ivan Rybkin, was in and out of the parliament building, but he was careful not to be present when the government troops began their attack on the building. The fact that the leaders of the left-wing opposition were not directly involved in the fight with the government meant that afterward, when the leaders of the parliamentary resistance were jailed, they were able to fill the power vacuum in the opposition. Some left-wing leaders, especially Rybkin, would become influential actors in the next acts of the drama.

WAS THE CONFLICT INEVITABLE?

Some may argue that violent conflict between the two branches of government in post-communist Russia was inevitable. Perhaps restraint and balance were lacking in Russian politics because they had been destroyed by seventy years of communism. Yet in other newly independent states with the same communist legacy, such as Ukraine, the struggle between the executive and legislative branches did not lead to comparable upheavals. Changes of leadership and even changes in the type of government there have followed a more civilized path, proving that violence is not the only possible way to resolve conflicts in the post-Soviet environment. Thus one must look further for the causes of the conflict.

It is beyond debate that the system of government that had been established in Russia in 1991 was far from ideal. There was no clear delineation of power among the branches of government; responsibilities overlapped in confusing ways and generated conflicts, and this incoherent governing system lacked a mechanism for resolving such conflicts. The confrontation between the branches of power had its roots in the period when the president's team was trying to create a new structure of government for Russia. As early as May 1991, Yeltsin's advisers had included an article in the law, "On the Russian Presidency," that vested Russia's supreme authority in the parliament. Yeltsin and his group understood that without such a provision, the Russian Congress of People's Deputies would never agree to the establishment of a presidency in Russia. After that law was approved, however, Yeltsin's supporters demanded more and more authority for the president while beginning to restrict the role of the legislative branch. In 1992 Yeltsin proposed an amendment to the constitution to make the president the supreme authority in Russia. This naturally roused a storm of opposition from the deputies. Nobody was ready for power sharing in Russia; the very idea sounded ridiculous.

A genuine multiparty system might have channeled competing social interests and facilitated the resolution of conflicts; its absence reinforced those conflicts. Local interest groups had to focus their efforts on the top echelon of power, since there was no opportunity to resolve conflicts or to negotiate at lower levels. Pressure on the top leadership was thus greatly intensified. Instead of serving to reconcile positions that had been worked out in advance by the interested parties, the institutions of national authority turned into superparties that were increasingly polarized between the liberal-technocratic and the national-populist camps.

The two-tiered parliament, comprising the Congress of People's Deputies and the Supreme Soviet, allowed deputies to block decision making and to use the legislature's podium for their own aggrandizement. This complicated the political process and introduced an element of showmanship into policy making. The existence of a strong opposition to the reforms in the parliament forced Yeltsin to rule by decrees—not the best way to create a legal basis for market reform. The sheer size of the Congress and the multiplicity of its factions gave Yeltsin a considerable potential advantage in maneuvering and negotiating compromises, but

89

this approach demanded a genuine willingness to work with the deputies, which the president's team had rejected from the very beginning.

Everyone was also using the infighting to advance his own interests. Both sides wanted to control the process of privatization, which
was mostly in the hands of the executive authorities; the parliamentary
leadership constantly sought ways to get what it viewed as its fair share.
Yuri Afanasyev, one of Yeltsin's former supporters and a member of
DemRossiya, said at the time:

> I do not want to participate in this war. This is biological warfare
> for survival. If the Supreme Soviet wins, it will begin criminal
> proceedings against the president's team. The same will happen
> to the Khasbulatov group if Yeltsin's team comes out on top.
> This is not a confrontation between two power centers, but a
> clan struggle within a single social stratum. I view this stratum
> as the neo-Soviet *nomenklatura*, which is engaged in stealing
> property that once belonged to the state.[20]

The zero-sum mentality of the leaders in both camps, their
efforts to secure a monopoly of power, their inability to engage in
dialogue, and the personalities of the main political actors and their
advisers contributed to the confrontation. Yeltsin, Khasbulatov,
Rutskoi, Burbulis, Gaidar, Shakhrai, and others liked best to operate
in an environment of confrontation. Another factor that contributed
to the clash was that the Yeltsin group was looking for scapegoats
in the opposite camp on whom to heap blame for the failures and
mistakes of the liberal reform program. Khasbulatov and the other
parliamentary leaders, meanwhile, escalated tension without consideration of the consequences.

Yet there also had been some positive developments by September 1993: a political structure had emerged that contained elements
of a balance of power. After more than seventy years of communist
unanimity, no one had a monopoly on power, which was now split
among several competing institutions, including an independent parliament and a Constitutional Court. Such pluralism could work only
if the members of the emerging elite could learn to come to terms
with each other, and they had not yet done so. The inability of the
participants to reach agreement on policies that all participants could
accept and follow was destructive. Fundamentally, they had not
agreed on rules of the game, which could have tamed the ambitions
and aggressiveness of the political leaders and the competing forces
they represented. Instead, all were ready to fight to the end.

THE VICTORS GET AWAY WITH IT

T he peaceful course of political transformation in post-Soviet Russia had been broken. Blood had been shed, and the political and psychological consequences of this tragedy would influence the future both directly and indirectly.[21] The events of September–October 1993 destroyed the long-standing taboo against the use of brute force in political struggle in Moscow. Neither Gorbachev nor the instigators of the August 1991 coup attempt had dared to bring about such a fierce confrontation for fear of its unpredictable and irremediable consequences. Breach of this taboo complicated the establishment of civilized politics and of predictable rules of the political game. The events of September–October 1993 created fears over the subsequent transfer of power. Many observers assumed that those in power who were responsible for the bloodshed would try to hold on to their power.

The official government version of the events of course blamed the opposition for provoking Yeltsin to dissolve the parliament. The most active propagandist for this version was Yegor Gaidar. His explanation was that "the leaders of the 'irreconcilable opposition' were waiting for just such a step from Yeltsin, and they were preparing for it. More than that, they clearly provoked it." He said that the leaders of the opposition "are as scared of elections as the devil is of incense and do not want to participate in them. If we need order and stability for victory, they need tension, struggle, and preferably blood."[22] This version can be disputed. The actions of the anti-Yeltsin opposition were indeed provocative in many ways; however, why would the opposition strive to provoke a direct clash with the president, for which it was not prepared and for which it clearly did not have the necessary resources? Khasbulatov understood that Yeltsin was ready to use any pretext to finish off the parliament, and in the last days before the clash, various groups of deputies constantly sent signals that they were ready for dialogue with the president.

The thesis that the opposition did not need elections is also inaccurate. On the contrary, Khasbulatov and others called for elections but insisted that the parliamentary and the presidential elections be simultaneous. Many members of the opposition actually wanted elections, believing that the mood of society had swung in their favor (indeed, the December 1993 elections proved that a large part of the population was actually not on the side of the executive branch). Nevertheless, it is true that it was the opposition leaders, especially Rutskoi, who provoked street violence by sending crowds to attack Moscow's mayoral building and the Ostankino television station. It is also true, however, that the executive did not use all possible means for the peaceful resolution of its conflict with the parliament.

Following the dissolution of the parliament (the Congress of People's Deputies and the Supreme Soviet), a new chapter began with the election campaign for the new parliament (the Duma) and preparation for the referendum on a new constitution drafted by Yeltsin's team. The liberal radicals quickly formed the Russia's Choice electoral bloc, led by Yegor Gaidar. Russia's Choice aspired to be the party of the president, and it came to represent such a party in the public's view. This characterization, however, was no guarantee of success in the elections.

The second echelon of Kremlin politicians, those who had been elevated by Yeltsin himself, decided that it was time to seek leading roles. The first to try to play an independent game were Sergei Shakhrai and Aleksandr Shokhin, another deputy prime minister. Together they formed the Party of Russian Unity and Accord (PRES), supported by Chernomyrdin, who was evidently beginning to think about building his own base of support. In effect, this was the first attempt to set up something akin to a two-party system, in which political power could be passed on from one cooperative group to another. It soon became clear, however, that the relationship between Russia's Choice and PRES was anything but friendly. The division of personnel within the ministries into the Russia's Choice and PRES camps caused a split in the government. The polarization did not stop there, as Aleksandr Zaveryukha, the minister of agriculture, joined the agrarian electoral bloc—the Agrarian Party of Russia (APR)—which consisted of members of the former communist *nomenklatura*. The government had evidently turned its full attention to the election campaign. Antagonism reached the point where ministers who represented rival parties would not even greet each other in the morning.

Yeltsin approved a merger of executive and legislative branch responsibilities to allow government ministers to become voting members of the parliament (a practice that was later ended). This was a de facto rejection of the division of powers and a return to the old communist practice whereby ministers sitting in the parliament adopted laws to their own liking, implemented them, and also exercised oversight over their implementation. Ministers and deputy prime ministers threw themselves into the electoral fray en masse, running as candidates for the Duma, the lower chamber of the new Russian parliament. Some headed the party lists of the various electoral blocs, which gave them a substantial advantage over other candidates, as they would have a seat guaranteed for them in the Duma if their bloc won.

On November 8, 1993, Yeltsin personally made an amendment to the draft of the new constitution to allow republic presidents and heads of administrations of the regions, who were usually appointed by the president, to become automatic members of the Federation Council, the upper house of the new parliament. Allowing concurrent membership in the executive structures and in the legislature created a remarkably corrupting environment for the high-ranking members of the executive branch. Parliamentary status conferred legal immunity from criminal prosecution, so the powerful bureaucrats could use their powers to enrich themselves without fear.

For the president, the crucial task at this point was winning the referendum on his new draft constitution. This was more important to him than the details of the election campaign, to which he was at best indifferent. After all, if his constitution was adopted, the president would not have to worry about the new parliament. Yeltsin had no constitutional power to organize this referendum, but that did not bother him. At this time, he appeared to be in a position to shape the political structure of the country in any way he wanted.

After some revisions, the presidential draft of the new constitution was finally published on November 10, 1993, in *Rossiiskaya gazeta*. This was actually the fourth draft, the result of a long constitutional epic. Fresh from their victory in the September revolution, Yeltsin's associates had returned to the superpresidential model and even strengthened it. According to this draft, the president was the head of state and the guarantor of the constitution; he appointed the prime minister and all other ministers. Only the appointment of the prime minister needed the approval of the Duma. The president had the right to dissolve the Duma if it thrice rejected the candidacy of his proposed premier and if it twice expressed no confidence in the government within three months. The procedure for removing the president was practically impossible to carry out; it required a two-thirds majority in both houses of the federal assembly, as well as the approval of the Supreme Court and the Constitutional Court, based on a serious proof that the president had committed high treason or criminal acts. Moreover, this complicated procedure had to be completed within three months of the charges being brought against the president by the Duma. Yeltsin's proposed constitution directly violated the principle of division of power and gave the president enormous executive, legislative, and judicial authority. With these powers, the president could evade any responsibility for his decisions.

Besides destroying the incipient balance of power, Yeltsin's draft constitution substantially increased the role of the upper house, the Federation Council, which included regional governors appointed by the president (they later would be elected) and heads of regional legislatures. Many Russian analysts were concerned that, because of the rather conservative mentality of the majority of the members of the Federation Council, the body would become an obstacle to the reform process and its members would clash with the government. These fears proved to be exaggerated, however: the upper chamber on many occasions demonstrated readiness to cooperate with the executive.

An even more crucial aspect of the new constitution was the difficulty of amending it; its authors sought to eliminate this possibility altogether.[23] The passage of ordinary amendments or of federal constitutional laws required a two-thirds majority in the lower house, a concurring three-quarters majority in the upper house, and the president's signature, followed by ratification by two-thirds of the legislative assemblies of the federation's subjects. Only after this final approval would a ratified amendment be included in the constitution. This procedure meant that representatives of the regional bureaucracy could block any change to the constitution.

The draft gave the president and the leaders of the federation units (republics and regions) the ability to collude, and it excluded political movements and trade unions from the constitutional process. The most dangerous deficiency was that the new constitutional framework was designed to meet the needs of a specific political personality, Boris Yeltsin, and was based on the transitory interests of several specific groups that had succeeded in dominating the power structure as a result of the events of September–October 1993. There was serious concern that any new leader who might succeed Yeltsin could use the new constitution to build a dictatorial regime. Instead of taming authoritarian ambitions, the new constitution only provoked them. Yeltsin's constitution liberated the president from all constraints.

The new constitution curtailed the role of the judicial authorities. The new provisions limited the right of the Constitutional Court to judge the activities of the government, senior government officials, and, above all, the president, who was not subject to its jurisdiction. The court, which had been created in July 1992, had the power to rule on the legality and constitutionality of government acts, bringing Russia a great step closer to a democratic and accountable system of government. In the fall of 1993, however, Yeltsin disbanded the Constitutional Court, and Russia remained without such a judicial body until 1995.

Yeltsin's supporters argued that strong presidential regimes based on direct elections are the most effective and stable form of government—especially during the transition period. This opinion, however, was contradicted by reality. Parliamentary systems almost invariably have the best records, particularly with respect to representation, protection of minority interests, and voter participation. The conclusion that economic development requires a strong presidency free of legislative interference is also highly suspect. As Arendt Lijphart noted, "To be sure, we do have a few examples of economic miracles brought by authoritarian regimes, such as those in South Korea or Taiwan, but these are more than counterbalanced by the sorry economic records of just about all the non-democratic governments in Africa, Latin America and Eastern Europe."[24] Moreover, economic development requires not so much a strong hand as a steady one. What is needed is "greater stability and continuity" and "greater moderation in policy," which could be provided by a shift to coalition government, which is more likely to be centrist in orientation.[25] Besides, in economic policy, according to Arendt Lijphart, speed is not particularly important: quick decisions "are not necessarily wise ones." In the short run, presidents may well be able to formulate economic policy with greater ease and speed. In the long run, however, policies supported by a broad consensus are more likely to be successfully carried out than policies imposed by a strong president against the wishes of interest groups.[26]

It is true that a traditional parliamentary system in Russia—when there is no viable multiparty system and when the major political force is still the Communist Party—may not be the ideal solution. A mixed parliamentary-presidential system might be more effective. On the one hand, this model would be flexible and would create conditions for the development of political pluralism; on the other, it would guarantee stability and strong and unified leadership.

Many analysts expected a parliamentary election win by the pro-presidential Russia's Choice bloc, which overwhelmed all the others with its mass advertising. Gaidar and the other leaders of Russia's Choice were already behaving like victors. The communists and their agrarian allies pursued their campaign less vigorously, but they were more active at the local level. Two reformist groups—Sergei Shakhrai's PRES and Grigory Yavlinsky's democratic-opposition group, Yabloko—appeared to be much less dynamic.[27] The old populist and nationalist opposition was unable to recover from the September shock and remained lethargic. Among the newly emerging parties, Vladimir Zhirinovsky's nationalistic Liberal Democratic Party of Russia (LDPR) attracted particular attention. Zhirinovsky had tried to scale the heights of political leadership several times before, without much success—including the presidential campaign of 1991—and many in Russia considered him more of a joke than a serious contender.

ELECTIONS TO THE TAMED PARLIAMENT

The first results of the voting on December 12 from Siberia and the Far East sent shock waves through the presidential structure, and analysts were completely bewildered, confirming how little the political establishment knew about the changing Russian society. Many regions that had earlier been loyal to Yeltsin and his reforms now went either to Zhirinovsky or to the communists and their agrarian allies.

The election results showed that 53.2 percent of the eligible voters had participated, 58.4 percent of whom had voted for, and 41.6 percent against, the new draft constitution. Thus the constitution was supported by about 30 percent of the Russian electorate. In twenty-four out of eighty-nine units of the federation, including eight of twenty republics, voters rejected the draft. In Chechnya the elections did not take place; and in seventeen of the eighty-nine regions, the referendum was not valid because less than 50 percent of the eligible voters showed up. A record number (7 percent) of ballots were disqualified, and 17 percent of the voters marked their ballots "against all candidates." Yet the constitution was approved, and this was the most important victory for Yeltsin.

Almost immediately, however, experts began to express suspicion that the approval was fraudulent. Particular concern was focused on a mysterious loss of nearly 7 million ballots. The presidential team never got around to explaining this loss and generally ignored all protests and demands for an investigation. The report of the Central Election Commission was never published, and it appears to have been destroyed. Even Yeltsin's closest allies later admitted that there had been electoral fraud. The entire Moscow political community talked about how, after a meeting between Yeltsin and Nikolai Ryabov, the chairman of the Central Election Commission, the figure of 50 percent in support of the new constitution suddenly metamorphosed into 60 percent. Sergei Kovalyov, the former chairman of the Committee on Human Rights, has charged that nearly 8 million votes were falsified in the December 1993 referendum.[28]

The schism in the democratic forces allowed several democratic groups to win seats in the new legislature (see table, p. 101). Yavlinsky's Yabloko and Shakhrai's PRES received the votes of many who were dissatisfied with the radical-liberal course and might otherwise have remained home. Thus, paradoxically, the splintering of democratic forces expanded rather than narrowed the number of democrats and liberals in the new parliament. The election produced two surprises. The first was that the pro-presidential bloc received only 15.4 percent of the votes cast. The second was the stunning number of votes received by Zhirinovsky, who now suddenly became one of Russia's leading politicians.

The elections were a clear vote of no confidence in the radical liberals. While a majority of the electorate voted for the presidential constitution, many of them rejected the pro-presidential political bloc, Gaidar's Russia's Choice. People voted for stability and order; rejection of the constitution, they feared, might lead to an intensification of the power struggle or to an authoritarian regime. The results of the elections also indicated that public support for the president was weakening. Yeltsin himself, however, did not display any particular anxiety over the results of the parliamentary elections. Moreover, he must have taken a certain satisfaction in knowing that his intuition had been right when he had refused to put his authority, or what remained of it, behind Russia's Choice. Immediately after the election, Yeltsin gradually began to distance himself even further from his liberal associates.

The crude official propaganda and the incompetence of the electoral campaign mounted by Russia's Choice played a part in both the bleak performance of the reformers and the appearance of the Zhirinovsky phenomenon. Voters were constantly told that Gaidar's Russia's

Choice was the president's party, and there could be no alternative. Russia's Choice claimed, "Either we will rule, or it will be bad for everyone." This reminded many of the days when the Communist Party had used similar arguments. However, the principal cause for the poor showing of the radical liberals was the failure of the policies that were introduced under the slogan of liberalism. Moreover, Russia's Choice fell into a trap: it was in most cases unfairly assigned blame for the failed government policies at a time when Gaidar had been out of power for more than a year and the cabinet had been headed by Chernomyrdin.

The success of Zhirinovsky indicated a strengthening of the Russian public's nostalgia for the USSR. It expressed the widespread feeling that the collapse of the Soviet Union was a national defeat. This sentiment was amplified by dissatisfaction with Russia's two main political currents, democratic and pro-communist. Thus a significant part of the electorate gave its vote to Zhirinovsky's Liberal Democratic Party of Russia (LDPR), which had several characteristics that appealed to the masses at this time: its outsider status; its great-power rhetoric; and its rejection of both liberal radicalism and communism, with an attempt to play the role of a third force.

Zhirinovsky's success was also abetted, in part, by those around the president. During the summer and autumn of 1993, Zhirinovsky was given ample opportunity to take center stage in the Russian political theater. Yeltsin himself gave the LDPR leader political legitimacy by inviting him to participate in the Constitutional Conference. Zhirinovsky's full access to the airwaves during the campaign must have been given with the consent of Yeltsin's circle, which controlled radio and television. Zhirinovsky also gained votes that might otherwise have gone to Rutskoi and the other nationalists who were, at that moment, sitting in jail. Zhirinovsky tried with some success to convey the impression that he was against the government's course but that he at the same time supported Yeltsin's new constitution. Indeed, those who voted for Zhirinovsky contributed to the passage of the president's draft constitution.

The president's advisers were evidently expecting a victory for Russia's Choice, but they tried to make it a certainty by characterizing the alternative, in the person of Zhirinovsky, as a dangerous endorsement of radical nationalism. Voters faced the dilemma of voting for Russia's Choice or facing the threat of fascism, and even voters who could not accept Gaidar's Russia's Choice could at least vote for the draft constitution, which would create conditions for stability and give the president the means of constraining Zhirinovsky or anyone else like him. Zhirinovsky's triumph could neutralize Yeltsin's former opponents, like Rutskoi, since they appealed to the same social base. His nationalist, semi-farcical presence in the parliament could be useful to the presidential team in the longer term as well, providing a handy pretext for dissolving the parliament or turning to authoritarianism to curtail the demands of the public.

The president's strategists had miscalculated, however. They clearly had not expected the LDPR to have such a resounding success. They had apparently intended to have a pocket jester whom they could silence at any time, but manipulating Zhirinovsky turned out to be more difficult than they had expected. His position was enhanced after several influence groups, including some from the former military-industrial complex, placed their bets on him. The Yeltsin team's strategy had created an outlet for society's extreme views and had also created a potential rival for democratic leaders, at least for a time. In the December 1993 elections, however, Zhirinovsky, perhaps not entirely consciously, did help the president accomplish one of his goals: the adoption of the new constitution.

THE FINAL DEPARTURE OF GAIDAR

After his September revolution, Yeltsin increasingly relied not on political parties or public politicians with well-known names, but on those who had been faithful to him for a long time, who made his life comfortable, and, most important, who had his own and his family's absolute trust. Among these solidly entrenched figures were the head of the presidential security guard, Aleksandr Korzhakov, and the commandant of the Kremlin, General Mikhail Barsukov. These behind-the-scenes operators formed the nexus of a group of people who began to play a decisive role in the Russian corridors of power between 1993 and 1996, as Yeltsin's circle of close associates became smaller and smaller. Yeltsin was gradually cut off from outside contacts (or he himself cut off these contacts); he became largely unreachable and distant. His behavior began to resemble that of a stereotypical old czar: isolated from everyone, dictatorial, intolerant of criticism, aloof from the society yet playing the role of the "father of the nation," commanding in manner, and terse in expression. Yeltsin referred to himself exclusively in the third person, as "the president." Even people close to him shrugged their shoulders as he began to use elaborate czarist procedures, such as emerging before audiences to a special presidential fanfare played by the Kremlin orchestra.

On the public side of the political scene, the opening of the new parliament, called the Federal Assembly, was under way. The two chambers of the new parliament, the State Duma and the Federation Council (also called the Senate), were assigned two buildings completely unsuited for their work. (The White House, where the old parliament had sat, was now occupied by the offices of the Russian government.) Despite neglect and poor conditions, the new legislative body began to function. Ivan Rybkin, a member of the agrarian electoral bloc and one of the leaders of the left opposition in the previous parliament, was elected speaker of the lower house, the State Duma. Rybkin, who always thoroughly weighed all sides of a question, was a compromise figure. His election reflected not only the weakened position of the liberals and democrats, but the readiness of a majority of the parliamentary blocs to compromise on moderate positions. In the eyes of many, Rybkin did not belong to the post–August 1991 establishment and was not among those responsible for the war between the branches that had gone on for the two preceding years. Partly because of that, it was easy for him to deal with all of the factions. Soon, however, Rybkin began to lean toward support for Yeltsin, which would complicate his career as an independent political leader.[29]

In December 1993, the State Duma was chosen by a mixed electoral system. Half of the seats (225) were allocated through a system of proportional representation (that is, party lists). To win seats through this system, a party had to get a minimum of 5 percent of the vote throughout Russia. The other half of the deputies were elected to represent single-mandate, territorially defined districts.

The major factions[30] formed in the new Duma are shown in Table 4-1. Deputy groups (which had less impact on the activity of the Duma than factions) also were formed; of these, New Regional Policy had sixty-four deputies; Union of December 12, twenty-two; The Russian Way, thirteen; and Derzhava, five.

Vladimir Shumeiko, first deputy prime minister, was chosen speaker of the Federation Council, the upper chamber, after direct pressure from the Yeltsin circle. The regional representatives assembled there had apparently agreed to have a close associate of Yeltsin preside over

Table 4-1. Parliamentary Election Results, 1993

Party	Party Leader	Party-List Seats	Single-Mandate Seats	Total Duma Seats	Percentage of Party-List Vote
Russia's Choice	Yegor Gaidar	40	26	66	15.4
Liberal Democratic Party of Russia (LDPR)	Vladimir Zhirinovsky	59	5	64	22.8
Communist Party (KPRF)	Gennady Zyuganov	32	16	48	12.4
Agrarians	Mikhail Lapshin	21	12	33	7.9
Yabloko	Grigory Yavlinsky	20	7	27	7.8
Women of Russia	Alevtina Fedulova	21	2	23	8.1
Party of Russian Unity and Accord (PRES)	Sergei Shakhrai	18	1	19	6.8
Democratic Party of Russia	Nikolai Travkin	14	1	15	5.5
Other Parties		0	22	22	–
Independents		0	127	127	–
Total		**225**	**219**	**444**	

Note: Russia's Choice, Yabloko, PRES, and Union of December 12 represented pro-reform forces. The Liberal Democratic Party, the Communist Party, and the Agrarian Party represented the opposition. Women of Russia and the Democratic Party of Russia represented centrist forces.

Source: Election of Deputies of the State Duma 1995, Electoral Statistics (Moscow: Ves Mir, 1996), pp. 202-204.

them in order to preserve good relations with the federal authorities, but that did not mean that they would submit completely to Yeltsin's wishes.

Gradually Russia became used to the new political configuration. This period witnessed a consolidation of a new political regime in which most political players were the same as in the previous one; there were few new faces. The old breeding ground of confrontation had disappeared, however. Differentiation within the Soviet ruling elite—a process begun under Gorbachev—and the elite's breakup into sometimes opposing interest groups, had run their course. All of these groups, however, were still defining their interests while incorporating representatives of the various social strata, including members of the intelligentsia, into their ranks.

The emerging balance of power did not favor the radical liberals. Despite their having been at the center of decision making and having had the opportunity to exercise a decisive influence on the president, they had failed to attract supporters from the old *apparat*, the army, or the regional bureaucracies and had also failed to widen their base in society. They could not help recognizing their failures. This explains, to a large extent, their active support of a strong presidential regime, aimed at the elimination of any countervailing forces; they apparently hoped that they could regain influence over Yeltsin and continue the reform effort. Developments went in another direction, however, and others would exploit the fruits of Yeltsin's September revolution.

After December 1993 the growing role of Chernomyrdin reflected the triumph of the groups that represented the interests of the natural resources and agrarian lobbies, members of the enterprise-director elite, and the federal bureaucracy. The weakening of the radical liberals, who had been supported by the financiers and commercial entrepreneurs, diminished the latter group's opportunities to control the redistribution of property and power. Yeltsin watched calmly as Gaidar and his allies lost their influence. Under these conditions, retaining the leaders of the radical liberals in the cabinet did not make political sense. At the beginning of 1994, therefore, Gaidar and his supporters who still remained in the government—the social welfare minister, Ella Pamfilova, and the finance minister, Boris Fyodorov—understood, or were forced to understand, that their departure had become inevitable. They left reluctantly, hoping against the evidence that the president would again support them. This did not happen; Yeltsin clearly wanted to close the Gaidar chapter of the transition manual. Gaidar's presence had been necessary to give liberal cover at a particular point in Yeltsin's September "revolution"; later, however, Gaidar became a hindrance to Yeltsin, who wanted to begin a stabilization period. Many in Moscow felt that Yeltsin had used Gaidar to justify, particularly to the West, the liquidation of the parliament. After this had been done, Gaidar and the most prominent remaining members of his team were squeezed out of government.

One Gaidarite, however, remained: Anatoly Chubais. Over time, he had succeeded in getting closer to Prime Minister Chernomyrdin and joining the new ruling group. Deputy prime ministers Aleksandr Shokhin and Sergei Shakhrai, who entered the cabinet at the same time as Gaidar, had distanced themselves from the liberals even earlier. With the second departure of Gaidar from the government came a more cautious political and economic course. Bureaucratic groups connected with sectoral interests, mainly with the oil and gas group, began to dominate.

YELTSIN ALLOWS HIMSELF TO RELAX

The year 1994 brought Russia some calm. There was cause for cautious optimism because none of the apocalyptic prophecies— of which there had been many in recent years—had come to pass. Russia did not break apart into warring principalities; it did not suffer an economic collapse; and there were no mass disorders, let alone a civil war. The social and political life of the country took on a more peaceful aspect. The opposition, including its irreconcilable minority, became quiescent, and appeared for a while to have lost its bearings and even its raison d'être. Some of the opposition leaders gave up active political struggle, while others just disappeared from the political scene. Within the ranks of the opposition, leaders of a more moderate cast, such as Gennady Zyuganov of the Communist Party of the Russian Federation (KPRF), came to the fore. Moderate members of the opposition began to force out the extremists who gave them a bad name: the combative Viktor Anpilov, head of the left-extremist movement Working Russia; Aleksandr Prokhanov, publisher of the nationalist newspaper *Zavtra* (Tomorrow), which had previously been called *Den* (The Day); and former Vice President Aleksandr Rutskoi, hero of the defense of the White House and unsuccessful Kremlin power seeker.

The new parliament behaved quite peacefully, perhaps because it had few means to oppose executive authority. The deputies refrained from direct confrontation with the president, but Yeltsin could not count on their loyalty. The State Duma's voting record shows that the majority of the deputies, 256 of 449, usually voted against the executive's proposals. Only 200 of them were adamantly anti-Yeltsin, but a mere 188 of the deputies could be counted on to support the president's policies.

Although a majority of Duma deputies were hostile to Yeltsin, they at the same time tried not to provoke him. The most striking evidence of this was the State Duma's passage of the law granting amnesty (on February 23) to Rutskoi, Khasbulatov, and other leaders of the opposition, as well as to the instigators of the 1991 coup attempt, who were still in prison. Some took this as an openly anti-Yeltsin gesture. Others speculated that this amnesty was part of a deal between the president's team and leaders of the new parliament. Although Yeltsin protested against the amnesty, he did not do so very vigorously. If there was a deal, which does seem likely, it provided freedom for the opposition leaders in exchange for the parliament's agreement to avoid discussion of questions relating to the 1993 September revolution or the possibility of election fraud in the adoption of Yeltsin's constitution. Such discussions would have been rather disagreeable to Yeltsin and his entourage.

The voting record of the Federation Council showed that, of 178 members, there were 48 reformers, 23 moderates, and 58 representatives of the opposition, as well as several dozen independents. Even though the majority of the Russian senators owed their positions largely to Yeltsin (as he appointed the heads of regional administrations at that time), and even though their speaker, Vladimir Shumeiko, was a man thoroughly loyal to Yeltsin, the senators did not feel particularly indebted to the president when it came time to vote. They did defer consideration of the president's proposed candidate for the position of prosecutor-general several times, as well as consideration of the proposed members of the Constitutional Court, the proposed chairman of the Central Bank, and so on. Yet the senators at the same time skillfully avoided open conflicts with the president.

The relatively peaceful mood of the parliament in 1994 was explained by the lamentable fate of its predecessor and the deputies' desire to avoid repetition of that course—as well as by purely practical calculations by the deputies, to whom the Yeltsin administration had given substantial perquisites of office. In their daily needs, the new deputies were completely dependent on the president's largesse. The flexibility of the Duma speaker, Ivan Rybkin, also accounted for the absence of open confrontation with the president. Thanks to his ability to compromise, Rybkin was able to establish good relations with all parliamentary factions, although the new speaker began to be regarded by many as the president's man.

Even the deputies who were loyal to Yeltsin, however, were constantly uneasy about the limitations on their scope of action and the largely ceremonial role of the Federal Assembly, or parliament. Gaidar's recognition of this fact was especially significant. Having been elected to the Duma, he soon noted the futility of his efforts to influence the political process. "Without any doubt," he complained, "the role of the legislative organs, including the Duma and the Federation Council, is extremely limited, even for a presidential republic."[31] Gaidar, it should be recalled, had been an active supporter of the constitution that had turned the parliament into a merely decorative appendage of the Russian government.

At the beginning of 1994, having obtained the constitution he wanted, Yeltsin burrowed deep underground, as he always did after a victory. In January he hardly left his dacha while his assistants explained his absence as an attack of the flu. The press again spoke of the president's poor health and of impending changes. Sergei Filatov, the head of the presidential administration, was compelled to deny rumors of Yeltsin's physical incapacity. As usual, such denials had the opposite effect. Yeltsin's assistants feverishly sought ways to show that the president was able to work. The dominant popular explanation of Yeltsin's disappearances, both in Russia and abroad, was that they related more to his life style and some presumed pernicious habits than to serious illness.

There was, however, something more serious behind Yeltsin's disappearances and erratic behavior. It may be true that he lived impulsively and after every victory had to lapse into lethargy, out of which only a new struggle for survival could rescue him. Yet it often seemed that the president was not just seriously tired from the constant strain, but that he had ceased to pay attention to developments. His experience as a provincial Communist Party boss who had spent a major part of his life in the hinterlands of Siberia did not equip him to grasp national events and to control them. He still was the best fighter in the political arena, but, when dealing with events and trends on a more conceptual level and faced with the need to think strategically, he more and more often displayed an utter lack of understanding. He may well have felt helpless yet unable to ask for advice—and may for those reasons have begun to sequester himself, to skip meetings, and to escape his responsibilities. Moreover, he really was unwell and exhausted. The depressions from which he was known periodically to suffer could only have added to the burden.

Despite some consolidation of Russia's governing mechanisms, policies remained inconsistent and incoherent. This was the case, for example, with the question of Russia's participation in NATO's Partnership for Peace program: one Russian official kept repeating that Russia would join the program in April; another declared that the question had not been decided. There appeared to be a variety of serious disagreements between the Ministry of Foreign Affairs and the Ministry of Defense. To add to the confusion, Yeltsin unexpectedly published a decree on the creation of Russian military bases abroad, including one in independent Latvia. The decree shocked Russian diplomats and even the military and caused an international uproar. In an attempt to quiet things down, the Yeltsin team, as usual, blamed it all on a technical error. There was no doubt that the Russian government lacked an adequate system of coordination. The lack of professionalism of the government's staff could be seen in its constant mistakes and blunders. All of these lapses could no longer be written off as the intrigues of the opposition.

The September revolution finally concluded with the signing of the Agreement on Social Accord. After the opposition had been crushed and the Yeltsin group was not constrained by rivals on the horizon, reaching such an agreement with loyal forces was not difficult. The agreement was signed on April 28, 1994, with pomp and ceremony, by nearly all of the main political forces. Exceptions were the defeated opposition and several abstaining democratic groups, notably Grigory Yavlinsky and his followers. The signatories to the agreement pledged to refrain from any destabilizing activity, and above all from proposing either changes to the constitution or early elections. This step indicated that the victor's camp was still unsure of itself. Possibly the open rumors that the government had cheated in the constitutional referendum unnerved the president and his allies, and they sought to protect their positions by means of yet another new document. As 1994 progressed, Yeltsin would continue to look for ways to unite society around his regime. He would fail to unite the society but would definitely succeed in creating a new political establishment that would demonstrate, despite its diversity of interests, a unique ability to pull together in moments of danger.

CHAPTER FIVE

MOSCOW'S CHECHEN WAR: 1994-95

AFTER THE 1993 ELECTIONS, SEVERAL KEY INFLUENCE GROUPS
began a struggle for domination: the pragmatists, headed by Viktor
Chernomyrdin; the loyalists, represented by the emerging alliance of
Aleksandr Korzhakov, Oleg Soskovets, and Mikhail Barsukov; and the
Moscow group, led by Mayor Yuri Luzhkov. The struggle among these
groups gave Yeltsin a lot of room to maneuver, which he used with
tactical brilliance. Playing off various individuals and groups against one
another and provoking tensions, Yeltsin would then act as arbiter to
create order both in his own entourage and on the political scene. A
typical Yeltsin ploy was to bring the most zealous of his associates to
their knees and then help them get back on their feet. This game helped
him neutralize possible opponents and avoid becoming hostage to any of
the interest groups. But permanent maneuvering and constant intrigues
could not substitute for coherent policy; nor could they help create new
political institutions for Russia.

A NEW GAME

The most significant development in Russian shadow politics at
this time was the alliance of Korzhakov and Barsukov with first
vice premier Soskovets, who was already trying on the mantle
of leader of the cabinet.[1] This group soon dominated the president's
entourage.[2] At times it appeared that Yeltsin was using the new favorites
for his own purposes; at other times they appeared to be manipulating
him. Korzhakov's team began to intervene directly in cabinet affairs,
and Korzhakov himself even attempted to gain control from Chernomyrdin of the lucrative allocation of licenses and quotas for the export and
sale of petroleum products.

Korzhakov, whose official role was chief of the president's security service, was gradually becoming an independent power broker. According to public opinion ratings in October 1994, Korzhakov was the seventh most influential person in the country (not counting Yeltsin); in November, he was in fourth place; in December, third; and in January 1995, he was second only to Chernomyrdin. Korzhakov later said of those days, "Yeltsin again went to sleep. And I sat up and began to 'rule the country.'"[3] Korzhakov, with his unimpeded access to the president and enormous influence over him, gradually began to be feared by democrats and pragmatists alike. Many had the illusion that if his favorite could be removed, Yeltsin would become more open and engage more actively in the reform process. The problem, however, was Yeltsin himself, with his predilection for intrigue, his unwillingness to rely on institutions, and his inability to conduct himself openly. Yeltsin could change his favorites, as he had done on more than one occasion: before Korzhakov, there had been Gennady Burbulis and Yuri Petrov. Korzhakov or any other "gray cardinal" could maintain his position at Yeltsin's side only as long as he did not show political ambitions of his own, was devoted to the boss, and did not in any way endanger Yeltsin's position. Yeltsin's habits of making policy in the shadows, of relying on select clans and on his cohorts, was not just a legacy of his *nomenklatura* past; his political habits were to a great extent a reflection of his deep distrust of people, and especially of the Moscow political elite. This permanent state of suspicion compelled him to surround himself with people who were devoted to him. Thus Yeltsin himself fostered favoritism and dependence on personalities rather than reliance on rules.

Meanwhile, power and authority continued to disperse from the center to the regions. This process should have been a generally healthy trend; decentralization of power was necessary for Russia's political development. The character of the regimes that were forming in the provinces, however, was not very encouraging. After a brief period during which democrats and other groups not beholden to the Soviet *apparat* assumed leadership in a number of regions, the old guard of the provincial *nomenklatura* regrouped and managed to regain most of the ground it had lost. The weakening of the federal structures and the constant struggle for power in Moscow permitted the rise of powerful regional clans, some of them associated with local criminal groups. This process had nothing to do with real democratization. Having acquired power and property, the local "barons" and their associates began to rule even more harshly and imperiously than when they had been dependent on Moscow. In some regions and republics, the old elites were now in complete control. The newspaper *Izvestiya* wrote that, in the regions, "the foundations of *nomenklatura* absolutism have grown stronger, and there are dangerous signs of Russia's growing division into regional-territorial entities."[4]

Part of the old establishment, however, appeared to have learned how to adapt to new conditions. Some could, when necessary, look like liberals, then turn into nationalists, and then become leftists. While they continuously shifted their allegiances, rules of conduct, and rhetoric, they were consistent in their sustained attempt to preserve their dominant positions in the regions, where not much had changed since the collapse of communism.

STABILIZATION RUSSIAN STYLE

C onstant turf struggles in the president's circle notwithstanding, Russian political and social life entered a period of relative calm in 1994. Yeltsin's regime had gradually turned into a unifying force, although the business of building a new state remained unfinished. This led even critics of Yeltsin's regime to fear that its fall would create a vacuum of power or a struggle among potential successor groups. The multiplicity of political groups in the federal center and in the regions was not only a source of conflict but also a factor of stability: competition among them prevented any one group from dominating the others, and this forced them all to bargain and to make compromises, which relaxed political tension.

Ironically, feelings of fear also contributed to the period of calm—fear of possible new confrontation and bloodshed, fear of accession to power of people whose behavior was hard to predict and to control, fear of military intervention in the political process, fear of new competitors for power and of their demands for a new redistribution of property; and fear of social outburst. In the months following the events of September 1993, such fears compelled even the most antagonistic opponents to seek some form of compromise in the name of mutual survival. Previously militant opposition groups were beginning to switch to civilized parliamentary struggle, and even to consider the possibility of dialogue with the moderate elements of the regime.

The apparent calm in Russia was also partly a consequence of social disillusionment or depression, brought on by the lack of a compelling alternative to the president and his course and the absence of a clear vision for the future. Public disenchantment with all political forces and institutions led to apathy and unwillingness to react to any political events.[5] The widening rift between the government and the nation served at least one useful purpose: it promoted the independent development of society, pushing people to look to their own survival. This widening gap threatened to make implementation of any government policy difficult, however, and it increased hostility toward the authorities. There was nothing to provoke a widespread social eruption, but the appearance of calm was deceptive. A stability grounded in fear, frustration, and alienation could only be fragile.[6] The fundamental problems of creating a new state and a new federation, as well as determining Russia's role in global and regional affairs, had yet to be resolved.

On "Black Tuesday," October 11, 1994, there was a sudden wake-up call when Russia's national currency collapsed. The ruble lost about a quarter of its value, and the economic shock upset the political equilibrium as well. The parliament called for the resignation of the cabinet, but a vote of no confidence failed to pass. Black Tuesday showed how fragile Russia's political and economic stability really was. For a year, the Russian government would be coping with the consequences.

THE FIRST STEPS IN THE CHECHEN CONFLICT

This relatively peaceful period of Yeltsin's consolidation of power ended with the unexpected outbreak of war in Chechnya, a Russian republic in the northern Caucasus. In 1991, General Dzhokhar Dudayev, a former Soviet officer, came to power in Grozny with the tacit support of Yeltsin's group, which hoped to have a loyalist in place in the capital of the Chechen Republic.[7] Yeltsin and his advisors had miscalculated, however: Dudayev made no attempt to maintain loyalty to Moscow. On the contrary, the general immediately began to push Chechnya toward independence. Preoccupied with their internal struggles, the Moscow authorities for several years ignored the deteriorating situation in Chechnya and its dangerous precedent for the central government's relations with other republics. Only after his victory over parliament did Yeltsin turn his attention to Chechnya.

The federal authorities hesitated for some time over whether to begin negotiations with Dudayev or to use force against him. Until the summer of 1994, Moscow gave the impression that it was ready to negotiate with Dudayev,[8] while it became involved in complicated political intrigues in the northern Caucasus. The president's advisors convinced him to create an anti-Dudayev opposition group, headed by Umar Avturkhanov (a former militia man) and Salambek Khadzyev (a bureaucrat working in Moscow). A force of anti-Dudayev volunteers was assembled by Russia's Federal Counterintelligence Service (FSK), the successor organization to the KGB, under the personal supervision of the head of the FSK, Sergei Stepashin.[9] According to the FSK's plan, a puppet government was to be set up after the volunteer force had taken Grozny. This puppet regime would then legitimize the introduction of Russian troops into Chechnya. On November 26, 1994, the volunteers began to march on Grozny, the capital of the rebellious republic. However, Chechen troops loyal to Dudayev routed the ill-assorted pro-Moscow force without much difficulty.

As John Kenneth Galbraith has said, politics is not the art of the possible; it consists in choosing between the disastrous and the unpalatable. Yeltsin in 1994 chose the disastrous option. The collapse of the FSK operation set dramatic events in motion. Yeltsin apparently regarded Dudayev's victory as a personal insult. On November 28, he demanded that the Chechen leader disband his armed units and threatened to impose a state of emergency in the republic if Dudayev failed to comply. Then, without waiting for any response to this demand, Yeltsin issued a decree ordering the Chechens to lay down their arms by December 15, an impossible target. No one in Moscow was very concerned about the feasibility of the deadline, however. At a meeting chaired by Yeltsin on November 29, the Security Council without much debate approved a plan to use the Russian army against the mutinous republic.[10] On December 2 the Russian military began air strikes against targets on Chechen territory. The decision to resort to air strikes suggests that Moscow was not interested in securing negotiations, but rather wanted to intimidate the separatists and to send a warning to other recalcitrant republics. On December 11, 1994—four days before the ultimatum deadline—three columns of Russian army units moved into Chechnya.

Moscow's actions in Chechnya reflected a Soviet-style approach to the crisis. The Chechen scenario was remarkably similar to Gorbachev's

111

attempt to suppress unrest in Lithuania in January 1991. Gorbachev's team had first created an opposition (the Committee of National Salvation); then artificially provoked disorder; and finally introduced military forces under a mandate of "restoring order and preserving the territorial integrity" of the USSR.[11] Yeltsin did much the same in Chechnya. The thinly disguised excuse for the use of force in Lithuania had accelerated the collapse of the USSR and marked the beginning of Gorbachev's fall from power. The suppression of Chechnya, in its turn, strengthened hostility toward Moscow in the Caucasus, led to a sharp drop in Yeltsin's popularity throughout Russia, and complicated the transition to democracy.

Paradoxically, the federal center's military involvement in Chechnya strengthened Dudayev's position. By the summer of 1994, many observers had begun predicting a severe crisis in Chechnya due to the failure of Dudayev's policies. There were signs that the Chechen people were tired of Dudayev and that his government had been weakened. Resentment toward his regime was fueled by economic difficulties and by the spread of corruption and criminal activities. A well thought out policy by the federal authorities might have led to a relatively peaceful removal of Dudayev by the Chechens themselves. Moscow's decision to use force, however, had the opposite result: the Chechens rallied around the rebellious general.

It is still unclear who started the war in Chechnya, how the decision was made, and what reasons were behind it. The chairman of the Duma Defense Committee, Sergei Yushenkov, has said, "I think that it was Lobov, Shakhrai, and Yegorov [who started the war]. The latter undoubtedly was the ringleader of the operation. Certainly Grachev and Stepashin were involved." Yushenkov also spoke of the motives for starting the war: "Oleg Lobov told me, 'Why shouldn't we carry out the same kind of operation in Chechnya that the [United States] carried out in Haiti? The president's prestige will rise.' The time had come for a show of force."[12]

Those who backed Russia's incursion into Chechnya were quickly dubbed the "party of war." Lev Ponomaryov, a democratic activist and former Yeltsin supporter, described the party of war as "the 'power ministries' and their leaders among the president's aides, the same kind of people who, in other times, had organized the August coup of 1991. Korzhakov and Barsukov, the heads of the Presidential Security Service, gave it a special flavor."[13] Nikolai Yegorov, who had replaced Sergei

Shakhrai as minister for nationalities, also played an important role. Yegorov, a regional boss, had risen rapidly to the inner circle of Moscow's ruling elite; like much of the southern Russian regional elite, he was strongly anti-Caucasus. He, too, insisted that the Chechen problem should be resolved by force.[14]

The military, in the person of Minister of Defense Grachev, is widely thought to have been an active instigator of the Chechen war. Indeed, contrary to the advice of the general staff, Grachev assured Yeltsin that the Chechen campaign would be "a piece of cake." It was Grachev's incompetence and disrespect for human life that made the war, once started, a bloody nightmare.[15] Yeltsin, however, had the last word on the decision to go to war. Perhaps Yeltsin's subordinates withheld information from him or distorted it in some way, but the president was the person who decided everything. The Security Council merely ratified a decision that had already been made by Yeltsin himself, first voting for the military option and only afterward discussing it. At the end of 1994, in an address on Russian television, the president acknowledged that he was completely in charge of all decisions made in regard to the Chechen problem. When they committed Russian forces to the war, the president and a majority of the members of the Security Council were convinced that what awaited them was an easy victory—almost an unimpeded tour of the Caucasus.

WHAT CAUSED THE WAR?

The former minister of nationalities, Valery Tishkov, believes that the decision to begin the war was not inevitable. "I am firmly convinced that until November 23, 1994, the Chechen war was not fatally inevitable and there were possibilities for resolving the crisis. All Yeltsin had to do was lift the telephone receiver and call Dudayev, who would immediately have flown to Boris Nikolayevich's side for discussions. Yeltsin merely needed to overcome his personal ambitions."[16] Yeltsin, however, never made the call. According to sources close to the president, Yeltsin decided to attack Chechnya after a television broadcast that showed dramatic images of captured and humiliated Russian officers and soldiers following the first assault on Grozny. Yeltsin's assistants deliberately drew the president's attention to these reports, which infuriated him and hastened his decision to take revenge. Sometime during the period November 26-29, he resolved to initiate an all-out attack on Chechnya and attended the Security Council session with the intention of announcing this decision.

Yeltsin and his associates were most likely moved by a combination of motives, both political and psychological, to launch what amounted to a civil war. At the time of the Chechen crisis, the president's popularity rating had fallen precipitously. Many of his old promises remained unfulfilled, and his new promises were no longer believed. Whereas previously all his failures could be blamed on his enemies, especially the parliament, Yeltsin now lacked strong opponents. He was sole master of the political situation, and thus sooner or later he would have to answer for the country's unsolved economic problems, the deteriorating living standard of a substantial part of the population, and the collapse of people's hopes. This made the outlook for Yeltsin's regime dim, especially with the approaching December 1995 parliamentary elections and the June 1996 presidential elections. The president also needed a means of placating regional and republic leaders who were becoming restive.

The traditional Soviet solution to such circumstances was to find an enemy to distract people's attention from explosive social problems, and somewhere in the back of his mind, Yeltsin may have hoped that a successful solution of the Chechen problem would strengthen his position and help to solve urgent domestic issues. It also meant he could strike back at the irritating upstart, Dudayev. Yeltsin's advisors, who had little knowledge about conditions in the northern Caucasus and the psychology of its people, convinced the president that it was a matter of an easy victory and that the entire military engagement would not take more than eight days.

The president's decision to begin military actions in the northern Caucasus was presumably accelerated by the fear that Ruslan Khasbulatov, who was Chechen by birth and who had become active in Chechen politics in recent months, might come to power there.[17] Khasbulatov could have become the new Chechen leader, which would automatically have made him a member of the Federation Council and an active participant in Moscow politics. Moscow politicians, especially Yeltsin, did not want to permit their former arch-rival to return to center stage.

Political goals were uppermost in the decision to begin the Chechen operation, but there were also economic factors, chief among which was the question of oil from Azerbaijan and the route of the pipeline to carry it. Moscow was trying to preserve its control of Caspian oil and oil transportation routes, which meant that either a new pipeline would have to be built close to Chechnya, or an existing pipeline on the territory of Chechnya would have to be used. In either case, it would be necessary to pacify Chechnya. In addition, Russia had left an unspecified quantity of arms in Chechnya in late 1991 and early 1992, and sooner or later these arms were likely to be used.[18]

None of Dudayev's machinations could have succeeded without cooperation from powerful forces in Moscow. All of the competing criminal groups in Chechnya had their protectors and connections in Moscow. Some Moscow clans supported Dudayev and contributed to his financial and other operations. Others supported the general's opponents and were eager to see his regime destroyed.

One opinion widely shared in Moscow was that the decision to go to war in Chechnya was part of a cover-up of an unprecedented financial fraud involving the sale of petroleum from Grozny. *Moskovskiy komsomolets*, a usually well informed newspaper with a reputation for sensationalism, wrote:

> Dzhokhar Dudayev has been in power for almost three years. All this time Chechnya was selling petroleum abroad without any regulation. Even if one assumes that the "black gold" was sold at dumping prices, the amount of profit would still be considerable, about one-half billion American dollars. It is understandable that those in Moscow who protected this illegal fountain earned enough for a lifetime, and thus were prepared to risk much to be able to continue to do it a hundred times over. [Then] at a certain point Dudayev apparently felt powerful enough to stop sharing the profits, and all of a sudden everyone [in Moscow] recalled that there were violations of human rights in Chechnya, and separatism, hostage taking, falsified documents, and fields sown with hemp. It remains to be learned just who stood behind the Russian president and who persuaded him to send forces to disarm the "unlawful" Chechen units. Then it would not be difficult to identify these new Russian billionaires. But we will never learn this.[19]

It would be too simplistic to try to explain the reasons for the Chechen war by this reasoning alone, but it would also be a mistake to ignore it.

Yet the entire blame for the Chechen war cannot be put on Moscow's shoulders. Dudayev and his entourage were not innocent victims. In fact, Dudayev's Chechnya had become a crime-infested zone where illegal trade in arms and narcotics flourished. Chechen criminal groups had become more active across Russia, including Moscow. Chechnya could have developed an agreement with the federal authorities similar to Tatarstan's federal agreement, which gave it a great deal of independence in solving its internal problems. Instead, the vain and power-hungry Dudayev chose to challenge Moscow, thereby provoking the bloody events that followed. Like some of the Russian politicians involved, Dudayev did not suffer excessively from pangs of conscience for what happened afterward, as evidenced by the statement that he would "sacrifice every last Chechen" to gain independence for Chechnya.[20]

THE REACTION TO THE WAR

The Chechen invasion was expected to last for a week, during which the problem of the obstinate Chechens would be resolved with practically no casualties. The blitzkrieg did not succeed. The second assault on Grozny foundered, and the battle became protracted. The setbacks revealed with merciless clarity the degradation and demoralization of the Russian troops. Russia's senior military commanders were inept; the troops were unprepared to conduct a winter campaign in mountainous conditions; and there was poor coordination among the individual military units and the power ministries. The most serious problem, however, was that the politicians threw the soldiers into battle without any clear explanation of the war's goals. Moreover, the Russian army never expected to fight on Russian territory against civilians. As a result of these factors, young, inexperienced boys, mostly poorly equipped draftees, died by the hundreds and thousands, while thousands of innocent civilians were also savagely killed.

The war itself lacked logic. Its origins were based on hearsay, irrationality, and cynicism. The Russian generals had decided to begin the second assault on Grozny during the night of December 31, 1994–January 1, 1995, under the worst winter conditions. *Izvestiya* reported:

> The editors received information from military sources in the war zone: "January 1 is Pavel Grachev's birthday. On the eve, Soskovets and another general [Mikhail Barsukov] visited him. There was a party in progress. Afterwards the lead units received their order—he who takes Dudayev's palace [in Grozny] will receive no less than three hero's stars." Thus, the

bloodbath took place on New Year's Eve. Many were killed both Chechens and our men—but the palace was not taken.[21]

The Chechen war increased the army's dissatisfaction with both Defense Minister Grachev and the commander-in-chief, President Yeltsin. Top military leaders openly spoke out against the president for the first time, condemning the war and its execution. A number of flag officers, such as the first deputy commander of ground forces, Colonel-General Eduard Vorobyev, chose to resign rather than assume any responsibility for the bloodshed. Grachev's deputies, most notably General Boris Gromov, who had led Soviet troops out of Afghanistan and was one of the most popular leaders in the army, also issued critical assessments of the defense minister and, indirectly, of the president himself.[22]

The miseries that the war brought to Russian society were unmistakable.[23] Every public opinion poll showed that the majority supported a peaceful solution to the conflict. In one poll, 54 percent supported withdrawal of Russian forces from Chechnya, while just 27 percent supported sending the troops. Popular disapproval of Yeltsin's policy in the northern Caucasus was evident in the further sharp drop in his popularity: 63 percent of the respondents disapproved of the president's actions, while only 8 percent approved of them. Seventy percent of the respondents were unfavorably disposed toward General Grachev; only 3 percent supported him.[24]

The Chechen war produced the same effect as the Soviet invasion of Afghanistan. As the number of dead and wounded grew, so did fear of personal loss. The Russians became more and more critical of the war in Chechnya. Moreover, the war also forced former Yeltsin allies from the democratic camp to reconsider their attitude toward him. They had already begun to reevaluate their support during his struggle with the parliament; the war was now added to the growing list of his failures. When the Chechen campaign began, Yuri Burtin, a representative of the intelligentsia who had long and consistently opposed the president, wrote: "Now it is absolutely certain that Russia has lost Chechnya. If Chechnya means something, not only in the sense of territory . . . but as the sum of the Chechen people, then this people will for many generations be alienated from Russia, at least spiritually."[25]

Regardless of the general disapproval of the Chechen war, the protest rallies organized by the democrats drew pitifully few people. The activist democratic movement had gradually been exhausted by the events of the past few years. The leaders of the democratic camp now appeared pathetic and helpless, and their appeals moved ever fewer supporters. People did not forget that the democrats had approved, through either their actions or their silence, the use of force in Moscow against the parliament in 1993. Many of the democrats had paved the way for Yeltsin to come to power. Perhaps because of this, the democrats' sudden accusatory fervor against Yeltsin and the regime weakened their credibility. The absence of mass protest against the events in Chechnya was also a consequence of the growing weariness of society. Individuals had begun to think only of themselves and of survival.

YELTSIN FINDS SUPPORT

Yeltsin, however, was not isolated on the issue of the Chechen war. Boris Fyodorov, former minister of finance and an active liberal, wrote, "If laws are not obeyed and bandits are allowed to arm themselves openly and to kill people on Russian territory, then the government is obliged to stop it. It must oppose such actions even though it means the use of force. We must restore order [in Chechnya]."[26] A number of other well-known democrats also supported this argument. One of the leaders of the Yabloko faction, Vladimir Lukin, a former ambassador to the United States and later the chairman of the State Duma Foreign Affairs Committee, wrote with approval:

> At the time of the Chechen war, the executive branch showed itself and society that it could act independently, without regard for political pressures and in spite of them. . . . In an ideal world, the absurd and dangerous notion that the army should not be used for internal conflicts should be pounded out of the heads of our military. . . . Using the army inside the country in extreme situations, when threats to the state appear, is the norm in democratic states.[27]

Lukin argued that Yeltsin's decision to use force against Chechnya was justified, and some democrats went along with this argument, provoking a split in the democratic camp.

The Chechen war also forced the right to reconsider its attitude toward Yeltsin. As Yeltsin adopted the opposition's patriotic great-power rhetoric, Russian nationalists were left without a basis of legitimacy: their store of ideas was used up. On the subject of Chechnya, Yeltsin's formerly irreconcilable enemies had few ideological differences with him. The barriers that remained were those of purely personal enmity, and some patriots began to condemn the president for simply appropriating issues that they had been advocating all along. Nationalist leaders and ideologues like Aleksandr Prokhanov, the editor of the nationalist newspaper *Zavtra*, argued that the use of force was necessary to restore the territorial integrity of Russia. Igor Shafarevich wrote:

> The main goal of the Russian nation now is to preserve and restore the Russian state. . . . The question of Russian unity must be resolved in Chechnya. Certainly, we patriots are uncomfortable with the fact that we now share a policy goal with Yeltsin and Grachev. But if we were to take the opposite position, we would be in the same boat as Gaidar. Such a consideration pales when compared to the question of the unity and existence of Russia which is being decided now in Chechnya. And that unity is being defended by the army.[28]

Nationalistic groups of various shades, notably Sergei Baburin's Russia's Way and Aleksandr Barkashov's extreme neofascist group, also supported the president's new direction. Zhirinovsky always backed Yeltsin at critical moments. Few issues divided Yeltsin and the nationalists during this period. One step further by either side, and the gap might have disappeared altogether.

At this point few people or political forces posed a serious threat to Yeltsin. He had more freedom of action than ever. Although many segments of the population opposed the president's policies, they did not protest, preferring to wait and see what would come next. The public's focus on the war might even have benefited Yeltsin, as it helped distract the country from its serious social problems and gave it a new enemy, the Chechens.

CHECHNYA GRIDLOCK

From December 1994 to the spring of 1995, Yeltsin became more irascible. Unable or unwilling to listen to reason, he would not consider compromise. Despite the failures, costs, and bloodshed in Chechnya, and although he may already have understood that he was caught in a political trap, he could not admit a mistake, and he stubbornly continued along the same path.

Yeltsin's undemocratic tendencies had been noted in the past, but they had been kept in check by political circumstances. It was not possible to establish one-man rule while the executive and legislative

119

branches were actively competing for power; the president had needed the support of the democratically oriented groups. After the October 1993 victory over the parliament, however, Yeltsin's authoritarian habits became more prominent. He began behaving like a monarch, apparently convinced that Russian society wanted him to rule this way. His isolation from society and from democratic forces, the growing influence of the intermediaries who regulated his contacts with the outside world, and the constant flattery and deference of his subordinates all had negative effects on Yeltsin's personality and policies.

Few people now saw the robust, smiling person of broad gestures that Yeltsin had once been. He was often gloomy and preoccupied, and he appeared in public less and less frequently. His associates constantly had to come up with excuses for Yeltsin's skipping official meetings. "The president is working at his dacha" and "the president is working with the documents" were the most common, but implausible, explanations for his frequent disappearances. He began to show increasing signs of suspiciousness, irritability, and harshness. His conduct worried many, even those in his own entourage. After Yeltsin's behavior in Germany on August 30, 1994, when, in an apparent state of intoxication, he conducted an orchestra, even his closest aides and speechwriters felt compelled to write him a letter in which they tried to persuade him to behave with more dignity. This provoked an indignant outburst from Yeltsin. Previously the president had shown recklessness, for which he could be forgiven; many people even considered it part of his charm. But now he became more and more stubborn as he insisted on getting his own way even when he himself could see the disastrous results. This began to change perceptions of him, even among his closest allies and supporters. One admitted, "The burden of power deformed Yeltsin's personality." During his increasingly rare television addresses, Yeltsin appeared absent-minded and terse. His face looked like a mask. Though occasionally his eyes lit up with the old spark, it would quickly be extinguished. He had too many problems that he did not know how to solve.

During this period, Yeltsin's health was deteriorating. In February 1995, during a visit to Kazakhstan, he looked physically worn out. His speech was weak, and the television cameras showed several instances in which he had to be supported on both sides. Moreover, behind his arrogant, self-assured manner he probably felt dismay and uncertainty: the reality around him was too difficult for an aging provincial *apparatchik* to understand, and the problems too complicated. As his press secretary, Vyacheslav Kostikov, and his bodyguard, Aleksandr Korzhakov, later said, he wanted to escape people, to avoid making decisions, and to hide from everybody.

War in Chechnya and the deterioration of the living standard of a significant part of the population were bound to affect attitudes toward the government and the president. Polls conducted in early 1995 showed that the "party of power" would be in serious trouble in the upcoming elections. Until 1994, Yeltsin had been in the "confidence zone"; that is, the number of people who had complete faith in him exceeded the number of those who had no faith in him. In 1993, for example, polls had indicated that 28 percent of those queried trusted him completely, and 32 percent trusted him in part, while just 24 percent distrusted him completely. In 1994, 20 percent trusted him and 26 percent distrusted him. In February 1995, however, the proportion of those who had complete faith in him fell to 8 percent and of those with some faith to 31 percent, while the number of those with no faith in Yeltsin rose to 48 percent. According to the same poll, if the presidential elections had taken place in February 1995, Yeltsin would have lost to all of the other major politicians. Even Gennady Zyuganov, who at that moment did not stand very high in public popularity polls, would have beaten Yeltsin by a small margin (20:18). Many analysts agreed that "Boris Yeltsin appears to be a political corpse whose activity and reputation have gone into an irreversible tailspin."[29]

Meanwhile, the war in Chechnya forced everyone to choose sides and clarify his or her political beliefs. The war showed what each player on the Russian political scene was worth. Yeltsin's associates, especially those who had previously been known for their democratic convictions, including his advisers Yuri Baturin, Aleksandr Livshits, Georgi Satarov, and Emil Pain, were in a difficult situation: they had to approve Yeltsin's Chechen policy or—if they wished to retain their democratic credentials—to resign. In the end, although they temporized and made efforts to escape responsibility for the bloodshed, none of Yeltsin's closest advisors jumped ship.

The Chechen war also provoked a growing unease among the local elites in the republics and regions of the Russian Federation. Moscow's Chechen policy signified for them the federal center's determination to reestablish strict control over the regions. It also hinted at the possibility of a reevaluation of all the agreements that had been reached between

121

the center and the republics, such as the one between Tatarstan and the federal government.

Only a few provincial leaders openly showed their disagreement with the way Yeltsin had chosen to resolve the problem of preserving the territorial integrity of Russia. In January 1995, several provincial representatives met in Cheboksary, the capital of the Republic of Udmurtia, to try to organize a collective protest against the war. A secondary goal of the meeting was to try to resuscitate the Council of Heads of Republics. This was the first open attempt by republic leaders to express their disapproval of the president's Chechen course, but it did not elicit much enthusiasm from other federation subjects. The regions were anxious not to irritate the Kremlin.

Some of the leaders of the ethnically Russian regions, particularly those nearest to the Caucasus, such as Stavropol and Krasnodar, actively supported the president. Many local leaders downplayed their demands for autonomy in exchange for more economic aid from the federal center. Thus Yeltsin had achieved at least one of his goals with the war: he managed to intimidate the subjects of the federation.

Several of Russia's neighbors welcomed Moscow's harshness toward the intransigent northern Caucasus republic. The first to express support was Georgian President Eduard Shevardnadze, as this now gave him a green light to solve his domestic problem in Abkhazia. He probably hoped that Moscow would stop the Chechens from helping the Abkhaz separatists (fellow Muslims). Moscow's actions also played into the hands of other multiethnic states with analogous problems, especially Moldova, Ukraine, and Azerbaijan. Kiev could use the example of the Chechen war to halt the quest for independence of the rebellious Republic of Crimea and to abolish the institution of the presidency in Crimea.

Yeltsin had not thought through a strategy for dealing with the effects of the Chechen adventure on Russia's interests in the outside world. The consequences were particularly sharp in Central and Eastern Europe, where Moscow's policy in the Caucasus gave former communist states a powerful trump card in their quest for admission to NATO, the enlargement of which now became practically inevitable.

The initial response of the Western governments to the war in Chechnya was rather restrained. The West was apparently taken by surprise both by the military actions and by the fact that the Russian federal troops failed to achieve a fast success. The major political forces in the Western capitals at first treated the invasion of Chechnya as an internal affair of Russia. Their restraint had several causes. The Western leaders were concerned about the threat of Russia's possible disintegration. No less important for them was loyalty to Yeltsin, whom they considered a main guarantor of liberal reforms in Russia. The Western leaders' failure to raise the Chechen issue in high-level discussions with their Russian counterparts gave Yeltsin a free hand in politics in the Caucasus for a long time.[30] Only after continued reports about the shelling of the civilian population and numerous casualties did the response of the West become more critical. Finally, in January 1995, Chancellor Helmut Kohl called it "sheer madness" and asked Yeltsin to resolve the conflict through peaceful means.

THE FIRST HOSTAGE CRISIS
AND THE PRIME MINISTER

For a time, Russian society became used to the war, and public attention turned to problems of daily life. It took a dramatic event to bring the war in the northern Caucasus back into focus: on June 15, about 100 Chechen kamikaze fighters conducted a raid deep into Russian territory and fought their way to the small town of Budennovsk in the Stavropol region. There they seized a local hospital, taking hostage more than 1,000 people—both staff members and patients. The Chechens were led by Shamil Basayev, a Chechen guerrilla leader who became a hero as the man who brought "the enormous bear" to its knees. (After the war he would become deputy prime minister of the new Chechen government, while he continued to be reviled in Russia.) After barricading themselves and their victims in the hospital, the Chechens demanded the immediate withdrawal of Russian troops from Chechnya and unconditional recognition of Chechen independence.

This action by the Chechens, unprecedented in its audacity and desperation, rocked all of Russia and temporarily paralyzed its leadership. Yeltsin himself, however, took the situation rather calmly; despite the brewing political crisis and the real threat to the lives of thousands of his fellow citizens, he traveled to Halifax, Canada, to attend a meeting of the G-7 (Group of Seven leaders of the major industrialized nations). While Yeltsin was in Canada, he approved military actions by elite Russian military troops to free the hostages, but this operation failed badly, with a large loss of life on both sides, including many of the hostages. Television viewers could see the hostages, mainly sick people,

123

waving white sheets and begging the Russian military not to shoot, while the Chechens placed Russian women at the windows of the building to use them as living shields.

In Yeltsin's absence, Prime Minister Chernomyrdin emerged at center stage. At the most dramatic moment of the siege, on June 18, when elite troops had failed to free the hostages, Chernomyrdin began to negotiate with the terrorists. He succeeded in reaching agreement for the release of the hostages in exchange for giving Basayev and his fighters safe passage back to Chechnya. They also agreed to a cease-fire between federal forces and the Chechen irregular forces and to begin negotiations toward a peaceful settlement.

Chernomyrdin's efforts to negotiate with the separatists met with criticism, however—even from some who considered themselves democrats. Reflecting the opinions of the liberal intelligentsia, *Literaturnaya gazeta* wrote:

> Both "victory at any price" and "peace at any price" are not what we need. They are dangerous and ambiguous. Only in Russia can one think that it is possible to forget a year and a half of war, and the deaths of hundreds and thousands of people. The very position declared by the authorities—that there will be no vengeance—puts the government on the same level as the gang of thugs, and makes the law a plaything in the hands of politicians. The public was not consulted when the war began, and it was not consulted when it was ended and the "negotiations" began.[31]

After Budennovsk, the Chechens no longer aroused sympathy.

Meanwhile, the communists in the Russian parliament, taking advantage of the drama in Budennovsk, drafted a resolution on the impeachment of the president. This was the first opposition attempt to test the strength of the government since the events of 1993. The temporary cease-fire between the two branches of power was at an end. On June 21, the communist draft resolution got only 172 votes of the 300 needed to pass an impeachment resolution, but on June 22, by a vote of 241 to 70, with 20 members abstaining, the Duma passed a vote of no confidence in Prime Minister Chernomyrdin's government (only 226 votes were necessary to pass a no-confidence motion). Thus, at the very moment when his political fortunes seemed to be soaring, the prime minister found himself in danger. According to the constitution, in case of a second vote of no confidence, the president would have to decide whether to dissolve the parliament and hold early elections or to dismiss the cabinet and appoint a new prime minister.

The vote of no confidence in the prime minister, however, was not directed so much against Chernomyrdin as against the president. Such a step served to consolidate the opposition and to test Yeltsin's power. But in this game Chernomyrdin might easily have become a victim. Showing emotion for the first time, the prime minister went on the offensive and demanded that the Duma immediately take a second vote on the no-confidence motion. This was an astute move, since the opposition was not ready for further confrontation. The president also warned the Duma that he would not accept the government's resignation and threatened to dissolve the parliament.

Thus the deputies were faced with a difficult choice: either to vote confidence in the government, which would make it hard for them to criticize it before the elections, or to let the president dissolve the parliament and set a date for new elections. With the possible exception of the communists, the deputies were not ready for elections as early as the summer. Yeltsin, for his part, did not want to lose his loyal prime minister. This created the possibility of a compromise. Yeltsin took the initiative and organized a meeting with representatives of all parliamentary factions on June 27. The discussion appeared almost serene: the president promised the deputies additional authority to participate in the elaboration of the draft budget for the next year, and he promised to resolve the Chechen crisis. In exchange, the president asked the Duma to reconsider its vote of no confidence in the Chernomyrdin cabinet, to agree not to propose any amendments to the constitution, and not to undermine his regime.

The Duma deputies, in order not to lose face, wanted reciprocal concessions from the president. They demanded the resignation of all of the power ministers, who were under attack after the Budennovsk events. Yeltsin had difficulty refusing. On June 29, at a meeting of the Security Council devoted entirely to the events in Budennovsk, Yeltsin replaced the director of the federal security service, Sergei Stepashin, and, with reluctance, his devoted interior minister, Viktor Yerin. Against expectations, he left Defense Minister Pavel Grachev in place, not able to afford the luxury of losing a faithful defense minister on the eve of the elections. Thus, by making partial concessions, the president and the parliament laid the groundwork for the resolution of the most serious crisis since 1993. Both sides displayed common sense, maturity, and a desire to avoid pushing things to the extreme.

At the beginning of July, Yeltsin suddenly became ill again, this time seriously, and was hospitalized with heart disease. The tensions of the previous weeks had evidently taken their toll. The outside world, however, knew practically nothing about the true state of the president's health. The situation closely resembled the era of Brezhnev, Andropov, and Chernenko. The televised snippets of Yeltsin's appearances only raised more questions and concerns about his health. Many began to doubt that the next parliamentary elections would take place. To calm public fears, Yeltsin, from the hospital, signed a decree setting December 17, 1995, as the date for the next parliamentary elections. The electoral campaign was launched. Everyone understood that these elections would be a warm-up before the main event, the presidential elections that were to take place in June 1996. No one was sure whether Yeltsin would be able to run.

DOES MOSCOW KNOW HOW
TO CONDUCT NEGOTIATIONS?

Meanwhile, negotiations between the Russians and the Chechens had begun. In June the delegations met in Grozny and began discussion of a complicated package of issues related to the conclusion of the war and the future of Chechnya. The goals of the two sides were difficult to reconcile. For the Kremlin the most important points, especially after Budennovsk, were to avoid making large concessions to the Chechens and to guarantee the primacy of the laws of the Russian Federation on Chechen territory. The Chechens, despite the havoc that the war had brought, sought only one thing: the creation of a sovereign state.

The Russian delegation found itself in a paradoxical situation: it was conducting formal negotiations with representatives of Dudayev—who was not present and was the object of a nationwide manhunt. Therefore the fate of the negotiations to a great extent depended on the willingness of the Russian authorities to declare an amnesty for Dudayev and his fighters. Also difficult were the issues of elections in Chechnya and the formation of a new Chechen political regime. It was clear that in the event of a fairly free election, Dudayev had every chance of preserving his power. The inevitable question arose: What had been the purpose of the months of war and bloodshed?

126

In the middle of July, after many troubling interruptions, the Dudayev delegation agreed in principle to a formula stating, "The status of Chechnya after the elections will be determined on the basis of the Russian and new Chechen constitutions in the framework of the Federation Treaty," which did little to clarify matters.[32] Both sides agreed to a new transition status for Chechnya that limited its independence and to a delineation of powers through a federal agreement between Moscow and Grozny that would be similar to the Tatarstan formula. There was, of course, a significant difference: while Tatarstan had secured its rights by means of skillful political pressure and negotiations, the Chechens achieved theirs as the result of a brutal war.

Soon it became clear that the negotiation and its results did not command full support on either the Russian or the Chechen side. It was entirely possible that the Russian military as well as the Chechen field commanders, who wanted full independence for Chechnya, would not accept the results of negotiations and would continue the war.

No less important was the opposition to the peace settlement in Russian political circles. "Certain forces are openly trying to disrupt the talks. Never before has the delegation felt such powerful pressure. Most of all, this has come from the part of the military. . . . Even some commercial organizations have become active [in opposing the settlement]. The end of the war will prevent certain highly placed people from continuing to line their pockets with impunity,"[33] said Arkady Volsky, the head of the Russian delegation at the negotiations with the Chechens. The problem was no longer the inability of Moscow or Dudayev to negotiate, but the resistance of powerful groups on both sides for whom the war was a means of survival or enrichment.

Within Russian political circles, there were three points of view concerning the future fate of Chechnya. The official side continued to insist on keeping Chechnya in the Russian Federation. Other forces advocated Chechnya's separation from Russia—an idea first expressed by Aleksandr Solzhenitsyn some time earlier. "We cannot keep Chechnya, and we should not keep it. This is unpleasant, but true. The attempt to 'keep' it at any price is yet more self-delusion," said Federation Council member Nikolai Gonchar, who suggested that at least part of Chechnya, namely the Dudayev-controlled south, be separated from Russia. "You dream of complete independence," Gonchar addressed the Chechens. "Didn't you fight for that? You will get that independence. . . . Why should we drag you along with us, and develop inferiority and guilt complexes while you play the part of the 'enfant terrible' before whom all are guilty and who is allowed to do anything he wants?"[34] There was a large dose of realism in this view, but it also grew out of a strong wish to punish the Chechens. The third, more balanced position, did not receive much support in Moscow. Its proponents advocated giving Chechnya an association with the Russian state, without final definition of its status, and with a high degree of autonomy in maintaining external ties. It was the most reasonable option, but in the highly charged atmosphere, such a compromise position was not popular.

By the end of July 1995, after a torturous process of conciliation, the Russian delegation and the Chechen side signed an agreement on a package of military measures, but they had not reached closure on the political issues related to Chechnya's future. Even this was a triumph that few had expected. Most of the Russian troops were to be withdrawn from Chechen territory, while the Chechen fighters were to be disarmed. The Chechen side received the right to organize self-defense units in residential areas. These steps were to lay the groundwork for the election of a new government in Chechnya. Unfortunately, optimism about the military agreement was short-lived. Everyone quickly realized the difficulties of its implementation in the atmosphere of mutual suspicion. Dudayev was not prepared to disarm the groups of fighters that he controlled. Moreover, after his delegation signed the agreement, he unilaterally proposed a fundamental change to the agreement itself, stating that Chechnya was and would remain a sovereign and independent state. It was clear that the Chechen fighters, who obeyed no authorities, would not voluntarily give up their arms. The federal forces were not consistent in observing the peace agreement either; they violated it periodically.

Soon the Chechen situation became even more confusing. Lieutenant General Anatoly Romanov, commander of the unified group of Russian forces in Chechnya, and General Aslan Maskhadov, a former Soviet colonel who was now chief of staff for the main contingent of the Chechen armed formations, became the main actors on the Chechen scene. The fragile cease-fire depended in large part on these two generals and their relationship. "We can no longer shoot at one another," announced the two military leaders after many sleepless nights and heated, almost explosive, arguments.[35] It was immensely difficult for them to sustain a thin thread of dialogue when contradictory instructions were coming at them from the central authorities. Dudayev had threatened to destroy Maskhadov if he went along with the Russians. At the same time Moscow was dissatisfied with Romanov's independence and popularity. But both generals resolutely tried to cooperate. "I will fulfill the terms of the agreement to the end," Maskhadov proudly declared after another volley of criticism from his chief, Dudayev.[36] After Yeltsin's demand that rebel units be disarmed by force, Romanov defiantly stated that the disarming would be carried out by peaceful means only.

The situation in Chechnya remained tense, and soon the peace process was broken by the attempted assassination of General Romanov on October 6, 1995, which left him in a coma. Clearly the assassins did not want to see the war end, and in this they succeeded.

CHAPTER SIX

RUSSIA CHOOSES
A NEW PARLIAMENT: 1995

THE PLAYWRIGHT ALEKSANDR GELMAN accurately captured the mood of society in the summer of 1995 as the parliamentary elections approached:

> The country is in the grip of a sharp sense of foreboding. No one believes in anything—not in the past, not in the future. They do not even believe in their own sanity. In 1993, there was no question in my mind about who to vote for—clearly it was for [Gaidar's party] Russia's Choice. Today I cannot answer with such certainty. People don't know how to react, what to do, who to vote for. More than half the citizens of our country have not bothered to vote for a long time, and will not do so again. Others, accustomed to the old Soviet ways, will go to the polls, but without understanding what they are voting for. They will choose someone at random according to party affiliation, or because of a familiar name, or they will vote for whomever the propagandists tell them to, or for a dollar tip.[1]

THE HEROES OF THE OPPOSITION FADE

By the time the parliamentary election campaign began in the fall, the public had lost faith in most politicians, but few people were ready to show their dissatisfaction openly or to participate in protest actions. In polls, a majority of Russians said they expressed their unhappiness only in discussions within their circle of friends, on trains and buses, in shops and stores. In the summer of 1995, only 12 percent of respondents in Moscow said they were ready to take part in political demonstrations and rallies, and only 3 percent said they would

131

participate in a strike. In other large cities the corresponding numbers were 4 percent and 3.5 percent, and in smaller cities and villages, even less—1 percent and 2 percent. Only 2 percent of respondents thought that people were ready to take violent action against the government or to clash with the police. On the basis of these polls, observers speculated that, after a rise in dissatisfaction at the beginning of the 1990s, a certain calm had set in, as people adapted to their new life.[2]

During this period, the political parties concentrated on preparations for the parliamentary elections to be held, according to the constitution, on December 17, 1995. DemRossiya, the first Russian democratic movement, could not even secure the number of signatures required to participate in the elections. Its demise had become inevitable when it would not go over to the opposition against the government of Yeltsin, whom it had promoted during the struggle with Gorbachev, but at the same time could not secure power or influence in its own right. The end of DemRossiya meant the end of the era of democratic idealists and revolutionaries.

Russia's Choice was also on its way off the political stage, despite Gaidar's heroic efforts to maintain its position. Politicians began leaving its ranks in droves. Pragmatists left because the president no longer openly supported the movement. Others left because they felt that Russia's Choice had not distanced itself far enough from the president, whom they blamed for the war in Chechnya. Russia's Choice gradually lost the support of federal and local government authorities as well as funding from bankers, who began to put their money into more promising organizations, including the Communist Party. In addition, a significant part of the population continued to blame Gaidar for the costs of reform, although he had not been in the government for some time. Thus Russia's Choice was penalized for both its proximity to power and its inability to influence this power.

The Yabloko movement and its leader, Grigory Yavlinsky, attracted more public attention. Yavlinsky, who had taken no part in formulating or implementing Yeltsin's policies, succeeded in increasing his influence among the democratically oriented segments of society. He was also the only politician who consistently tried to build up a democratic opposition to the current regime. In preparation for the elections, Yavlinsky decided to remain independent, refusing to form a coalition with other democratic and liberal associations. This decision provoked substantial criticism, most prominently from Gaidar. In response, Yavlinsky wrote in

Izvestiya, "What is the point of uniting movements such as Yabloko and Russia's Choice for the parliamentary elections? These political forces have many differences—in the first place, on economic issues. How can two parties unite when one of them [Russia's Choice] supports the policies of the government, while the other opposes it. . . . Why confuse voters?"[3] Yavlinsky was convinced that an alliance with Russia's Choice would damage Yabloko's electoral chances, and he did not want to take the blame for the mistakes that Gaidar and his team had made while they were in power.

Yavlinsky's decision not to join forces with Gaidar or other groups that supported Yeltsin helped him gain support for Yabloko among those democratic voters who were frustrated with Yeltsin's policies and would otherwise not have voted. It was the only way to build a democratic alternative, which Russia badly needed. Yabloko succeeded in preserving its position and in gaining a stable electoral base, whereas all the other democratic and liberal groups gradually vanished from the political scene.

The dark horse of the election campaign was the Congress of Russian Communities (KRO). The main source of its influence was one of its leaders, General Aleksandr Lebed. Lebed had commanded the 14th Army in the Trans-Dniester, where he became a thorn in the side of Defense Minister Pavel Grachev. When Grachev decided to reorganize the 14th Army in order to rid himself of the maverick general, Lebed used the reorganization as a pretext to resign from the army, and Yeltsin, who could have compelled Lebed to remain, accepted his resignation. Lebed appeared in Moscow on June 14, 1995, and immediately dove into Russian politics, joining the camp of his old acquaintance Yuri Skokov and becoming one of the leaders of the Congress of Russian Communities.

Lebed proved to be a strong-willed, charismatic personality. He was now popular and had a reputation as a man with a sharp and original mind. He had long been waiting to break out of the army and to declare himself a national politician. His views were openly authoritarian: "There is the right of the strong. If the state is strong, it is respected by the outside world." Concerning leadership, he stated: "I do not praise Pinochet in principle. But what did he do? He succeeded in bringing order and preventing the total collapse of the state, and he put the army on top. With its help, he forced everyone to go about his business. The critics shut their traps. Everyone began to till his own field. Now Chile is one of the most successful countries." Lebed also declared, "I am not a democrat since I think that in the near future Russia will remain an empire."[4]

The general's popularity in the summer of 1995 was extraordinary. To some extent, his political career recalled that of Yeltsin in the late 1980s. In Moscow, Lebed quickly became the center of attention. Many, including those from powerful lobby groups, began to study him carefully to determine whether the general could become the heir to the weakened Yeltsin and whether it was time to change sides.

KRO's two other leaders, Yuri Skokov and former Minister of International Economic Relations Sergei Glazyev, did not enjoy much popularity and were hardly an asset to the movement. Besides, the "Russian idea"—the notion of Russian supremacy—on which the KRO's program was based had no appeal for the populations of Tatarstan, Bashkortostan, and other non-Russian republics, and it also worried those who feared the consequences of an explosion of Russian nationalism.

In the new struggle for power, or at least for representation, all the more or less well-known politicians rushed to create their own parties. Among these were Svyatoslav Fyodorov, Boris Fyodorov, Irina Khakamada, and Ella Pamfilova.[5] A majority of these parties were merely small political clubs, some existing only on paper. The explanation for such a profusion of political organizations was simple: party leaders received funds from the state budget for conducting their campaigns and television time for publicity. This increased their chances of getting into the parliament in single-mandate areas, where nearly all the leaders of the mini-parties stood for election so they could be sure of a safe seat. The president's team also had an interest in seeing the political arena highly divided and therefore helped to create and finance these dwarf parties, which might later be gathered under the president's wing in the State Duma.

THE COMMUNISTS BECOME
THE CENTER OF ATTENTION

The communists, as the largest opposition party with any real expectation of gaining power, became the center of the political scene. The ideology of Gennady Zyuganov's Communist Party of the Russian Federation (KPRF) was an eclectic mix of old communist dogma, nationalistic-chauvinistic ideas, and social-democratic slogans. The KPRF tried to satisfy the most diverse segments and groups in the population—from those who had lost everything in the course of reform to those who were its real winners. Within the ranks of the Communist Party could be found both former leaders of the last Soviet parliament, such as the communist dogmatist Anatoly Lukyanov, and pragmatic new Russian capitalists, such as Vladimir Semago. Under strong pressure from the influential pragmatists, the KPRF adopted a minimal program, which aimed to attract as much support as possible from the non-communist camp. In the new program, Zyuganov's party approved a mixed economic system and allowed for private property during an extended transitional period. The goal of this minimal program was to help neutralize the radicalism of the Communist Party's conventional ideological slogans, which were meant to elicit the support of the traditional communist electorate.

Zyuganov managed for a while to become a notable political figure. He was able to strengthen the organizational foundations of his party and to keep it from sliding into extremism. Under his guidance, the KPRF began to learn the essentials of parliamentary action. The collapse of communism was, in a way, useful to the Communist Party: it was now forced to look for allies and to reach out to the electorate. It outpaced the campaign efforts of the reformers, who were at this time incapable of concerted action.

Soon Zyuganov and other communist leaders became figures on the Moscow political and social circuits. Everyone wanted to meet them, including foreign ambassadors and journalists. They demonstrated ideological flexibility: when they met with Western and liberal audiences, they tried to show that they did not represent any threat to democracy and that they supported a parliamentary form of struggle. Zyuganov impressed everyone with his good manners, speaking ability, and elegant attire. Mindful of the polls that showed the continuous rise in the KPRF's ratings, Zyuganov apparently had no doubt of victory in the parliamentary elections. He often mentioned the results of the presidential elections in Poland at the end of November, when Solidarity firebrand Lech Walesa had lost to a former communist, Aleksandr Kwasniewski; the Polish elections led some observers to expect a leftist victory in Russia as well. However, the Polish leftists were much closer to Social Democrats than were their Russian counterparts. Kwasniewski was a typical pragmatist whom one could not suspect of harboring a secret longing to restore a communist regime. In contrast, Zyuganov's party—despite the evolution of its leader's views and his attempt to appear civilized in the eyes of the West—had not really broken with the past.

THE "PARTY OF POWER" PREPARES
TO DEFEND ITS POSITIONS

On April 25, Yeltsin proposed that Chernomyrdin form a center-right electoral party to prepare for the upcoming parliamentary elections. This was part of a strategy to create two centrist blocs: a center-right group headed by the prime minister and a center-left group headed by the speaker of the State Duma, Ivan Rybkin. The strategy was based on the premise that a two-party system comprising representatives of the major groups close to the government would splinter or neutralize the opposition. It would thus strengthen a political system based on forces friendly to one another and, more important, loyal to Yeltsin.

Some observers saw this move as part of Yeltsin's preparation to hand over the reins of power to the prime minister. Rumors that leaked out of Yeltsin's closest circle suggested that the president sometimes spoke of Chernomyrdin as his preferred heir. These rumors were misleading, however. Those who understood Yeltsin's nature knew that such leaks were probably part of the president's game. He was not a person who would leave his post voluntarily. Moreover, as there were no signs of any immediate danger to the president's position, such talk of an heir was premature. The discussions resembled a reconnaissance and disinformation mission into the enemy camp—all the more so since Yeltsin's entourage had no particular liking for the prime minister.

Chernomyrdin and the new bloc, Our Home Is Russia (NDR), were meant to serve two of Yeltsin's goals simultaneously: to push aside the groups that were opposed to him and to consolidate the "party of power"—a term that became popular at this time and was used to describe the political and bureaucratic groups that took part in exercising power. In any case, Yeltsin's experiment could not lose him anything. If Chernomyrdin's NDR failed in the parliamentary elections, Yeltsin could always distance himself; if it won, Yeltsin knew how to neutralize the prime minister and to make use of his bloc. It was not immediately clear, however, how Chernomyrdin and Rybkin were going to be able to create new electoral blocs loyal to the president. Memories were still too vivid of the previous unsuccessful attempt to organize a similar two-party system with Yeltsin's blessing which had involved Gaidar's Russia's Choice and Shakhrai's Party of Russian Unity and Accord.

In the summer of 1995, this attempt to form a two-party political system and to squeeze all the remaining political parties into irrelevance was at the center of the political community's attention. Journalists managed to get hold of a memo by the president's staff containing a plan to manipulate the Russian electorate, in which the views of Yeltsin's advisers were openly laid out. The authors of the memo formulated a goal "to straddle the wave of leftist sentiment, weaken the opposition's camp, and ensure that part of the ruling elite becomes fertile ground for a loyal mini-opposition." This would provide, they argued, "a higher degree of insurance to the authorities." The president's analysts warned, however, that the two-bloc option would not capture the organizations that espoused the great-power ideology. To neutralize those forces, the authors of the document proposed to finance some nationalist-patriotic candidates, to "ensure [their] relative loyalty . . . in the event they are successful in the elections." Thus the Kremlin advisors were proposing, in effect, to buy off and control everyone. However, those who devised Yeltsin's two-bloc system from above proved that they had little understanding of Russian reality. Soon it would become evident that the manipulation of political life from the center was no longer feasible, and the political genie could no longer be put back into the bottle. It was impossible to return to the previous system, in which political life had been controlled from the top. Attempts to do so could only discredit the new parties that the president's team was organizing and financing.

On May 27, Yeltsin's strategists launched the center-right Our Home Is Russia (NDR) under Chernomyrdin's leadership. The methods of organizing NDR were reminiscent of the Soviet days. Officials of the central and regional administrations busily engaged in independent party-building during their working hours. Such a convergence of government and party functions clearly violated the president's decree on de-politicization, which forbade any partisan activity in government institutions and places of work. In fact, however, it was difficult to differentiate between the government and the NDR, whose leading members included most of the senior officials in the government. Thus the taxpayers financed yet another semi-governmental but allegedly independent structure. In trying to deflect his critics, Chernomyrdin argued that NDR "will not dissolve into the government right away and

137

will not support its actions unconditionally.'"⁶ That is, Chernomyrdin claimed that, as the NDR leader, he would not necessarily endorse everything he did as prime minister. He was, in effect, committing himself to act and speak both as the head of the government and as the opposition to it. The success of such a split-personality exercise was doubtful, and the prime minister's arguments persuaded no one.

Meanwhile, the NDR leaders decided to concentrate on working with the regions, which, many thought, could guarantee the needed votes. In many regions, especially those with large rural populations, the local leaders had strong influence and could help attract voters to the party they favored, but none of them would do it for free. In exchange for a promise of support, each of the governors, presidents, and mayors made demands. Usually these demands were that the federal government pay the region the subsidies it owed, but since sixty of the eighty-nine subjects of the federation were entitled to such subsidies, the federal center could not satisfy everyone.

Chernomyrdin's NDR initially received the support of one of the most important regions, Moscow, and its mayor, Yuri Luzhkov. After the elections, however, when it became clear that Yeltsin himself was not going to associate with NDR, Luzhkov distanced himself from the organization as well. The Moscow mayor evidently did not care about consistency in his political commitments, and, in this case as in many others, he accurately detected which way the wind was blowing. Besides, he had his own political game to play, and he had no interest in assisting Chernomyrdin.

While the prime minister's NDR built up its organizational network and attracted financing, things were going badly from the start for the left-center bloc formed on June 22 and headed by the Duma Speaker Ivan Rybkin. The task he was given—to woo voters away from the Communist Party and other leftist groups—was simply impossible to carry out. With great difficulty, Rybkin managed to attract some small groups to his bloc, whose existence few noticed. The majority of the big political movements found Rybkin's bloc too pro-Yeltsin, and everyone was well aware that the president had assigned Chernomyrdin and Rybkin the task of creating friendly parties. This had not impeded the prime minister's party-building efforts, as the NDR's potential members already belonged to the governing class and were willing to join any government-centered organization or movement to show their loyalty and to get access to the attendant benefits. Assigning such a task to

Rybkin's bloc, however, killed its prospects from the beginning, as any viable left-center organization was by nature opposed to the government. No matter how hard the speaker tried, the formation of a left-center party as a friendly opposition could never have succeeded.

In August 1995, a rehearsal for the future Duma elections took place. This was the election of the governor of Yekaterinburg (formerly Sverdlovsk), one of Russia's largest cities and Yeltsin's birthplace. The two main contenders for the position were the former governor, Eduard Rossel (whom Yeltsin had fired in 1994, when Rossel had proclaimed the independence of the Urals Republic in direct violation of the constitution), and the incumbent, Aleksei Strakhov (head of the local branch of Our Home Is Russia). The elections were a test of the popularity of the pro-government forces and a general indicator of the regions' attitudes toward Moscow politics. The victory of Rossel, who represented local interests, showed that the party of power under Chernomyrdin's leadership would have a hard time winning the regions' support. Some provincial leaders would support the prime minister in exchange for promises of future rewards, but they also had to think of their own upcoming regional elections at the end of 1996. To win local support, the potential governors had to appear cool toward—even critical of—the federal authorities.

The summer of 1995 drew to a close with an annual event that had become a measure of the public's attitude toward the authorities and the president: this was the anniversary of the August 1991 attempted coup d'état. The results of a poll conducted among Moscow's inhabitants indicated that they were trying to forget whose side they had been on and where their sympathies had lain in those memorable August days. The number of those who responded that they did not remember whose side they took in August 1991 grew from about 8 percent on the first anniversary of the coup to 18 percent on its fourth anniversary in 1995. The number of those who responded they had hoped for the defeat of the August coup declined from 26 percent to 7 percent. Disappointment in politics was accompanied by an increase in nostalgia for the USSR: 74 percent of Muscovites regretted its demise (an increase from 69 percent in 1992), while only 18 percent did not (a decrease from 25 percent in 1992). The president's favorable rating had fallen from 55 percent in May 1991 to just 16 percent in August 1995 in Moscow, a city traditionally favorably disposed toward him.[7] For Yeltsin, this was practically a defeat.

YELTSIN REHEARSES HIS REBIRTH

On September 8, 1995, before going on his regular vacation, Yeltsin held a press conference at which he tried to compensate for his rare appearances before the Russian public and to accomplish several political tasks. First of all, Yeltsin apparently wanted to prove before a wide audience that he was still a tough and strong leader. He stated that Russia supported the Serbs, and that it would not accept the expected NATO enlargement. "When NATO approaches Russia's borders, one must acknowledge the existence of two military blocs," the president warned, hinting at the possible creation of a defense alliance with the other post-Soviet states, although he failed to specify which, if any, former republics might want to join a new defense alliance against the West.[8]

Yeltsin also announced that he had directed the Central Bank to pay out 2 trillion rubles in pension arrears. For a long time the president had shown little interest in the problems of the elderly, most of whom did not receive their niggardly pensions for months at a time. Now that the elections were approaching, Yeltsin remembered the millions of votes that might go to the communists and took a populist step. Even more surprising was Yeltsin's prediction in the press conference about the prospects for Chernomyrdin's Our Home Is Russia, given that it was created at the president's behest. The president's unexpected declaration that the NDR would win no more than 8-12 percent of the votes signaled that he had no intention of identifying himself with it. This was a severe blow for the NDR's creators, who considered the president's conduct a betrayal. In addition, the president spoke disparagingly of the government's achievements. It appeared that he had suddenly become dissatisfied with the prime minister's too-active electoral campaign and was trying to rein him in—even though it was Yeltsin himself who had pushed Chernomyrdin into public politics.

Each of the president's words and actions at the press conference had a specific goal in the context of the electoral campaign: his statements reflected his efforts to show that he controlled the situation in Russia. Yeltsin had seen that some lobbies and regional bosses were beginning to look for a new leader, and he had decided to demonstrate that no one should write him off. Throughout the press conference, Yeltsin was energetic, and his speech was firm although sometimes slow. The president reacted swiftly to the journalists' questions and remarks and even reverted to his somewhat crude humor.

Yeltsin displayed total disregard for his former allies, not mentioning either DemRossiya or Russia's Choice. Instead, he turned toward great-power rhetoric and populist action. Yet this attempt to look for a new political base for the upcoming presidential elections might easily backfire. It was doubtful that he could win the opposition over to his side, and, meanwhile, his turn to the right would not be supported by his former democratic allies. The powerful corporations, including Gazprom (which had put up the money for the prime minister's parliamentary campaign), supported Chernomyrdin, whom they at that time wanted to see in the president's chair. The other groups, small associations consisting of several tens or hundreds of people, could not prop up a president whose ratings had fallen so precipitously. Thus, as Yeltsin turned away from his old democratic allies, it was not obvious where his new support would be found.

Having demonstrated his vitality, however, and leaving political observers guessing what he had in mind, Yeltsin left for his vacation in Sochi on the Black Sea. As soon as he returned, tanned and rested, he flew to New York to join world leaders for celebrations of the fiftieth anniversary of the United Nations and an opportunity to meet with President Clinton. After Yeltsin's hard-line speech in Moscow, many expected cool personal relations between the two presidents, but their meeting was most cordial, and Clinton managed to break through Yeltsin's wariness.

Indeed, Yeltsin's rhetoric often fluctuated between open hostility toward the West when he spoke in Russia and a friendly and constructive tone when he dealt with Western leaders in person. He was by nature a populist; he knew how to play to the public's feelings, and he tried to use anti-Western sentiment to his own advantage. As a pragmatist, however, he tried to maintain a measured tone when it came to the actual conduct of inter-state relations, and he did not want to wreck relations with the West. Moreover, when he personally liked someone such as President Clinton or Chancellor Kohl, he could be more flexible in resolving political issues. Thus when he was in Moscow he would heatedly and sincerely make a scapegoat of the West, but when he was in the West, under the influence of the friendly attention of his host, Yeltsin would make concessions that were unanticipated even by his closest foreign policy associates. This pattern was repeated in 1995, when Yeltsin and Clinton managed to avert a serious downturn in Russian-American relations.

141

A TIME OF TROUBLE FOR THE PRESIDENT

As soon as he returned from his trip to the United States, where he had seemed to be in excellent physical form, Yeltsin again unexpectedly collapsed. He lost consciousness on October 26 and was rushed to the hospital by helicopter. After an examination, it was officially reported that he had aggravated ischemic heart disease. This confirmation of grave illness caused alarm and confusion. Rumors quickly spread; some people began to doubt whether the president was alive at all. This brought to the fore the question of his possible successor. According to the constitution, that successor could only be the prime minister, Chernomyrdin, who was to assume temporarily the responsibilities of the president in the event Yeltsin was incapacitated and to organize new elections within three months. Chernomyrdin's advisors and allies urged him to take power immediately. There was, however, no official mechanism in place for the transfer of power from the president to his successor. The prime minister apparently got cold feet, remembering what had happened to all those whom Yeltsin suspected of being too ambitious, and for some time he avoided saying anything on the subject in public.

On October 30, 1995, however, after visiting Yeltsin in the hospital, Chernomyrdin unexpectedly showed firmness. He announced that, with the president's agreement, he would be coordinating the activities of the power ministries and of the foreign affairs ministry, which up to this time had been subordinated directly to the president, and that he was ready to help Yeltsin with the "accumulated business." This appeared to be a breakthrough: Russia might have a new leader. The prime minister's statement shocked the president's entourage, which immediately decided to act. On the very next day, Mikhail Krasnov, the president's assistant for legal matters, announced that the prime minister could not be "put in the position of taking on functions that were not in the nature of his position. The president and the prime minister were, after all, not the director and deputy director of a factory."[9] Minister of Defense Grachev declared that the army would continue to take its orders from the president. It was clear that the president's cohorts had decided to resist any attempts to transfer power to the prime minister. On November 3, evidently under the pressure of his assistants, Yeltsin appeared on Russian television for the first time since being hospitalized. He looked stiff and slurred his words. It was obviously hard for him to make this effort, and it was apparent that a fight was going on behind the scenes. Finally, on November 4, presidential spokesman Sergei Medvedev announced that the power ministers and the foreign affairs minister would remain directly subordinate to the president. As for Chernomyrdin's earlier declaration, the spokesman, backed up by the prime minister himself, blamed the confusion on journalists' misinterpretation of the prime minister's words. Thus the fight ended with a victory for Yeltsin's entourage. The nuclear suitcase, the most important symbol of power in Russia, remained at Yeltsin's bedside in the hospital. Chernomyrdin's ascent to the top was averted. He did not have Yeltsin's thirst for power. Meeting resistance, he did not fight back, but retreated into the shadows again.

Meanwhile, tension among Yeltsin's associates was growing. They had two possible courses of action: to delay any transfer of power to Chernomyrdin for as long as possible, or to come to an agreement with the prime minister on their personal security in the event of a peaceful transfer of power. The president, by all accounts, was not in any condition to resolve the question of his powers and the issue of succession independently. Yeltsin's associates chose to delay, hoping that the president would recover, while simultaneously trying to create the impression that Yeltsin was in control of the situation. The propaganda machinery began to work, claiming that the president only needed time to regain his strength. Numerous decrees allegedly signed by Yeltsin were issued from the hospital. From time to time, political figures close to Yeltsin, for example Shumeiko, visited him and attempted to persuade the public that the president was going to be playing tennis again soon.

Nevertheless, it was hard to fool Russians in such matters. Everybody understood that Yeltsin was in no condition to govern. The general concern was not so much with the lack of control over events as with the threat of a struggle for the seat in the Kremlin. At the beginning of December 1995, however, Yeltsin again astonished everyone by shaking off his illness, proving that he had enormous reserves, both physical and political. Short television reports from the hospital showed that Yeltsin was indeed better.

The main political issue in the autumn was the requirement that a party must gather 200,000 signatures to be registered and to have its candidates on the parliamentary ballot. The process of collecting signatures turned into another farce. The party of eye surgeon Svyatoslav Fyodorov gathered signatures at clinics, and Women of Russia collected them at pedagogical institutes, but the majority of parties, lacking any organization at the local level, simply bought signatures. Thus the Beer Lovers' party handed out mugs of beer at the rate of two signatures a minute. Professional teams of signature collectors made a business of it. In the end, forty-three electoral associations were registered to take part in the parliamentary elections, promising considerable chaos. Having such a crowded field was to the benefit of the authorities, who would be able to take advantage of the confusion and then "correct" the results of the voting.

After the parties were registered, representatives of the small groups that had no chance of passing the 5 percent threshold to enter the Duma launched a campaign to defer the date of the elections. They were actively supported by Yeltsin's advisers, who in the middle of the campaign began to press for revision of the electoral law under the pretext that it was inconsistent with the constitution. They were evidently afraid that Yeltsin would not recover completely and that he would not be ready to participate in the presidential election. The postponement of the parliamentary election was a way to defer the presidential elections. The president, however, would have lost more than he would have gained by such a turn of events. The elections to the Duma would be a barometer of public emotions. Besides, whatever the composition of forces in the new Duma, the legislature would not be able to threaten his position, given the limits on its powers. But putting off the parliamentary elections would put a stamp of illegitimacy on the regime, heighten tensions in the country, and help consolidate opposition to the government.

Groups with an interest in seeing the elections deferred included the small parties, especially those of a democratic orientation loyal to the president, which expected to lose heavily and thus find themselves excluded from the parliament; deputies from the previous Duma who were not on any party list and might lose in single-mandate districts; and a segment of the entrepreneurs' lobby that feared the communists and nationalists would win. Taking the other view were the stronger and more confident political actors, such as the Communist Party, Yabloko, and the Congress of Russian Communities. Chernomyrdin and NDR also increasingly leaned toward holding the elections.

The Constitutional Court finally put an end to the indecision by determining not to review the question of whether the electoral law was consistent with the constitution. This meant that the elections would take place on the basis of the existing law. Considering the Court's dependence on Yeltsin, it was clear that the president approved of the decision to hold the elections and that he was ready for battle.

THE ELECTIONS AND THEIR OUTCOME

I n October 1995, the Public Opinion Foundation conducted a poll asking, "Which parties are close to you in spirit, and which would you like to see in the Duma?" Among registered voters between eighteen and twenty-four years of age, 21 percent wanted to see Women of Russia represented in the State Duma; 18 percent wanted Yabloko; 16 percent, Our Home Is Russia; 11 percent, Zhirinovsky's Liberal Democratic Party of Russia (LDPR); and 9 percent, Democratic Choice of Russia (the renamed party of Yegor Gaidar). Among voters in the fifty-five years and older bracket, 30 percent preferred the Communist Party of the Russian Federation; 23 percent, Yabloko; 21 percent, Women of Russia; 17 percent, Our Home Is Russia; and 15 percent, the Agrarian Party of Russia (APR).[10] No analyst doubted that among the winners in the parliamentary elections would be Zyuganov's Communist Party, Yavlinsky's Yabloko, and Chernomyrdin's NDR. In the opinion of many observers, Women of Russia, the Agrarian Party, Zhirinovsky's LDPR, and the Congress of Russian Communities also had good chances of gaining seats in the State Duma.

A new turn of events in Chechnya spoiled the authorities' upbeat pre-election mood, however. By September the dialogue with Dudayev's supporters had again collapsed. Not knowing what to do, Yeltsin's team decided to restore the Soviet-era powers in Chechnya. At the end of October, they forced the two figurehead Chechen leaders, Salambek Khadzhyev and Umar Avturkhanov, to resign (as a reward for their loyalty, both were instantly transferred to Moscow and given government jobs). Their successor was Doku Zavgayev, who had been the last Soviet leader of Chechnya and who had until that moment held a very comfortable position on the president's staff. Thus the Russian government had apparently decided to distance itself from the war and to turn it into an intra-Chechen confrontation. The federal authorities began to help their new henchman, Zavgayev, who was quickly installed as the new leader in Grozny. Shortly before the elections, Zavgayev and Prime Minister Chernomyrdin signed an agreement on basic principles governing relations between the Russian Federation and Chechnya. The document gave the republic considerable powers. Chechnya was the first of the Russian Federation's subjects to have its own representatives in foreign countries, a goal beyond even the dreams of the Dudayev leadership.

The next step in the implementation of the government's plan was to organize elections in Chechnya. It was clear that most Chechens considered elections impossible as long as Chechnya was occupied, the war continued, and the status of the republic was unclear. The fact that the Chechen population was not at all ready to take part in elections did not deter the federal center. Moscow resolved the problem by announcing that the federal troops located in Chechnya would vote there. This made it clear why the leadership in Moscow was so confident: it had decided to replace the votes of the Chechens with those of its own soldiers.

Russia's parliamentary elections, meanwhile, were nearing. Yeltsin was still at the Barvikha rest home outside Moscow. From time to time he addressed the nation in televised messages. Russian citizens were also treated to an unusual sight: Aleksandr Korzhakov, chief of the president's Security Service, came out of the shadows for the first time to give an interview. Korzhakov no longer bothered to conceal his influence over the president. He excoriated a series of key Russian political figures, starting with Defense Minister Pavel Grachev and Moscow Mayor Yuri Luzhkov, openly warning Luzhkov against entering the presidential race then or even in four years' time. Korzhakov made it clear where the sympathies of the president's entourage lay, stating that he personally planned to vote for Rybkin's bloc during the parliamentary elections. This was one more sign that the president was distancing himself from Chernomyrdin. Korzhakov also indirectly answered the question about whether Yeltsin would stand in the next presidential elections. If Yeltsin did not, Korzhakov said, "I think that something bad would happen," making it clear that Yeltsin's circle would stop at nothing to ensure that he was reelected.[11]

On December 17, 1995, the elections to the Sixth State Duma took place with a higher turnout—64.4 percent—than in the 1993 elections (when 54.8 percent had voted). The new State Duma was chosen by a mixed electoral system, with half of its 450 seats allocated according to the results of the party-list proportional representation vote, and the other half by the results of the single-mandate vote.

146

Of the six or seven parties that had been expected to enter the State Duma, only four crossed the 5 percent threshold in the party-list vote: the Communist Party of the Russian Federation (KPRF), the Liberal Democratic Party of Russia (LDPR), Our Home Is Russia (NDR), and Yabloko. More than 51.4 percent of the voters voted for these parties. None of the remaining thirty-nine groups gained the necessary 5 percent threshold of support, and they were thus excluded from the Duma. The first results coming in from Russia's Far East confirmed predictions of a communist lead. The surprise was which party came in second: predictions that Zhirinovsky's Liberal Democratic Party was in serious decline were proven wrong. Our Home Is Russia, the so-called party of power, came in only third, despite its enormous organizational and financial support; such a showing practically amounted to a defeat. (See table, p. 148).

The process of bloc organization in the new Duma was dominated by the leaders of the four main factions: Zyuganov for the KPRF, Zhirinovsky for the LDPR, Sergei Belyaev for the NDR, and Yavlinsky for Yabloko. As expected, the communists became the leading faction. They also helped two allied deputy groups come into being: the Agrarians, headed by Nikolai Charitonov, and Power to the People, established by the nationalist Sergei Baburin and former Soviet prime minister Nikolai Ryzhkov. The communists directed some of their members to join these groups in order to increase the communist representation on some Duma committees. A group of independent deputies also formed Russia's Regions, headed by Artur Chilingarov and Vladimir Lysenko, which did not have a clear ideological orientation; some of its members supported the communists, while others voted with NDR or with Power to the People. In addition, at the start of the new State Duma, some 77 deputies elected from single-mandate districts did not specify a party affiliation.

In the 1993 elections, pro-reform forces (including Russia's Choice, Yabloko, the Democratic Party of Russia, PRES, and the Union of December 12) had won 147 seats; in 1995, however, pro-reform forces (NDR, Yabloko, and Democratic Choice of Russia) won only 109 seats. In 1993, the opposition (LDPR, communists, and agrarians) had won 145 seats; in 1995, this increased to 228 seats (LDPR, communists, and agrarians).

According to Michael McFaul's analysis, reformers got 43 percent of the vote in 1993, but only 38.2 percent in 1995; the opposition got 42.8 percent of the vote in 1993, but 52.8 percent in 1995.[12] According

Table 6-1. Parliamentary Election Results, 1995

Party	Party Leader	Party-List Seats	Single-Mandate Seats	Total Duma Seats	Percentage of Party-List Vote
Communist Party (KPRF)	Gennady Zyuganov	99	58	157	22.7
Liberal Democratic Party (LDPR)	Vladimir Zhirinovsky	50	1	51	11.4
Our Home is Russia (NDR)	Sergei Belyaev	45	10	55	10.3
Yabloko	Grigory Yavlinsky	31	14	45	7.0
Democratic Choice of Russia	Yegor Gaidar	0	9	9	3.9
Women of Russia	Yekaterina Lahova	0	3	3	4.7
Agrarians	Nikolai Charitonov	0	20	20	3.8
Party of Russian Unity and Accord (PRES)	Sergei Shakhrai	0	1	1	0.4
Other Parties		0	32	32	—
Independents		0	77	77	—
Total		**225**	**226**	**450**	

Source: *Election of Deputies of the State Duma 1995, Electoral Statistics* (Moscow: Ves Mir, 1996), pp. 202-204.

to the analysis of the Central Electoral Commission of the Russian Federation, in 1993, 20.4 percent of the voters expressed a communist orientation, 22.9 percent voted national-patriotic, 29.1 percent voted centrist, and 23.4 percent expressed a democratic orientation. For 1995, the Electoral Commission's figures were: 32.8 percent, communist orientation; 21.1 percent, national-patriotic; 22.6 percent, centrist; and 21 percent, democratic.[13]

The new Duma became more oppositional than the previous one, but this time the deputies behaved more cautiously. The political divisions in the new parliament were very ambivalent. Ironically, it was often the opposition (the LDPR, and sometimes even the communists and their allies) that helped the government out of difficult situations— for instance, by saving the budget and preventing a no-confidence vote.

The elections in Chechnya also took place as scheduled. According to official statistics, 50.43 percent of the Chechen population took part in the elections, with the majority supporting Our Home Is Russia. About 40,000 Russian soldiers voted and, of course, helped Zavgayev considerably. In an outcome reminiscent of Soviet times, it was claimed that Zavgayev won about 93 percent of the vote for president.

The elections to the Sixth Duma revealed the emergence of definite party preferences in Russia's slowly restructuring society. Those who had been the main participants in the 1993 elections had been able to preserve much of their support. The surprisingly large voter turnout suggested the beginning of a new politicization of Russian society, but one that would not benefit the authorities. The campaign also showed the radicalization of a rather wide segment of the population, demonstrated by the support received by radicals such as Viktor Anpilov and Ivan Tyulkin, and by the unexpected failure of Women of Russia to reach the threshold needed to enter the Duma. The elections showed that the swing vote (known as the "swamp") had moved over to the opposition. In this environment, the Women of Russia movement, inclined to support the executive branch, could no longer satisfy its former base. Predictions about the Agrarian Party, which everyone had expected to clear the 5 percent threshold, also proved wrong. Voters viewed the agrarians as communist fellow travelers and voted instead for the Communist Party.

The most unexpected result of the elections was the defeat of the Congress of Russian Communities (KRO), which some observers had expected to place second after the Communist Party. The fate of KRO was reminiscent of the demise of Civic Union, which had been considered the most influential movement in Russia in 1992-93, but was a loser in the 1993 elections. The KRO failed in part because some voters saw it as an additional "party of power." Those who wanted to support the government voted for Chernomyrdin's NDR. The pressures applied by the ruling team, especially in the regions, because of fear of KRO leader Aleksandr Lebed, played a role in the KRO's defeat. Falsification of the electoral results was also a possibility.

The KRO itself, however, was mostly to blame for its own lack of success. The triumvirate of leaders (Skokov, Lebed, and Glazyev) was not effective at structuring a political organization. Lebed's appearance on the party list in second place after the unpopular Skokov substantially lowered the KRO's potential appeal. Finally, the Russian nationalist idea was not very effective in mobilizing the electorate. Nevertheless Aleksandr Lebed, the KRO's principal figure, gained a seat in a single-mandate district even though his movement made a poor showing in the party-list voting. His brother Aleksei Lebed was also elected to the parliament from the Republic of Khakassia (he soon became the leader of this republic). A complete newcomer to the region, without any organizational support, Aleksei Lebed defeated all his better-known rivals, owing largely to his sibling ties, which he exploited in a very simple slogan that substituted for an electoral program: "Brothers—Soulmates." This was evidence of Aleksandr Lebed's appeal and helped to raise his profile as a possible presidential candidate, despite the KRO's poor showing. Some people felt that Russia needed a Bonapartist-type leader, and the pugnacious general became the leading candidate for the role.

Gaidar's Democratic Choice of Russia did not reach the 5 percent threshold to enter the parliament. Russians still could not forgive Gaidar—not only for his real mistakes, but also for their own unrealized hopes. That Gaidar and his people continued to support Yeltsin in the face of widespread popular dissatisfaction with the government also contributed to their defeat.

Yavlinsky's Yabloko failed to widen its support, but, considering that the environment was one of general disenchantment with democrats, the party did well, showing that it had a fairly stable base. People voted for Yabloko not for lack of choice, but on the basis of convictions; this distinguished these votes from those for other parties. Yet Yabloko's base was too small for a successful presidential campaign.

The Zhirinovsky phenomenon was instructive. The LDPR was able to achieve a great deal through the energetic grass-roots activities of its adherents. It was the only party besides the communists to pay attention to organizing at the local level. The LDPR's support came from a segment of the population that was emphatically opposed to the government and its policies and that had a nationalist and great-power viewpoint. These were people who had failed to find a place for themselves in the new Russian reality, and the ideology and activity of the LDPR and Zhirinovsky's rhetoric expressed their protests against those who succeeded. The LDPR opposed the authorities and was in some senses an anti-establishment party. Yet Zhirinovsky often used the LDPR in the State Duma to help the government out of difficult situations—while, many in Russia believed, extracting substantial rewards for himself and for his associates.

Chernomyrdin's NDR attracted the government *apparat* and its family members in both the capital and the provinces. The masses, however, ignored NDR—a development that affected Chernomyrdin's presidential prospects. Nevertheless, the conduct of the 1995 Russian parliamentary elections on the whole solidified the formation of a new "party of power" and its efforts to form its own political representation.

Despite their greatly strengthened position in the Duma, it was clear that the communists would be hard pressed to become the decisive factor in the new Duma, even with their potential allies. Passing a law in the Duma required 226 of 450 total votes (fifty percent plus one vote); changing the constitution required the votes of two-thirds of the deputies. It was practically impossible for the communists to control so many votes. In addition, other levels of approval were required to pass constitutional changes. Yeltsin's 1993 constitution had placed many limitations on the Duma's activities, making it extremely difficult even for a parliamentary majority to change the balance of power: the Federation Council, the president, and the Constitutional Court would all stand in the way of any attempts by the communists to influence the course of politics. No matter how much the communists attacked the government and the president, there would be few visible results. Yet it was evident that the communists could use their foothold in the new Duma to prepare for the presidential elections.

151

After the parliamentary elections, Yeltsin found himself in a difficult position. He did not have his own party from which to launch his election campaign. He apparently could not turn to Our Home Is Russia; he had demonstrated several times that he did not consider it a serious political party—and in any case it did not do well in the parliamentary elections. Moreover, there was no guarantee that those in the *apparat*, which had tied itself to Chernomyrdin, would now race to the aid of a weakened Yeltsin. It was doubtful that Yeltsin could create an effective second "party of power," as some of his allies tried to persuade him to do. The president had already used every possible way to attract the masses. Reformist slogans in Yeltsin's mouth were unlikely to move many people. He was viewed as the main culprit not only for the failures of reform but also for the continuing war in Chechnya, and his ratings were low.

Nevertheless, one could not yet write Yeltsin's political obituary. His political isolation, lack of party support, and distance from all political groups could be his secret weapons. His chance, it appeared, was to use the quarrels among the other presidential hopefuls, playing off the disagreements among them, and then to present himself to the nation as the lesser of evils. The weaknesses of his opponents played into his hands. He could assure Russia's emerging powerful political clans and lobbies that he would not interfere in their affairs if they would support him and help him retain his office. The struggle for the presidency and its results depended on Yeltsin; he still was the major political actor on the Russian scene.

In sum, however, 1995 was a sad year for Russia. The main positive step was that the Duma elections had been held on time. This modest achievement, which should have been a natural part of the political process, did not make up for all the failures. The war in Chechnya continued; according to some estimates, more than 50,000 people had died there on both sides. The war had become a constant factor in Russian life, bringing with it demoralization, violence, and intolerance.

Other events of 1995 only increased the frustration of the Russian people. The country had experienced the hostage drama in Budennovsk; an earthquake that had demolished the Siberian city of Neftegorsk; a series of aviation disasters that took hundreds of lives; the collision of three Russian fighter planes in the air over Vietnam as they were returning from an air show in Malaysia, with the loss of some of Russia's best air crews; and the sinking of a fishing trawler near the shores of Norway.

Nearly all of the events that made an impression on people were somehow connected to suffering and loss.[14] The crisis that gripped the country—as well as the lack of resources and will to turn it around—had become immense. The parliamentary elections showed that the authorities had lost a great deal of support, but there was no viable alternative.

CHAPTER SEVEN

YELTSIN'S STRUGGLE FOR REVIVAL BEGINS: SPRING 1996

THE FEVERISH POLITICAL ACTIVITY of the parliamentary election campaign increased in anticipation of the presidential contest, set for June 16, 1996. A new act in the political drama had begun: the campaign for the first presidential election in post-communist Russia. The campaign would demonstrate not only Yeltsin's amazing capacity for political survival, but also the failure of the fragmented Soviet establishment, which still dominated Russia's political process, to produce any real alternatives to Yeltsin.

THE PRESIDENT RETURNS FROM HIS SICKBED

On New Year's Eve 1995, Yeltsin appeared before the public for the first time since October. His appearance was staged as in Soviet times. Returning to his residence from the convalescent home, Yeltsin halted his motorcade and walked onto the Kremlin grounds, stopping along the way to chat with a carefully selected crowd of "ordinary people." He asked them whether he should run for the presidency again, and naturally he received "enthusiastic" support. He declared that all of Russia's problems would soon be solved and the country would begin to flourish. This optimistic assessment, which Yeltsin himself apparently believed, would become a constant theme in his speeches.

The winner of the presidential contest would be the candidate who received half of the votes cast plus one, but it was clear that no one was likely to win in the first round. A second-round run-off between the top two candidates would be held, according to the election law, within two weeks of the tabulation of the first-round votes. Even Yeltsin's closest associates doubted that his candidacy could survive the first

Table 7-1. Public Opinion Polls on Likely Presidential Votes, 1996 (percent)

January[a]		March[a]		Late March[b]	
Zyuganov	21	Zyuganov	25	Zyuganov	20
Yavlinsky	11	**Yeltsin**	**15**	**Yeltsin**	**14**
Zhirinovsky	11	Yavlinsky	11	Yavlinsky	11
Lebed	10	Zhirinovsky	9	Zhirinovsky	8
Yeltsin	**8**	Lebed	8	Lebed	7

[a] Poll organized by VTSIOM, with 1,500 respondents.
[b] Poll taken by Public Opinion Foundation.
Source: National News Service, April 16-17, 1996; and National News Service, press conference of All-Union Center for Study of Public Opinion (VTSIOM), April 17, 1996.

round of voting; his popularity rating was hovering at 5-8 percent, and he trailed behind Aleksandr Lebed, Grigory Yavlinsky, Vladimir Zhirinovsky, and Gennady Zyuganov (Table 7-1). Some of his supporters had already started looking around for another candidate who could compete against the growing strength of Communist Party leader Zyuganov.

Yeltsin began his campaign effort with his usual dramatic gesture: he fired some of his unpopular associates, to general public acclaim. He dismissed Foreign Minister Andrei Kozyrev, who was disliked by most of the political establishment; even liberals considered Kozyrev weak and ineffective. Yeltsin's dismissal of his faithful associate was carried out crudely—Yeltsin did not even deign to meet with him. Kozyrev's post was taken by Yevgeny Primakov, who had been head of the Foreign Intelligence Service. This appointment dismayed many, especially in the West, partially because of Primakov's warm relations with Iraq's President Saddam Hussein. In Russia itself, however, the appointment was generally supported. This rather conservative policy maker was seen as a foreign affairs professional who belonged to no political camp and who would not rock the boat. The political atmosphere in the country had clearly shifted in a moderately statist direction. Most political actors were turning to more conservative values, believing that liberal ideas were no longer popular with the electorate.

Yeltsin also moved to strengthen his regional support. On January 12, 1996, Prime Minister Viktor Chernomyrdin and the governor of the Yekaterinburg (Sverdlovsk) region, Eduard Rossel, signed agreements allocating powers between the federal authorities and the region. The federal center agreed to some of the demands for autonomy that Sverdlovsk had been making since 1992 (for which demands Rossel had previously been fired as governor). Moscow even allowed the region to establish some independent international economic ties. On the same day, Moscow signed similar agreements with the Kaliningrad region. These agreements indicated that the president had cut a deal with the regions for their support in the upcoming elections. But many analysts questioned whether Yeltsin could rely on the governors' promises of support. The regions had also been strengthened by the recent elections of several governors, which rendered them less dependent on presidential power.

Yeltsin was also forced to deal with the war in the northern Caucasus, which had entered a new phase. In December, Moscow had installed Doku Zavgayev as head of the Chechen Republic. This ended any possibility of negotiations, because the supporters of Dzhokhar Dudayev would never recognize the regime of a Kremlin vassal. Zavgayev could not move around Chechnya unless accompanied by Russian federal troops in armored personnel carriers. Moscow's manipulations had served only to consolidate the popular base of the Chechen separatists.

Moscow had not wanted armed confrontations before the Duma elections but now believed that it must destroy Dudayev's armed groups before Russia's presidential election. The iron-fisted Lieutenant-General Vyacheslav Tikhomirov was appointed the new commander of Russian forces in Chechnya. The conciliatory mood of the previous year was gone, and the embraces of Generals Anatoly Romanov and Aslan Maskhadov were forgotten.

The Chechens did not wait around to be chased back into the mountains, but dealt Moscow a preemptive blow. On January 9, two hundred Chechen fighters, led by Dudayev's son-in-law, Salman Raduyev, repeated the Budennovsk formula. They seized about 3,000 hostages at a hospital and a maternity home in the city of Kizlyar, in the neighboring republic of Dagestan, and fled with some of them, ending up in the Dagestani village of Pervomaisk.

In a glaring error, Yeltsin named his close associate Mikhail Barsukov, chief of the Federal Security Service, head of the operation to free the hostages. Barsukov had spent his entire career in the Kremlin on guard details and had no experience with operations in the field. His appointment indicated that Yeltsin had no idea what to do. This impression deepened when Yeltsin held a press conference at which he claimed that the operation to free the hostages would be over in a single day, and that all of the hostages would be alive. He demonstrated before the television cameras just how the separatists would be attacked and defeated by thirty-eight snipers. The president's approval rating again dropped sharply as millions of television viewers saw him telling clumsy lies and looking as if he were absolutely out of touch with reality.

Yeltsin's televised tactics notwithstanding, the Russian military launched a full-scale operation, complete with fighter planes and Grad missile launchers, against the Chechens holed up in Pervomaisk. The Russian forces announced before the operation that the hostages were no longer alive, which meant that they had already written them off. Raduyev and his fighters were able to elude the federal forces, however, and escaped to Chechnya, taking a number of the hostages with them. Although dozens of hostages had been killed during the fight, Yeltsin hastened to label this humiliating fiasco a "success."

Popular dissatisfaction in Russia increased throughout the winter. In December the patience of the most long-suffering of the intelligentsia had snapped: teachers and researchers at the Academy of Sciences institutions demanded months of back pay. Leaders of the unions representing educational establishments in St. Petersburg went on a hunger strike to demand that the government pay its debt. The ruling team ignored them all.

Yeltsin's team reacted immediately, however, when representatives of Russia's mining regions traveled to Moscow in January and began to picket government headquarters in the White House. Recalling how striking miners who supported Yeltsin during his 1987 confrontation with Gorbachev had dealt a serious blow to Gorbachev's leadership, Yeltsin's team feared that the miners might do the same to him. The government quickly acceded to their demands, but everyone understood that this only deferred the inevitable; the underlying problems of the mining sector had not been solved.

YELTSIN'S GAME

On January 15, Yeltsin fired Sergei Filatov, who had given an intellectual air to Yeltsin's entourage and who represented the president's ties with the democrats, which by then were purely symbolic. Filatov's departure signified the victory of the group headed by Yeltsin's bodyguard, Aleksandr Korzhakov, who now had no influential rivals within the president's inner circle. Filatov was replaced as head of the presidential administration by the hard-line former nationalities minister, Deputy Prime Minister Nikolai Yegorov. He had been the president's representative in Chechnya from November 1994 to February 1995, during the most intense stage of the war, and was noted for his nationalist views. Yegorov's promotion confirmed Yeltsin's turn toward statism. The president also apparently hoped that Yegorov, the tough former head of a collective farm and a representative of the conservative southern Russian governors, would be able to mobilize the support of the regional elites to help him in the upcoming elections.

The next day brought the long-expected departure of Anatoly Chubais, who was blamed for all the unrealized promises of the government and of the president himself. Chernomyrdin was also expected to resign, but as Moscow analysts hastened once again to write him off, Chernomyrdin left for a meeting in the United States with Vice President Al Gore. The unsinkable prime minister remained as head of government. Yeltsin could not afford to lose a faithful premier before the decisive moment. The new appointments, however, did little to improve Yeltsin's image.

The small group of favorites around Yeltsin now included the two chiefs of the security services, Korzhakov and Barsukov; Deputy Prime Minister Oleg Soskovets; and Yeltsin's personal tennis trainer and head of the National Sports Fund, Shamil Tarpishchev. The rise of Soskovets had been remarkably rapid. He was a typical representative of the younger generation of Soviet industrialists, with strong ties to the lucrative and criminalized aluminum industry. Soskovets had already come close to replacing Chernomyrdin as prime minister in late 1994. The decree had been prepared and placed on Yeltsin's desk, but Yeltsin apparently decided to keep both Soskovets and Chernomyrdin in place to balance one another. Still, Soskovets was becoming very powerful, in part because he was loyal to the president and in part because he was more acceptable than Chernomyrdin to Korzhakov and his cronies. As the new favorites at the top grew stronger, an atmosphere of suspicion permeated the Kremlin. People did not trust each other, and those who tried to discuss dangerous topics in their offices did so only by writing notes.

Yeltsin also worked on other potential allies. For example, after many ups and downs, his relationship with Moscow Mayor Yuri Luzh-kov had warmed again. Television cameras frequently showed them together at a Russian bistro, a church construction site, or a road-building project. Yeltsin allowed the mayor to show off his successes, and Luzh-kov, in turn, appeared pleased with the new political alignment. An understanding evidently had been reached between the president's team and Luzhkov: the mayor probably renounced his own designs on the presidency, at least for the time being, and guaranteed that he would try to ensure electoral support for Yeltsin in Moscow. It was not clear, however, what Luzhkov received in exchange. He already had a free hand in the city of Moscow. He may have been promised the prime ministership, but if so, that promise had been made to several others as well, including Soskovets and Chernomyrdin.

Although Yeltsin had yet to make an official announcement of his candidacy, he threw himself into campaigning. He tried to persuade Russian voters that only he could guarantee Russia's survival. "I do not need power," he declared. "But we must not permit the country to be deflected from the path on which it has embarked. The country needs strong presidential power for this." He also said, "As we promised, 1995 was the year of stabilization. Next year will be the beginning of an upturn, which will continue in the future."[1] People were tired of prom-ises, however, and did not react to these speeches.

A campaign team had been created with Soskovets at its head.[2] However, using taxpayer funding for the president's reelection campaign and putting its staff under the direction of a member of the government were unconstitutional actions, and the State Duma immediately sum-moned Soskovets for an explanation. The deputy prime minister claimed that there had been a mistake, and that there was no "campaign staff." Evidence to the contrary was plentiful, however. Soskovets used the traditional Soviet-type electoral tricks; for example, in some enterprises salaries were withheld until people signed the statements supporting Yeltsin's candidacy that were required to register Yeltsin as a presidential candidate. Even with such manipulations, the collection of the one million required signatures progressed slowly.

Gradually Yeltsin began to see that Soskovets's team was not up to the task of running a modern campaign. The pragmatists, especially Chernomyrdin and Viktor Ilyushin, the president's principal assistant, as well as representatives of the financial circles who feared the president's defeat, pressed Yeltsin to set up a second campaign team. The bankers Boris Berezovsky, Vladimir Gusinsky, Pyotr Aven, Mikhail Fridman, Mikhail Khodorkovsky, Aleksandr Smolensky, and Vladimir Potanin, meeting in February 1996 at the Economic Forum at Davos, persuaded Chubais to help organize the new campaign team.[3] The bankers' group was referred to ironically as the "Group of Seven"—after the G-7 group of leaders of the seven major industrial nations. Their bargain with Chubais and representatives of Yeltsin's team was later called the Davos Pact, and Berezovsky was its main architect. Ilyushin, Filatov, and Yeltsin's daughter, Tatyana Dyachenko, joined the new team, which immediately began to raise money from private capital and to recruit high-powered people to conduct the campaign. The result was that Yeltsin had two presidential campaign staffs—headquartered on different floors of the prestigious President Hotel in Moscow—competing against each other.[4]

The two groups differed on the necessity of the election itself. The Korzhakov-Soskovets group was not optimistic about Yeltsin's chances for a victory, or about his ability to withstand the physical rigors of the campaign. This group was looking for an excuse to cancel or defer the election. The less they were able to cope with the tasks of organizing the campaign, the more they tried to persuade Yeltsin to reject the election altogether. Cancellation of the election would also make Yeltsin more dependent on his entourage. Thus the campaign became an arena for the political struggle between the Chubais-Ilyushin-Filatov team and the Korzhakov-Soskovets-Barsukov group.

THE DEMOCRATS AT AN IMPASSE AGAIN

In the Duma, the process of selecting the speaker and committee chairmen revealed some unexpected alignments among the various factions. Zhirinovsky supported the NDR's (party of power) choice of Yeltsin loyalist Ivan Rybkin, while the leaders of KPRF and Yabloko, not wishing to have a speaker who was too close to the government, voted against Rybkin. The process demonstrated a dilemma

161

for Yavlinsky and Yabloko: they had to play the role of opposition to the government and to keep up their anti-communist image even while sometimes voting with the communists. Maintaining their positions was all the more difficult because the ruling team constantly tried to discredit Yavlinsky. It accused him of a secret conspiracy with the communists, while it simultaneously negotiated with Zhirinovsky. The compromises and corridor games of NDR and LDPR further muddied the waters. The support that NDR got from Zhirinovsky only discredited it in the eyes of the public. In the end Rybkin failed to receive the requisite number of votes, and Gennady Seleznyov, a representative of the Communist Party's moderate wing, was chosen speaker instead.

In contrast to the lower house, the Federation Council was able to select its speaker quickly. There was only one strong candidate: Yegor Stroyev, the head of the Orel region. When he had visited Yeltsin in December 1995, political observers had figured that this was a "viewing of the bride." The senators also supported Stroyev, who, as a pragmatist, could adapt to new realities and compromise with various political forces. He avoided sharp turns, was predictable, and preferred to use wait-and-see tactics, which pleased most of the regional leaders in the Federation Council. Stroyev was one of them and knew their problems well. He had gone through the typical Communist Party and Soviet training schools, had waited out the stormy Gaidar years in Orel, and had easily won election as the head of the local administration in that region. He had left the Communist Party just in time and now supported Chernomyrdin's NDR yet continued to have good relations with the communists. He liked to remind people that "the Erhardt government asked experts from the old regime to join them. Everyone worked together to improve the economy and help Germany get back on its feet."[5] Although Stroyev was inclined to cooperate with the president, he would not necessarily take orders from him.

In early 1996 the Chechen war forced those in the democratic camp who considered themselves reformers to review their attitude toward the president. Many of them acknowledged the contradictions between their support for Yeltsin and their opposition to the war and began to distance themselves from Yeltsin. One was Yegor Gaidar, who, breaking at last with Yeltsin, announced his resignation from the Presidential Council. He called on the president not to run for reelection, saying that his candidacy would be a gift to the communists. In January 1996 the prominent human rights activist and former Yeltsin supporter

Sergei Kovalyov wrote a sharp letter to Yeltsin. "At the present time, your administration is trying to reverse the direction the country has taken since August 1991. You have actually stopped basic reforms. . . . You stated that your goal was the preservation and strengthening of the Russian Federation's territorial integrity. What were the results? A shameful and unproductive civil war has been raging for more than a year in the northern Caucasus. The decision-making mechanism has become almost as non-functional and secretive as it was in the Politburo's time."[6]

The unavoidable question was why the democrats had taken so long to break with Yeltsin—long after he had stopped any democratic reform. Even when the war in Chechnya had been under way for more than a year, democrats were still flocking to the president, joining his moribund consultative bodies and allowing themselves to be used as front men by a person who showed little respect for democratic principles. Even though they were effectively excluded from the decision-making process, many democrats continued to support Yeltsin, enabling him to maintain an image as a democratic leader even while he discredited the very idea of reform in the eyes of Russian society.

The choice facing the democratic forces was not an easy one. Although it was difficult to continue supporting Yeltsin after the bloodshed in Chechnya, there was no other leader who could oppose the resurgent communists. Politicians who could claim to lead the democratic forces, such as Yavlinsky and Gaidar, were relatively weak and had little popular appeal. Thus the democrats and their supporters began to cast about for a lesser evil. Part of the democratic community began to view Chernomyrdin as a possible moderate successor to Yeltsin. Gaidar was the first to acknowledge publicly the possibility that democrats and liberals might unite behind Chernomyrdin and form a union with Our Home Is Russia. The prime minister, however, categorically refused to compete for the presidency.[7] Gaidar actually did Chernomyrdin a disservice by urging him to run, since this forced Chernomyrdin to convince Yeltsin of his loyalty.

Gaidar himself, caught up in the heat of the anti-communist struggle, did not seem to realize that some members of the new Russian bureaucracy, particularly those connected to sectoral interests, did not regard KPRF as so terrible and were not greatly concerned about a communist revival. Gaidar also probably did not realize that Chernomyrdin could make deals with Zyuganov (in fact, meetings between their

163

representatives had been going on for some time). The sectoral interest groups did not need the liberals and democrats, nor did Chernomyrdin. If Chernomyrdin had suddenly decided to run for the presidency, he would never have tied himself to them, especially not to Gaidar. It would not have helped him in any way. Instead, he would probably have turned toward the moderate wing of the Communist Party.

In the end, however, despite pressure from his own staff, Chernomyrdin refused to take part in the presidential election, although he had already gathered the requisite number of signatures and had tentative support from some democrats and industrialists and even from some circles in the West. He constantly repeated, "We are working with the president." Chernomyrdin knew perfectly well that Yeltsin would never approve of his participation in the presidential contest, and he was not ready to compete with the Boss.

Several leading intellectuals who spoke out against Yeltsin were in the end forced to back him because they could find no acceptable replacement. One such figure was Lev Timofeyev, who was always critical of the president. On the eve of the presidential elections, however, he came to the conclusion that the democrats and liberals should again support Yeltsin. "The president's situation is by no means hopeless," wrote Timofeyev. "Although it may sound dubious and even terrible, President Yeltsin remains the principal (if not the only) guarantor of democratic reform in the country." He argued, "To be without a leader today would be to deliberately bring the communists back to power. . . . Even if we support the president, we cannot guarantee that there will not be a communist victory. We find ourselves in a situation of unprecedented powerlessness."[8] The majority of the democratic community in Russia, feeling this helplessness, would turn in the end to Yeltsin, fully understanding the nature of his political leadership. Gradually, therefore, the gap between Zyuganov and Yeltsin began to decrease: in January it was 20 percent; in February, 12 percent; in March, 8 percent; and by April the gap had narrowed to just 3 percent.[9]

MOSCOW WANTS TO END THE WAR

Soon after the fiasco of the hostage crisis in January, Yeltsin signed a decree to rebuild Chechnya. About 16.2 trillion rubles ($3.24 billion) was to be set aside for this purpose. Many Russian observers believed that the hard currency sent to Chechnya came at least partly from foreign credits, mainly from the International Monetary Fund (IMF); the aid to Chechnya was obviously being offered under pressure from Russia's commercial banks, which made money by channeling such assistance.

Yeltsin's decree caused outrage among those who received their salaries from the state budget. People were furious that the government—which could not pay salaries on time or pay the army's outstanding debts—was so generous to the Chechens while the war was still going on. The decree was the last straw for the miners, who called a strike. If the government had enough money to destroy and then to rebuild Chechnya, they reasoned, it had enough money to pay them.[10]

Meanwhile, observers began to wonder where the money allocated to restore Chechnya had gone. A large part of it appears to have gone to Moscow commercial banks and to Chechen groups with close ties to the Russian ruling center. The rest found its way into the hands of Chechen fighters: even though they were at war with Moscow, they bought their weapons from the Russian military, often with federal money. Akhmet Zakayev, one of the Chechen field commanders, said, "If it were not for the authorities [in Moscow], we would long ago have died of starvation. It is astonishing that we are fighting the Russian army while holding Russian automatic weapons and dressed in Russian camouflage gear bought from the Russians with Russian money."[11]

Yeltsin understood that his fate might depend on what happened in Chechnya. The war had to be stopped, at least temporarily, before the elections. He was also afraid that the withdrawal of the Russian troops would not solve the problem. He summarized his dilemma: "Withdraw the troops from all of Chechnya, and the slaughter will begin. Don't withdraw them, and my chances of winning the presidency disappear, since the country will not support me."[12] The president then made a surprise announcement that he had seven options for resolving the Chechen problem. Soon afterward he created a group to develop these options, and he put Chernomyrdin in charge, thus ensuring that any blame would fall on the prime minister should the effort fail. Hints of dissatisfaction with the prime minister had again crept into Yeltsin's speeches; he was evidently distressed by the frequent calls for Chernomyrdin to take his place—the kind of thing he neither forgave nor forgot.

Yeltsin's new attempt to achieve peace in Chechnya met with controversy. On February 23, 1996, great-power Russia advocates, including well-known nationalist writers and cultural figures, published an open letter to the president. They demanded that the government take harsh measures against Dudayev and that it continue the war until victory is achieved. "Mr. President, your duty is to end this humiliating and feckless policy of conciliation toward criminal forces [in Chechnya]. You should know that political capitulation will not lead to peace," they wrote. "Political negotiations with murderers are unacceptable and unthinkable."[13]

Meanwhile, there was open skepticism about the sincerity of Yeltsin's efforts. Ruslan Aushev, the pro-Chechen president of the neighboring republic of Ingushetia, stated a view shared by many: he was convinced that the president, while using the rhetoric of peace, had given a secret order "to carry out bombing raids to weaken the Chechen position so much that, when the elections are closer and it becomes politically impossible to continue bombing, it will no longer be necessary to use much force." Aushev also pointed a finger at those with financial interests in the war. "One must ask where the money for the restoration of Chechnya went, how it was used, what is to be done with the oil pipeline and with the contract for transshipment of oil across Chechen territory, and why it took four years to suddenly decide that it was necessary to restore constitutional order in Chechnya."[14] Yeltsin was not, however, ready to answer these questions.

The war in Chechnya had confirmed the serious deterioration of the Russian army and made it obvious that the government had not carried out any effective military reforms. The army's growing dissatisfaction with the president and the defense minister alarmed the Yeltsin team. They understood that it was necessary to mollify the army; immediately after the parliamentary elections, Yeltsin took measures aimed at pacifying the top brass as well as the elite units based close to Moscow. He met with top military representatives and made several promotions, and he strengthened the elite Tamansk and Kantemirovsk divisions and the 27th Special Forces Brigade, which had participated in the siege of the White House and the dissolution of the parliament in 1993. These steps did not, however, neutralize dissatisfaction in the rest of the military, and analysts warned:

> In the event the Kremlin resorts to unconstitutional methods, the more politicized part of the military, namely the paratroopers and ground forces, could become ungovernable. Such developments are most likely in the Far East, in the Trans-Baikal Military District, in the Volga Military District, and in

the Siberian Military District, that is, in the so-called "red belt," where the standard of living is low and the military has not received its cash payments in a long time.[15]

Despite his efforts, Yeltsin could not count on the loyalty of Russia's military.

The president apparently understood this, and it was at least one of the reasons for the significant reductions in the regular army that he ordered. In 1991 there had been 186 army divisions; by 1996, there were one-sixth as many, and only ten divisions were battle-ready and fully staffed. Simultaneously, however, there had been an enormous increase in the number of internal troops. The Soviet Union had had about 8 million people under arms; the Russian Federation Defense Ministry and the interior troops now numbered 7.5 million, even though Russia's population was less than half that of the Soviet Union.[16] By the beginning of 1996, Interior Ministry forces consisted of twenty-nine divisions and fifteen brigades stationed in nine districts. Their numbers exceeded those of the army's ground forces. Minister of the Interior Anatoly Kulikov had become more powerful than Defense Minister Pavel Grachev. The number of police (militia) had also increased to half again their numbers during the Soviet period, but whereas two-thirds of them previously had been assigned to the needs of the civilian population, now only one-sixth were. Instead, most were now guarding government institutions and senior officials and being prepared to deal with mass disorders. It was clear that Yeltsin was expecting trouble.

YELTSIN BEGINS HIS OFFICIAL CAMPAIGN

The delay of the official announcement of Yeltsin's candidacy had helped spread confusion among his political competitors and diffused their criticism of him. It also gave him time to try to resolve some problems in order to deprive his opponents of their strongest arguments against him. As his team hoped, Yeltsin's ratings went up before the official announcement of his candidacy. In addition, Yeltsin, who knew well how to play the game of long pauses, took the opportunity to observe how his associates and his rivals conducted themselves. He was in no hurry to show all the cards in his hand, and he wanted to begin his official campaign with the right symbolism.

In the middle of February 1996, Yeltsin officially began his campaign in his native Yekaterinburg (Sverdlovsk) and neighboring Chelyabinsk. He wanted to demonstrate continuity, but it seemed to be of a

167

peculiar sort: by returning to his native city, Yeltsin reminded everyone of his communist past. When Yeltsin had been first secretary of the Communist Party in Sverdlovsk, he had been nicknamed "The Magician of the Emerald City" because, on his orders, all the fences from the airport to the city center were routinely given fresh coats of green paint before important conferences or the arrival of political leaders from Moscow. During his presidential campaign, Yeltsin proved that he had earned the nickname and that he could still create myths.

This time, however, it was difficult for him to begin the struggle. He had lost the ability to deal with people on a personal level, and he was no longer accustomed to meeting large crowds. Yeltsin had not made a personal appeal to the nation since the spring of 1993, when he had called on a large rally in Moscow for support against the Supreme Soviet. Now, as he turned to the public again, it was clear that Yeltsin was not in good shape for active campaigning. He appeared clumsy and beset by anxiety. Although he tried to hide it, he was in poor physical condition. It was reported that members of the president's staff had asked journalists and those who would be participating in a meeting at the local Palace of Youth not to spoil the president's mood and not to ask him any pointed and unpleasant questions.

In Yekaterinburg the president walked the streets and visited businesses, where he met people and joked with them. "If you elect me, I'll come back again," he teased. In the factories, he got right down to business and asked, "What's needed? Ask while I'm here." A candy factory wanted $10 million for modernization. "You've got it," Yeltsin said, and ordered the money to be handed over immediately. At a meeting with local managers, he gave money to one for a kindergarten, to another for computer equipment, and to a third for equipping a medical center. In exchange, the local bosses assured the president that he would have the support of their workers. Yeltsin brought with him some well-known entertainers. The spectacle resembled the travels of the secretaries-general of the Communist Party of the Soviet Union, as well as the customs of the Russian Imperial court, but even they had never dispensed such largesse with such profligacy.

Yeltsin's promises did not make the desired impression on everyone; even in his native city he was viewed with suspicion and often open hostility. For example, Eduard Yalamov, director of an optical-mechanical factory, said publicly during the visit: "The decree on [paying] the arrears is an attempt to defer the consequences. It will get bogged down in two or three months because the main reason for the non-payment cannot be eliminated by a decree. The main reason is the economic crisis, about which no one seems to want to do anything."[17]

As soon as he returned to Moscow, Yeltsin launched vigorous campaigning efforts. He promised that, beginning in March, there would be no more delays in the payment of salaries and that he would sign a series of decrees to compensate investors who had suffered as a result of bankruptcies and fraudulent pyramid investment schemes. The cost of implementing the decrees made by the executive and legislative branches during just one and a half months at this time was calculated by some observers at 80 trillion rubles—an amount equal to the entire budget deficit at that point, or nearly one-fifth of the whole 1996 budget of 448 trillion rubles. The government simply did not have the resources necessary to fulfill these promises; it would have had to print new money equivalent to 4-5 percent of the gross domestic product (GDP).[18] Although this would have made inflation unavoidable, it would not have appeared until well after the elections. Those who predicted that these presidential and parliamentary decrees would simply suffer the usual fate and vanish were soon proven correct.

In the meantime, Yeltsin's main opponents were developing their electoral tactics. The Communist Party leaders had decided to put up several sympathetic candidates in the first round of the presidential elections and to then have these candidates deliver their supporters to a single opposition candidate in the second round. Among these proto-communist candidates who would hand over their support to Zyuganov in the second round were Pyotr Romanov, the director of a factory in Krasnoyarsk, and Aman Tuleyev, the popular leader of the opposition in the Kuzbass coal mining region.

Zyuganov, the leading communist candidate, behaved cautiously, trying not to scare off the new Russian businessmen or the West. Not all communist activists were so restrained, however. The leftists in the Duma, for example, had created a commission to assess the results of privatization, and Seleznyov, the new speaker, demanded that "Chubais should give the commission explanations [and] comments."[19] This was a direct threat to the liberals. Other representatives of the Communist Party began to make plans for renationalization of newly privatized property and for limiting freedom of the press. Yuri Ivanov, an active communist deputy, said: "When we speak of nationalization, one of the options we are considering is to renationalize about two hundred

169

of the largest enterprises. Small businesses would not be nationalized. With respect to commercial banks, we have to be firm, since they pose a threat to all of society." Ivanov also said, "I am in favor of reconsidering the law on the press. What kind of a right is it for journalists to be allowed to conceal their sources of information? . . . Today that law allows the press limitless arbitrary rule. . . . The words of some radical democrats should be the subject of investigation by the security organs."[20] Such statements greatly increased fears of what the Communist Party would do if it came to power.

Gennady Zyuganov's chances of being elected president of Russia, however, were never as strong as some asserted. His sole strength was the fact that he was the only political figure in Russia supported by a mass party. Nevertheless, while the KPRF support had facilitated its candidates' victories in the parliamentary elections, it could be a millstone around Zyuganov's neck in the presidential elections. It limited his room for maneuver, preventing him from seeking broad compromises with non-communist segments of society. The conspicuous KPRF label, and his party's Leninist and Soviet roots, kept Zyuganov from becoming a national leader and complicated his ability to unify opposition forces, which included many non-communists and anti-communists.

Among Zyuganov's other disadvantages was the uncertainty his victory would have represented. No one—apparently not even Zyuganov himself—knew how he would conduct himself once in power. He might behave as Gorbachev and Yeltsin did before him, distancing himself from his party and relying on the state bureaucratic *apparat*. If he remained loyal to his KPRF comrades and tried to implement even a few of the communists' stated goals, Russia would be threatened with genuine instability. It would also be difficult, perhaps impossible, for Zyuganov to attract the urban intelligentsia and the media to his side. It was unlikely that he could, in the short time available, change the existing image of the leftist opposition as losers bent on revenge. Zyuganov's other major political shortcoming was his relative youth. No one wanted a leader who would remain in power for an unpredictably long time.

Yeltsin and Zyuganov faced similar dilemmas, which, judging by their actions, they both recognized: they had to play two different roles at the same time. Both had to convince the public that they would try to change the situation for the better yet at the same time had to persuade the powerful economic clans that there would be no great changes unfavorable to them. This compelled them to conduct a heated ideological struggle in public, sustaining the public division between left and right. At the same time, in private, they quietly moved closer together in the solutions they offered for concrete problems and in the struggle to win over various interest groups. Eventually they nearly converged on centrist positions. This game was complicated; it demanded inventiveness and the ability to transform oneself and to persuade others. Even in poor health, Yeltsin was far better at the game than Zyuganov.

International political circles, which had been wavering, began to come down on Yeltsin's side. Western policy makers had probably concluded that, while the current Russian president was far from ideal, the communists were much worse. At the end of February, IMF Managing Director Michel Camdessus visited Moscow to announce the deal on the release of the long-awaited IMF tranche of a $10-billion loan to Russia (which the government had already counted in its 1996 budget). The credit was part of a program of macroeconomic stabilization worked out between Moscow and the IMF. This deal underlined the support of the Western economic community for the group that was in power. Chancellor Helmut Kohl and President Bill Clinton also let it be known in Moscow that it was Yeltsin who had the support of the West.

Meanwhile, Duma Speaker Gennady Seleznyov suddenly proposed that if Yeltsin would offer an amendment to the constitution abolishing the presidency after 1997, many parties and movements would agree, in exchange, not to hold the presidential elections in 1996. This was a trial balloon floated by the KPRF to test Yeltsin's willingness to compromise. The leaders of the Communist Party apparently were not confident of their own victory—or perhaps they feared what might happen whether they won or lost.

THE STRUGGLE FOR THE ELECTION

The electoral struggle heated up following the most remarkable event of the spring of 1996: the State Duma, on March 17, 1996, renounced the Belovezhskiy Forest agreement that had liquidated the Soviet Union in December 1991. The communists had raised the issue unsuccessfully many times in the previous Duma. This time, however, with a leftist majority in the new Duma, the renunciation passed. The resolution was legally meaningless; without the Federation Council's ratification and the president's signature, it meant nothing from the constitutional point of view. Moreover, Russian political institutions were no longer in a position to decide this issue unilaterally; the resolution could change no geopolitical realities. Nevertheless, the move made Russia seem threatening to the other states of the former Soviet Union.

The KPRF's sponsorship of the resolution seemed to confirm everyone's worst fears about what would happen if the communists returned to power. This was the best gift the leftist opposition could have given Yeltsin. It also nearly created an excuse to cancel the elections. Immediately following the Duma's vote on renunciation, the president ordered his security services to occupy the parliament building. Using the threat of terrorist actions as a pretext, they searched the offices of Valentin Kuptsov, the number-two man in the Communist Party, who was head of Zyuganov's election campaign.[21] Meanwhile, Yeltsin consulted with his closest associates about what to do next. The Korzhakov group tried hard to convince Yeltsin to defer the elections, while the liberals— Chubais, Ilyushin, and Filatov—opposed this. Chernomyrdin evidently hesitated and, as usual, tried to avoid taking a strong position.[22] Yeltsin finally allowed the electoral campaign to proceed as scheduled only after Grachev and Kulikov expressed doubt about their ability to guarantee the loyalty of troops in case street clashes broke out.[23]

Thus the Chubais-Ilyushin-Filatov team won the internal dispute over holding the elections, but their success occurred mostly for reasons other than democratic convictions. Having wagered on Yeltsin's reelection, the Chubais team hoped to neutralize the influence of Korzhakov's group (who for their part were collecting compromising materials on the members of the Chubais team) and to push them away from the president. Even the liberal technocrats on Yeltsin's team, however, had considered the option of canceling the elections, apparently not believing that he might win. The victory of the liberal technocrats was partly due to the collaboration of Yeltsin's daughter, Tatyana Dyachenko, who was rapidly becoming one of the most influential individuals in the president's entourage. Yet the Chubais-Dyachenko team's victory could not be final while Korzhakov and his group were still close to Yeltsin.

Yeltsin's worsening health was another source of concern for the president's team. He refused to undergo a heart operation before the elections, and he was pushing the limits of his strength. He kept on going, but anyone could see that complete physical collapse was possible. Thus his team, including both Chubais liberals and Korzhakov loyalists, had another reason to look for a pretext to postpone the elections: the possibility that he might collapse during the race.

While the Duma was playing on nostalgia for the USSR, Yeltsin's team was attempting to use the integration card in its own interests. In Yeltsin's electoral platform, unveiled in March, integration was the third highest priority, coming just after the issues of back pay and the Chechen war. In response to critics who accused him of destroying the Soviet Union, Yeltsin claimed in a television address that he himself had voted to preserve the Union during Gorbachev's March 17, 1991, referendum on the fate of the USSR. He said that he had believed, at the time the Belovezhskiy Forest agreements were signed in 1991, that a new federation would eventually be created, and he hinted that it was not his fault that it had never happened.

The presidential team also floated the idea of integrating Russia and Belarus. Teams in Moscow and Minsk began to prepare an agreement on the creation of a new Union. The Russian government proposed to form a coordinating structure at the deputy prime ministers' level that would plan further integration of the two countries. Yeltsin also discussed with Kazakhstan's president, Nursultan Nazarbayev, who happened to be vacationing near Moscow at the time, the possibility of Kazakhstan's joining such a structure. This hasty proposal did not impress most observers: the process appeared too artificial and forced, and it was clearly being done just to knock the integration card out of Zyuganov's hands. Moreover, if something went wrong with Yeltsin, the creation of a new Union might well have provided another pretext, ostensibly constitutional, for canceling the elections. The ploy did, however, gain some support. Nationalists and great-power advocates like Sergei Baburin, who had long denounced the Belovezhskiy Forest agreement as high treason, responded to the integration initiatives of the KPRF and the president, and some as a result decided to support Yeltsin.

As the date of the elections approached, Zyuganov tried even harder to play leader of a united opposition. It was not clear to what extent he was still a leftist and to what extent he had gone over to the side of the nationalists. Yavlinsky also made an attempt to broaden his base of support, drawing not only from the other democratic groups but also from the left-leaning electorate. Leaders of all major political groups toyed with the smaller parties, whose votes could substantially alter the outcome in the second, if not the first, round. The followers of eye surgeon Svyatoslav Fyodorov and of Aleksandr Lebed suddenly found themselves in great demand as Yeltsin, Zyuganov, and Yavlinsky began to fight for their support. The struggle for the electorate, which would decide on the next occupant of the president's seat, had begun in earnest, and Yeltsin was gaining.

THE OLD-NEW PRESIDENT OF RUSSIA: SUMMER 1996

COMMUNIST PARTY CANDIDATE GENNADY ZYUGANOV was the first to gather the necessary 1 million signatures required to register as an official candidate, but Yeltsin soon caught up. The candidates' list eventually included Vladimir Zhirinovsky, Mikhail Gorbachev, Grigory Yavlinsky, Aleksandr Lebed, Svyatoslav Fyodorov, Martin Shakkum, Yuri Vlasov, and Vladimir Bryntsalov as well. A genuine alternative never materialized to the power struggle among interest groups engendered by the communist *nomenklatura*: the main candidates basically came from the same old ruling class. The only two real contenders for the presidency in Russia, Yeltsin and Zyuganov, were both representative of the former communist elite. The battle for third place was also important, since whoever came in third might be able to swing the vote to Yeltsin or Zyuganov in the second round.

THE SERIOUS CANDIDATES EMERGE

The race was difficult to predict. Yeltsin was in poor physical health, had alienated many of his allies, and had lost the support of broad segments of the population. Polls taken in January showed him trailing Zyuganov by 15 points: if the second round had been run then, 18 percent would have supported Yeltsin and 33 percent Zyuganov, while 22 percent said that they would vote against both. In February Yeltsin had come up a few points (21 percent to Zyuganov's 34 percent), and in March he had gained a bit more (24 percent), while Zyuganov had lost a bit (32 percent), but 21 percent of the electorate would still have voted against both.[1] Even Yeltsin's supporters and close associates were not certain that he would win, but neither were they ready to reconcile themselves to defeat. The president himself seemed to believe that he was destined to continue to lead Russia. For many, the question was just how he would ensure this: by means of an honest election, by falsification of the voting results, or by resort to force.[2] Yeltsin's entourage was busy developing options in the event of Yeltsin's defeat at the polls. The Russian media, which were controlled by the presidential team, began to claim that the communists were planning massive falsification of the election results—a strange assertion considering that it was Yeltsin who controlled the Central Election Commission.[3] The Yeltsin team was clearly preparing the way for invalidation of the elections in case the results were unfavorable to the president.

The atmosphere contrasted sharply with Russia's first presidential elections. In 1991 the country had been full of enthusiasm, and the elections were the focus of lively interest. People had discussed the candidates heatedly, argued in the streets and on buses and trains, and were constantly caught up in rallies. This time, people scarcely reacted to the political struggle under way. None of the candidates inspired much enthusiasm. The most visible and irritating signs of the upcoming elections were billboards and a constant stream of television advertising.

Yeltsin, meanwhile, continued his frenetic activities. He was seen constantly on television. For several years he had rarely set foot in the rest of Russia, but now he began to travel all about. Some trips were relatively successful, but others were not. In April, for example, as he faced a hand-picked crowd in the Kuban region, some old-age pensioners in the front presented a petition calling on him to give up power. A flustered Yeltsin responded by saying, "I cannot agree. Whom do you propose in my place?" An elderly man replied from the crowd, "We'll elect someone younger!"[4]

Realizing that liberalism had become discredited in the eyes of most of the population, especially in the provinces, Yeltsin's team turned to the Russian tradition of state paternalism. Yeltsin came up with new promises practically every day, and a shower of decrees rained down, meant to preempt the opposition's demands and to eliminate the sources of dissatisfaction among the leftist electorate. There were promises to liquidate the state's arrears in salaries and pensions, to compensate people for inflation, and to introduce a new initiative for indexing pensions. Yeltsin promised to restore the savings people had lost as a result of price liberalization; to compensate defrauded investors; to implement a whole series of protectionist measures to help indigenous

producers; and to aid those who worked in agriculture, science, education, and culture. These promises, however, often generated not gratitude but suspicion. People saw these efforts as simply pre-election pos-
turing.

The enormous activity of Yeltsin's campaign staff was not enough
to neutralize Zyuganov. By the end of April, Yeltsin had managed to
narrow the gap between Zyuganov and himself to 5 percent, but he
was still behind. The outcome would depend on the extent of voter
turnout. The opinion polls showed that if people under forty participated
actively in the election, then Yeltsin would beat Zyuganov in the second
round. Zyuganov, however, would be the victor if there were a substantial turnout of older, less educated voters, who made up the largest
group of voters (53 percent) and voted in a disciplined manner. If
Yavlinsky, rather than Yeltsin, made it to the second round, he was
more likely to beat Zyuganov.[5] Other poll results, however, were more
encouraging for the president. A poll on April 20, 1996, showed 22
percent of respondents ready to vote for Yeltsin and the same number
for Zyuganov, with 6 percent for Yavlinsky and a similar number for
Zhirinovsky.[6] But no polls could guarantee that Yeltsin would win. His
campaign urgently needed to find new ways to attract wavering voters.

The campaign of Communist Party candidate Zyuganov was more
traditional. He did not appear frequently on television but traveled
widely around the country. A year earlier he had looked for support
mainly to the left, but now he began to move actively toward the
statists and the moderates. Unlike the majority of communists, Zyuganov
believed that the presidency should not be abolished and that Russia
needed a strong government. His electoral platform became sharply
different from the one the KPRF had adopted in January 1995. In his
campaign speeches, Zyuganov did not use the word socialism at all, and
he mentioned communism only once (as an idea analogous to "the
Russian tradition of community and collectivism"). The leader of Russia's
Communist Party was clearly trying, with limited success, not to appear
too "red."[7]

The Communist Party had also evolved; it was no longer mono-
lithic but had divided into statist, social-democratic, and orthodox currents. Zyuganov himself was a statist, and his supporters dominated the
Central Committee and the Presidium of the Communist Party. The
statists had allies in the leadership of the Russian security agencies and
the highest circles of the military and in nationalistic members of the

entrepreneurial class. Duma Speaker Gennady Seleznyov, the most influential member of the party after Zyuganov, and Valentin Kuptsov, the head of Zyuganov's campaign staff, had a social-democratic orientation. The orthodox wing of the Communist Party included Anatoly Lukyanov, Albert Makashov, and Valentin Varennikov, but they were being eased out of positions of leadership.[8] Despite this quiet purge, however, the communists' intransigent and unconcealed thirst for vengeance prevented Zyuganov from establishing a moderate image.

Zyuganov managed to keep his party under control and to suppress its divisions, and his campaign had many volunteers, but it was an old-fashioned campaign. The communists invented no new techniques, other than gatherings at pedestrian crossings near the subway and going from apartment to apartment to solicit votes. This face-to-face approach was fairly effective in the provinces, where there was still a disciplined body of leftist voters, but on the whole the communist campaign was uninspired and reminiscent of Soviet times.

None of the other candidates had the funds or the staff to mount an active campaign. Their only hope was to unite the many voters who disliked both Yeltsin and Zyuganov. Mikhail Gorbachev, among others, called for an alliance of those opposed to both Yeltsin and Zyuganov. During March and April, Yavlinsky, Lebed, and Svyatoslav Fyodorov attempted to form a third force, but they wanted nothing to do with Gorbachev, whom everyone considered a ghost from the past. Their negotiations soon foundered on the question of who would withdraw from the race. At the beginning of April, however, Yavlinsky and Lebed came to an agreement, which was never made public. Each agreed to drop out of the race and support the other if the latter's poll standing was higher on the eve of the election. Fyodorov also, rather reluctantly, agreed to withdraw his candidacy in favor of Yavlinsky or Lebed—whoever was leading.

Any third force, however, required more than self-sacrifice by candidates; it also needed to establish its leader's public image in order to draw votes away from Yeltsin and Zyuganov. But the leaders of the third force were not good organizers, and precious time had been lost. The major financial institutions had already chosen between Yeltsin and Zyuganov, and they were not prepared to spend much on an alternative. Moreover, potential voters for Yavlinsky, Lebed, and Fyodorov were not interchangeable, and the supporters of one candidate could not automatically be transferred to the pocket of another.

WHAT IF THE COMMUNISTS WIN?

Two different views emerged in Moscow of what might happen after the elections. One was that the election would make little difference. A Zyuganov victory would not be a revolution, supporters of this view said; it would only mean a transfer of power from one ruling group to another. Zyuganov's supporters were not trying to restore communism, just to get for themselves some control over property and power. There might be changes in the pace of privatization and in the balance of powers, but even Zyuganov and the communists could not reverse the economic and political developments of recent years. Moreover, the argument went, a KPRF victory would split the communists, thus perhaps doing more to foster a pluralism of power than a Yeltsin victory. It might even remove the communist alternative from the political agenda. In that case, the competition in the year 2000 would not involve the communists and Yeltsin supporters, but other, more mature political forces.[9]

Those who disputed this view argued that, while Yeltsin was a known quantity, Zyuganov was not. In this view, the leader of the KPRF would sweep out the current elite and reward his supporters—unqualified and bent on revenge—with high positions. This wholesale change in the cast of characters would destabilize the already fragile government system. Even more dangerous would be a renationalization or a new redistribution of property, which many liberals expected of the communists and which could lead to civil war. Zyuganov's opponents were also convinced that, once the communists reclaimed power, they would do anything to retain it and would cancel all future elections.

A poll in March sought to ascertain the public view of the possible consequences of a communist victory in the presidential election. The results showed a broad range of expectations, while rejection of the communists was far from certain. From 14 to 17 percent of respondents expected that a Zyuganov victory would bring a return of peace and order, regular payment of salaries, lower prices, and nationalization of property, while 14-16 percent expected it to bring a return of empty shelves and limitations on freedom. One in ten (9-11 percent) expected that a communist victory would result in international isolation for Russia, civil war, and conflicts with the other newly independent states, while 11 percent expected a Zyuganov win to result in the restoration of the Soviet Union.[10]

In reality Zyuganov and his supporters would never have been able to impose an entirely new regime, although they could have changed things to their own advantage and enrichment. Even such alterations, however, would have had far-reaching consequences by increasing the tensions in an environment where social conditions were unstable and both the market and democratic transitions were incomplete. The economy would certainly have suffered a deep crisis. Many were forced to the conclusion that stagnation under Yeltsin might be the lesser of two evils.

As the presidential elections drew nearer, various groups expressed fear about the possible outcome. On April 13 the press carried a "Letter from the Thirteen," a leading group of Russian financiers and entrepreneurs, that spoke of the inevitability of confrontation between the government and the communists and called on the parties to find a peaceful way of resolving their differences.[11] The letter did not specify how such a reconciliation could be achieved, and it could be interpreted either as a call for the cancellation of the elections or the formation of a coalition government that included the leftist opposition.[12] This was the first time that the financiers and entrepreneurs had spoken as an independent political force. The "Letter from the Thirteen" only added to the considerable disarray on the political scene, and right up until June 16 no one was sure whether the elections would take place.

YELTSIN'S COMEBACK

Without a resolution of the Chechen question, Yeltsin was afraid he would lose the election. On March 31, in a televised speech, the president revealed an improvised plan, evidently one of several options that he claimed to have developed for the settlement of the Chechen problem. He expressed his readiness to engage in dialogue with Chechen leader Dzhokhar Dudayev, although only through an intermediary: Yeltsin still could not bring himself to agree to a personal meeting with the Chechen leader. As possible intermediaries, he mentioned "an Arab sheik," President of Kazakstan Nursultan Nazarbayev, or former dissident Yuri Orlov. The offer of a dialogue was not part of Yeltsin's speech until just before he went on the air, and "not all the members of my team agree with this," he admitted.[13] All of his suggestions seemed to have been ill-prepared and improvised.

The president also promised to end all military operations in Chechnya by midnight on March 31 and to begin withdrawal of forces from Chechen territory. Local authorities would be allowed to resume control in Chechnya. The future status of Chechnya had been the major stumbling block to any settlement. Yeltsin dealt with it by suggesting that the status of any Federation subject could be changed by mutual agreement "between Russia and the subjects themselves." This formula offered some hope to the Chechens, and at the same time it did not mean much. Yeltsin promised that a transition period in Chechnya would begin with demilitarization, the assembling of a representative body, and amnesty for the separatists. Yeltsin's proposals were greeted by Dudayev's representatives as well as by Moscow with caution and reserve. Many saw this as simply an electoral ploy to appease the democratic segment of the electorate.

The military's reaction to the peace plan was strongly negative. The army thought it a treasonous sellout, because it would allow the Chechen fighters to regroup. After its humiliating defeats and setbacks, the army wanted an unambiguous victory, and if it did not get one, it could take it out on Yeltsin in the elections. The pacifist mood in Russia had subsided, and combative references to "the obstinate Chechens" could be heard throughout the country. The peace initiative indicated that Yeltsin felt he could disregard these nationalists for the moment in an attempt to hold on to the democratic segment of the electorate.

General Aslan Maskhadov, one of the Chechen leaders, was skeptical about Yeltsin's plan, saying: "Despite Yeltsin's announcement of the cessation of operations, we are convinced that the decree will not be fulfilled. Wide-scale military operations, including the use of aircraft and artillery, are continuing. Obviously, there are forces out there that refuse to obey presidential decrees. Perhaps this is being done on purpose or perhaps the situation in the Caucasus is really out of Moscow's control."[14] Maskhadov insisted that the negotiations be bilateral; the Chechen combatants would never accept the participation of Doku Zavgayev, the figurehead president.

Despite Yeltsin's peace initiative, the war in Chechnya continued, and it became unclear which side was responsible for its continuation. Each side blamed the other. Perhaps Yeltsin deliberately closed his eyes to the actions of his military, or perhaps he could no longer control his generals. His offer of negotiations with Dudayev had come to nothing.

Soon, however, the federal forces achieved one goal they had sought for a long time. On April 21, Chechen president Dzhokhar Dudayev was killed by a rocket. He had been speaking on a cellular telephone to his intermediary in Moscow about conditions for the negotiations, and the telephone transmission signal helped the rocket find its target.

Dudayev's heir was his deputy, Zelimkhan Yandarbiyev, not a leader who could become a strong symbol of the Chechen resistance. Moscow hoped that Dudayev's death would bring about disarray and chaos in Chechnya, but, despite their internal divisions, the Chechens continued their war.

A few days after Dudayev's death, Yeltsin threw his last trump card on the table. He invited Yandarbiyev to Moscow, where, quickly and unexpectedly, they concluded an agreement ending military actions in Chechnya. The swiftness of this step was astonishing, yet it made sense. At this critical point in his campaign, Yeltsin needed to show that he was seeking peace. The Chechens achieved direct negotiations, which they had long sought, at a time when they badly needed breathing space to regroup and rearm. Soon thereafter, in Nazran, the capital of Ingushetia, an agreement was signed that provided for the withdrawal of Russian forces from Chechnya by the end of August 1996 and free elections in which all political forces would be allowed to participate.

In another move aimed at restoring his popularity, Yeltsin and his team orchestrated a series of ceremonies for the signing of agreements with the Russian regions on the delineation of powers. The federal center had signed more than twenty such agreements in two years, and eight of them were concluded during the presidential campaign. Some of the regions, such as Sverdlovsk, gained the right to keep up to 25 percent of the taxes they collected. In exchange for these concessions, Yeltsin asked the local authorities to support him during the presidential elections. Such presidential generosity led to the proliferation of regional rights and autonomy at the expense of the stability of the federation. Moreover, the required ratification by the Duma was not ensured, and there was no guarantee that Yeltsin's attitude toward the agreements and privileges secured by the individual regions would not change after the election. At the moment, however, his team was not concerned with the logic of the rather complicated federal arrangement that was evolving; their focus was on the approaching presidential elections.

By May 1996 it had become evident that the much discussed third force was a non-starter. None of the potential participants in such an alliance was ready to follow it—neither Yavlinsky nor Lebed would withdraw his candidacy on the eve of the elections. Instead, negotiations between Lebed and the president's team began in May. It was impossible to keep such a secret in Moscow. The results were soon apparent: Lebed began to appear constantly on television, which would not have been possible without approval from the president's team. The maverick general suddenly seemed to have the finances to conduct his campaign; he had clearly found important backers. There was no doubt about the bargain. The presidential team helped Lebed to get more support in order to take potential votes away from Zhirinovsky and Yavlinsky, and possibly even Zyuganov. In return, Lebed was expected to call on his supporters to vote for Yeltsin in the second round. Presumably the general expected his political reward after the elections.

During this period Yavlinsky was again under attack from all sides, and especially from the liberals and democrats still loyal to the president. He was criticized for refusing to follow the example of Gaidar, who, despite his earlier harsh statements about Yeltsin, had once more come around to support the president. Meanwhile, Yavlinsky declared that he was prepared to endorse the president's candidacy only if Yeltsin would guarantee a change of policy. Seeking to win the votes of Yavlinsky's supporters, Yeltsin forced himself to begin negotiations, and even held two private meetings with Yavlinsky, but he could not persuade him to withdraw his candidacy or to hand over his supporters to Yeltsin.

Yeltsin's associates, still not confident of his reelection, began to develop various other options for keeping him in the Kremlin. Presidential aide Georgi Satarov continued warning that the communists were "preparing militant volunteers to seize power."[15] The liberal newspaper *Nezavisimaya gazeta* published a provocative report describing how the Communist Party was making preparations for a coup.[16] The courts and the police urgently investigated the matter, but they could find no evidence of clandestine activities by Zyuganov's supporters. Yeltsin's team was simply restaging its 1993 experiment: creating the appearance of a threat so there would be a pretext for reaction in case the results of the elections were unfavorable to Yeltsin.

The economic situation on the eve of the elections was disheartening. Despite the massive budget outlays, people in many regions of the country were still not receiving their salaries on time. The problem of tax arrears had also increased significantly. By June 1996, only 60 percent of taxes due had been collected, while 70 percent of the budget expenditures for the year had already been allocated. The government's effort to keep inflation low merely deepened the old problems: enterprise arrears continued to grow, and delays in the payment of salaries out of the state budget increased. For the first four months of the year, GDP fell by 4 percent, production decreased by 4 percent, and investment fell by 10 percent. More than 50 percent of budget outlays went for the payment of salaries and pensions; in 1995, these had accounted for only 27 percent of the budget. The amount spent on production and capital investment dropped sharply. Desperate attempts to break the vicious circle of economic stagnation failed.[17]

Everything that the president could possibly promise he had already given away. He had no political reserves left. He had exhausted all possible electoral tricks. The night before the election, Yeltsin appeared on television and announced with great conviction that his intuition had told him that he would win in the first round. He did this despite the protests of his advisers.[18] This was a very imprudent move; it brought him no benefits, but it so reassured his supporters that some of them did not bother to vote.

Yeltsin, however, did have grounds for at least some optimism. Although he had been politically defunct in January, by June he had managed to turn himself into an active politician who was once again the most popular leader in the country. Polls showed that the number of those ready to vote for Yeltsin had risen from 8 percent in January to 34 percent in mid-May, and by June 1 it had reached 36 percent. Poll results from rural areas were, however, still worrisome to Yeltsin's team: only 14 percent of those questioned trusted Yeltsin, while 33 percent trusted Zyuganov. The incumbent president had, however, been able to regain much of his former support in the cities. Zyuganov's popularity, in contrast, grew slowly, from 20 percent in January to 24 percent in June.[19] June polls indicated just 10 percent support for Lebed, 8 percent for Yavlinsky, and 6 percent for Zhirinovsky; and most polls predicted a substantial turnout—two-thirds of the eligible voters.

The first round of elections took place as scheduled on June 16. The turnout was 69.8 percent, slightly more than predicted. Yeltsin led (see Table 8-1) with a margin of just over 3 percent. The president's advisers hoped that this narrow lead would serve a useful purpose by

**Table 8-1. First-Round Election Results, Principal
Candidates, June 16, 1996**

Candidate	Percent of Votes Cast	Voters (millions)
Yeltsin	35.28	26,664
Zyuganov	32.03	24,200
Lebed	14.52	10,974
Yavlinsky	7.34	5,550
Zhirinovsky	5.70	4,300
Fedorov	0.92	699
Gorbachev	0.51	386
Shakkum	0.37	277
Vlasov	0.20	151
Bryntsalov	0.16	123
Against All	1.54	1,163

Source: *Election of the President of the Russian Federation, Electoral Statistics*
(Moscow: Ves Mir, 1996).

alarming anti-communist voters and forcing them to support Yeltsin in
the second round.

There were several surprises in the first round. The first was the
sharp rise in Lebed's standing and Yavlinsky's drop to fourth place. Most
of those who voted for the general had not intended to vote at all, but
Lebed also drew some voters away from Zyuganov and Zhirinovsky,
and perhaps from Yeltsin as well. He became an overnight sensation
and, in political terms, the principal victor in the first round of the
elections. Yavlinsky, on the other hand, could no longer claim a place
in the political leadership troika, which would have given him influence
over the makeup of the new governing coalition. Yet the results of the
first round were not a humiliation for Yavlinsky and his party; he proved
that he had a fairly solid and permanent base of support. He received
700,000 more votes than his party had gotten in December 1995, and
1.3 million more than in 1993. For the first time, voters in small cities

and the provinces voted for Yavlinsky, although his losses in Moscow and St. Petersburg were heavy blows. As for Zhirinovsky, it became clear that, with Lebed addressing the same nationalist electorate, the LDPR leader had no chance. Zhirinovsky's influence was waning.

THE PRICE OF VICTORY AND THE VICTOR'S SPOILS

Events unfolded swiftly after the first round. The day after the elections, Yeltsin met with Lebed, and their secret pact came out into the open. Lebed joined the president's team and called on his supporters to vote for Yeltsin in the second round, which was scheduled for July 3. In the euphoria following his success at the polls, Lebed increased his demands on the president. He wanted to stand alongside Yeltsin as an equal partner. This would have meant a complete reconfiguration of power and the creation of a new position for Lebed. The president was not ready for such concessions, but he wanted to keep Lebed in his camp at least until the next round.

After some bargaining, Lebed agreed to accept the post of secretary of the Security Council and assistant to the president for national security affairs. His decision showed his inexperience: he had accepted a bureaucratic position with no constitutional standing. The Security Council was a consultative body without specified functions; it could make decisions only if the president wanted it to do so. The post of assistant to the president also had little leverage; moreover, Yeltsin was accustomed to changing his assistants frequently and without explanation. Lebed had placed himself in a position that was totally dependent on Yeltsin's whims. Although Yeltsin had promised Lebed full authority and the right to affect personnel appointments in the power structures, such promises from Yeltsin were generally empty.

By joining the president's team, Lebed disappointed many of his followers and placed himself in an unfamiliar and hostile environment. At first he did not seem to notice. He felt like a hero, and he allowed his ambition free rein, soaking up the limelight, appearing often on television, and expressing his opinions on various issues. In his view his responsibilities were broad and included not only oversight of national security structures but economic questions as well. For a while, Yeltsin did not contradict him: he needed Lebed until the second round of elections. The old hands around Yeltsin snickered at the general's supercilious attitude and enjoyed his blunders and embarrassments. They understood that he did not have any real power and that soon he would not be in the Kremlin at all.

When Lebed began to demand more authority from the president and spoke of the need to create security councils in the provinces, Chernomyrdin sharply rebuked him. He said, "One does not demand additional authority from the president, one asks for it. Lebed may ask for it, but not demand it." He added that Lebed already had all the authority he needed. Other influential figures, including Speaker of the Federation Council Yegor Stroyev, also spoke out against increasing the powers of the Security Council. Lebed had thus received his first warning, but, judging by his actions, he either did not understand or chose to ignore it.

Public attention soon turned to new developments that would have a profound effect on Russian politics. On June 19, two close associates of Anatoly Chubais were detained by agents of Korzhakov's security service as they were leaving the White House, the headquarters of the Russian government, with a cardboard box containing $US 500,000. Chubais, startled and apprehensive, immediately understood what was afoot. He struck back, publicly accusing Korzhakov and Barsukov of planning to disrupt the second round of the presidential elections. Chubais reached Yeltsin through his daughter, Tatyana Dyachenko, and gave his side of the story. Soon after, Korzhakov, Barsukov, and Soskovets, all much hated in democratic circles, were dismissed. At a press conference that day, Chubais, looking triumphant, declared that he had "hammered the last nail into the coffin" of communism. He said that the Security Service chiefs and their "spiritual godfather," Soskovets, had been dismissed because of their attempt to disrupt the second round of the elections and "to achieve their goals through the use of force." He did not, however, provide any explanation for the detention of his two associates, why they were taking money from the White House, or whose money it was; nor did he detail how Korzhakov was supposedly going to disrupt the elections.

The story was not pursued, perhaps because no one wanted to uncover more unpleasant facts about the financing of the presidential campaign.[20] In any case, the results seemed more important: the long-running conflict between the loyalists, headed by Korzhakov, and the liberals and pragmatists, represented by Chubais and Chernomyrdin, was over, and the latter had won. Although Yeltsin gave up Korzhakov and his loyal buddies, he did so with reluctance, but he apparently was persuaded that this step was necessary if he wanted to win the election. His bodyguard's group was discrediting him, so Yeltsin performed the surgery.

Yet the victory over Korzhakov's group left a bad aftertaste. Russian democracy had gained little from these behind-the-scenes intrigues. One group of favorites was simply replaced by another—this one headed by Chubais. The power structures continued to work with little public or parliamentary oversight of their activities.

Meanwhile, Zyuganov, who had nothing new to offer in response to Yeltsin's continuing activism, proposed the formation of a "government of national accord" that would include Lebed, Yavlinsky, Svyatoslav Fyodorov, Stroyev, Murtaza Rakhimov (president of the Republic of Bashkortostan), and Eduard Rossel (governor of Yekaterinburg), and would be headed by Moscow Mayor Yuri Luzhkov. The proposal greatly angered these political leaders, whom Zyuganov had not consulted before announcing his plan. It was obviously a desperate effort by Zyuganov to attract part of the non-communist electorate that had voted for other candidates in the first round, and it was undertaken in such a heavy-handed manner that it only hurt Zyuganov's chances. The KPRF was evidently losing ground, and after the first round it appeared to stop trying.

At the beginning of the presidential campaign, the communist leader had appeared invincible. Zyuganov had had the highest rating in the country without having done anything special to earn it. But he failed to take a number of obvious steps. For example, he should have gotten rid of the extremist and orthodox communists, specifically Viktor Anpilov and Ivan Tyulkin, and then tried to unite all oppositionist forces into a genuine coalition that voluntarily rejected domination by the KPRF. He could have proposed such an alliance to Lebed and Svyatoslav Fyodorov and made some concessions to them. In the early stages of the electoral battle, when they had no financial backing, they might have agreed to such an alliance. Zyuganov should also have recruited experts who knew how to organize and run a contemporary political campaign, but he took none of these steps. Instead, the communists relied on the course of events to carry them to victory. When this failed, after the first round of elections, they simply gave up and allowed Yeltsin to win. It is possible that they did not want victory, since it would have meant a dangerous conflict with Yeltsin. Even if they had won, they would hardly have known what to do in power.

Yeltsin needed Yavlinsky's and Lebed's voters, but within Yeltsin's circle, some believed that Yavlinsky's supporters could be taken for granted. They were reassured by predictions that 58 percent of Yavlinsky's electorate would vote for Yeltsin in the second round. Polls also indicated that 47 percent of Lebed's supporters might vote for Yeltsin.[21] Thus Yeltsin's advisers continued to court Lebed while harassing Yavlinsky.

At the end of June, the event that Yeltsin's team had most feared came to pass. Several days after the first round, Yeltsin, who had been under considerable pressure, physically collapsed. Many were amazed that the elderly and unfit president had managed to withstand so much grueling stress for so long. As usual, Yeltsin's aides tried to calm the public by offering a variety of reasons for his disappearance. Some said he had a cold, others that he had lost his voice. Yeltsin's wife, Naina, appeared on television and explained that her husband's absence was due to fatigue from the taxing presidential race, but her worried demeanor suggested that Yeltsin was seriously ill.

Yeltsin's failure to attend the G-7 meeting in Lyons on June 27 and 28 confirmed the fact that he was not well. He was fond of these gatherings, which gave him an opportunity to feel that he belonged to the world's political elite. The loyal press downplayed the gravity of the situation, but there were rumors that he had suffered another heart attack, possibly even a stroke. Everyone anxiously waited to see whether Yeltsin would come out to vote in the second round, which was scheduled for July 3. The president's team was in panic.[22] On election day, Yeltsin showed up at a voting booth specially constructed for him near his dacha at Barvikha, moving stiffly and with great difficulty. He appeared partly paralyzed; his face was swollen, immobile, and devoid of expression. Far from reassuring people, his appearance increased fears. His illness was not, however, decisive in the voting: many voters, especially in the provinces, did not even know that he was unwell.

Yeltsin's success depended to a great degree on voter turnout: the larger the turnout, the greater his chances of defeating Zyuganov. Until the middle of the day, voter turnout was low. By the end of the day, however, it had increased, and the first returns showed Yeltsin in the lead. Soon it was clear that he would win, and with a margin much larger than expected. Suspicions were aroused, however, because usually turnout fell at the end of the day. Even more curious, Zyuganov's support in many regions had dropped, compared with the first round.

In Dagestan, for example, where more than 66 percent had voted for Zyuganov in the first round, only about 45 percent did so in the second; in Mordovia, his votes fell from 51 percent to 47 percent; and in the Karachayevo-Cherkesskaya Republic, from 56 percent to 45 percent. Preferences appeared to have changed quite drastically in just a few days. Subsequently, it came out that the central authorities had applied strong pressure to force regional leaders to manipulate votes in Yeltsin's favor.[23] There were threats to withhold subsidies and even to shut off electricity and energy supplies. Under the circumstances, it was surprising that all political forces, including Zyuganov's KPRF, accepted the results of the voting without raising official challenges. Perhaps Zyuganov really feared victory and did his best to avoid it.

Zyuganov was one of the first to congratulate the president on his reelection, which meant that the left opposition was not going to provoke confrontation with the government. Instead, Zyuganov and his associates set their sights on the gubernatorial elections scheduled to take place at the end of 1996.

DEMOCRACY RUSSIAN-STYLE

Yeltsin's victory was truly remarkable. In January and February 1996, no one had believed it possible, not even those closest to the president. Yeltsin's slight margin over Zyuganov in the first round had hardly prepared anyone for his resounding victory in the second. Turnout in the second round was more than 68.89 percent of registered voters. Yeltsin got 53.82 percent of the vote, and Zyuganov, 40.31 percent. Another 4.83 percent voted against both candidates.

Several considerations accounted for Yeltsin's success. Russians were voting against Zyuganov more than they were voting for Yeltsin. They voted for the present and against the past not because they were satisfied with the present, but because they were afraid that any change would be for the worse. The vote was a vote for stability, in the absence of any real and satisfactory alternative; it was clearly a vote for the lesser of two evils. Even the president's former associates in Gaidar's Russia's Democratic Choice (RDC) supported Yeltsin only with great reluctance. At an RDC conference before the elections, the running theme was "the president is a liar, but the communists are far worse."[24] Many voted for Yeltsin primarily out of a sense of hopelessness. Yet, in voting for Yeltsin, Russians showed that they were becoming accustomed to

the new realities. Those realities might be dissatisfying and even confusing, but many people had found ways to survive and did not want
change. They feared new revolutions, especially any led by the communists. A few of those who voted for Yeltsin, however, especially in the
large cities, did so because he would guarantee their well-being. Yeltsin's
rule had served the interests of a few people very well.

Yeltsin's victory was also the result of an expensive electoral campaign—a campaign that cost between $700 million and $1 billion. In
the first six months of 1996, during the presidential campaign, Russia's
external debt rose by $4 billion while its internal debt grew by $16
billion—sums at least partially attributable to Yeltsin's campaign expenditures. All of the government's organizational and financial resources
were engaged to ensure the president's victory. Yeltsin's team had used
the newest technology, even calling in American campaign experts. All
of the democratic press and, more important, all of the television channels, worked on Yeltsin's behalf.

Yeltsin's campaign strategies were effective. Portraying the contest
as a bipolar struggle, Yeltsin against Zyuganov, had pushed all the other
candidates to the sidelines. The sharp rhetorical confrontation strategy
forced the average voter to choose between the government and the
opposition forces. Many ordinary citizens, despite their unhappiness
with the official course, were not ready to join the camp of the open
enemies of the regime.

Other factors contributing to Yeltsin's victory were the collapse of
the third force; the drafting of one of its leaders, Aleksandr Lebed, to
the president's side; financial assistance to Lebed's presidential campaign;
and Lebed's inclusion in the president's team. The removal of Korzhakov, Barsukov, and Soskovets from his entourage demonstrated Yeltsin's
ability to clean house. Yeltsin managed to win over some of Yavlinsky's
supporters in the second round, and he also benefited from the support
of local regional leaders who forced their electorates to vote for the
president. He was also assisted by some degree of falsification of the
voting results, which was confirmed in Tatarstan and several other
regions.[25]

The communists' unsuccessful campaign and their decreased activism after the first round also helped Yeltsin. The fact that they did not
take full advantage of their opportunities may be explained by their
ideological and social conservatism, their lack of understanding of the
campaign techniques necessary to reach sophisticated electorates in large

cities, their gross incompetence in political planning, and their inability to see farther than one step ahead.

Some of the communists were overconfident, but others felt that they would not win no matter what they did, and that Yeltsin would never voluntarily give up power even if they did win. The latter busied themselves preparing scenarios in case of defeat, even planning to register as a new party. Some of the Communist Party's leaders behaved as if they did not want victory but instead wished to remain in the role of an opposition force, with no responsibility for anything, able to criticize the government as much as they wanted.

The 1996 elections, the first in an independent Russian state, were significant for the institutionalization of Russia's political life and for the establishment of a certain political routine. Within the chaos, a tradition of governance was gradually developing. The presidential elections in and of themselves were not, however, compelling evidence that Russia had moved very far along the path of democracy. Elections had enabled part of the dominant ruling class to keep its power, but if at some other time elections were to contravene its interests, there was no guarantee that the ruling class would support them again. Thus the debate over democratization continued: would it be best for Russia to choose its president through national elections, or should the president instead be chosen by the legislature or some other select gathering?

Popular attitudes toward the elections and their aftermath were mixed. The massive voter turnout was partly an indication of a commitment to democracy, but it also resulted from a Russian tradition of obeying and supporting the existing state authorities, whoever they might be. Many people voted for those in power simply because they could not imagine it possible or even legal to vote against them. Yeltsin, consistent in his anti-communism if nothing else, ironically benefited from habits and traditions formed under communist rule.

The large voter turnout did not disguise the fact that many ordinary citizens viewed the elections as simply a game of the ruling group. There was a rift between politicians and the rest of society. Many people questioned the purpose of holding expensive elections when they did not result in any change for the better.

The elections also demonstrated contradictions in Russian society. On the one hand, great restraint and moderation were displayed by those who did not want any eruptions and who were trying to avoid extremism. On the other hand, many voters fell victim to the most primitive forms of manipulation by the government. The fluctuations in Yeltsin's approval ratings suggested that many Russian voters cast their ballots on the basis of their moods and emotions rather than their rational interests. Skillful propaganda and clever gimmicks could turn some people toward democracy and liberalism or just as easily toward nationalism and populism.

BATTLING FOR A PLACE IN THE KREMLIN SUN

The battle for positions in the new administration began immediately. The members of the winning team could hardly wait to receive their rewards and to establish their influence. After the elections, during Yeltsin's incapacity, several people on the scene considered themselves the real victors. If the political victor in the first round of elections had been General Lebed, the victors of the second round were Acting Prime Minister Chernomyrdin and Anatoly Chubais, who had no official government position at the time. Immediately after the election, Yeltsin authorized Chernomyrdin to form a new cabinet. The communists let it be known that they would support Chernomyrdin's confirmation by the Duma. They hoped that if Yeltsin's incapacity or death brought early elections, they could either defeat the sedate and inarticulate Chernomyrdin in a direct contest or incorporate him into their coalition. Thus Chernomyrdin became the president's heir apparent with support from the left-wing opposition.

Lebed also had a claim to be heir apparent to the presidency, and he had demanded a promise from the president, before the second round of elections, that he would be given additional power and that the Security Council would have a broader sphere of influence. Lebed was not shy about announcing that he still hoped to be president, that he believed it would be a good idea to have a vice president again (although the new Russian constitution did not provide for one), and that he considered himself suitable for that position. Lebed's broad interpretation of his role naturally provoked opposition from the prime minister, who again rebuffed Lebed, stating that he was not prepared to share his powers with anyone. Chernomyrdin also adamantly objected to the idea of resuscitating the vice presidency.

A struggle within the ranks of Yeltsin's associates at this moment was useful to the president. He preferred to have Chernomyrdin and Lebed neutralizing each other. Yet serious confrontation at the top could

193

be dangerous for the balance of power. For this reason, Yeltsin decided to create a new power triangle, with the Security Council, the presidential administration, and Chernomyrdin's government counterbalancing one another. To this end Yeltsin named Chubais as the new head of the presidential administration, replacing Nikolai Yegorov, the last holdover of the Korzhakov group. This was a sensational appointment. The polished and well-spoken Chubais still had a strongly negative reputation in certain political circles and among the population at large. Everyone recalled the humiliating impression created when Yeltsin had fired him in January of 1996, swearing that "the privatization czar" would never again "return to power."[26]

The appointment of Chubais to a position that gave him constant access to the president can be explained by several circumstances. Yeltsin wished to counterbalance the competition between Lebed and Chernomyrdin and also to have an effective organizer for the gubernatorial elections at the end of the year. This appointment reflected the growing influence of Yeltsin's family, especially his daughter, Tatyana Dyachenko, who soon joined Chubais's staff. Her activities suggested that a new dynasty was establishing itself in Russian politics.

Chubais also had the backing of powerful financiers and representatives of the electronic information media, the so-called Group of Seven, under whose pressure Yeltsin had included Chubais on his election team. Chubais's appointment was to some extent an expression of gratitude to the bankers and the media barons for their support. A still more important factor in Yeltsin's decision was that, while he was ill, it was in his interest to have someone at the top who was loyal to him, had strong administrative abilities, and yet, being generally unpopular, would be unable to establish his own power base. Chubais was ideal for such a role.

To satisfy Lebed's enormous appetite for influence on national security matters, Yeltsin appointed one of Lebed's protégés, Lieutenant-General Igor Rodionov, as the new minister of defense. The logic of the system of counterbalances soon led to the creation of yet another new federal organ, the Defense Council, to neutralize the influence of Lebed's Security Council. However, Lebed's unbridled ambition and inability to play by the rules of the game made it doubtful that any system of checks and balances could survive for long.

CHAPTER NINE

THE PRESIDENT RETURNS: THE SECOND HALF OF 1996

IMMEDIATELY AFTER YELTSIN'S VICTORY, the struggle for the formation of a new government began. Viktor Chernomyrdin, backed by the natural resource monopolies and especially the oil and gas lobbies, tried to form a cabinet that would consolidate all central political and economic power. The other group, led by Anatoly Chubais, included those closest to Yeltsin; it favored a cabinet with limited responsibility that would, like the previous government, concentrate on managing the economy and leave the political decisions to the president's circle.

DIVIDING THE SPOILS

I n this dispute, the president's circle inevitably won. Yeltsin needed a government whose authority was limited, subject to direct control by himself and his team. Chubais and the Russian financiers who backed him established a group within the cabinet that was responsive to their influence. It included Deputy Prime Minister Vladimir Potanin; the president of Oneximbank, one of the country's most powerful private banks; and Deputy Prime Minister Aleksandr Livshits, the former presidential adviser for economics; as well as Economics Minister Yevgeny Yasin. Thus there were opposing groups: a macroeconomic one, drawn to Chubais; and one that represented sectoral interests, especially the "natural monopolies" connected with gas, oil, electricity, and transportation, under the leadership of Chernomyrdin. A government split from the beginning could hardly be expected to work as a team, but it did fulfill one purpose. It gave representatives of the main interest groups— most important, the financial and energy lobbies—an arena for debate and negotiation.

195

The Duma quickly approved Chernomyrdin as prime minister, mainly because of his support from the communists, who justified this on the grounds that the alternative was Chubais; in addition, since the communists could not take power directly, they were seeking allies within the regime, attempting a gradual infiltration of the executive branch. The prime minister was the most congenial figure to the communists, especially since they now had common enemies in Chubais, who was increasingly insinuating himself into the prime minister's domain, and in Lebed, who was trying to assume the mantle of national leadership. The ascendance of Chubais and Lebed forced the moderate pragmatists in the government and the moderate members of the Communist Party to seek dialogue. They were drawn together by their mutual desire to form a power base that would prevent radicals (of any orientation) from influencing Yeltsin or from seizing power if Yeltsin weakened.

On August 7, 1996, the presidential inauguration took place. For this momentous occasion, the doctors got the president back on his feet, but it was impossible to conceal the seriousness of his illness. He came on stage feebly, read the brief oath of office haltingly, and left the stage like a sleepwalker. At that moment, it was plain that the president was so ill that he could not govern. As during his previous illness, Yeltsin did not entrust his power to anyone. Again he tried to have his closest associates create the appearance that he was still able to run the country. Yeltsin's youngest daughter, Tatyana Dyachenko, was his main source of information, and she began to exercise great influence.[1]

Anatoly Chubais, not Prime Minister Chernomyrdin, was clearly in charge while Yeltsin was ill. Chubais became the guardian of the president's seal and the purveyor of access to the head of state. Not a single document could reach Yeltsin without Chubais's approval, and he controlled the president's schedule and contacts with the outside world. He gradually acquired more and more responsibilities, both formal and informal, not only because of his official status but also because of his administrative abilities. He took part in all kinds of decisions, from the economy to personnel matters, and began to make public statements on any and all subjects. Chubais also began putting his own people into influential positions.[2] It was even rumored that he was preparing for a presidential bid of his own, but this was improbable; he was generally disliked and could never have been popularly elected. The increasing influence of Chubais and the financiers forced other interest groups that had previously not shown much desire or ability to cooperate with each other to form coalitions against the new favorite.

The election was hardly over when the war in Chechnya broke out with renewed force. On July 6, General Vyacheslav Tikhomirov, commander of the Interior Ministry troops in Chechnya, issued an ultimatum to Chechen leader Zelimkhan Yandarbiyev, whom he called a "bandit," ordering the Chechens to stop their resistance and to surrender. Federal troops opened artillery fire on the civilian locations occupied by separatist forces and began to attack Chechen villages in a desperate attempt to smash the separatists and destroy their bases. It was soon apparent that Lebed, as executive secretary of the Security Council, was behind this. He was evidently eager to end the Chechen war with a decisive thrust like those that had been successful for him in Baku and the Trans-Dniester.

The separatists responded by trying to recapture Grozny, Chechnya's capital. By the beginning of August, downtown Grozny had become a hell. Chechen fighters surrounded all the government buildings. Chechen president Doku Zavgayev took hasty leave of his few supporters and instructed them to "hold fast" while he fled to Moscow. The civilian population came under heavy fire; people began to flee their homes in droves. In August alone, more than 1,500 people were killed in Grozny, and many more were wounded or disappeared. Desperately trying to restore federal control of Grozny, the Russian military set a deadline for separatists to leave the city, threatening that otherwise it would destroy the Chechen capital by bombing.

This threat could not have been made without the complicity of the federal authorities, and its implementation would have represented a new wave of brutal and uncontrollable bloodshed. At the last moment, however, Aleksandr Lebed prevented the assault on Grozny. It is not clear what moved Lebed to change his position; perhaps he finally understood that the war could not be ended by military means. Perhaps he also realized that continuing the war would mean the further moral and physical deterioration of the Russian army. After a night-time excursion to Chechnya, he said, "I had assumed that the situation was not ideal, but I did not know just how bad it was."[3]

LEBED ENDS THE CHECHEN WAR

On August 10 Yeltsin appointed Lebed his representative in Chechnya, and four days later Lebed had authority over all federal powers in the intransigent republic. Such a high-

profile assignment for Lebed suggests that Yeltsin realized the hopelessness of the situation. Lebed himself said, probably correctly, that someone obviously wanted to see him "break his neck" in Chechnya. Many
people in Moscow were giving more thought to ways of getting rid of
Lebed than they were to ways of solving the raging civil war.

The president asked Lebed not to comment on this issue in the
mass media. Yeltsin also insisted on a return to the status quo before
the seizure of Grozny by the Chechen fighters, which could not be
achieved without new bloodshed. Lebed, instead, set his own course.
He conspicuously removed Moscow's puppet, Doku Zavgayev, from the
negotiations and began meeting, in complete secrecy, solely with the
leaders of the separatists. On August 31, after hours of negotiations in
the tiny village of Khasavyurt, Lebed and Aslan Maskhadov, one of the
separatist leaders and chief of the Chechen general staff, signed a "Joint
Statement" and "Principles Governing Mutual Relations Between the
Russian Federation and the Chechen Republic." Their agreement cov-
ered withdrawal of federal troops; deferred the definition of Chechnya's
status for five years; and called for a unified commission to supervise
implementation of the agreement. "There are no victors in this war!"
declared Lebed.[4] This was more of a wish than a realistic assessment,
as the Chechens, and many others, interpreted the agreements as a
Russian capitulation. Lebed, however, felt that he had achieved the
impossible, and he was bursting with pride. In a speech to a crowd of
Chechens he boasted that the agreement proved that "generals know
how to make deals, while politicians do not."[5] His words were greeted
with cheers for himself and Maskhadov, and shouts of "Hurrah" and
"Allah Akbar" ("Allah is great"). Lebed had achieved what no other
Russian political leader had done—he stopped the war, and for several
days after the signing there were practically no casualties.[6]

Lebed's pride was premature, however. His position in Moscow
had changed drastically after the second round of elections. The general
had served his purpose: now that he had helped get Yeltsin reelected,
the president had no intention of supporting a would-be successor.
Lebed attempted to demonstrate that he was independent. When asked
whether he could manage without Yeltsin's support, however, Lebed
replied that, while "everything is possible," he would not refuse
"open support."[7]

Lebed had been rebuffed in his attempt to meet with Yeltsin before
negotiating the final agreement with the Chechens. On his return to

the capital, Lebed met not with a victory parade but with coldness. Individuals as diverse as Chubais, Yuri Luzhkov, and Gennady Zyuganov spoke out sharply against the agreements Lebed had negotiated. Russia's political and intellectual elite also expressed its disapproval of this "defeat" for Russia. Some feared that Lebed, having returned as a victor, would try to grab power like "a Russian de Gaulle."

The main argument against the Khasavyurt agreements was that they contravened the Russian Federation's constitution. Communists, patriots, and liberals alike feared that Chechnya's separation would mean the collapse of the whole structure. If Russia lost control over the Caucasus, it could face an arc of unfriendly Muslim states: Turkey, Iran, Azerbaijan, Dagestan, and Chechnya. Gleb Pavlovsky, a democratic analyst, warned: "A region of a new kind has now entered Russian politics—Chechnya—whose official ideology proclaims victory over Russia as the basis for its sovereignty. . . . It will implement its interests by killing everyone who gets in the way."[8] Many seemed to forget that the agreement with Chechnya had settled only a single issue: it had stopped the war, leaving unresolved the relationship between Russia and the breakaway republic. Many who expressed concerns about the strength and integrity of the Russian state seemed oblivious to the fact that the main threat had been the war itself.

In early September, Chernomyrdin announced that Yeltsin had approved the agreements. The government had apparently decided that it had no choice, but its support was conditional. The prime minister insisted that the agreements did not constitute a violation of the territorial integrity of Russia. Meanwhile, with tacit approval from the Kremlin, Minister of Internal Affairs Anatoly Kulikov began to criticize the agreements publicly. "I have personal concerns," said Kulikov, "that behind this tactical victory we may have suffered a strategic defeat for the future. If we lose Chechnya, we lay the foundation for the creation of an Islamic belt to the south of the country."[9]

When the Duma returned from vacation, a majority of deputies also spoke out against the Khasavyurt agreements. Yabloko was the only faction to support them. The Federation Council took up consideration of the agreements at the beginning of October. It passed a resolution that approved ending the war but reaffirmed the territorial integrity of Russia. This was equivalent to negating the agreements, because the Chechens had viewed them as the basis for independence from Russia. They had already begun creating their own local government administration.

During the summer and fall of 1996, Lebed was constantly in the news, and he became the most popular person in Russia. Although he was still a member of Yeltsin's team, he began to attack the president openly. Yeltsin did not react: his public statements said that Lebed was "acting on the president's instructions." This suggests that the Yeltsin team did not want to give the maverick general any grounds for reenacting the Rutskoi scenario. For a brief period, Lebed was in a no-lose situation: as an insider, he could create his own power base and obtain financing, yet he felt no obligation toward the regime or the president. The situation resembled Rutskoi's position before his rebellion and fall, but it also resembled that of Yeltsin himself in the late 1980s, when he was on his path to the top.

Lebed declared that it was time for Yeltsin to hand over the reins of power to Chernomyrdin. "Otherwise a dangerous precedent will be established in which [Chubais] rules the country in the name of the president," said Lebed. "This does not suit me. I prefer to do business with the chief, even if he is only a temporary one."[10] He predicted that the issue of handing over presidential authority to Chernomyrdin "will be settled, and we will work with the prime minister." He tried blackmail, threatening that the army was on the verge of revolting and that the country "in the near future might simply explode."[11] At a press conference, Lebed offered an assessment of his first hundred days "in power," a step that would normally have been taken only by the president himself. Clearly expecting Yeltsin's speedy departure from the scene, Lebed had begun his own presidential campaign, and few could doubt that he would have an easy victory if there were early presidential elections.

Lebed's conduct made it clear that there was a paralysis of power at the center. The president did not have the strength to rein in his Security Council secretary, and the upper circle of the Russian ruling class was busy with a different struggle: Chubais, Chernomyrdin, and Lebed, called "three bears in a den" by journalists, were fighting over who would give the president recommendations on personnel assignments, who would meet with him without previous notification, and who would be number two in the informal chain of command. Another wave of compromising disclosures about Yeltsin's entourage was released to complicate the situation: the press reported on payback deals the presidential administration had cut with the banks that financed the presidential campaign, giving these banks illegal advantages during the new round of privatization.[12] Such revelations only increased popular irritation with the ruling team.

YELTSIN'S REVIVAL

During August, Yeltsin's closest associates still tried hard to conceal the president's poor health. The president's press secretary spoke of his "firm handshake," Chubais of his "energetic voice." Yet by September, it was impossible to hide the precariousness of affairs. When Chancellor Helmut Kohl announced that he was preparing to visit Moscow to check on "his friend Boris," the presidential team decided to tell the truth. The president appeared on television to acknowledge publicly that he had heart disease and had agreed to an operation, although the Kremlin continued to obfuscate the nature of the operation and the specifics of his diagnosis.[13] On September 10, the eve of the operation, Yeltsin delegated some of his authority, including control over the power ministries, to the prime minister. However, Yeltsin kept the symbol of supreme presidential power, the "nuclear briefcase," at his side in the hospital.

Meanwhile, Lebed went off to NATO headquarters in Brussels, where he was received almost like a head of state. His bluntness and openness made a favorable impression on his first trip to the West. He no longer bothered to hide his desire to occupy the highest position in Russia, and his public approval rating continued to rise. Kremlin patience with Lebed was wearing thin. The possibility of an alliance between Lebed and the disgraced Aleksandr Korzhakov, who had begun to blackmail the president and his family, was a threat. Lebed accompanied Korzhakov to Tula, where Korzhakov took part in the campaign to fill the Duma seat that Lebed had vacated upon joining the president's administration. This probably sealed Lebed's fate with Yeltsin, and the last straw was Lebed's reception as a future leader during a visit to paratrooper headquarters. With the concurrence of the presidential circle, Interior Minister Anatoly Kulikov publicly accused Lebed of preparing an armed coup.[14] It was not clear whether Kulikov and the presidential entourage really believed this; what was clear was that they were tired of Lebed and fearful of his potential power. The mass media they controlled began to attack Lebed, and Lebed's inexperience led him into blunders that gave them plenty of ammunition.

201

The president, preparing for his operation, chose this time to get rid of the bothersome general, and Lebed found himself pushed out the Kremlin door. His expulsion was accompanied by considerable official tension. Authorities in Moscow imposed a virtual state of emergency, with increased militia patrols and armed detachments guarding the streets. The governing group was concerned that the military might support the ousted security chief. The prime minister instructed the power ministries to hold information sessions among its personnel and to "maintain peace."

These precautions were probably unnecessary; there were no public protests against Lebed's dismissal. Only in Chechnya was his removal viewed with great anxiety. Aslan Maskhadov had warned, "If they get rid of Lebed, we will have to prepare for war."[15] The Chechens feared that the agreements signed by Lebed on behalf of the Russian government would become null, but Lebed's firing led to no significant changes either in Chechnya itself or in Moscow's policies toward Chechnya.

Meanwhile, Lebed continued to be a charismatic figure, and he could not yet be dismissed altogether.[16] His expulsion from the official power structures might even have worked to his benefit if the next presidential elections had been held soon. The farther off they were, however, the more the existing regime could consolidate, leaving little room for an anti-establishment figure like Lebed to rise to the top.

Ivan Rybkin, former speaker of the Duma and a Yeltsin loyalist, was appointed secretary of the Security Council to replace Lebed. In 1994, Rybkin had supported the decision to send troops to Chechnya, but now it was his turn to play the role of peacemaker. His appointment did not make many waves. However, the appointment of Boris Berezovsky—one of the so-called Group of Seven bankers who had financed Yeltsin's campaign—to the post of deputy secretary of the Security Council caused a sensation. An instigator of numerous intrigues, one of the richest men in Russia, and one of its most controversial figures, Berezovsky now had responsibility for the economic restoration of Chechnya, which suggested that he hoped there was money to be made there.[17] Berezovsky's appointment was seen as an attempt by the financiers' group to increase their influence and power, taking advantage of Yeltsin's incapacity. It also meant that the presidential team was beginning to pay back those who had helped Yeltsin to victory.

Berezovsky's appointment was an indicator of new trends in Russian politics. A generation not linked with the old Communist Party *nomenklatura* had risen to take over economic as well as political power. These "new Russians" were aggressive, pushy, and unprincipled in the pursuit of their private interests. They could readily adapt and survive in any conditions. Their rise presented the old interest groups, which had formed in Soviet times and prevailed during the first stage of the transformation, with a dilemma: they had to either share their power with the newcomers, or fight them. But most of the old guard were not crafty enough to struggle successfully with powerful, sophisticated, and wealthy upstarts such as Berezovsky. Nor did they have the vital support of the president's family and its circle. Berezovsky's emergence on the political scene and the appointment of Oneximbank president Vladimir Potanin as deputy premier reflected the increasing influence of powerful business interests and put some focus on their efforts to use the weakness at the federal center to secure permanent political influence.

On November 5, Yeltsin underwent a successful quintuple coronary bypass operation.[18] On the same day, by coincidence, the unions called a general protest, in which tens of thousands of people took part, demanding that the government solve the country's social problems and that the president fulfill his campaign promises, especially payment of wage and benefit arrears. The government generally ignored them, however. Just before his surgery, Yeltsin had signed a decree temporarily transferring some of his powers to Chernomyrdin, but his first words, the second day after the operation, were "Give me a pen," and he signed a new decree reclaiming all his powers.

While Yeltsin was in the hospital, a Chechen delegation headed by General Aslan Maskhadov met with Chernomyrdin in Moscow, and the two signed an agreement that completely satisfied the Chechens. Before this meeting, the president had unexpectedly signed a decree removing the remaining two brigades of Russian troops from Chechnya. This was a real breakthrough. The Russian ruling group had finally rejected the option of resolving the conflict with Chechnya by means of force. Instead, it sought to engage the Chechens in negotiations, especially on the creation of an economic free-trade zone and of a security zone around the oil pipeline planned to transport Azerbaijan oil to the Russian port of Novorossiisk. The new agreement was greeted with hostility by the public, but the government stood firm. The military conflict in Chechnya had thus ended, and the Chechens began to prepare for local elections set for January 27, 1997.

During the fall and winter of 1996, regional elections took place in Russia. For the first time, the Russian people elected the heads of their local executive branches and legislative bodies. No longer appointed bureaucrats but popularly chosen politicians, local leaders gained new legitimacy and were no longer dependent on the whims of the president. This fundamentally altered the relations between the federal center and the regions. The president could not remove elected local leaders, even those whose policies did not suit him. Local governors thus acquired unprecedented rights to dispose of resources, to direct financial flows in their regions, and to hire and fire local officials. One result was the increasing importance of the Federation Council as a vehicle for forging compromise between the center and the provinces.

Against this background, the decline of national party politics and state-wide political movements became inevitable. The previous divisions between the "party of power" and the opposition had lost their significance. The public was moving away from party affiliations, instead often supporting moderate candidates who were good managers but did not have the backing of a party—local Luzhkovs. Local political preferences still remained: Moscow, St. Petersburg, the industrial center, and the less productive central agricultural regions traditionally voted for pro-reform leaders, while the richer agricultural regions, small towns, and southern Russia usually voted for "red" candidates. Yet the majority of those who came to power in the regions, even those supported by the leftist opposition, tried to behave like moderate pragmatists. Most tried to cooperate with the president, because they could not solve their local problems without Moscow's help. The most striking example of such pragmatism was General Aleksandr Rutskoi: at one time Yeltsin's vice president and later his worst enemy, Rutskoi—following his release from prison—had been elected governor of Kursk, where he became one of the regional leaders loyal to the Kremlin.

IS THERE LIGHT AT THE END OF THE TUNNEL?

Meanwhile, economics assumed ever greater importance in Russian life. The transition to a better future still had not come about, and behind the economic statistics were strikes, demonstrations, and even suicides. The only success of 1996 was that the rate of inflation went down to 22-24 percent a year. This was achieved in great part because the state reneged on its obligations toward the population. Pension arrears were equivalent to $12-15 billion. At the end of 1996, back wages due from the federal budget totaled

100 trillion rubles ($17.9 billion), while debts owed by enterprises and other organizations equaled 500 trillion rubles ($89.5 billion). This meant that the country would be paying off government debt for many years.

In 1996, Russia's GDP fell 7 percent, almost twice as much as 1995 (4 percent). Retail trade fell by 4 percent and industrial production by 5 percent. The decline even affected sectors that had performed well in 1995, including oil, chemicals, and ferrous and non-ferrous metallurgy. The volume of foreign investment was less than $4 billion, or $27 per capita (in Hungary, by comparison, the figure was $12 billion, or $1,150 per capita). According to *Finansovye Izvestiya* (Financial Izvestiya), "A structure for rebuilding and retraining the country's work-force has not been created. . . . In the course of four years, not a single plan or mechanism to encourage investment was developed at the federal level. Although a program of de-monopolization was announced, in fact, various government agencies nurtured new monopolies. And the officials who helped them in this way prepared 'parachutes' for themselves."[19]

In the autumn, there were indications that the government was finally beginning to understand the complexities of the economic situation. A letter from Economics Minister Yevgeny Yasin to Chernomyrdin noted that the optimistic predictions of a surge in the Russian economy immediately after Yeltsin's victory had not materialized. The minister blamed the 1996 reduction in tax revenues not on taxpayer refusal to pay but on "a reduced tax base as a consequence of the worsening of enterprises' financial situation." He went on to say that, "currently, we collect only 28 percent of the taxes owed. . . . [Thus] the struggle to collect taxes from the bulk of industrial enterprises that are already on the rocks might lead to a further deepening of the crisis. Clearly that would destroy the basis for the revival of production and for attracting investment. Taming inflation by increasing government debt rather than balancing the budget is not a solution and only defers inflation." He warned that "the previous policy of balancing among various interest groups, and handing out concessions and spoils to one lobby group or another, resulting in unaffordable expenditures, was justified, to some extent, before the elections. Now, however, it has completely outlived its usefulness, and continuing on this path will lead the country into a prolonged depression, increasing the threat of new political upheavals."[20]

These stark facts did not necessarily mean that the Russian economy was completely dysfunctional. Many enterprises continued to operate, but they avoided paying taxes in order to survive. The business would ask its buyers not to pay in cash, but to barter with goods and raw materials "invisible" to the government. "If people paid their taxes honestly, they would perish," wrote journalist Aleksandr Minkin.[21] No one knew the volume of this shadow economy. Enterprises deliberately underestimated the volume of their production by an average of 20 percent and their sales by an average of 40-50 percent. The existence of the shadow sector attested to the astonishing ability of Russian society to overcome government obstacles and to survive. Yet this did not change the overall picture of economic stagnation.

During the reform years that began in 1991, 40 percent of the population in Russia experienced a sharp drop in income. The ratio of poor to rich had increased to 20:1. According to official data, about 32 million people, or 22 percent of the population, received less than a subsistence wage. Independent researchers reported an even worse situation: the rich and super-rich (people with incomes of more than $3,000 a month) made up 5 percent of the population; 15 percent were well off ($1,000-$3,000 per month); 20 percent were moderately well off ($100-$1,000 a month); 20 percent were poor ($50-$100 a month); and 40 percent were impoverished (less than $50 a month).[22] Moreover, 10 percent of those in the impoverished category were at the very bottom, with virtually no income, and many others were close to it, including elderly retired people, single mothers, large families, the unemployed, refugees, and Russians who had fled other states of the former Soviet Union.[23]

Even those with jobs were in a precarious position because of the delays in the payment of wages. Polls at the end of 1996 indicated that only 24 percent of Russian workers received their wages on time; 27 percent experienced short delays of up to a month, and almost half— 49 percent of all workers—experienced delays of more than a month. The most fortunate workers were those in Moscow, where only about one in four suffered long delays in receiving pay. The situation in the regions was considerably worse, especially in the north, Siberia, and the Far East, where about 55 percent of all workers faced long delays in receiving their pay, and only 20 percent generally were paid on time. Nearly one in ten Russian workers (8-9 percent) experienced delays of more than three months in receiving wages.[24]

The widely anticipated new middle class was not thriving. Its weakness meant that those on the lower rungs of the social ladder had no prospect of moving up; mobility was increasing only in a downward direction. The possibility of social mobility based on an individual's education and capabilities was also decreasing. Special cliques began to form. Entire socioeconomic zones experienced widespread poverty: the army; enterprises of the military-industrial complex; medical, cultural, and scientific workers; and inhabitants of the rusting "company towns" in Ivanovsk oblast, Vorkuta, northern Russia, and elsewhere. During the period of reform, the governmental sector suffered a braindrain: about one-third of the best-educated people left underfunded research institutions, cultural establishments, universities, and institutes for other jobs, private enterprise, or abroad.[25]

The situation in the military continued to deteriorate. Military personnel did not receive their pay for many months at a time, and their level of discontent was rising. Even officers openly hinted at the possibility of insubordination. "It would be enough to find just one decisive commander to rally his regiment and head for Moscow as an act of protest against prevailing conditions—and further events might take an unpredictable turn for the authorities."[26] It was a dangerous situation.

The health of the Russian population had also suffered. For the first time during peacetime, Russia's mortality rate exceeded its birth rate. Between 1987 and 1994, average life expectancy for men declined from 65 to 58 years and for women from 75 to 71 years. The suicide rate in 1996 was 43 percent higher than in 1988. More than 30 percent of newborns were in poor health, reflecting shortcomings in prenatal nutrition and medical care.[27] A survey undertaken by the Prosecutor-General showed that in 1996 half a million children were not attending school. A quarter of those who were in school had only half the textbooks they needed; millions more had none at all. Such shortages of learning materials had never occurred before—even in wartime. "The health of Russia's children has become a national tragedy," the survey concluded.[28]

In these circumstances, a broad segment of the population was deeply dissatisfied. Polls showed that 62 percent considered their situation to have become more difficult in 1996, an increase of 55 percent over the 1995 figure. In 1996, only 5 percent of those polled thought that the next year would be better, a decline from the 17 percent of the previous year.[29] Nevertheless, there was no sharp increase in social protest. The Russian people seemed to have become accustomed to a state of constant dissatisfaction.

Yeltsin addressed these issues when, just before the new year, he achieved the impossible and returned once again to the Kremlin. In a radio address, Yeltsin was harsh: "The guilty parties in the leadership will have much to answer for: if you steal, you will go to jail; if you are not up to the task, you will be fired." Back in the Kremlin, he announced that he was ready to fight. "Things have come to a sorry state of affairs. There is a real mess here!"[30] He convened the members of the government and demanded that they resolve the arrears in payments of pensions and reestablish the state monopoly on the sale of vodka, evidently hoping that this would generate the necessary funds. "The coming year will be better for Russia—that is the word of the president," Yeltsin promised.[31] Few people, however, still believed his promises.

THE PRESIDENT FAILS TO COPE

Just eight days after his return to the Kremlin, Yeltsin was back in the hospital with pneumonia. In the belief that his days were numbered, even those politicians who had previously refrained now began to prepare for a new presidential campaign. The communists launched a campaign in the Duma to have Yeltsin removed from office. The Russian constitution contained no clear guidance on how to proceed in case of a prolonged presidential illness. The second provision of Article 92 of the constitution states: "The President of the Russian Federation shall cease the exercise of his powers early in the event of his resignation, persistent inability to exercise his powers for health reasons, or removal from office. Furthermore, the election of the President of the Russian Federation must take place no later than three months after the early cessation of the exercise of power." The constitution did not specify, however, who was to make the decision on the president's "persistent inability to exercise his power for health reasons," and Yeltsin's associates argued that only the president himself could make this call.

Yeltsin's new illness added momentum to the debate over constitutional reform. Even his loyal forces began to seek ways to limit the immense powers of the presidency in order to prevent those powers from falling into the hands of an authoritarian successor. On January 22, Yegor Stroyev, the usually cautious speaker of the Federation Council, announced that the constitution was "not an icon" and must be amended, specifically with respect to the distribution of power between the president and the parliament. This statement was interpreted as a signal that Yeltsin's condition was very bad, and the political elite began to speak of the "post-Yeltsin era." For practically everyone at the top, the highest priority was to avoid early elections that might bring Lebed to the presidency, but there was no agreement on how to escape that fate or how to preserve their respective positions.

The Communist Party hoped that either power would be transferred to Chernomyrdin or the post of vice president, to which Zyuganov aspired, would be reestablished. They also proposed that the Federation Council govern for a transitional period until the next elections, a proposal that Stroyev and the regional elites supported. Chernomyrdin's supporters preferred a transfer of presidential powers to the prime minister until the end of Yeltsin's term of office, with no early elections. Yeltsin's associates and advisors, headed by Chubais, worked out various options: substituting the Security Council for the president; having the cabinet, augmented by more Chubais allies, rule in Yeltsin's name; or naming a loyalist to the post of prime minister with the expectation that he would become Yeltsin's successor in the case of an early conclusion to Yeltsin's term. Others tried to develop alternative procedures for the selection of a new president by either the parliament or a constituent assembly.

Yeltsin's public approval rating was falling catastrophically, and the political situation in the country was deteriorating, while Yeltsin's team maintained that he was "doing paperwork." His new illness started an unofficial presidential race. If the presidential elections had been held at the beginning of 1997, no candidate would have won in the first round of voting, but either Lebed or Zyuganov would have won in the second round. Moscow Mayor Yuri Luzhkov had not yet succeeded in forming a national base of support. In January and February, Lebed began to travel to Western capitals, presenting himself as the leading contender for the Russian presidency, and Luzhkov worked at establishing his national image. Polls indicated that 58.4 percent had confidence in Lebed, 42.7 percent had confidence in Luzhkov, and 34.9 percent had confidence in Yavlinsky. Yeltsin was in seventh place (22.6 percent)—after Nizhnii Novgorod Governor Boris Nemtsov, Zyuganov, and Chernomyrdin.[32]

In the winter of 1997, General Aslan Maskhadov was elected president of Chechnya—the best possible outcome from Moscow's point of view. Victory by the second-place contender, Shamil Basayev, a terrorist who was wanted by the Russian authorities for the Budennovsk hostage crisis, would have been too much for the federal authorities to countenance. The presidential elections in Chechnya created a virtually independent state within Russian borders that nonetheless had no chance of being recognized by Russian authorities or the international community. Without Moscow's assistance, Chechnya would face an economic and social catastrophe, the results of which would have been felt throughout the Russian Federation. Thus Moscow and Grozny—now dependent on each other—entered a new stage of sorting out their relations. On May 12, after difficult negotiations, the two sides signed a new peace agreement, opening the way for the resolution of the economic issues between them, especially the fate of oil and its transport. It was clear, however, that a complete settlement would be a difficult process that would test the ability and willingness of both sides to negotiate and to compromise.

ANOTHER CABINET RESHUFFLE

As spring approached, there were signs of growing tension. On March 27, the unions called a general strike to protest the government's incompetent handling of economic problems.[33] Confidence in Yeltsin continued to fall. By March 1997, it had dropped to 16 percent, less than half its level (37 percent) in July 1996.[34] The political and economic clans had already begun an open struggle for Yeltsin's legacy when the president, again showing his customary keen sense of timing, made a miraculous return to the political scene.

On his return to the Kremlin after his bout with pneumonia, Yeltsin appeared much thinner, but his voice was firm and his mood was resolute. To convince everyone of his ability to control the situation, Yeltsin made his usual move: he announced his determination to reshuffle the government. He may also have had more sincere motives. He told Boris Nemtsov that he did not want to live in "a bandit state." A new reform agenda would require a new team of reformers: Chernomyrdin and his type would never be able to solve the country's urgent economic and social problems.

Government reorganization benefited the president's inner circle, particularly Chubais and his group, who sought to control the most powerful official institutions in case Yeltsin became ill again. The idea of a new cabinet was also supported by the financial oligarchs who had fully exploited the opportunities for enrichment through the purchase of government debt at extremely high interest rates. Now they hoped to broaden their influence within the government so they could begin raiding the powerful sectoral groups, starting with Russia's richest corporations, Gazprom, UES (Unified Electric System) Russia, and the railroad system. The financiers also had to take into account the fact that the next elections could take place at any moment, and elections required money. Control of the natural resource monopolies would give them tremendous sources of revenue.

The reshuffling of the cabinet resulted in the formation of a powerful reform wing under the leadership of two new first deputy prime ministers: Boris Nemtsov and Anatoly Chubais. Chubais became responsible for economic strategy, and his place as head of the presidential administration was taken by Valentin Yumashev, a journalist close to Yeltsin's family who had helped Yeltsin write his memoirs. The portfolio of deputy Prime Minister Nemtsov, who had been governor of the Nizhnii Novgorod region, included social security reform and the restructuring of the natural resource monopolies. As a result of the reorganization, Chernomyrdin lost a number of trusted associates, including Agricultural Minister Aleksandr Zaveryukha and Energy Minister Pyotr Rodionov. He also lost control over the government's economic ministries, which were now dominated by people close to Chubais, especially representatives of the so-called St. Petersburg clan.[35] The liberals managed to persuade Yeltsin to remove Lebed's crony, Defense Minister Igor Rodionov, and to replace him with General Igor Sergeyev, commander of the Strategic Rocket Forces, who was more likely to cooperate with the reformers. The struggle for influence in the cabinet now coalesced around Chernomyrdin and the industrial and natural resource lobbies on the one hand, and Chubais and the liberals on the other. The balance initially favored the latter, and Chubais, with Nemtsov as his front man, acquired considerable power.[36]

The formation of the new cabinet did not inspire any particular public optimism.[37] Boris Nemtsov, however, was becoming a favorite of journalists, and he won supporters because of his directness, intelligence, energy, and integrity, as well as his youth and good looks.[38] Nemtsov's first step in office was to make a populist gesture: he ordered federal officials to replace their foreign cars with Russian-made Volgas (although this step actually cost more than it saved). Nemtsov published his income declarations, recommended that all officials be required to do so, flew on regularly scheduled commercial flights instead of special government charters, and scolded officials for slipshod work in front of the television cameras. Such actions quickly brought Nemtsov considerable popularity, as he artfully drew lessons from Yeltsin's successful struggle for power. Nevertheless, his prospects for further success were limited, because he soon ran out of relatively harmless populist actions to exploit.[39] To go any further, Nemtsov would have to turn to unpopular measures.

Meanwhile, the March 1997 poll demonstrated that if there had been early presidential elections, and if Yeltsin had not participated, 31 percent of those polled would have voted for Zyuganov; 18 percent for Lebed; 14 percent for Nemtsov; 11 percent for Luzhkov; 5 percent for Yavlinsky; 4 percent for Chernomyrdin; and 4 percent for Zhirinovsky.[40] Even though Zyuganov and Lebed maintained their leading positions in the popularity ratings, it became apparent that the KPRF leader would not be able to expand his base of support, and the general's star was waning.

THE RISE AND FALL OF A NEW LIBERAL REVOLUTION

Throughout the summer, the liberals were active. Their first priorities were to solve the budget crisis, to pay wage arrears and pensions, and to begin social and housing reform. One way to resolve the budget crisis would be to force the "natural monopolies" to pay their taxes. By July 1, the government had largely succeeded in paying out the pensions it owed, mainly from taxes that Gazprom finally paid. This was a success for the reformers, and especially to Nemtsov's credit. The liberals also managed to get prompt approval in the first reading in the State Duma of a new tax code. The government itself began to operate more energetically and professionally. There was a glimmer of hope that some economic issues might at last be solved.

By many measures, liberals had more government power in the summer of 1997 than they had had in the Gaidar government. They had almost a monopoly of influence on the president, having pushed other interest groups out of his entourage, and they formed the most powerful force in the cabinet. The Chubais group could count among its supporters the presidential administration, members of Yeltsin's family, and the mass media, especially the three main television networks. Yeltsin had no other team in reserve. The "young reformers," as they were called in Russia (the West called them "the dream team"), also had the support of international financial organizations and Western governments. They were experienced in bureaucratic infighting and political action, and they had a charismatic leader in the person of Boris Nemtsov, whom they could groom as a candidate for the next presidential elections.

The liberals also had weaknesses, however. A government dominated by Chubais and his people could not count on the support of parliament, but Duma approval was crucial for many issues, such as revision of the 1997 budget, the 1998 budget, the new tax code, and social welfare reform. Public support for the liberal team was lukewarm; Chubais and his cohorts were widely disliked. Moreover, Russia's social situation during the summer of 1997 had heated up. Strikes broke out in various regions, and many of them were political rather than purely economic. New forms of protest appeared: people blocked railway lines, resorted to hunger strikes, or took their supervisors as hostages. In this unsettled environment, the new government would need to carry out unpopular reforms, limit social welfare payments, and raise rents and rates for housing, all of which would further diminish living standards.

The powerful industrial lobbies and regional governments began to oppose even the partial reforms that Chubais and Nemtsov were trying to implement. The financial interests that had backed the reformers were demanding more control of state property and economic resources. The new reformers' actions were thus jeopardized from the start not only by the opposition, but also by some of their supporters, who were seeking to advance their own personal interests. Moreover, astonishingly, the new cabinet did not have support from Russia's democratic elements, and the Federation Council and many governors and regional executives also viewed it with caution. Democratic critics of the government pointed out that some of the reformers' actions were unlikely to be successful. For example, requiring a declaration of income was not much of a weapon in the battle against corruption; since officials routinely registered their holdings in the names of relatives, this requirement would not improve accountability. The proposed tax code drew widespread criticism because it would not help ordinary people or small and medium-size businesses. Democrats also criticized the reformers' failure to eliminate "insider" banks and the continued sale, under privatization, of the country's natural resources to banks and other favored groups at cut-rate prices.

In June, Yabloko called for a vote of no confidence, even though Nemtsov was a Yabloko adherent and Yavlinsky's personal friend. Yavlinsky explained: "The government cannot collect taxes; it is in no condition to develop a budget; it cannot prevent the dangerous collapse of the armed forces; it is not protecting the security of its citizens; it is in no condition to reverse stagnation; it is not paying pensions and salaries."[41] The Yabloko leader further pointed out that the reformers were incapable of distancing themselves from interest groups, that they were careless with democratic processes, and that they continued to rely on shadowy centers of power and political manipulation.

It was also becoming evident that the actions of the new government were increasingly more statist than liberal. For example, Chubais and Nemtsov, like Chernomyrdin, increasingly spoke of the necessity of strengthening government regulation of the economy. The presumed liberals' efforts to increase state control in the economic sphere, over the regions, and even over the media proved that the reformers behaved like technocrats who (perhaps against their own better judgment) had begun to play a stabilizing role within a system that secured the positions of the richest and most powerful.

The appearance of a new team of reformers and the powers that they received in March of 1997 cannot be explained merely by Yeltsin's love of favoritism. He could just as easily have surrounded himself with people like Aleksandr Korzhakov. To his credit, however, Yeltsin twice chose to advance those who, in his opinion, were capable of radical reform. Apparently he understood that loyalists like Korzhakov, although able to ensure his safety, were not close to him in spirit, while natural pragmatists like Chernomyrdin, who could maintain stability, could not stimulate development. Thus, in critical moments, Yeltsin called on those with the potential to make reforms: people such as Burbulis, Gaidar, Chubais, and Nemtsov. The rapid advancement of a new group conformed to a Russian and Soviet political tradition. Such revolutions in government had taken place frequently under Lenin, Stalin, Khrushchev, Andropov, and Gorbachev. Changes were carried out by young technocrats who were unencumbered by ideology or dependence on public popularity; because of this they were able to take risks and to act without looking over their shoulders. "Not burdened by moral complexes, social prejudices, the inertia of the 'rules of the game,' the youthful descendants of yesterday's Soviet middle class received maximum advantages as a result of the downfall of the old establishment," wrote analyst Andrei Fadin. "They enjoyed a dizzying political rise at the beginning of the 1990s and were also the winners during the period of privatization and property auctions, in the financial arena, and in the economic opening of the country."[42] The groups that had seized leading positions in the banking realm and their representatives were now beginning to conquer political terrain as well.

Yeltsin's "young wolves," however, were operating in a political environment quite different from the one that existed during Gaidar's time. In 1991 and 1992, there had been euphoria about the complete collapse of the communist state. The opposition was then weak, and the unsettled political and economic scene gave Gaidar an open field for maneuver. By 1997, however, powerful interest groups had been formed, and the security services and the interior ministry had been strengthened. The possibilities for reform breakthroughs were limited. It was becoming ever more apparent that the old guard, the communists, the nationalists, and even the pragmatists such as Chernomyrdin and Luzhkov were unhappy with the rise of the young wolves. The only firm support that Chubais and Nemtsov had was from Yeltsin, who, however, was notorious for never placing his bets on just one horse. Moreover, as soon as the reformers were forced to seek support among the powerful business interests, they lost their main asset, their neutrality.

The changing of the guard in Yeltsin's camp shows the emergence of a certain pattern in Russia's development: the alteration of periods of change and periods of stabilization. The changes were carried out by young technocrats, but the fact that the reformers were unpopular and had no base of mass support sets them apart from their counterparts in most other societies in transition. This isolation made them dependent on the president, thus allowing him to influence the course of events, while Yeltsin's practice of bringing in outsiders allowed him to maintain a certain degree of independence from the ever-growing bureaucracy around him. Once their task was completed, the reformers would leave, and their departure would be followed by a period of stabilization as moderate and conservative bureaucrats corrected their "excesses." Yeltsin, consciously or not, understood this cyclical system and the recurring need for new "breakthrough" teams. It was obvious that Yeltsin was fond of his reformers, but that did not keep him from getting rid of them whenever he considered it necessary.

CHAPTER TEN

1997: NEW REFORMS OR STAGNATION?

IN THE EARLY SUMMER OF 1997, CHUBAIS AND HIS COHORTS were still full of optimism and confidence. Addressing the council of Democratic Choice of Russia, Chubais said, "We have a clear plan of action and a solid, united team. We have enormous intellectual potential—the best not just in Russia, but in the whole world. We are convinced that we can attain the goals we set for ourselves back in 1992."[1] Gaidar was also fairly optimistic, announcing that the situation in Russia had "changed radically."[2] Chubais and his team immediately launched an active campaign to build their own political and financial base. Their first goals were to take control of the most influential arms of the mass media, to tame the natural monopolies (especially Gazprom), to find allies among the regional bosses, and to neutralize their rivals in Yeltsin's camp. During the March government reorganization, Chubais had been unable to place his people at the heads of the defense, interior, and foreign ministries, but he had succeeded in obtaining control of some major sources of influence, particularly the finance ministry, the economics ministry, the State Property Committee (GKI), and the fuel and energy ministry.

THE BANKING WARS

The alliance between Anatoly Chubais and the popular Boris Nemtsov became a powerful political force. Another important alliance was that between the young reformers and the financial group Oneximbank, headed by former Deputy Prime Minister Vladimir Potanin—but this one link soon created problems for the reformers. Here, for the first time, Chubais violated his principle of neutrality, which had served as the basis for the respect accorded him by the financial community. "The government now has a favorite bank, Onexim, which

217

is in a privileged position," wrote financial observer Mikhail Berger "This love has manifested itself in the fact that this bank was awarded the account of the State Customs Committee."[3] Potanin also began actively buying up newspapers; he acquired controlling interests in *Izvestiya* and *Komsomolskaya pravda* and control of Russian Television (RTR). These media immediately became a channel of influence for the Chubais group. It was becoming apparent that the group's members were going to seek a greater role in the next presidential race, although it was far from clear which one of them would be their candidate.

The expansion of the Chubais team's power was bound to annoy other interest groups. The auction of Svyazinvest—the monopoly that controlled the Russian telephone and telecommunications market—served as the turning point. Former allies found themselves on opposite sides, and this marked the end of the "Davos Pact" (the deal between the so-called Group of Seven Russian bankers, Chubais, and Yeltsin that had helped ensure Yeltsin's 1996 victory). Chubais provoked the dissolution of the pact by refusing to help Boris Berezovsky, media tycoon Vladimir Gusinsky, and their associates acquire shares at a bargain price—though even so the auction was hardly pristine. Many independent observers believed that Potanin was given preferential treatment. The Potanin group had long had a reputation for amassing capital in shady ways, and Oneximbank had been the first private bank to acquire large amounts of money through the 1995 loans-for-shares schemes, whereby its managers secured for their own benefit an array of enormously valuable state assets for almost nothing.[4] After the Svyazinvest auction, Yeltsin fired the head of the State Property Committee, Chubais associate Alfred Kokh, who had been responsible for conducting the auction.[5]

Even apart from the consequences of the Svyazinvest auction, several factors were bringing about fragmentation within the Russian ruling class: the new stage of privatization, which revealed the competing interests of various powerful figures; preparations for the next presidential elections and the search for candidates for the post; a new round of struggle for influence with Yeltsin; and differing ideas about the priority of Russia's problems. Major interest groups were busy trying to ensure favorable positions for themselves in the period after Yeltsin's departure from the scene. This very fragmentation was evidence that there was no serious threat to the ruling class; a threat would have caused them to pull together. Potanin's group, backed by Chubais and his team, openly squared off against the Berezovsky-Gusinsky group, which had developed a close relationship with Chernomyrdin.

The battle soon became harsh. It was, first of all, a struggle over private interests, but as the conflicts intensified, they were also reflected in ideas about public issues. Part of the business elite was trying to establish rules of the game that would favor the entrepreneurs over the bureaucracy. Berezovsky, for example, wanted oligarchs like himself to have a pocket government. Conversely, the bureaucrats and part of the political establishment were trying to limit the influence of business and to subordinate it to government or to their own needs. Chubais and Nemtsov became symbols of this new statism. These were new conflicts for Russia, and they reflected the appearance of a new social class that had arisen from the privatization process and was now trying to dominate the government. Chubais's attempts to rein in the entrepreneurial class might have won over to his side previously hostile democrats—if they had believed that the privatization czar was sincere and not just attempting to favor Oneximbank, the financial group that supported him.

The "banking war" resulted in immediate clashes within the branches of the media controlled by the banks. The young reformers came under attack from the Berezovsky-Gusinsky press group. On August 20, Berezovsky charged that Chubais and Nemtsov were "making a serious error" by not heeding the views of the business community (that is, Berezovsky's views). *Komsomolskaya pravda*, supported by the Potanin group, fired back at Berezovsky, accusing him of mixing power with business. *Nezavisimaya gazeta*, sponsored by Berezovsky, accused Chubais of "striving for complete control over Russia and [therefore] strengthening oligarchic instead of democratic tendencies in Russia's development."[6] It was evident that the Berezovsky-Gusinsky group was trying to force Yeltsin to fire the young reformer. The former allies had become enemies.

As the war within the banking and media worlds spun out of control, the president was forced to intervene. On September 15, Vladimir Potanin of Oneximbank, Vladimir Gusinsky of Media-Most, Vladimir Vinogradov of Inkombank, Mikhail Fridman of Alfa Bank, Mikhail Khodorkovsky of the Rosprom group, and Aleksandr Smolensky of SBS-Agro attended a meeting with Yeltsin. The president tried to force the oligarchs to conclude a truce while he maintained that he would not give up his young reformers. But he did not then fire Berezovsky from his post as deputy secretary of the Security Council, as Chubais and Nemtsov requested. It was evident that the president relished the opportunity to resume his role as arbiter, and the war between the oligarchic groups was useful in broadening his field for maneuver.

To some degree this battle was also healthy for Russian political life. It prevented the financial community from monopolizing power and influence over Yeltsin. Much more destructive was another development that became obvious during the banking war: most of the major Russian mass-media outlets had lost their independence.

PRESIDENTIAL MANEUVERING

Meanwhile, the major political players did not believe that Yeltsin would be able survive physically, let alone politically, until the end of his term. Some political leaders wanted Yeltsin's support and blessing during the transition period, believing that the role of heir apparent would give them a greater chance of success in the next election. Many began to lay the groundwork for future campaigns. Moscow Mayor Yuri Luzhkov used the celebrations surrounding Moscow's 850th anniversary, on September 5-7, 1997, to boost his popularity. Grigory Yavlinsky openly declared his intention to run.

Yeltsin began his own game. On September 1 the president stated unequivocally that he would not seek a third term in 2000. He said that a younger and "more energetic" generation would govern Russia after his term expired. Few, however, believed that the statements were sincere. On October 2, Yeltsin told reporters: "My friends and colleagues have forbidden me to talk about this," a statement that stimulated even more speculation. Yeltsin's allies immediately assumed this indicated that the president was ready for a new campaign.

Article 81 of the Russian constitution forbids a president to serve more than two consecutive terms, but there is a loophole that could allow Yeltsin to run again. Yeltsin was elected in 1991 under the Soviet constitution and therefore had served only one term under the new Russian constitution. Presidential spokesman Sergei Yastrzhembsky argued that Yeltsin could, under the constitution, serve a third term, but shortly thereafter, Yeltsin declared: "As president, I am the guarantor of the constitution. I should be the first to give an example of how to abide by the constitution." He promised that he would not seek a third term and again expressed the hope that he would be succeeded by "a young, energetic democrat."[7] However, since Yeltsin is well known for changing his position, this did not put an end to the speculation.

Yeltsin was perhaps wondering how to end his political marathon in the most effective way and to secure an honorable place in history. If so, he could afford to ignore populist sentiments and to forge ahead with some urgent tasks. But some observers argued that Yeltsin would never resign voluntarily. Moreover, he now had his family's economic and political interests to protect. For these reasons, they argued, Yeltsin would, health permitting, run again; and, if his health was too fragile, he would find other means to preserve continuity of power. In any case it would have been dangerous for Yeltsin to appoint an official heir; he might soon have found himself in the role of King Lear, watching his associates betray him and switch their allegiance to a new boss.

The fall of 1997 brought the usual speculation as to how the government could persuade the Duma to approve the 1998 budget, a new tax code, and welfare reforms. Yeltsin chose his typical carrot-and-stick approach. He began hinting that he might disband the parliament. The loyalist press was full of articles outlining what would happen in case of dissolution—as if it were a foregone conclusion. Yeltsin also tried to play the two legislative chambers against each other. On September 24 he met with the Federation Council, the upper house of the legislature, where he advocated concessions to the regions and promised that the government would consult with them on revising the draft tax code and the 1998 budget.[8] Yeltsin praised the Federation Council as a "stabilizing force" while he accused the Duma of "political anarchy."

THE BUDGET CRUNCH

At the beginning of October, the parliament began to discuss the 1998 budget. As expected, on October 9 the Duma rejected the draft budget, and the deputies began to prepare a no-confidence vote.[9] The communists and the democrats from Yabloko were equally dissatisfied with the government's performance, although for different reasons. The communists' aim was not merely to force the government to forsake reforms and to become more populist in its policies; they wanted to realize their dream of a gradual accession to power. Having their representatives included in the government would

221

create a base from which to launch a fight for Yeltsin's mantle. Yabloko, meanwhile, criticized the cabinet for slow and inconsistent reform.[10]

The two sides were not prepared to cooperate in preparing a vote of no confidence in Chernomyrdin. Moreover, the communist opposition itself was split on the issue. Its moderate members, such as Duma Speaker Gennady Seleznyov, warned that if the prime minister stepped down, Yeltsin might appoint Nemtsov or Chubais in his place. For this reason they thought that the Duma had to find common ground with the prime minister.

On October 15 the Federation Council adopted a resolution calling for cooperation between the president, the government, and both houses of parliament. It became clear that part of the communist opposition, together with the Federation Council, was looking for a peaceful solution while trying to save face before the electorate. On the same day, at a critical moment in the Duma discussion, Yeltsin phoned Seleznyov twice, asking the deputies to withdraw their motion for a no-confidence vote. "I don't want another round of confrontation; I don't want new parliamentary elections," Yeltsin was quoted as having said to the speaker. "In the name of calm in Russia, I ask each of the 145 deputies who launched the no-confidence vote to remove the issue from today's debate. I guarantee that the government will take heed of the Duma criticism. Don't put me in a difficult situation," Yeltsin said, referring to the constitutional provision that would force him to dismiss the government or to call new parliamentary elections if the Duma passed two no-confidence votes within three months.[11]

On October 17, in his weekly radio address, Yeltsin made one more attempt to downplay the growing tension. "I want to reassure you, there will be no surprises. There is no disaster in Russia today." He vowed that there would be no repetition of the bloody 1993 clash between the Kremlin and the parliament. "Today we can say that we have a stable political system. Even though it has not been obvious, our way of life has changed fundamentally. Although our political passions boil and bubble, they boil and bubble within the strict framework of the law," he said.[12]

The president was in an uncharacteristically conciliatory mood—all the stranger because, just a few weeks earlier, he had been ready to strike a blow at the parliament. What had changed since then? He may have concluded that it was time to alter the pattern and play father to the nation. He may have recalled that he had declared this to be a year of peace and accord and thought that now was a chance to implement his slogan. Perhaps he realized that the communists no longer presented a serious threat to his regime. He may also have recognized that the reformers had failed to fulfill their promises, and he may have been afraid of confrontation with the opposition at a moment when social tensions were high. In addition, the eightieth anniversary of the October Revolution was approaching on November 7, and Yeltsin may have wanted to minimize the danger of mass demonstrations.

On October 21 the president met with representatives of the major Duma factions. After some bargaining, they reached agreement on a list of opposition demands. Yeltsin also agreed to withdraw the tax code legislation. This appeared to be a major concession and came as a surprise to most. Thus Yeltsin secured a truce with the Duma. Immediately after the meeting, Yeltsin released a letter agreeing to the major demands of the communist opposition. These included regular meetings of the Council of Four (the president, the prime minister, and the speakers of the Duma and the Federation Council) and round-table meetings of major political forces; acknowledgment that housing policy needed work; and formation of a commission of government and parliamentary representatives to discuss amendments to the law on government.[13] Yeltsin also increased parliamentary access to the media, allowing parliamentary activities two hours of air time each week on state-controlled radio stations and two hours on Russian Television (RTR); and he created public oversight councils at the two state-controlled nationwide television networks, Russian Public Television (ORT) and RTR, as well as invited parliamentary representatives to join these councils. In addition, the president agreed to amend the draft 1998 budget to provide funding for a new parliamentary newspaper.

On October 22 the communists removed their no-confidence motion from the Duma agenda. Gennady Zyuganov announced that his party was satisfied with the compromise, which, he said, would lead to better mutual understanding and a more rational balance between the branches of power. Zyuganov, however, warned that his faction reserved the right to pursue a no-confidence vote in the future if the round-table talks and the Council of Four meetings produced no results.

At the height of the government's October crisis, only 7 percent of respondents across Russia fully trusted the parliament, while only 10 percent fully trusted the government. But only 11 percent of respondents supported dissolution of the parliament, while just 12 percent supported

223

the resignation of the cabinet. Polls indicated that support for the Duma and support for the government were equally low but that the majority opposed radical measures to solve the crisis.[14]

According to polls conducted in October, most Russians did not expect much confrontation on the political scene. Surveys showed a growing sympathy for Yabloko, and increased chances for Aleksandr Lebed to form a strong faction in a new Duma should elections be held very soon. Of those surveyed, 40.6 percent said they trusted Luzhkov; 32.9 percent, Nemtsov; 31.8 percent, Lebed; 28.2 percent, Yavlinsky; 22.5 percent, Zyuganov; 18.4 percent, Yeltsin; and 17.4 percent, Chernomyrdin.[15]

THE RESULTS OF THE AUTUMN GOVERNMENT CRISIS

There were differing opinions in Moscow's political circles about the significance and the consequences of the "October compromise" Yeltsin had reached with the Duma and the leftist opposition. Some observers thought Yeltsin was simply playing his usual game, giving the opposition minor concessions without changing the essence of his own policies or his decision-making mechanism. They noted that the creation of consultative bodies with the participation of the opposition did not oblige either Yeltsin or his government to heed their recommendations. Moreover, the inclusion of the opposition in the work of these consultative bodies tended to neutralize the opposition parties, forcing them to share responsibility for the actions of the government. The other concessions were merely symbolic. These observers maintained that Yeltsin had thus successfully managed to neutralize the opposition, to achieve a political truce, and to create a basis for stability for 1998.

Other observers saw more significance in Yeltsin's October compromise. In reaching an agreement with the left, they said, the president had abandoned his former reliance on pragmatists and technocrats and had broadened his base by including part of the opposition. This could, in the future, lead to significant changes in his policies. There were those who went even further in their assessment, saying that the communists could henceforth even enter the government and assume major posts. Supporting this view was the fact that, on December 9, Yeltsin promised to consider an idea advanced by the communists, namely the creation of a "government of national trust" based on a parliamentary majority.

It would soon become clear, however, that those who thought Yeltsin was simply playing his games were right. Nevertheless, it was a positive development that Yeltsin had decided not to strain his relations with the parliament and, for the first time, had sought a dialogue with the legislature. The compromise between the executive and the legislature undoubtedly defused a tense political situation. Russia would have gained nothing from the dissolution of the parliament, since the next parliament would likely have been even more solidly oppositionist, with more Lebed supporters and other unpredictable forces, and would have brought even greater tension into the country's political life. Sooner or later, the executive and legislative branches had to learn to talk to each other. But everything depended on what was behind this urge toward dialogue: was it intended to further reforms, or was it meant to preserve the status quo and to keep Yeltsin and his team in power?

Soon it would become evident that the creation of new consultative bodies strengthened the backroom nature of Russian politics and contributed nothing to urgently needed constitutional and political reforms. By participating in such bodies, the leaders of the Communist Party and the Federation Council lent their support to a form of government in which the deciding role was held by the president. Yeltsin had become, in essence, a monarch.

The autumn events and the dialogue between the two branches of power also illustrated a contradiction facing the Russian government. On the one hand, normal political development dictated that the parliament should assume a greater role in adopting decisions. On the other hand, given that the communists and their allies were in the majority, a greater role for the legislature would only slow down economic and social reform. Indeed, although a compromise between Yeltsin, the leftist opposition, and the regional elites guaranteed temporary stability and reconciliation, it also meant postponing necessary economic measures. But for the Russian ruling elite, it was more important to preserve the peace today than to worry about what could happen tomorrow.

The conflict between the Duma and the administration, and its resolution, demonstrated that the majority of political actors had no interest in deepening the crisis, but everyone wanted to save face. The major victor was Yeltsin, who managed once again to strengthen his political role. Profiting from Chernomyrdin's fear of acting independently and his unwillingness to take responsibility for resolving the crisis, Yeltsin took a decisive role in the conflict, showing that he was indispensable.

225

But Yeltsin was becoming more and more of an obstacle to the development of independent political institutions. He was trying to preserve his key role at a time when his physical weakness regularly left him unable to cope with the decision-making process.

Zyuganov showed that he and his entourage were ready for far-reaching compromise with the president. Although communist candidates won elections in a number of regions in the fall of 1997, Zyuganov admitted that "the Communist Party has not yet been able to digest the piece of power it has attained."[16] During 1997 he spoke more and more often of the need to "insert ourselves into power" and seemed to doubt that the communists would ever come to power independently. Zyuganov developed certain tactics: he praised Yeltsin in private meetings while continuing to blast the "anti-populist regime" in public, realizing that he had to conserve his party and its base. "He doesn't really want to be president—being president of Russia is very difficult and dangerous," wrote observers.[17] According to opinion polls conducted in September-November, Zyuganov was still in the lead: if presidential elections were held early, 17 percent of the voters were prepared to cast their ballots for him, but this was no guarantee of victory, nor did it mean that Zyuganov himself was ready for the fight.

Dmitri Furman, observer of the Russian political scene, wrote that "Zyuganov and his cohorts are 'brilliant politicians' who did everything they could to avoid coming to power." He continued, "It is not even really an opposition, but a functional element of the power structure."[18] It seemed that Russia had gradually developed what Yeltsin had tried to create in 1995: a tame two-party system. One of its components was the bureaucracy, with Chernomyrdin's Our Home Is Russia as its mouthpiece, while the other was Zyuganov's communists. This system was able to provide a certain political stability, but it could not stimulate constructive development.

The fall compromise could, in the final analysis, only weaken the position of the Communist Party. Zyuganov's willingness to give in and the fact that he deliberately refused a confrontation with the government gradually eroded the loyalty of his radical supporters, who were already calling him a traitor. His colleagues, among them Aleksandr Kuvayev, a member of the Communist Party leadership, had this to say about the compromise with Yeltsin: "At the last congress we announced a policy of attack on the regime and gathered 10 million signatures calling for the president's retirement. How do we now explain to our electorate why we backed off from the no-confidence vote in the government?"

He charged, quite accurately: "Yeltsin is playing a game with the opposition, a game in which he holds all the cards."[19] It was true: Yeltsin was
able to outmaneuver everyone, especially Zyuganov.[20] As further events
would show, Yeltsin did not take the compromise with the opposition
seriously. The president followed Bismarck's precept that, when you
agree to a thing in principle, you mean you have no intention of carrying
it out in practice.

At the same time, it was important to the government that Zyuganov retain his influence over the disaffected—to prevent them from
abandoning him for a more intractable and dangerous leader such as
Lebed. The government also needed Zyuganov as the main opponent
in the next elections. "Having the leader of the Communist Party as a
rival in the second round is the dream of every candidate for the presidency," said analyst Vyacheslav Nikonov.[21] But in order to retain the
Party and its support, Zyuganov had to go on the attack against the
government.

THE REFORMERS' MISTAKE

Hard on the heels of the October battles came a new shock to the
political establishment. On November 5, Yeltsin unexpectedly
signed a decree removing Deputy Secretary of the Security
Council Boris Berezovsky from his post. The departure of the powerful
bureaucrat was even more sensational than his appointment had been
a year earlier. On November 4, Chubais and Nemtsov had taken advantage of the absence of Chernomyrdin (who was favorably disposed
toward Berezovsky) and evaded the eagle eyes of Berezovsky allies
Tatyana Dyachenko and Valentin Yumashev, the head of the president's
administration. They went to see Yeltsin at his dacha, bringing with
them a draft decree dismissing Berezovsky that they persuaded the
president to sign.[22]

The young reformers risked everything and won. Yeltsin's move
was explained by *Obshchaya gazeta* in this way: "Yeltsin most likely
understood that there were quite a few other people like Berezovsky
associated with the policy known by some as stabilization and by others
as stagnation. Losing him would not cause any serious imbalance in
the upper echelons. But after Chubais's prolonged fall from grace, Yeltsin
decided to make it up to him."[23] That Yeltsin removed a man who was
supported by the president's family, especially the influential Tatyana

227

Dyachenko, showed that he could still make decisions independent of the interests of his family. Yeltsin, knowing of the closeness between Berezovsky and Chernomyrdin, also may have been aiming a blow at the prime minister, who was then being touted in the press as a presidential candidate. Such maneuvering is quite his style. Yeltsin's motives also may have been much simpler—perhaps he was just indignant at Berezovsky's use of his position to further his own financial interests.

These efforts to get Berezovsky out could also be perceived as Chubais's abandonment of the fragile peace that had begun to take hold after the August conflict over Svyazinvest. Chubais had decided to go on the attack. He had been successful with this tactic in the past, but soon success would elude him. The reformers would realize just how important it was to have friends in the president's family and in his administration. A return strike against Chubais came along very quickly.

On November 13, journalist Aleksandr Minkin, known for his exposés, reported on the radio program "Ekho Moskvy" about a book-publishing deal involving high-ranking government officials, who were immediately dubbed "the new writers' union." Chubais and his allies— Maksim Boiko (a new deputy prime minister and the head of the State Property Committee); Pyotr Mostovoi (chairman of the Federal Bankruptcy Committee); Alfred Kokh (former head of the State Property Committee); and Aleksandr Kazakov (deputy head of the administration)—had supposedly written a book together about privatization in Russia. No one had seen this book, but the authors had already been given an advance on royalties for the manuscript. Each received $90,000. Even more significant than the princely sum was the fact that it had been paid by a group close to Oneximbank, just before the Svyazinvest auction.[24] Those who had accused Chubais and his cohorts of lobbying for Potanin thus had confirmation of their suspicions. Minkin's assessment was harsh: "If the deputy prime minister receives honoraria that smell like bribes, it is not merely compromising, it is grounds for opening a criminal investigation."[25] In principle, this honorarium was small change compared with the fantastic sums that others, including the leaders of the "natural monopolies," were earning. But on moral and ethical grounds, the reformers should not have taken the money, especially from a group on the winning side in the privatization process. Chubais, too sure of himself, had taken a false step and slipped.

According to journalists, the president was enraged by the tale of the manuscript.[26] Beginning November 14, he fired all the "writers" but

Chubais from their posts. Chubais also wrote a letter of resignation, but Yeltsin did not accept it, making it known that he still needed Chubais. Nevertheless the affair marked the beginning of Chubais's downfall: he lost a significant portion of his team, and he soon lost his job as finance minister. The new candidate for that post was an old foe of Chubais's, Mikhail Zadornov, a representative of Yabloko and chairman of the Duma budget committee. The opportunity had arrived for Chernomyrdin to take control of all the major economic ministries, and he acted quickly. His influence was at its highest at the end of 1997 and the beginning of 1998, but Yeltsin was not happy when someone was too obviously out in front. This partly explains why he decided, for now, to leave Chubais in the government (as deputy prime minister)—to counterbalance Chernomyrdin. The other reasons for not firing Chubais were simple: Yeltsin believed that Chubais was a bridge between Russia and the West, and, in addition, Russia had a serious shortage of good administrators.

Public opinion polls revealed society's reaction to the book scandal: 57 percent of respondents said they knew of the scandal; 55 percent approved of the firing of the reformers; 25 percent termed Chubais's action theft; 15 percent called it a bribe; 15 percent thought it was money laundering; 16 percent considered it a violation of ethical norms; and only 3 percent called it a normal honorarium. Of the respondents, 53 percent called for Chubais's resignation, while just 13 percent approved of the president's decision to let him stay. Only 10 percent believed that the scandal had been drummed up by Chubais's enemies; 48 percent felt that journalists were telling the truth; and 73 percent approved of the journalists' role in exposing the affair.[27]

Chubais's story is emblematic of Yeltsin's style of governing—helping favorites to rise very rapidly, making them the focus of envy and hatred, and then stepping back as they are transformed into scapegoats who fall as suddenly as they rose. Chubais was certainly not the first "temporary worker"; Burbulis and Gaidar had also been similarly advanced by Yeltsin only to be dropped some time later.

THE REFORMERS IN DANGER

In 1997 Chubais and his team were hampered on all sides: first, by the demands of the financial clans that their interests be protected; and second, by the scarcity of government resources and the team's complete lack of social and political support. In fact, the only resource they really had was Yeltsin's support, which was always conditional. The president would not allow his reformers to expand their influence beyond the ministry of economics and the finance ministry, and he counterbalanced them in economic policy with Chernomyrdin. The presidential administration was becoming increasingly critical of Chubais and his people, and Chubais, in transferring to a cabinet position, had lost the ability to control access to Yeltsin. Deprived of real power, Chubais could no longer be effective.

The second generation of reformers was also quite different from the first. One could hardly accuse them of idealism, a quality that had still clung to many of Gaidar's team. Chubais and his cohorts had both feet on the ground and were no strangers to personal interest, a fact that would make them vulnerable. But even with limited resources and Yeltsin's conditional support, the Chubais-Nemtsov team had the chance to design honest rules of the game, at least in the economy. They failed to carry out their program, however: their tax bill was not approved; social reform was postponed; housing reform provoked criticism; they were unable to break the dominance of the "natural monopolies"; tax collection did not improve; and the non-payments crisis, although it had abated somewhat, was not solved.

But what exactly caused the downfall of Chubais's team in 1997? It was not, after all, the book scandal that caused heads to roll. Other members of the "party of power" had much greater sins on their souls. The prime minister had also been unable to cope with economic problems, but he continued to head the government. Chubais and his associates did nothing that smacked of liberal radicalism: all of their reforming zeal was spent in half-measures. Chubais himself acted the part of a typical administrator. His attempt to ease the crisis by firming up fiscal policy and by working through the emergency commission could hardly be seen as an excess of liberalism. There were accusations that the reformers had a special weakness for Western capital, but the deal between Gazprom and Shell showed that the same could be said of Chernomyrdin. If bolshevism can be understood as acting according to the principle that "the ends justify the means," then Chubais and his team were no more guilty than all other Russian politicians—from the president on down. And if the reformers were suspected of having begun to prepare themselves to do battle for the presidency, others were certainly doing this as well. Luzhkov, Chernomyrdin, and Zyuganov had openly entered the fray. The prime minister had had his own party for a long time, as well as a large financial base and loyal media. But Chubais's attempts to expand his influence immediately provoked a storm of protest.

The real causes of the Chubais team's collapse were a bit different. In a way, they dug their own grave. They ignored the basic rules of politics, alienating almost everyone—the presidential administration, Yeltsin's family, Chernomyrdin, Luzhkov, the Duma, the communists, Yabloko, and many of the financial clans. In fact the entire "party of power" came out against Chubais's team. The special services were also beyond their control and had gathered compromising material against Chubais to give to Berezovsky.[28] No less significant was the fact that the reformers had alienated the general public as well, by saying they were going to raise rents, lower social spending, and raise prices and taxes. The reformers were poor strategists, and the fact that they were caught by this "book story" shows that they were too sure of themselves.

Of course Yeltsin could have protected the reformers instead of giving them up to the lions. He had defended Gaidar and former foreign minister Andrei Kozyrev for a long time before sending them into retirement. Yeltsin has never liked to give up his people under pressure, but this time he was himself annoyed with his young team, which had promised to solve all the problems but was unequal to the task. Yeltsin had already begun to distance himself from Chubais in October, when he refused to support Chubais's pet project, the tax code.

There is yet another reason, perhaps the most important one, for the defeat of the reformers in 1997. Despite all the modern trappings, Russian society as a whole remained highly traditional. Patrimonialism, old patron-client relationships, typical Soviet habits and symbols, and populist sentiments retained their hold. The very fact that the country was still governed by representatives of the communist *nomenklatura* showed the depth of the roots of the past. For a significant portion of society, the members of Chubais's team—with all of their self-assurance, their lack of a sense of proportion or of respect for the old symbolism, their conviction that they could do anything, and their disdain for all roots—were an alien growth. Also alien to the establishment was a large part of the new business world, especially those who had not gone through the Soviet school and were not familiar with the habits of the old establishment. The parvenus were able to attain power and to make money. They could be assigned certain tasks—they could become functionaries, like Chubais. They could be liked by Yeltsin, and some of them, like Nemtsov, could even became his favorites. But they could not rise above that level—they could not overcome the old establishment and get to the point of dictating their own laws.

Thus one possible conclusion is that the fall of Chubais's team was the result of an unofficial, spontaneous apportioning of roles within the Russian ruling class. This was reflected in the fact that the technocrats, who were given the task of overcoming obstacles and energizing the system, could not aspire to greater roles, much less try to gain a monopoly on power. If they tried, they were immediately rejected by the system. This is the trap for all Russian reformers. On the one hand, they have to have political resources in order to take action, and the support of the president alone is not sufficient. On the other hand, all of their attempts to build their own power structure and financial base meet with resistance from the bureaucratic machine already in place and may be opposed even by the president. To succeed, the reformers need the support of the pragmatists among the bureaucrats and interest groups, but to provide that support, the pragmatists would have to let go of their traditional notion of stability as the preservation of the status quo. Thus, much depended on whether the pragmatists would have the courage to launch themselves into the unknown, cutting their old ties. Five years of Chernomyrdin's government had shown that they were incapable of pushing through reforms by themselves, even if they understood the need for radical measures. Some of them were occasionally capable of subordinating their own interests to the general good, as when Chernomyrdin forced Gazprom to help the government pay out pensions, even though it had to borrow money from abroad to do so. This, however, was not enough to continue real reforms.

THE ECONOMIC BURDEN

The Russian economy continued to present a controversial picture. Throughout the spring and summer, interest rates and inflation fell, making the economy look better. Stock market improvement was evident. Consistently tight monetary policy finally was producing positive results, and prices rose more slowly. The government was gradually solving at least some of the problems of nonpayments and wage arrears, especially with the military, funded by the proceeds of the huge privatization auctions.

Yet everyone understood that only stable economic revival and the improvement of tax revenue collection could prevent arrears in pensions and wages from occurring again. This demanded further restructuring of the economy. The country badly needed to rid itself of overregulation, arbitrary administrative rule, and unpredictable changes in tax legislation. Only this would prompt investors, both domestic and foreign, to risk their money in the Russian economy.

In the fall it became apparent that the economic picture was not quite as rosy as it had seemed. Chubais nonetheless continued to say, as late as October, "Russia is just a half-step away from the beginning of real economic growth."[29] But Aleksandr Livshits, former finance minister and now a representative of the presidential administration, gave a gloomier assessment. He identified "consistently unsatisfactory" tax collection as the basic problem: in October 1997, only 67 percent of planned tax revenues were received (and this was from the sequestered budget).[30] It took the government two quarters of 1997 to collect the amount it had collected in one quarter in 1996. The IMF even delayed a scheduled tranche of its loan to Russia because of the critical tax-collection situation.

But poor tax collection was unavoidable: the economy had not yet begun to work. Factories and other enterprises were in a pathetic state, and the shadow economy paid no taxes. Despite all its promises to correct the situation, the government was unable to pay its debt to the military (it owed 9 trillion rubles, or $1.5 billion in October). Livshits did not foresee real economic growth for 1998. More likely, he said, would be a continuation of 1997 conditions—that is, a combination of stagnation with limited areas of success and continuing elements of crisis.[31] Academician Nikolai Petrakov wrote: "Our industry has collapsed. We sell oil and gas, and we plug the holes in the supply system with imports. But this is a dead end: we are using up our natural resources in the most primitive way. The country is infected with an economic immune-deficiency disease. Some areas of industry have almost disappeared."[32] Economist Grigory Khanin said: "The population is managing a tolerable standard of living only by consuming the national wealth, including working capital and reserves, which have decreased by a factor of seven."[33]

These developments marred the hopes aroused in the spring and summer, when the government had developed certain priorities and announced its readiness to act, and when it had begun to shake payments out of those who had not paid their debts. Internal troubles were not entirely to blame: the Asian financial crisis that exploded in the fall affected Russia as well.

Meanwhile, the reformers left in government, and Chernomyrdin himself, tried their best to project an image of self-assurance. They continued to forecast an imminent economic boom, but few believed them. The president himself, having in September professed to be satisfied with his cabinet, began to understand that not everything was going well. In his radio address on November 28, Yeltsin announced that he planned to call his government to account. The president was harsh: "I want to look our ministers in the eye. . . . It is not out of the question that there will be some personnel changes as a result of this accounting. It is a bad thing when people in the government are constantly changing. But it is still worse when bad ministers remain at their posts."[34] Yeltsin also demanded that the government pay all wage arrears by January 1, 1998.[35] When at the end of November 1997 the world financial crisis had swept a significant number of foreign investors out of the Russian market, Chubais himself admitted: "We have been thrown back six months."

At the end of the year, the government managed, with extreme difficulty, to pay all debts to state workers, which meant that the money left Moscow and went to the provinces. In practice, this did not mean that all state workers got their pay, since the regional authorities were highly inefficient and often held back the funds. Everyone was left with a feeling of anxiety, since it was unclear how pensions and wages would be paid in 1998. Tax collection was still poor, and the economy continued to stagnate.

YELTSIN STRUGGLES ON

With all of this going on, Yeltsin remained quite vigorous. In the fall he made a series of quick visits to Europe and China. In Krasnoyarsk, Siberia, he met with Japan's Premier Ryutaro Hashimoto and agreed to conclude a peace treaty with Japan by the year 2000. It was amazing to see a man who just one year earlier had been in such poor health now able to carry out such an active program. On December 5, Yeltsin suddenly appeared in the Duma and asked the deputies to pass the 1998 budget. "I am asking you not to delay, but to go ahead and adopt the budget," said the president in a conciliatory manner.[36] Instead of threats and demands,

234

Yeltsin pursued his new tactic of conducting a dialogue with the Duma, and it worked brilliantly. The budget was adopted in the first reading (with 231 deputies voting for, 136 against, and 6 abstaining). It was even supported by the communists, although Zyuganov had repeatedly declared that "the faction cannot and will not vote for the budget." All Yeltsin had to do was go to the Duma, and everything changed; the president could still persuade almost anyone. An exception was Yavlinsky, who remained inflexible; Yabloko voted against the budget.[37]

By all accounts, Yeltsin did not get involved in the details of the budget; they did not really interest him, nor, apparently, did he understand much about them. He simply wanted the Duma's approval of the budget at any price. By demonstrating his ability to prevail on the Duma, Yeltsin looked like a winner, and he evidently enjoyed his success. But again fate seemed to play tricks on him: his most successful periods have invariably been followed by stretches of inactivity or failure, and, indeed, the president soon began to show signs of the enormous stress he had been under throughout the year. In December, during a visit to Sweden, Yeltsin appeared weak; he made constant blunders and conducted himself in ways that made those around him wonder whether he was up to the job. In Stockholm, Yeltsin confused Sweden with Finland; he announced, to everyone's surprise, that he would reduce the number of Russian warheads by one-third; he conferred nuclear status on Germany and Japan. He looked as bad as he had before his operation. His team said, "The president is tired," but sometimes they just shrugged their shoulders.

At times during this period Yeltsin was lively and sharp, demonstrating his quick mind and great memory; at others, he began to confuse simple things and to come up with nonsensical statements. Yeltsin had always loved to make impromptu remarks, which often were right on the mark. He loved to play to the public, expecting delight and applause, a quality that had helped him to break the ice with other leaders and to reach agreement or compromise on numerous occasions. But in December his jokes seemed strange, to say the least. Moreover, Yeltsin did not seem to realize how he was coming across and tried to appear majestic. He began to compare himself, in all seriousness, to Peter the Great, and to refer to himself as "Boris the First" (apparently forgetting that Russia had already had Czar Boris the First, Boris Godunov). These gestures and his bumbling behavior were becoming more and more pathetic.

At the end of December, after his return from Sweden, Yeltsin again took to his bed, this time, according to his press service, with "a respiratory illness." It became more than apparent that Yeltsin needed constant backup. Faithful Chernomyrdin provided this. He was loyal to Yeltsin and his family but appeared to be incapable of making decisions independently or thinking strategically. Surveys on December 13-14, 1997, asked, "Who would you vote for if the presidential elections were held next Sunday?" Only 3 percent of respondents favored Chernomyrdin; 4 percent were against all the candidates; 5 percent favored Zhirinovsky; 6 percent, Yeltsin; 7 percent, Luzhkov; 9 percent, Yavlinsky; 10 percent, Nemtsov; 10 percent, Lebed; 11 percent would not vote; 14 percent could not answer; and 20 percent would vote for Zyuganov, who still had the most stable base of support.[38] According to this and other polls, Yeltsin had little chance of winning a third term, but this was no worse than at the start of his last presidential campaign.

The year ended in a mood of dismay. In December, there was an explosion in a mine in the Kuzbass region, and sixty-seven miners died when safety precautions failed. A huge Ruslan aircraft crashed into apartment buildings in Irkutsk, causing many casualties. "Catastrophes are becoming an everyday occurrence. Horror and panic are becoming chronic," wrote the press.[39]

But Russians perceived 1997 as the most stable and least difficult year of the reform period, perhaps because they had neither a war nor elections to contend with. Polls revealed that 46 percent said that they were no worse off in 1997 than in the previous year—a huge increase over the 1996 figure of 27 percent. Only 37 percent felt that they were worse off, again a great improvement over the 1996 figure of 62 percent. Seventeen percent said that 1997 was better for them, an increase from 11 percent in 1996. At the beginning of the year, 49 percent of respondents had said that the president should resign, but by November the figure was down to 21 percent.[40]

As in previous years, however, Russians had little faith that the next year would be better. The feeling that nothing would change had become more widespread, but the fear that things would get worse had decreased. Russia thus finished the year with at least the hope that there would be no radical worsening of the situation. But all the unsolved problems of 1997 carried over into 1998, which was expected be the last relatively calm year before the run-up to the 1999 parliamentary elections and the presidential elections set for 2000.

CHAPTER 11

YELTSIN STRUGGLES FOR A RESURRECTION: 1998

ON FEBRUARY 26, 1998, THE CHERNOMYRDIN GOVERNMENT delivered the long-deferred annual report to the president. Throughout the meeting with the cabinet, Yeltsin's expression was gloomy, and he coughed persistently. In a short speech to his ministers, he demanded to know who was guilty of failing to solve the country's economic problems. Chernomyrdin, imperturbable, gave a speech in the best Soviet tradition, trying to convince everyone that things were going well and that 1997 had marked a breakthrough. He said that the economic indicators of half of the eighty-nine Russian regions showed marked improvement, and that the gross domestic product (GDP) was 1.3 percent higher in January 1998 than in January 1997. He promised that 2000 would be a boom year, with 5 percent economic growth. "The economy has begun to broadcast good news for the first time," Chernomyrdin concluded.[1] Anatoly Chubais and Boris Nemtsov said the same thing, in solidarity with the prime minister. Although the delivery of the government's report took place without incident, it was clear that Russia's economic affairs in no way resembled the cloudless picture Chernomyrdin had painted.

A LULL, THEN A THUNDERCLAP

After the government report, there was a lull, during which Yeltsin became ill once again (with laryngitis, according to his press service). Chernomyrdin was clearly now a powerful political figure with whom all would have to contend, and his position was growing stronger. Everyone took him for Yeltsin's official successor.

Curiously, after Chernomyrdin had redistributed power in the government to his advantage and had deprived Chubais and Nemtsov of their independence, his relations with his young colleagues were no longer characterized by jealousy but by loyalty. He did not seem to treat them as rivals. Instead, he tried to give the impression that the government was working as a coordinated team of like-minded people. The reformers, too, constantly affirmed that they had no real differences with Chernomyrdin, and they were never heard criticizing him. Those close enough to know, however, were aware that a struggle was continuing behind the scenes, and that this time the balance favored the experienced players in Chernomyrdin's group. The prime minister was not openly preparing to run for the presidency, but Yeltsin was clearly weakened, and Chernomyrdin—who suited many people as a moderate and predictable figure—automatically began to be considered the main candidate for president.

Despite the government's triumphant report, the Russian people had not noticed much improvement. Polls asked them to rate the cabinet's work during 1997, and 41 percent called it merely "satisfactory," while 40 percent gave the government the lowest grade, and 10 percent considered its performance "very bad." Only 9 percent thought the cabinet's work "excellent."[2] Opinion polls showed that the public was not ready to demonstrate dissatisfaction actively, but that, after a period of guarded hope during 1997, discontent with the authorities had once again begun to grow. At the end of 1997, 60–69 percent of those polled were not prepared to take part in protest activities, but 17 percent (one person out of six) were predisposed toward openly expressing dissatisfaction with the authorities, and public opinion of the president was very negative.[3] Polls at the start of 1998 showed that 31 percent considered massive workers' demonstrations against the decline of living standards to be possible. Twenty-five percent said that if such demonstrations did take place, they were prepared to participate.[4]

Then Yeltsin loosed a thunderbolt. On March 23, 1998, he dismissed the Chernomyrdin government, and deputy prime ministers Anatoly Chubais and Anatoly Kulikov, inveterate enemies of one another, were fired by special decrees. To some, this dismissal was not unexpected. Rumors of Yeltsin's dissatisfaction with the reformers and pragmatists alike had been circulating since the end of 1997. But previous government failures to manage the economy had not necessarily given Yeltsin cause for dismissal; he had often put up for a long time with comrades-in-arms who could not tackle the country's social and economic questions. As usual, this dismissal was provoked by the president's attempts to solve his own problems. Everyone who had noted the increasing power of Chernomyrdin knew that Yeltsin would not voluntarily hand over the reins of government to him. This would have been entirely out of character for the president, who tolerated neither rivals nor overly strong collaborators.

The decision to dismiss the government had been prepared in the strictest secrecy. Only a small circle of insiders—above all Tatyana Dyachenko and Valentin Yumashev (the president's head of administration)—were informed of the details. The top-secret planning and the way the dismissal was carried out led Kremlin watchers to call it a "presidential coup." The secrecy was meant to forestall resistance. The president had, as usual, struck without much thought for the consequences—without even having chosen a successor for Chernomyrdin. Yeltsin first announced that he himself would assume the duties of the prime minister, but this was unconstitutional. During his meeting with Chernomyrdin, Yeltsin offered him a position in the Duma, even though Chernomyrdin was not a deputy.[5] The decree dismissing the government said that "the president was instructing Chernomyrdin to concentrate on political preparations for the presidential elections in 2000," which implied that the president was charging Chernomyrdin with preparing the campaign of an as-yet-unidentified candidate.[6] The prime minister struck back, saying that he would indeed organize a campaign, but it would be his own. To make matters worse, Yeltsin—having fired Chernomyrdin and provoked an emergency—announced that economic policies would remain the same.

What in fact had precipitated Chernomyrdin's dismissal? Many pointed to the March 1998 Gore-Chernomyrdin meeting in the United States, which had been called a "meeting of future presidents." The head of the foreign intelligence service, Vyacheslav Trubnikov, reportedly had provided Yeltsin with an account of the meeting and even of the private negotiations between the Russian prime minister and the U.S. vice president.[7] And Chernomyrdin's trip to Odessa to meet with the presidents of Ukraine and Moldova had aroused Yeltsin's rage. He had allegedly telephoned the prime minister and asked: "Who sent you there?" This was a sign that Chernomyrdin was on the very edge of the precipice.[8]

Yeltsin and his advisers tried to justify their actions after the fact and to create the impression of advance planning, and many analysts consequently assumed that the president was engaging in Machiavellian intrigues. In fact, Yeltsin's actions had been typically improvised and

239

based on emotions and instincts. As usual, his improvisations fitted in with his plans for political survival.

This time, unlike the March 1997 cabinet reshuffle, Yeltsin really did rearrange the political scene. A partial renewal of the cabinet (as in the previous year) no longer made sense; his actions had to be decisive and sweeping. Moreover, the tasks that Yeltsin faced in the spring of 1998 were also different from those of the previous year. If in 1997 Yeltsin was most worried about social and economic problems, now he was above all concerned with his own power and the question of succession. Yeltsin also wanted to get rid of the influence of the financial heavy hitters, who had established excessively close relations with members of the cabinet. The government shake-up also may have been a way for the president to get over a bout of depression.

Whatever explanations were offered, everyone in Russia knew that Yeltsin had once again decided to assert himself and to affirm his exclusive right to power. The president's step meant that he did not want to have any successors—especially not strong ones. He wanted to be his own successor. This was the main idea of the new Yeltsin "revolution." Many saw this move as the beginning of his presidential campaign. Few people defended the government that had been dismissed, but many reacted negatively to the way Yeltsin had gone about sacking it and to the way he had behaved during the crisis he created. Yavlinsky said: "This is not democracy; it is Byzantium."[9]

THE "YOUNGSTER" PRIME MINISTER: KIRIYENKO

On March 23, 1998, Yeltsin unexpectedly put forward the virtually unknown thirty-five-year-old Sergei Kiriyenko as prime minister. Starting off as a Komsomol leader in Nizhnii Novgorod, Kiriyenko, like many others from the communist youth organization, had learned how to be an entrepreneur and had become the leader of a regional oil company. Boris Nemtsov had brought Kiriyenko with him to Moscow. He was a talented organizer who advanced quickly in government. In November 1997 he had become Russia's fuel and energy minister. Once nominated to be prime minister, he sought the support of various forces by demonstrating his flexibility, finding the right words for all those who could influence the confirmation process in the Duma. To make himself acceptable to the communists, for example, he admitted that he had not thrown out his party card, saying "I am not ashamed that I joined the Communist Party."[10]

Even though Kiriyenko's candidacy arose by chance, it soon became clear that he completely fitted in with Yeltsin's plans. The president was looking for a neutral candidate not linked to any interest group, and Kiriyenko was just such a person. He was also young and energetic, and he could set forth his ideas convincingly. These characteristics had always pleased Yeltsin, who liked young technocrats. But Kiriyenko did not have much national political experience, having spent only about a year in Moscow. Moreover, he had no political base, which made him entirely dependent on the president's support—which also suited Yeltsin. But could a government that was politically weak and dependent on the president and his administration solve the country's problems? Could this untested young man gain the respect of such experienced political hands as Yuri Luzhkov, Mintimir Shaimiyev, Gennady Seleznyov, and Yegor Stroyev? Many had their doubts.

Despite the fact that his choice caused much surprise and opposition, Yeltsin stubbornly announced that he was not about to change his mind. Now it was up to the Duma to confirm the new prime minister, but the Duma voted against Kiriyenko twice. Those most opposed to him were the communists and Yabloko, although each had different reasons. The communists demanded that their members be included in the government. Yabloko leaders did not believe that Kiriyenko could get the country out of its crisis. They felt that he was only a convenient tool in the hands of Yeltsin's immediate circle and that a change in government was the president's means of shifting responsibility for the country's collapse. Before the third and decisive vote, however, Yeltsin brought out his customary tactics of frightening and buying off the Duma. Sergei Shakhrai, a close ally of Yeltsin, warned the deputies that if the Duma did not confirm Kiriyenko, the president would dismiss it and carry out elections according to new rules, such as eliminating party lists; this would be a blow to the parties, particularly the Communist Party and Yabloko.

Before the third vote, Yeltsin gave a televised speech in which he remarked that he had told Pavel Borodin, the head of the Kremlin's powerful household affairs directorate, "to solve the problems of the deputies," but to do so only after the vote.[11] This was both a threat and a bribe: deputies who voted for Kiriyenko would be compensated personally. Kiriyenko was surely right when he said, "The president

241

has a mass of possibilities and experience in knowing how to convince his partners."[12]

The president's arm-twisting tactics were effective, and on April 17 the Duma voted for Kiriyenko, with 251 votes in his favor and 25 against; the rest either did not take a ballot or abstained. The deputies were not ready for a dissolution of parliament and new elections, and they preferred approving the unwanted Kiriyenko to angering the president. Once again, Yeltsin had won.

Kiriyenko's confirmation did not mean that Yeltsin had given over the government to a team of reformers, however, and this was soon confirmed by a new nomination: Yeltsin named Berezovsky acting executive secretary of the Commonwealth of Independent States (CIS). "He is a spirited man. To many, this is unexpected. But I swallow it. This is for the sake of the job," said the president, explaining his choice.[13] Almost simultaneously, at a special session of their board, the directors of the giant power utility Unified Energy Systems of Russia chose Chubais as their chairman, which could not have happened without pressure from the president's team.[14] This could only mean that Yeltsin was still influenced by various groups, and he was trying to set up a new system of counterbalances by getting representatives of the sworn enemy clans into influential posts.

ONEROUS TASKS FOR YELTSIN AND THE KIRIYENKO GOVERNMENT

Kiriyenko quickly formed a new government. The economic ministries were staffed by liberally oriented people. The troika of deputy prime ministers—Nemtsov, Oleg Sysuyev, and Viktor Khristenko, an entirely new figure—had all come from the provinces. The political figures at the foreign affairs ministry and the armed forces, however, were well known from the old cabinet: Defense Minister Igor Sergeyev, Foreign Minister Yevgeny Primakov, and Interior Minister Sergei Stepashin. These appointments confirmed that the president was ready to take risks, to experiment, and to give a free hand to the young reformers in the running of the economy, but that he was not about to change horses in foreign policy and the armed forces ministries. Yeltsin continued his practice of giving much freedom to his prime minister in the economic sphere while keeping the political side of the cabinet subordinate to himself. He reserved the right to decide personnel questions; the prime minister could not choose his own deputies.

Thus Yeltsin's new "revolution," which dragged the country into a political crisis, was complete. Many Western analysts were oddly optimistic about the president's actions, seeing them as proof of his adherence to reforms. But the immediate result was increased instability. Yeltsin lost Chernomyrdin, who had been able to compensate for the president's absences and who reflected the interests of a significant part of the ruling class. Even more significant, Yeltsin had destroyed the old system of counterbalances and alliances that had begun forming in 1993, which to a certain degree had made up for the lack of institutionalized political structures. This system had also helped Yeltsin hold on to his own position. If before the shake-up a good part of the ruling class had considered Yeltsin the leader best able to allow them to pursue their interests, now they were disgruntled with him. He was no longer perceived as a guarantor of stability.

Nor did the president's actions win him any public support. People increasingly saw Yeltsin as an autocrat who cared only about his own problems. Many agreed with the political commentator Aleksandr Bovin, who wrote, "The biggest losses of the political crisis were brought on by its initiator—Yeltsin. I don't rule out that he wanted to make things better. And again, I don't rule out that the change in government was to Russia's benefit. But how the president did what he did, how he behaved before the people who elected him, did a disservice to his image."[15] In fact, after getting rid of those who had backed him, particularly the pragmatists among them, and destroying the network of influence through which he had diffused tensions and avoided taking sides, Yeltsin for the first time found himself without support—indeed, in an even worse position than at the beginning of 1996.

Antagonism between the executive and legislative branches was growing, and all political institutions had been weakened. The Duma had discredited itself by appearing to give in to blackmail and bribes. Russia got a government of technocrats, but one without any political footing of its own—and thus fully dependent on the president and his whims—just when the deepening economic crisis required political will and influence. The president ended up more vulnerable, without anyone to whom he could shift blame for failures. Moreover, by forcing the communist opposition into an agreement, he had managed to discredit it in the eyes of its own electorate. Such weakening of an opposition entirely loyal to the regime was not necessarily a good thing: it could prompt the public to express its discontent by turning to more radical leaders.

Yeltsin's actions split the ruling class into various disoriented groups, each in search of a leader. Our Home Is Russia, which had been a loyal supporter of the president in parliament, was now distanced from Yeltsin. In the parliament, Yeltsin and the government could now look only to Zhirinovsky for help. The fragmentation of the ruling class would make it harder to gather support around a single, moderate candidate, which could open the Kremlin door for a radical, anti-estab-lishment leader. Yeltsin's actions weakened oligarchs of all stripes, and in this respect his revolution was successful. The crisis had revealed, however, that the Russian oligarchs were not nearly as powerful as many had thought. In any case, no single group could now significantly influence the actions of the president and the formation of a new cabinet. But neither was Yeltsin able to escape the embrace of some of the oligarchs: the nominations of Berezovsky and Chubais were evidence of this. Yeltsin's family was unable to free itself from dependence on Berezovsky, which raised many unpleasant questions about their finan-cial activities and their connections.

Moreover, the new members of the cabinet to one degree or another turned out to be linked to certain oligarchical groups: Nemtsov and Kiriyenko to media magnate Vladimir Potanin; Minister of Science and Technology Vladimir Bulgak to Chernomyrdin and the gas lobby; and so on.

Having torn down his former system of support and dependence, Yeltsin found himself backed by only a small circle of people besides the young technocrats. Perhaps Yeltsin was attempting to return to the Gaidar model of breakthrough, but the situation in 1998 differed fundamentally from that in 1991. The balance of power had changed, and, more important, the problems that Russia faced were different. If in 1991 it was necessary to break down the old system, now it was necessary to build a new one—to set right a chaotically developing market economy, to rebuild a social infrastructure, and to strengthen and rationalize the role of the state. Gaidar may have been able to destroy the old economy by revolutionary methods, using the confusion of the old elite to his advantage, but policies for putting the new economy in order could not be carried out without social and political support.

Yeltsin, too, was now in a different situation. In 1991 he could rely on a mass movement, but now he had no support even within his own bureaucracy. Yeltsin should, however, be given credit for the fact that, in his attempt to revive his regime, he had again turned for help to reformers—even though he could have chosen others. Yet every time that Yeltsin gambled on young technocrats without creating the political and structural conditions for their success, he put them in a complicated and perhaps impossible position. Their unavoidable failures brought discredit both to themselves and to their ideas.

Moreover, there can be no doubt that Yeltsin created a new government in 1998 as a means of ensuring his own survival rather than as an instrument of reform. This is what differentiated the Yeltsin of 1998 from the Yeltsin of 1991. Had he been thinking primarily of reforms, he would have tried to create a base of support for the new cabinet, particularly among the democrats and the pragmatists. He would not have humiliated the opposition and created antagonism between the Duma and the executive branch. He would have selected those reformers who already had political experience.

Having won a battle, however, Yeltsin was again full of self-confidence, which led him to say, when he was asked whether he would participate in the next presidential contest: "We shall see." Everyone in Russia took this to be the signal that he had entered the race. Yet he did so under conditions far worse than those he had faced at the beginning of 1996. Now he did not even have what he had then—the support of the main oligarchs. But this was not the first time that Yeltsin had begun a comeback.

The new cabinet was in a difficult position. Kiriyenko was forced to retract the optimistic statements made by Chernomyrdin and Chubais about economic growth. In February 1998, investment was down by 7.6 percent compared with a year before. Thirty percent of all government expenditures went to servicing the state's domestic and foreign debt, compared with just 13 percent in 1996. Kiriyenko pointed out that if those trends continued, by 2003, 70 percent of all federal revenues would go toward servicing the debt. Federal tax revenues amounted to less than 10 billion rubles per month, while budgeted expenditures were 25–30 billion rubles. The wage arrears to state workers for February alone rose by 21 percent.[16] The monthly budget deficit was more than 165 billion rubles.

245

Kiriyenko had three options. The first was to act in the style of Gaidar and Chubais, meaning harshly and decisively—lowering state debts, restructuring the "natural monopolies," and eliminating stagnating enterprises. But the more experienced and influential Chubais had been unable to carry through this option in 1997. For Kiriyenko, doing so would have required the unconditional support of the president, the elite, and at least some part of the population—but there was no hope of this. The second option was to follow the economic path laid out by Chernomyrdin, continuing to put out fires and to balance the interests of various groups against one another while leaving all of the sources of stagnation and crisis untouched. The third option was to implement a new model of reform with a more social emphasis, which would gain the support of the Russian people. This would require not only a great deal of consensus building but also the creation of a new political base for the government, and this was an activity that would never get Yeltsin's nod of approval.

The new government had far less room to maneuver than the previous one. Kiriyenko had to find a solution for the mounting problems, above all by reducing state expenditures—which in turn would cause all Russian citizens to suffer. But the president, worried about the re-election campaign, began to demand more socially oriented policies to avoid increasing popular discontent. This was a dead-end situation for the government. Kiriyenko, to his credit, took entirely reasonable first steps. He was able to get Yeltsin's assent to considerable independence of the presidential administration. His pragmatism began to impress even those who initially had no confidence in him. But this was not enough. In Russia, everyone expected Kiriyenko to fail—and to do so sooner rather than later. After several unsuccessful "liberal revolutions," Russians just did not believe that any new technocrat—especially one who had Yeltsin standing behind him—could succeed.

RUSSIA AGAIN AT THE EDGE OF THE PRECIPICE

Meanwhile, world oil prices dropped drastically. This had a severe impact on the Russian economy, greatly lowering the inflow of hard currency and increasing the budget deficit. Russia's dependency on the export of oil limited its field for maneuver and only deepened the economic crisis.

In May 1998 financial panic struck Russia. Stock prices took a 10-percent dive on May 20. Share prices for Lukoil and Unified Energy Systems dropped to half their October 1997 peaks. The pressure came from the foreign exchange market, and to meet it, the Central Bank raised interest rates sharply. The stock market continued downward, plunging 22 percent in a single week.[17] On May 28 the ruble came under the most serious pressure yet, prompting a Central Bank interest rate rise from 30 percent to 150 percent. This was a desperate and dangerous move, since it increased the cost of government debt service and deepened the budget deficit. But the government considered the alternative—devaluing the ruble—even more dangerous. By triggering a return to high inflation, devaluation could undo all that had been achieved during six years of painful reforms. The cost of living would soar, and investments would slump. Russian leaders were afraid that devaluation would lead to a collapse of confidence in the economy not just among foreign investors but also among Russian citizens.

Between October 1997 and July 1998, the Russian market lost more than 60 percent of its value. The country once more found itself at the precipice, and this time even the optimists lost hope. The crisis meant that growth in the Russian economy, long awaited, was unlikely to materialize anytime soon. Yeltsin, however, persisted in demanding that the government provide for a 2–4 percent economic growth rate.

Working day and night, the Kiriyenko government developed an austerity program. Yeltsin and his new team also went the usual route, trying to borrow from the West, mainly from the IMF, while promising again to collect overdue taxes. Anatoly Chubais was given the responsibility for coordinating Russia's relations with international institutions— an appointment designed to restore the confidence of foreign investors who had begun deserting Russia.[18]

In late May, Russia and the IMF negotiated over what Russia must do to receive the next $670-million disbursement of a three-year, $10-billion loan. The talks were difficult. The IMF officials complained that the Russian government was not making enough progress with reforms. While the negotiations dragged on, the financial crisis deepened. It took pressure from Washington to get the IMF to agree, grudgingly, to release the tranche.

President Bill Clinton stepped in on May 30, attempting to calm turmoil in Russia's financial markets by promising U.S. backing for additional funding from international lending agencies. The IMF had

247

been reluctant to step up its support. Its officials argued that Russia's financial turmoil was not severe enough to require massive external assistance beyond the $670 million it had agreed to release a week before. The IMF and others were concerned that, after the bailout, the Russian government would revert to its previous practice of promising fiscal and other reforms but failing to carry them out.

Meanwhile, the situation was becoming worse. Yeltsin told a special joint session of the cabinet and State Duma leaders on June 23 that Russia's financial situation was alarming, and that radical measures were essential to avert social and political danger. He asked the parliament to back a government rescue program before its summer recess, warning that if the package of laws in the program were not approved, other measures would be taken, and hinting that if the parliament resisted, he might dissolve it. But even Yeltsin admitted that, beyond this combination of measures to boost tax collection and to cut spending, no one had any new ideas.

At the same session, Prime Minister Kiriyenko acknowledged the seriousness of the situation:

> Today we are confronting the results of our hesitancy in the pursuit of reforms, and the problems which, due to political concerns, have been neglected and deferred. We can no longer do so. We need clear-cut, understandable, and practical solutions. . . . The impact of the world financial crisis on the Russian economy has cost us dearly, but it has also shown us how badly the country needs a sober and realistic budget policy, and the ability to live within our means. . . . The foundations of the present aggravation of the crisis were laid in 1995 when, after [the Central Bank] stopped financing the budget deficit, we lacked the courage to make fundamental changes to improve the budget situation. Instead of collecting taxes and cutting spending, we allowed state debt to grow.[19]

The new prime minister did not point out that, for more than a year, he had himself been a member of the very Chernomyrdin government he was criticizing.

In July Russia's finances were again on the brink of disaster. Short-term interest rates climbed back up to 80 percent per year, and a crash of the ruble became an immediate threat. The Kiriyenko government and Yeltsin himself were becoming increasingly desperate. The Finance Ministry's ruble reserves, necessary to pay off maturing Treasury securities, were fast shrinking. The Central Bank reserves of hard currency

248

and gold, used to support the ruble, were nearing $12 billion—down from double that level just one year earlier. Foreign investors were again close to panic. Moscow asked the IMF for urgent assistance, and the IMF—arguing that the Russian plan to cut the budget deficit went only half-way—handed back a list of tough demands, including reduction of the budget deficit from 5.5 percent to 2.0-2.5 percent of GDP.

On July 10 Yeltsin called the leaders of the major industrial nations to enlist their support for additional financial aid for Russia—up to $20 billion, much more than had been sought earlier. Reality in Russia was becoming even more grim. The crisis in Asia, political upheavals in Indonesia, and falling commodity prices triggered and exacerbated Russia's financial crisis, but its real causes were domestic economic failings. Notable among these were weak tax collection and the generally unhealthy state of Russia's finances.[20] The crisis was not just about economics but also about politics and power. Yeltsin's erratic behavior and aimless actions inspired little confidence. His abrupt firing of Chernomyrdin had made matters worse, and the inexperienced Kiriyenko government did not inspire much hope.

ONE MORE CHANCE

The political situation was no better. Among other powerful figures, former Yeltsin allies Boris Berezovsky and Vladimir Gusinsky, who had helped him to win the 1996 elections, demanded a promise from Yeltsin that he would not run for a third term. Radical measures were proposed. One of these was the creation of a temporary State Council, in which leading politicians would participate, to rule the country until new elections were held.

Never before had Yeltsin come under such fierce attack. Even some of his closest supporters appeared to be falling away. One of his longest serving advisers, Sergei Shakhrai, announced his support for the candidacy of Moscow Mayor Luzhkov in the next election. Yeltsin's popularity ratings were lower than ever, and the parliamentary opposition began impeachment proceedings. Some of the oligarchs attempted to form a consultative council, allegedly to help the government, but actually, some analysts suggested, to exploit the situation to serve their own interests. Major players, including the financial clans, influential regional bosses, and representatives of the oil and gas lobby, had decided to use the financial crisis to weaken Yeltsin and to force him to share power with them. Even politicians who were cautious and loyal to Yeltsin, including representatives of Our Home Is Russia, demanded a change in the constitution to give more power to the parliament and the government. But everyone had in mind a new government that would represent major political groups in Russia. Thus the Kiriyenko team was gasping for its life before it had even gotten started.

In July Moscow was full of rumors of a possible coup attempt by senior members of the security forces along the lines of the August 1991 coup that had resulted in Gorbachev's ouster. Political extremists were raising their heads, and it was looking more and more like Yeltsin's last hour.

The economic crisis prompted deepening social unrest. The government's failure to pay wages led to a costly blockade of key railway lines by striking miners. Coal miners came from Siberia to Moscow to demonstrate in front of the White House, where they thumped their helmets on the ground and waved banners with a blunt message for Yeltsin: "Boris—we raised you up. We will remove you!" The collapse of negotiations to privatize Rosneft, one of the largest state-owned oil companies, was the last straw; the revenues it would have raised were vital to public finance.

On July 13 Yeltsin met with leaders of the State Duma to urge them to approve the government stabilization program that was the main condition of the IMF loan. Yeltsin was in an unusually conciliatory mood. He backed away from previous hints that he would dissolve parliament and rule by decrees. He promised there would be no coups, no changes in the constitution, no dissolution of the Duma, and no early elections. To persuade the deputies to support the reform package, Yeltsin hinted that he was not going to run again; he also promised to hold regular round-table meetings of executive and legislative leaders.

On the same day it was announced that Russia would get about $22 billion from the IMF, the World Bank, and Japan. The Clinton administration had been a driving force behind the IMF decisions, pressing the Fund to double the amount of its loan. The IMF imposed as a condition of the new loan that Russia undertake tough structural reforms. Most of the money would be used to strengthen the Central Bank's reserves, which were at about $12 billion. The money would also be used to retire short-term treasury bills, which were commanding interest rates in excess of 100 percent a year. The government was to replace treasury bills with long-term, dollar-denominated loans at lower interest rates. The cash could not be used to pay striking miners or the bankrupt utilities; most of it would actually go to the foreign bankers, who held $16 billion of high-risk, short-term (one to two months' maturity) treasury bills.

On July 17 the Duma approved some of the government's proposed measures, including those that would reduce the tax burden on industry, but it rejected those aimed at shifting the tax burden onto the shoulders of individuals.[21] Yeltsin responded swiftly by decreeing additional tax-raising measures, and he vetoed two tax-cutting laws adopted by the Duma. All these decrees were unconstitutional. The constitution makes the Duma responsible for approving all federal taxes and levies, which must then be ratified by the Federation Council.

After weeks of haggling and admonitions, the IMF at the end of July voted to release the rescue package. It signaled its disquiet at the Duma's recalcitrance, however, by tagging only $4.8 billion of the anticipated $5.6 billion for immediate disbursement.

Meanwhile, some Western analysts began to criticize the logic of the bailouts. Jeffrey Sachs wrote that, "In the past three years, under IMF auspices, Russia has been borrowing short-term funds from abroad to keep a corrupt and mismanaged government afloat," and the new IMF loan "will likely do Russia more harm than good."[22] Sachs charged that "the IMF has become the Typhoid Mary of emerging markets, spreading recessions in country after country," arguing that:

> The IMF lends its client government money to repay foreign investors, with the condition that the government also jack up interest rates, cut the flow of credits to the banking system, and close weak banks. The measures are intended to restore investors' confidence. Instead, they kill the economies and further undermine confidence. It would be much more sensible to keep interest rates moderate and let the economies continue to grow [even if] currencies would lose value and speculators would lose their bets.[23]

In Russia as well, people were skeptical about the new IMF loans, which were perceived to mean merely "a delay of the death penalty" without eliminating the danger of a devaluation.[24] At the end of July, Russia's biggest energy companies, including Lukoil, issued a statement criticizing the government's "unreasonable and irresponsible" economic policy, which risked a social explosion "within the next three months."

The statement attacked the IMF austerity recommendations: "This deepens the crisis, aggravates the social situation, and will lead to the bankruptcy of those few enterprises capable of producing value."[25] These were the companies most squeezed by the government's attempts to raise extra revenues to narrow its budget deficit. Apparently they believed that devaluation would help them more than it would hurt them.

The loans did not, however, save the situation. On August 10 Russian stocks again dropped sharply despite the massive IMF–led bailout. Yields on long-term government debt rose to 130-140 percent, up from 90-110 percent the preceding day. Shares in some companies slipped by as much as 20-25 percent. The Central Bank reported a new sharp drop in foreign exchange reserves. Investors continued to flee, indicating lack of confidence in the government and its ability to overcome the crisis.

The presidential team was increasingly desperate. The state debt was unsustainable. Before the end of the year the government would have to find 113 billion rubles to redeem maturing Russian treasury certificates (GKOs) and bonds (OFZs). It would also have to deal with wage and pension arrears, which had been accumulating since the spring. Revenues were expected to reach no more than 160 billion rubles. Central Bank reserves were falling rapidly, as defense of the ruble cost nearly $0.5 billion a day.[26] When the average yield on GKOs exceeded 100 percent, it became clear that the financial system was on the verge of collapse.

On August 17 the government announced a dramatically new approach to currency policy. The main ingredients of this approach were a ruble exchange rate fluctuating within the new limits of the "currency corridor," set at 6.0-9.5 rubles per dollar; a ninety-day moratorium on international debt service; a halt to trading in GKOs; and restrictions on non-residents' foreign currency transactions. As a result of the new policy, the ruble would be devalued by up to 50 percent.

The team that made these fateful decisions included Kiriyenko, Central Bank Chairman Sergei Dubinin, Finance Minister Mikhail Zadornov, Chubais, and Gaidar (as an advisor). Thus the very people who began the reformist cycle in Russia in 1991—notably Gaidar and Chubais—in August 1998 participated in its calamitous end. It is a sad but unavoidable truth that the reformers who were instrumental in building a market economy in Russia took part in a decision that will for a long time undermine trust in Russia on the part of the West—and in Russia itself—and that has ruined the fragile base of the nascent market economy.

ANOTHER GOVERNMENT RESHUFFLE

W hen the government decided to devalue the currency and to default on its debt, it made the worst of a bad situation. The reformers were cornered. Kiriyenko was forced to deal with the consequences of a crisis that had been building gradually for months, if not years. Most of the economic problems plaguing Russia, including the GKO pyramid, arose and festered during Chernomyrdin's tenure from 1992 to 1998. His government ran large budget deficits, partly the result of excessive spending by the executive branch and partly the result of the legislature's unremitting populism. It financed these deficits with a mountain of high-interest, short-term debt. This deficit financing allowed the government to pursue a tight monetary policy, resulting in low inflation and a stable ruble, but the approach had other, disastrous, consequences. The government was repeatedly forced to issue new securities to repay the maturing ones. Because of economic stagnation and political uncertainty, the rate of interest that the government had to offer to attract investors was increasing sharply, so that government debt was spiraling higher and higher. By mid-1998, interest payments accounted for 34 percent of all federal expenditures. With low or negative real economic growth and serious failures in tax collection, the collapse of the GKO pyramid was only a question of time.

It is worth considering whether the Chernomyrdin government should bear full responsibility for the August disaster or whether Kiriyenko and his team were also partly to blame. Certainly, the latter were guilty of mistakes. The Kiriyenko government was constantly a step or two behind events. In May and June, when the depth of the economic crisis became evident, the reformers could have taken some pre-emptive measures; for instance, they could have partially devalued the ruble. But they evidently hoped that they would succeed in walking the tightrope. Chubais later tried to justify their policy, arguing that they wanted to use all available measures to avoid devaluation. In this, the reformers miscalculated fatally. The monetary decisions made on August 17 demonstrated all too clearly the illusory success of Russian market reform, which had been based entirely on macroeconomic stabilization but had

253

failed to create incentives for economic growth, honest competition, and small-business development.

As a result of the default and devaluation, the reformist government lost credibility, and its reputation at home and abroad suffered. Russia's ability to borrow money in the international market would be affected for a long time. Foreign investment would decrease. The door to the world's markets had closed, and opening it again would take time. Devaluation eradicated the government's major claims to economic success: the stabilization of the ruble and the taming of inflation.

The announcement caused an immediate panic in the domestic financial market. Both the exchange rate and the Russian stock market fell, triggering turmoil. Prices skyrocketed. Kiriyenko and his economic ministers decided to assume personal responsibility for the crisis and informed Yeltsin that they were ready to resign. Yeltsin rejected this offer and ordered Kiriyenko "to continue working to rectify the situation."[27] Rumors and leaks from the Kremlin suggested that Yeltsin had not anticipated the financial collapse and was demoralized. He remained secluded at his dacha outside Moscow and kept silent while the financial crisis escalated. It was evident that he hardly knew what to do.[28]

In a sudden move on Sunday evening, August 23, Yeltsin dismissed Kiriyenko and nominated Chernomyrdin to the post of prime minister. Addressing the nation in a televised speech on August 24, Yeltsin said that he wanted to replace Kiriyenko with Chernomyrdin because Chernomyrdin was better equipped to lead Russia out of the financial crisis. Yeltsin said, "I believe it necessary to bring in Chernomyrdin's experience and weight."

Much more important was the fact that Yeltsin spoke of the need "to ensure the continuity of authority in the year 2000."[29] It created the impression that Yeltsin was thinking about handing over the reins. Sources close to Chernomyrdin were quoted as saying that Yeltsin offered him a guarantee that he would be the Kremlin's official candidate in the next presidential election.[30] Chernomyrdin's nomination went to the Duma for confirmation hearings, which the Duma had one week to take up.

Yeltsin's decision caused alarm in the capital. Russian observers described the situation as a change of parachutes in the midst of a jump.[31] Of course the young reformers knew they were doomed and would soon be forced to resign. Few observers had expected that Yeltsin would fire them right in the middle of the crisis and return to power a former prime minister whom he had dismissed in a most humiliating way—or that Chernomyrdin would accept the offer.

The night they were fired, Kiriyenko and Nemtsov left the White House and met with striking coal miners who had been camped out protesting against government policy. The ousted reformers brought with them a bottle of vodka, but nobody drank. After they left, one miner smashed the vodka bottle against the ground, saying, "They came too late; they should have come earlier and not with vodka, but with concrete proposals."[32] Many Russians expressed sympathy for the ousted reformers, however, considering them victims and scapegoats who were forced to take responsibility for the failures of the previous government.

What were Yeltsin's motives in firing a prime minister he had fought so desperately to get appointed and in returning to power the prime minister he had fired five months earlier? The general perception in Moscow was that it had been Boris Berezovsky and other oligarchs who had orchestrated the removal of the young reformers—in an effort to force on Yeltsin a government beholden to their interests. According to Nemtsov, the government was preparing "to put a number of banks under government administration . . . and to begin bankruptcy procedures against major companies, including oil companies." This, in his view, "could lead to a displacement of the current elite . . . so they decided to replace the government. . . . Indeed, a significant role in influencing the decision to sack Kiriyenko was played by Berezovsky."[33]

This, however, is only a partial and subjective explanation of events. It was true that some of the oligarchs, first and foremost Berezovsky, were unhappy with the reformist government, which had been acting contrary to their interests, and pressed for a more pliant government. However, as became clear later, other oligarchs were successful in co-opting the Kiriyenko government. The decision to include among the August measures a moratorium on international debt service indicates clearly that Kiriyenko's team was set on rescuing several financial tycoons—among them Potanin, Smolensky, Khodorkovsky, and Gusinsky, who were unable to meet August deadlines on payment of external debt. Yavlinsky openly accused the government of trying to save six or seven people at the expense of the entire country's reputation.

The question thus remains: why were the young reformers fired? It is likely that a major reason for Yeltsin's decision to replace them had a personal basis: Kiriyenko could not guarantee Yeltsin and his family personal and financial security if the president resigned. Yeltsin's firing of Chernomyrdin in March had clearly shown that he was at that time thinking of re-election and had decided to get rid of a potential rival. The firing of Kiriyenko in August indicated that Yeltsin was ready to step down and wanted a successor who would guarantee his safety after leaving office—at the end of his term or sooner. The rapid deterioration of Yeltsin's health in August was a decisive factor in his recalling his loyal former prime minister.[34]

STALEMATE

By the end of August, the ruble was in free-fall, leaving Russia's entire economy in limbo. The market plunge was accelerated by the Central Bank's decision on August 27 to stop selling foreign currency indefinitely on a key exchange. Millions of Russians ran to the banks in an attempt to swap rubles for hard currency. Foreign-exchange booths ran out of dollars, the currency Russians relied on in hard times. People waited in line for hours at banks in the hope that someone would be arriving with dollars. The Soviet tradition of black-market currency trading reappeared. With the exchange rate of the ruble in flux, many stores and outdoor markets simply shut down, unable to keep up with the falling currency. Other shops began setting prices arbitrarily—partly as a hedge against a further fall in the ruble, partly to gouge over-eager consumers, who began buying up everything in sight. What had begun as a financial crisis swiftly spun into a broader economic collapse, seriously cutting into the availability of goods and services.

Pensioners and government-sector workers had been suffering for some time because of low or nonexistent pay. The August financial meltdown claimed a new, politically significant victim: Russia's middle and quasi-middle class. Workers who had gone unpaid for months were now joined by a middle class whose savings were eradicated by the banking crisis. The ranks of the losers expanded, and this became a serious threat to the regime.

The financial crisis also increased pre-existing centrifugal trends in the country. Regional leaders were outright defiant. The leader of Yakutia, a Siberian province rich in resources, ordered local gold producers not to send the precious metal to Moscow and to store it instead in the regional government's vaults. The governor of Kaliningrad imposed a state of emergency in his region and refused to send taxes to Moscow.

Meanwhile, Yeltsin's constant absence from Moscow intensified speculation about his imminent resignation. In the United States, the CBS television network reported that Yeltsin had allegedly signed a postdated letter of resignation, which would come into effect once the new prime minister was confirmed in his post. Under such a scenario, Chernomyrdin would take over as interim president until new elections could be called (within three months). According to commentators, Yeltsin was desperately trying to secure a "dignified exit." The entire Moscow establishment was preoccupied with discussion of conditions that would guarantee Yeltsin's status, personal security, and financial future—his own and his family's—as well as immunity from prosecution. The legislature began to prepare a bill that would make the former president a senator for life. Finally, on August 27, the Kremlin, after a long silence, issued an official statement denying that Yeltsin was resigning. Kremlin officials brushed off any suggestions of resignation, but of course no one believed them.

The Russian press was unanimous in its assessment that Yeltsin's days in the Kremlin were numbered.[35] Indeed, there was little remorse to be found in this consensus—for the first time analysts and observers openly expressed their desire to see Yeltsin go. Everyone, even the president's former allies and advisers, now looked upon him as a lame duck. Journalists ridiculed him. Ordinary Russians told jokes about him. Yeltsin himself continued to keep silent. Everything depended on whether he was ready to leave voluntarily, because impeachment would be practically impossible. Only Yeltsin's press secretary stood firm, repeating that the president's resignation had been and continued to be out of the question. But this could not calm the audience. *Komsomolskaya pravda* wrote: "President Yeltsin is still signing decrees, addressing the nation, or participating in military maneuvers. But this does not mean a thing. In essence, at the moment there is no president in Russia. . . . The financial crisis has made the situation drastically worse. The president's week-long silence has shown that he is not in any condition to take responsibility upon himself for getting the state out of crisis."[36] Many feared that the paralysis of power would lead to the rise of a military dictator or the collapse of the country into feuding regional fiefdoms—or that it would provoke the long-suffering population to revolt.

Finally, on August 28, Yeltsin appeared on television and stubbornly pledged to remain in office until the expiration of his term in

257

2000. "I will not go anywhere. I will not resign. I will work as long as the constitution allows," he said.[37] This short pre-recorded interview was the first time Yeltsin had addressed the nation since the onset of the economic crisis. He looked tired and ill. He spoke slowly, with long pauses, and appeared to be struggling to compose his thoughts. Only once—when he dispelled rumors of his resignation—did Yeltsin look the interviewer straight in the eye; at that moment he was his old self, defiant and dangerous. Russians were not persuaded, and predictions continued that Yeltsin would resign after getting sufficient legal and material guarantees.

The communist opposition, which had previously kept a low profile while registering Yeltsin's weakness, decided this was just the right moment to force the president to give up some of his extraordinary powers. The Duma, with active Communist Party participation, drafted economic and political agreements as informal treaties among the Kremlin, the Duma, and the government. These were intended to increase the powers of the parliament and of the cabinet.

The political agreement was in fact a political truce between the executive and the legislature. Both sides pledged to avoid dissolution of the lower chamber or a vote of no confidence in the government until the next parliamentary elections, due in 1999. The agreement also gave the legislators more say in government appointments. One provision called for amending the 1993 constitution to limit the powers of the president.

The economic agreement called for increased government management of the economy, protection of the banking system, and support for industry. The deputies also demanded a mass infusion of rubles. The adoption of the political and economic agreements by the president was the price for confirming Chernomyrdin. Yeltsin, facing a rapidly deteriorating situation and dwindling support, was ready to compromise with parliament.

Chernomyrdin apparently was sure that the Duma, regional elites, and major interest groups would support him. A majority of analysts also thought that Chernomyrdin would be confirmed in the first ballot. But in this case the unexpected happened. Before the first ballot, nearly all factions in the parliament expressed their disapproval of Chernomyrdin's candidacy and the manner in which Yeltsin's entourage had decided to guarantee continuity of power. It was evidently a major shock for the candidate, who had always enjoyed warm relations with the deputies and especially with the communists. What had changed? The answer was evident: previously Chernomyrdin had been supported as a prime minister, as Yeltsin's shadow, but this time the Duma was asked to vote for a possible acting president, and that changed everything. Confirmation of Chernomyrdin as prime minister, at a time when Yeltsin's grasp on power had weakened, would give him enormous leverage in the struggle for the Kremlin. This was the major factor that consolidated deputies who lined up against him. He was not even able to gain the support of the previously loyal oil and gas groups, which adopted a wait-and-see approach. Berezovsky's obvious support for Chernomyrdin's candidacy only increased the negative feelings toward Chernomyrdin. Nobody wanted to have Berezovsky as a gray cardinal.

Chernomyrdin, failing to understand the change in the deputies' moods, made a new mistake: he began to behave with self-assurance and even aggressively tried to dictate his own rules. It only worsened his chances. Until recently Chernomyrdin had been considered a guarantor of stability; now the prospect of his return sparked growing resentment. Not only the communists but also the democratic opposition were against Chernomyrdin. Grigory Yavlinsky said that Yabloko would reject him. "Chernomyrdin is fully responsible for the crisis in Russia. Total, full responsibility," Yavlinsky insisted.[38]

On the Sunday evening before the first ballot, communist leader Gennady Zyuganov, appearing on a widely watched television program, unexpectedly announced that the left opposition had decided not to sign the political agreement. "The document does not guarantee anything to anybody," he said, adding that Yeltsin's family "should convince him to resign and not drag the entire country into the grave with his bony hand."[39] Thus the opposition pulled back from a power-sharing agreement that would have salvaged Chernomyrdin's candidacy. Zhirinovsky and Yavlinsky said that their factions also would not support the agreement. This meant defeat for Chernomyrdin's nomination.

On August 31 the Duma rejected Chernomyrdin by a vote of 251 to 94, with 105 members abstaining (Chernomyrdin needed 226 votes in the 450-seat legislature for his appointment as prime minister to be approved). Chernomyrdin was humbled with the lowest level of support that a prime ministerial nominee has received in Russia's brief history. Yavlinsky, speaking at the Duma session, explained why the democratic opposition had decided to vote against him: "The reasons for making such a decision are that under Chernomyrdin, during the six years he was Prime Minister, an extremely inefficient economic system was created. It was under him that the use of barter and money surrogates reached 85 percent of economic turnover. It was under him that the payment of wages, pensions, and social subsidies stopped and huge unemployment emerged." Yavlinsky added, "The Russian government has one main problem: that there are thieves there."[40]

Chernomyrdin was rejected first of all because the left opposition in the Duma decided that Yeltsin was weaker than ever and that, if they held out, they could get more than the concessions offered in the political agreement. They hoped that they could not only force Yeltsin to propose a candidate more acceptable to them, but also force him to resign.[41] Zyuganov was surely under pressure from his more radical colleagues to push for revenge. In any event, Yeltsin was not ready to retreat, and the communists were now prepared for a confrontation with the president and for the dissolution of the Duma.

The question was whether Yeltsin would crack before the Duma did—whether he had a reserve of will power and toughness. This time Yeltsin did not hesitate and immediately resubmitted the nomination of Chernomyrdin. He apparently hoped that the deputies would surrender as they had done so many times before.

While the politicians were engaged in a tug-of-war, the ruble continued to fall, pushing Russia deeper into economic crisis. Russians were desperately forming lines outside banks trying to withdraw their savings. Many food markets and consumer-goods stores were running out of popular items. Retailers found it increasingly difficult to replenish their inventories. The potential for far worse shortages emerged. Panicked buyers snapped up everything. Supplies of sugar, salt, and cooking oil were dwindling, and the empty shelves were reminiscent of the first difficult days of reform. Food shortages threatened to become a national problem. The prices of almost all goods rose in relation to the free-fall of the Russian ruble, which by September 1 was trading at about 22 rubles to the dollar, or less than one-third its value scarcely a month earlier. Foreign firms were refusing to let Russian companies buy on credit. The edgy feeling of uncertainty prevailed. In September the Russian economy virtually collapsed.

Before the second vote, Chernomyrdin attempted to get the support of the Federation Council, the upper house of the legislature. In his address to the senators, he tried to satisfy everyone—liberals, nationalists, and communists alike. For the communists and nationalists, he offered the introduction of "economic dictatorship", for the industrialists, he made allusions to protectionism; for the reformers and the West, there were hints that he might impose a currency board. He succeeded in getting the senators' support, but that did not help him much with the lower chamber, where the confirmation vote would be held.

On September 7, the Duma rejected Chernomyrdin for the second time—with 273 against and 138 in favor (1 abstention and 38 not present). Not even Yeltsin's offer to install him for a six-month probation-like period softened the opposition. Chernomyrdin had gathered support only from Our Home Is Russia, and from an ultranationalist group led by Zhirinovsky, who this time decided to support the president's candidate. The communists behaved like victors, anticipating that they could succeed in bringing Yeltsin to his knees, though stopping short of demanding their own left-wing cabinet. Indeed, they recognized that it would be suicidal to form a government in such a deep crisis, with no guarantee of success before the parliamentary elections in 1999 and presidential elections in 2000.

FINDING A COMPROMISE CANDIDATE

The pressure was mounting on Yeltsin to choose a new candidate for prime minister—anyone but Chernomyrdin. Other candidates proposed for the job included Yegor Stroyev, a communist and head of the Federation Council; Yuri Luzhkov, mayor of Moscow; and former general Aleksandr Lebed, now governor of Krasnoyarsk. In the midst of the stalemate, Yavlinsky unexpectedly proposed Foreign Minister Yevgeny Primakov, a veteran diplomat and former chief of Russian foreign intelligence. Yavlinsky reasoned that only a candidate perceived as politically neutral and without presidential aspirations could gather the necessary support to become prime minister.

The reclusive Yeltsin heightened this tension by secluding himself in his dacha near Moscow while the Duma waited for his response. The left opposition declared flatly that Chernomyrdin would not be confirmed, no matter how many times Yeltsin submitted his nomination. And although Yeltsin could, according to the constitution, dissolve the Duma and call new elections if his nominee were rejected for the third time, the communists warned that they would begin an impeachment procedure against the president—during which the Duma could not be dissolved. A constitutional crisis and even a direct confrontation seemed to be in the offing. Many in Moscow expected eventually to see tanks in the streets.

Yeltsin faced unpleasant choices. Giving up Chernomyrdin would mean a loss of face and confirm the president's loss of clout. Dissolution of the parliament threatened turmoil and possibly violence. The nomination of a left-wing prime minister would signal a reversal of economic reform, which would only deepen the crisis. The appointment of an authoritarian candidate like Lebed could result in a dictatorship. And if Luzhkov became prime minister, Yeltsin would become a figurehead.

After three days of paralysis and a desperate behind-the-scenes struggle, Yeltsin proposed Yevgeny Primakov as his new candidate for prime minister. The nomination was a clear sign that the president chose to retreat, recognizing that he did not have the strength for confrontation. Nor did he have a political base—his own entourage had split, with part of it now supporting Luzhkov. For the cornered Russian president, Primakov became a last and only resort.

The Duma quickly indicated its readiness to confirm Primakov and on September 11 did so by a large margin: 317 to 63, with 70 abstentions. Thus, after several weeks of paralyzing stalemate, Russia finally got as its new prime minister a survivor from the Soviet past who had succeeded in staying above the fray.

To Western diplomats, Primakov had for quite a long time seemed a thorn in the side. Few among them could forget his role during the 1991 Persian Gulf War, when Gorbachev sent him to try to broker a deal with Iraqi President Saddam Hussein. As foreign minister, Primakov had for two years clashed with Washington on a range of key issues, including Iraq, Bosnia, and the enlargement of NATO. He had, however, at the same time pressed the Russian parliament for ratification of the START-2 arms control treaty.

The reasons for Primakov's overwhelming support in the Duma were clear: he was a moderate pragmatist with no party connections or ties to any oligarchic group. Even more important, he was believed to have no presidential aspirations, which made him acceptable to most political forces. Primakov was a compromise candidate—someone on whom everyone, communists and liberals alike, could agree. His nomination saved the parliament from probable dissolution and Yeltsin from possible impeachment. If Yeltsin did step down, Primakov would assume the presidency for ninety days, until new elections (organized by Primakov himself) could be called.

The biggest test for Primakov, of course, would be his handling of the economy. Much depended on the composition of his government. Primakov offered the post of first deputy prime minister with control of the economy to Yuri Maslyukov, a member of the Communist Party and the former head of Gosplan (the Soviet central planning body). He also proposed Viktor Gerashchenko, a prominent member of the old Soviet elite, as head of the Central Bank.

These and other early appointments discouraged liberals, who accused Primakov of assembling a government with a communist orientation. Grigory Yavlinsky rejected an offer to become a deputy minister because he did not believe he could work with the Primakov team. In fairness, it should be noted that Maslyukov and Gerashchenko were not dinosaurs who dreamed of returning Russia to a command economy. Maslyukov had actually been invited by Kiriyenko to join the reform cabinet because of his thorough knowledge of the military-industrial complex, and he agreed to do so even at the risk of being expelled by the communists. And Gerashchenko had worked in the Central Bank during the Gaidar reform period. But there was justifiable concern that the new pragmatists would rely too much on state regulation, which would be fatal to the fragile market. Nevertheless, Primakov had an extremely short list of candidates from which to choose. Many of the politicians he approached rejected invitations to serve in his cabinet for fear of damaging their own prospects in the upcoming parliamentary and presidential elections.

Primakov's cabinet—a hybrid, like those of Gaidar and Chernomyrdin—included pragmatists with Soviet credentials, moderate technocrats, and one regional governor. The difference was the domination of centrists, the virtual exclusion of liberals, and the fact that, for the first time, former members of the Soviet elite took over responsibility for the economy.

Despite nearly unanimous initial support for Primakov's candidacy, almost all political forces soon took a cautious position toward the new government, which began to work in an atmosphere of general acquiescence rather than full-fledged support. The communists opted for a wait-and-see posture, while the liberals adopted a position of deep distrust verging on open antagonism.

Primakov at once distanced himself from the previous liberal course, adopting a policy that sought to combine a "social-market" approach with increased state involvement in the economy. In his view,

263

"The government should intervene in economic affairs and regulate them, but this is not a return to the administrative and command system."[42]

But the new prime minister was forced to address incompatible tasks simultaneously. To lay the groundwork for economic recovery, he had to cut the budget deficit, allow inefficient banks and enterprises to go bankrupt, and impose tight fiscal discipline. At the same time, he had to pay off all debts and pension and wage arrears—a goal that seemed impossible without printing more money. Moreover, Primakov had to preserve a fragile political truce and to prevent a new crisis of power in the event Yeltsin became incapacitated. This meant demonstrating that he was both tough enough to make painful but necessary economic choices, and reasonable enough to compromise—all at a time when the situation in Russia was so desperate that even a gradual "muddling through" seemed like an optimistic outcome. The creation of Primakov's government signified that the chapter of liberal technocratic reform was over. Russia began a new experiment with more gradual and eclectic solutions—an approach that many liberals forecasted would end (like their own failed experiment) in a fiasco.

For the time being, the country stepped back from the precipice. The most positive thing that could be said of this period was that the worst did not happen. Russia avoided the introduction of a state of emergency or a coup d'état, though these possibilities continued to persist. At the decisive moment, Yeltsin proved that he still had a sense of historic mission. He backed away from a seemingly unavoidable confrontation toward which his deepest instincts had driven him. This was his personal victory over his own ego, pride, and ambitions.

The constitutional crisis continued, however, since there was no consensus in the search for the general rules of the game. Yeltsin emerged from the crisis even weaker than he had been at its start, and few believed that he would be in office at the end of his term in 2000. According to the constitution, Yeltsin should still have been a major player, but in Russia the Yeltsin era seemed over—except that the possibility of yet another outburst by the Russian president could not be completely ruled out.

In the beginning, Primakov tried to avoid making sharp departures and independent decisions. He appeared to be testing the political waters, perhaps recalling how Chernomyrdin's assertiveness had provoked Yeltsin to dismiss him from the same post. Within a few months, however,

264

the prime minister no longer seemed to be looking back for approval from Yeltsin's entourage. He began to act more independently in defining the government's political and economic course and more openly in his attempts to consolidate his own position.

Important sources of power within the country likewise began to express more openly their support for Primakov and his pragmatic policies. Suddenly, for the first time since becoming president, Boris Yeltsin was forced to agree to the curtailing of his vast powers. And Russia, for the first time in its modern history, seemed to have a political system in which the executive branch relied on the support of a parliamentary majority.

Although this partial move toward a system of checks and balances may suggest a maturing of Russian democracy, the process in fact has been driven not by the strengths of the democratic reformers but by the weaknesses of the Russian president. The changes have not been legitimized by law and constitutional amendment and thus remain vulnerable, unstable, and subject to abrupt reversal. Moreover, the immediate practical effect of the changes in the balance of forces benefits not the fragile liberal and democratic forces (who are still unprepared for effective parliamentary struggle) but the leftist opposition—that is, the former communists.

Whether or not Primakov was able to reinvigorate the transition toward liberal democracy and the market economy, his coming to prominence in the fall of 1998 reflected the fact that Russia's elected monarchy had all but exhausted itself. Yeltsin may still have occupied the office, but by the fall of 1998, the superpresidential model that he had tried to construct was revealed for what it was—a hollow shell. The Russian political class had already begun looking for a new model of governance to meet the demands of a new century.

Meanwhile, Primakov continued skillfully navigating the shoals of Russian politics. The key to preserving political stability was his determination to avoid making serious and potentially costly decisions. There were of course limits to such dilatory tactics—especially since it was evident that Primakov could not sidestep at least two formidable challenges in 1999. The first of these was linked to the 1999 budget, approved in late January. This budget was the toughest ever adopted in post-communist Russia—one that Gaidar, Chubais, and Kiriyenko could only dream about in their day. Paradoxically, this stringent budget was overwhelmingly approved by the left majority in the Duma, but it ran into difficulties with critics on the right. The economic situation in Russia was so desperate that even a rather tight budget by Russian standards was not considered tough enough by the International Monetary Fund, whose representatives criticized it as "neither sufficiently ambitious nor realistic." And without IMF support, Russia could not restructure its sovereign debt to other international financial institutions. That in turn could prompt a full-scale default on its external obligations.

This made for Primakov's dilemma. He knew that agreeing to IMF demands for a tighter budget would leave the government without support in parliament and would bring the cabinet under attack from different forces already engaged in the parliamentary campaign. He likewise knew that, by acceding to demands for a nonconfrontational and therefore unrealistic budget, he ran the risk of making Russia a pariah in the international financial community.

A second challenge Primakov would have to confront in 1999 was no less dramatic. To curb the demands of interest groups—especially the regional elites who were pursuing their own policies—the embattled prime minister needed to consolidate his power, to form his own base of support, and to extract greater authority from the ailing president. Primakov knew, however, that the moment he set such a process in motion, he would encounter the dissatisfaction and jealousy of the president as well as the disapproval of other political leaders. The Russian political community would refrain from attacking Primakov only as long as he kept a low profile and demonstrated at every turn that he did not have "excessive ambitions."

This was amply highlighted by the reaction to Primakov's January 26 proposal of a peace pact between the branches of power. In a letter sent to the Duma, the prime minister outlined a proposal under which President Yeltsin would refrain from dissolving the parliament, and the parliament would drop its impeachment hearings and agree not to hold a vote of no confidence in the government. The government, for its part, would also agree not to raise the no-confidence issue before the parliament.

Key political actors immediately reacted negatively to the proposal. Yeltsin was reportedly angered by Primakov's independent action and by the fact that his premier was attempting to curtail his presidential powers. The presidential hopefuls understood that the proposed peace would give Primakov a head start in the presidential race. The major political forces in Russia clearly preferred a weak government with a caretaker prime minister. Unfortunately, such a government could not address the country's myriad problems.

Despite these difficulties and the fact that he repeatedly rejected the idea of his candidacy, by early 1999 Primakov was considered one of the strongest candidates for Yeltsin's job. He usually trailed Zyuganov closely in voter-preference polls (but sometimes even outpaced him) and increasingly led Luzhkov, Lebed, and Yavlinsky as well. But Russian politics resembled Russian roulette: at any moment, the leading candidate could fall from grace into obscurity. Chernomyrdin's dramatic fall was still instructive.

In early 1999, as in previous years, a series of illnesses caused President Yeltsin to disappear from his Kremlin office for extended periods. But Yeltsin's comings and goings had ceased to be a sensation; the country had gotten used to its phantom president. Nonetheless, the president did not want the world to forget about him. The idea of early retirement angered him. Responding to constant demands that he step down, Yeltsin repeatedly asserted that he would neither leave his post nor transfer his powers to Primakov. Even more important, he said that he would not agree to any changes in the constitution—which meant that the crisis of the elected monarchy would continue. Early in 1999 the Russian president went even further: together with Aleksandr Lukashenko, president of Belarus, he declared the creation of a "union-state," a purposefully ambiguous phrase that set off a new wave of speculation in Moscow political circles that Yeltsin might try to become president of the new union-state when his term as president of Russia ended in 2000 (just as Slobodan Milosevic became president of Yugoslavia after his term as president of Serbia expired). The old warrior clearly did not want to leave the scene, and in this respect the atmosphere in Russia continued to resemble that of the late Brezhnev period. Russia still could not free itself from the grip of the past.

Meanwhile, early jostling for the 2000 presidential elections (as well as the 1999 parliamentary elections) had already begun. In the presidential elections, the choice would no longer be between the communist past and a different present. If communist leader Zyuganov were to win the first round of elections, other candidates could beat him in the decisive second round by uniting the anti-communist electorate. Only the failure to consolidate a non-communist base would present the communists with an opportunity to win.

The struggle in Russia still is not between the present and a different future. The country still has no influential forces ready to address its problems with a fundamentally new vision. Some of the leaders said to have the best chance of winning the next presidential elections (Luzhkov and Lebed, for example) are themselves variants of the Yeltsin model of charismatic, authoritarian leadership. This type of leadership caters to the needs of the weakest in society, who expect help from the state. In essence, it is a continuation of Russia's traditional patriarchal approach to social relations.

It is still possible that the "party of power" will unite around the less charismatic Primakov before the next presidential election (which might be before 2000). If that happens, Primakov would have a good chance of winning; and if he did, his presidency would represent a model of cautious leadership with a distinctly bureaucratic character. (To be sure, this scenario depends on Primakov remaining prime minister—by no means a foregone conclusion in Yeltsin's Russia. Were it not for his current position, few knowledgeable observers would consider Primakov a serious presidential contender.)

Grigory Yavlinsky is also expected to play a role in the next presidential contest, competing for Yeltsin's former electorate; his results will demonstrate just how strong liberal and democratic convictions and moods in fact are among Russians.

It is unlikely that any serious new contenders for the presidency will emerge in the near future: the time is too short for any newcomer to stake out a place on the political scene. (Of course, in Russia the unexpected can never be completely ruled out: in September 1998, no one could have predicted that Primakov would become prime minister.) Only in the presidential elections of 2004 will Russia finally get the opportunity to complete the transformation that so far has been carried out mainly by an aging elite that grew up under communism.

CHAPTER 12

BORIS YELTSIN AND THE FUTURE OF DEMOCRACY IN RUSSIA

THE POLITICAL HISTORY OF RUSSIA SINCE 1991 is intimately tied to the personal history of one man: Boris Yeltsin. Although the full account of Yeltsin's place in Russian history will not be written for some years, the record already available—the accomplishments and failures recounted in this book—allows us to make some summary assessments of Yeltsin the man and the president, the political class and regime that grew up around him, and the problems that Russia will need to address in the immediate post-Yeltsin era.

MYTHS AND REALITY

The Russian president is a most contradictory political leader. Indeed, it is difficult today to distinguish reality from the myths—myths that Yeltsin himself has had a hand in creating. It is difficult to identify which of his multiple incarnations reflect his deeper convictions and which were forced on him by the pressure of circumstances. Yeltsin began as a reformer, but he has ended up with a compromised regime that most Russians now describe as a "mafia state" or "criminal-oligarchic capitalism." He has managed an incredible number of personal transformations: first a communist, then a populist, then a liberal and a democrat who destroyed the Soviet empire. He later assumed the role of an elected monarch while his entourage ran the country.

Many controversial interpretations exist of Yeltsin's personality, his character, and his rule. Some see him as an impulsive and risk-seeking leader who has repeatedly plunged his country into crisis. Others, convinced that he is the only one capable of leading Russia through this turbulent transition period, see him as the "father of the nation."

Some note Yeltsin's flexibility and common sense; others, his stubborn-ness and propensity for fights. Still others see him as a dangerous and unpredictable personality—as an impulsive character who ruined Rus-sia's chances for a democratic development. A few, while recognizing his errors and failures, are nevertheless convinced that his presidency has been positive for Russia.

Who, then, is the real Yeltsin? Is he the reformer, whose achieve-ments have not been fully recognized by his countrymen, or is he a demagogue and populist whose only goal has been pure power? What posture reflects his innermost beliefs, if he has any? Perhaps Yeltsin himself would not be able to give an answer, and we can only judge him on the basis of what he has done, how he has done it, and what he has failed to do. Nevertheless, reflecting on Yeltsin's personality and his permanent psychodrama is irresistible—not only because it is intri-guing, but because this drama has profoundly influenced Russian politics throughout the Yeltsin era.

Yeltsin became Russia's leader due to his amazing ability to play two different roles simultaneously: that of rebel and that of adherent to the old system. This dual role drew the allegiance of both the masses and a part of the establishment, enabling him to lead a Russian version of the "revolution from above." Yeltsin fulfilled the urgent demands that were in the air, creating, in the process, an image of himself as a strong ruler, father to his people, and arbiter of the elites. For Yeltsin, power is more important than life itself; he acts as if he were Russia's destiny. He seems to perceive any division of power—any checks on and balances of the executive—as an insult. In this respect, he resembles the "father" of the Russian communist revolution, V. I. Lenin, who wrote: "He who voluntarily shares his influence with anyone is entitled to be left not only without influence but without the right to exist."[1]

Yeltsin took steps that were decidedly out of character for a former member of the Soviet *nomenklatura*. With his efforts to achieve the highest position, his obsession to reach his goals, and his straightforward-ness, Yeltsin was never a typical *apparatchik* for whom conformity is second nature. Even in Soviet times, he stood out from the rest by his behavior: he defied the norms, stirred things up, and shattered stereotypes.

Yeltsin was also more honest than many of his colleagues in the Soviet elite. He could not disguise the fact that he was in a hurry, that he wanted to achieve power immediately, without the long waiting or patient diplomacy at which he was not skilled. He refused to make his way to the top by stepping on each rung of the ladder; he wanted to get there in a single leap. The goal of power justified the means, which Yeltsin chose without much thought. He has never spent time in thinking and preparation; he is a politician by reflex. "When making a decision," Yeltsin himself has written, "I plunge in as if I were diving into water. I do not want to analyze whether this is a virtue or a fault." Others might point out that, in a politician, this clearly is more of a fault. But Yeltsin himself says with approval, "Play to win."[2] This may sometimes be admirable, but in Yeltsin's case it frequently has become an obsession, leading him to disregard the cost of victory. He likes to say, "I act as I see fit"—hardly a statement that describes a democratic leader.[3]

One feature of Yeltsin that raises no arguments is his amazing ability to survive. He has again and again risen from political extinction just when observers were writing his political obituary. The most astonishing of these resurrections was his victory in the presidential elections of 1996, only two or three months after even his own supporters had virtually written him off. His return to politics after a serious heart operation and subsequent illness was no less surprising. And in March 1998, he once again shook all of Russia as he tried to free himself from dependency on the oligarchy and to return to his reformist roots.

Yeltsin cannot live without a sense of urgency and danger. He must sense the approaching crash in order to scale the heights, and he constantly takes risks. He recognizes this himself: "In emergency situations, I am strong. In ordinary situations, I'm sometimes too passive. . . . I can only feel alive in a crisis."[4] To demonstrate that he controls the situation, Yeltsin himself creates tumult just to show that the bear is not sleeping. He hates situations in which nothing is happening; from time to time he himself stages a crisis so he can play his usual role of arbiter. Perhaps at some point Yeltsin began fearing his own physical weakness, and, in trying to look fit, he began to create the impression of movement without thinking much about its purpose. The means have never been important to him.

The question constantly asked by Russians however, is: what is the price of Yeltsin's frequent falls and revivals, and what is the cost of his victories? There have been times when Yeltsin has sounded a wake-up call, but more often he has resembled the proverbial bull in the china shop. Increasingly, observers are inclined to think that Yeltsin's personal victories and his struggle for survival have been at the expense of Russia's democratic development.

During major events—the 1991 liquidation of the USSR and the start of liberal reform, the violent struggle with the parliament in 1993, the beginning of the war in Chechnya in 1994, the cabinet reshuffle in 1997, the attempts to restart the reform engine in 1998, and desperate clinging to power in 1999—Yeltsin has always operated without much of a plan or much consideration of the consequences of his steps. Only later has he seemed to consider what to do next. Thus it is no wonder that he is often taken aback by outcomes he has not anticipated and begins to look around for scapegoats.

There is also little evidence that Yeltsin fully understands the major trends now shaping Russian society, the complexity of this transformation, or the main challenges the country faces. Fortunately, he has made some sensible choices. He has managed to avoid many mistakes urged on him by some of his advisors. He has not exacerbated relations with the West, for example, nor has he encouraged aggressive policies toward neighboring states (notably Ukraine and the Baltics), and he has not curtailed civil rights. He was, moreover, the main driving force behind the collapse of communism and the creation of the new Russian state in 1991-92. Perhaps the personal motives behind Yeltsin's actions—whether his personal antipathy for Gorbachev, or the desire to build a new Russia—are less important than their outcomes. The Russian public is now inclined to be critical of Yeltsin's role even during this early period—arguing that he never looked for the best options and thus pushed the country into the unknown. His attack on the parliament and the Chechen war turned him into a leader who provoked bloodshed and thereby lost his chance to be seen as a political hero.

Thus Yeltsin has rarely resembled the ideal leader capable of making rational choices, selecting optimal solutions, and elaborating successful strategies. Even his loyal supporters are forced to admit this. Certainly he never has had the political vision of Germany's Konrad Adenauer or the ability to forge compromises of Adolfo Suarez, who led Spain to democracy. He lacks the flexibility, the sense of humor, and the spontaneous charm of Poland's President Lech Walesa. He is the opposite of Czech President Václav Havel, for whom morality in politics is all-important.

To Yeltsin's credit, however, he has at some crucial moments chosen to take the reformers' side. In 1996 he decided to go ahead with the elections and fired the Korzhakov team. In 1997 and 1998 he again sided with the young reformers. In the fall of 1998 he decided to retreat, avoiding a potentially disastrous confrontation with the parliament over the appointment of a prime minister. While it would be a gross oversimplification to think that Yeltsin has been motivated solely by his thirst for power, it is also clear that he has chosen reformist goals when doing so could help him to survive.

The main argument offered in Yeltsin's defense by his few remaining supporters is that things might have been even worse with other leaders at the helm. Yeltsin is the kind of leader who, like many other promising politicians, begins by raising too many hopes and ends up being viewed with disappointment as the lesser evil. In Yeltsin's case, however, there is a difference: after failures during the first round of reforms, he managed to get back on his feet and to persuade the country to elect him a second time. This came about not only through political manipulation but also because a majority of the electorate considered that, at that moment, all other potential leaders were less suitable for the job.

Yeltsin's amazing survival in such a turbulent period is not due just to force of will or good luck. He cannot be faulted for a lack of political intuition or for a lack of understanding of human psychology, especially the mentality of the post-Soviet elite. He is a master at employing the tools of power. In 1990-91, against the background of a completely inert Russian political elite, Yeltsin stood out because his personal qualities were needed in the struggle for power. It was really the weaknesses of the many that made his leadership possible. He was more stubborn and clever than his competitors, and he knew how to capture and play on the mood of the population. He also had what a majority of other Russian leaders lacked: a desire to make a breakthrough to a new reality and sufficient courage to follow through on this desire.

Some may ask whether Yeltsin wanted to build a new Russia for all Russians, or only to satisfy his ambition to become a new Peter the Great. Clearly, when he began his reform in 1991 and started a new liberal revolution in 1997, he was thinking more about the problems of the country than about preserving his post in the Kremlin. His moves in 1998-99, however, seem to have been prompted more by a concern for his own survival than by any notion of how to resolve the country's crisis. Moreover, between his reawakenings, Yeltsin spent most of his time engaged in Kremlin intrigues.

273

Yeltsin's behavior has been marked by a personal conviction that he is destined to lead his country into the future. This type of messianic authoritarianism was all too familiar in Russia's past. Yeltsin does not conceal his belief that he alone has the right to exercise leadership; he displays amazement at the notion that anyone else might dare to compete with him. This conviction has contradictory consequences. On some occasions, it reinforces his reformist zeal; at other times, as in Chechnya, it leads him to pursue his goal out of sheer stubbornness and an inability to admit error.

Yet the impression of Yeltsin as a strong personality is at the same time misleading. He is a man with many weaknesses. The memoirs of his assistants reveal a president who suffers from bouts of depression and struggles to extricate himself from them by some familiar and traditional means. These weaknesses, which might be professionally fatal for a Western politician, did not initially cause much concern in Russia; they were even interpreted as manifestations of the Russian character. Only later did it become clear how much Yeltsin's ups and downs, and the ways in which he tried to reinvigorate himself, blunted the president's intuitions and analytical abilities. Gradually, power itself seems to have become his "drug of choice" to help him overcome his depressions. The prospect of losing power might, if he continues to believe that he is Russia's savior, turn him into a tragically destructive force for the country.

How, then, has this man of yesterday, with his provincial background and human weaknesses, often lacking firm convictions and unable to make truly strategic decisions, managed to remain at the top for so long at such a critical time?[5] Yeltsin has proved that he understands the nature of power and the rules of fierce political struggle better than any other contemporary Russian leader. Perhaps more important, he has also struck some invisible chord in Russian society. The first president of Russia embodies the features that ordinary Russians seek in a leader: he has shown himself to be strong, strict, tough and even aggressive, not a talkative busy-body, and not a refined urban intellectual but a typical Russian *muzhik*: a pragmatic peasant man who knows how to get things done—solid, simple, even somewhat crude, with down-to-earth common sense and a disdain for long deliberations and abstract thinking. Of all those on the Russian political scene, he alone has met these criteria.

Yeltsin never was a democrat. During his struggle with Gorbachev, he often spoke of democracy, but once in power he changed his opinion about what Russia needed. This can be seen in his pronouncements after 1993, like the following: "Everyone should be subordinate to one person, who is clearly designated by principle, by law, and by establishment. Roughly speaking, someone in this country should be the chief. That is all."[6]

Having come to power on a democratic wave, Yeltsin quickly got rid of the democrats. Moreover, having taken over the right to speak in the name of reformers, he made things much more difficult for the democrats, who found themselves in a quandary during his rule. If they criticized Yeltsin, they risked being accused of playing into the hands of the communist and nationalist opposition; but if they supported him, they were also supporting a regime with undemocratic elements, nepotism, and absolutism. Yeltsin's tremendous power—and, equally important, the influence of his circle—have accentuated some of his undemocratic characteristics. Those close to him have often encouraged him to think of himself as Czar Boris.

Yeltsin has never been a dogmatic person following a single course. He has often pushed forward stubbornly, trying to achieve his goal without much concern about the means or the effort required. Especially at the beginning, he hated to engage in dialogue with his opponents, and he considered long discussions a waste of time. Yeltsin disdained Gorbachev for having made too many compromises. Russia does not need compromises, he wrote, "but stronger, firmer, even forceful policy."[7] He saw in the process of making concessions only weakness, cowardice, and timidity rather than reasonableness. This does not mean, however, that Yeltsin has never made concessions; he has repeatedly maneuvered, advanced, and retreated—and even sacrificed his closest associates and advisers when circumstances demanded. After 1993, when he dominated the scene, he constantly made deals—first with one group, then with another. The proponent of confrontation became a master of intrigue and behind-the-scenes games. In 1997 he once again did the unexpected, beginning a dialogue with his most hated rivals, the communists. It was again a game, but through this game he managed to avert a new confrontation. It is true that a year later—in his new tug-of-war with the opposition—he was forced to surrender. Yet it was and remains unclear whether his surrender meant a victory for the left-wing forces; it may be that both protagonists needed each other to survive.

Beginning in early 1995, having cleared the field of dangerous opponents, Yeltsin began to take more of a wait-and-see course—acting only when a real or imagined threat to his position appeared, observing the scene with constant vigilance, and sometimes demonstrating amazing restraint with regard to the political intrigues around him. Yeltsin's resort to this tactic is largely due to his physical condition, as he now lacks the strength for open struggle and for day-by-day management of the country. Yet he has not stopped fighting; in early 1998 he demonstrated that he was still on the alert and ready to strike any time he felt in danger, underestimated, or not respected. By late fall 1998, however, it had become clear that the old warrior could not fight on forever. Yeltsin's "resurrection technique"—reshuffling the government and making new promises—long ago stopped impressing Russians. Most believe that he is no longer up to the task of governing and are convinced that he has become Russia's main problem. No one wants to have to endure Yeltsin's next resurrection.

The principal myth about Yeltsin—one that he personally helped to create—portrays him as the "destroyer of communism." There is no doubt that Yeltsin helped bring down the former system, yet his decisions helped keep in power significant numbers of the former ruling class. It would also be a mistake to overestimate the depth of Yeltsin's anti-communism and his hostility toward the old system. Yeltsin never openly revolted against communism: he was one of its cogs, and he suffered greatly in 1987 when he was ostracized by the Party because of his excessive ambitions. Yeltsin's approach to the communist system, as to the post-communist system, has been entirely pragmatic and based mostly on his assessment of its potential to fulfill his ambition for power.

Yeltsin's regime has been woven of paradoxes and conflicts that have been the means of his political survival. Thus, although the first Russian president formally has had colossal powers—surpassing those of some general secretaries of the Communist Party—he often has lacked the means to carry out his decisions. Inclined by nature toward populism, he has been deprived of mass support and of the resources needed to implement his authoritarian habits. A leader whose ideal governing structure is a "pyramid of power," he has had to operate in an epoch of ambiguity, pluralism, and disintegration. A politician who hates compromises, he has had to maneuver by making deals and concessions.

Having declared his goal to be the building of democracy, he has headed a system that many consider to be oligarchic or patrimonial. Having won in democratic elections, he has been forced to preserve his power by relying on clans.

THE SUPERPRESIDENTIAL REGIME

Russia's current system of presidential power took shape under the strong influence of Yeltsin's personality and ambitions. The Russian system of governance became, recalling Ralph Waldo Emerson's description of another time and place, "the lengthened shadow of one man."[8] Yeltsin meant to create a pure pyramid of power that needed no other institutions, but the emergence of pluralism in society and among the political elite and a devolution of power from the center to the regions precluded this design. The "presidential pyramid" is in fact a false front for a ramshackle regime built of ill-fitting parts. Although the president has tremendous prerogatives, he is in reality much weaker than the last of the communist leaders because he lacks the resources to realize his prerogatives. Paradoxically, the Russian presidency has been preserved only through a further devolution of power to the regions and to the oligarchic groups in exchange for their loyalty to the boss. The superpresidential regime is unstable; it can drift in any direction—changing its rhetoric, its goals, its balance of forces, and its major ideas. Fluidity, uncertainty, and ambiguity are becoming the mode of the regime's survival.

Until recently, Yeltsin's principal instrument for exercising power was his hands-on manipulation of his followers. Yeltsin resolved conflicts among the main interest groups, maintaining a balance on the Russian political scene. This mechanism is no longer effective, however—both because the president has become physically unfit to keep it going and because the complexity of challenges facing Russia demands a different way of responding. No arbiter can be effective without the main political actors' recognition and readiness to comply with his decisions. During the events of 1998, political actors began to show their fatigue with Yeltsin, and the system nearly stopped functioning. Some influential groups have already set their sights on the transition to a regime headed by a weak, symbolic leader.

The growing role of the wealthy has led many analysts to expect Russia to experience oligarchic rule. Russian oligarchs, however, are not yet the decisive political force that some assume them to be; they are dependent on the state and on their access to state resources. Yeltsin can still change the balance of forces, as he did in 1998, when he delivered a blow to the oligarchic networks by toppling the Chernomyrdin government. The financial crisis of the fall of 1998 left the previously powerful political and economic actors in the position of pleading with the state and the West to help them survive. In case of danger to himself in a struggle with the business elite or with the state apparatus, the president—Yeltsin or his successor—may address the nation and seek support from at least part of the population. The natural monopolies—Gazprom, the transportation system, and the Unified Electric System—do have a great deal of power, but they are trying to keep a low profile, at least for the time being.

Favorites other than the oligarchs (family members, for example) might also play a crucial role in the regime, as they did during the 1996 presidential campaign. They do not, however, dominate the political scene. The chief executive needs them in times of trouble, but he might just as readily diminish their role or shuffle his favorites from time to time when he feels strong. Another salient feature of Russia's presidential regime is the role of liberal technocrats who have been brought into the ruling structures by the president (for instance, in the creation of the Kiriyenko government).

Russia's presidential regime, with its strong patrimonial features, worked during the revolutionary stage of the transformation—helping to destroy the previous system, although not always in the most effective way. It is not, however, suitable for the challenges of the current stage of development. Yeltsin has tried to survive by shuffling personnel, resorting to emergency methods, and creating tension. Although such "stabilizing by destabilizing" or power sharing with loyal interest groups in exchange for their support has in the past temporarily solved some tactical problems for Yeltsin, it will in the end contribute to systemic decay or even bring about a collapse of the whole construct.

Numerous centers of power, which are now the principal channels for harmonizing the interests of the elite groups, have become an important element of Yeltsin's regime. These include the presidential administration, the Security Council, the Defense Council, and "the group of four" (the president, the prime minister, and the heads of the Duma and Federation Council). In some respects, the system of power that evolved around Yeltsin recalls the Soviet system: the president plays the role of the general secretary of the Communist Party; the presidential administration, the role of the Central Committee; and the government, the role of its Soviet counterpart, responsible only for managing the economy. Bureaucratic pluralism—a multiplicity of elite groups and their mutual patron-client relationships—is an important factor in the survival of the Russian system of government. Most interest groups were formed on the basis of previous sectoral, administrative, and regional divisions— such as, respectively, the fuel and energy lobby, the "power" structures, and regional groups, most notably the Moscow group.

The results of the 1996-97 regional elections are likely to lead to further decentralization of political and economic power. The multiplicity of the subjects of the Russian Federation and their inequality enable the federal center to manipulate them, especially when there are conflicts between rich, revenue-generating regions and poor, subsidy-receiving regions; between agrarian regions and industrial regions; or between ethnic republics and ethnic Russian entities. The federal center, however, continues to decline in power. The federal authorities no longer have sufficient financial resources to buy the loyalty of all of the regions; nor do they have their former powers of coercion. Moscow's invasion of Chechnya was a watershed event in the relations of the constituent parts of the Russian Federation with the center: the limits of the center's influence and capability became clear to all regional leaders.

There already are signs that the constitutional and political structure created during Yeltsin's time in power—designed expressly to ensure domination by the leader and his close entourage—no longer corresponds to reality. Any lapse in the president's command automatically creates a vacuum of power, and the system contains no efficient mechanism for the transfer of power. A superpresidential regime is incompatible with the loose federation that Russia may be becoming, and it prevents further state-building and the emergence of a viable party system. It creates no incentives for the development of civil society, tries to freeze an unstable situation, and produces permanent conflicts that it cannot resolve. The nominally democratic procedures used to preserve the status quo have only discredited democracy.

THE RUSSIAN POLITICAL CLASS AND ITS FAILURE TO IMPLANT DEMOCRACY

At the end of the 1980s, no one could have predicted that an independent Russian state would emerge with a vocal political opposition, relative freedom of the press, open political struggle, and no constraints on entrepreneurial activity. The influence of ideology has for the first time been removed from Russian life. Social and individual autonomy have increased. The old mechanisms and structures have been broken beyond repair. Russia's transformation would now be difficult, perhaps impossible, to reverse.

There is, however, a powerful legacy not only of the Soviet past but also of the pre-communist past. The old Soviet system is still evident in the preservation of a large part of the old ruling class and in the persistence of the patronage system. Some features of Soviet life linger on, though they have assumed new aspects. Communism merged politics and economics through an administrative mechanism for managing the economy. Today, a similar merger of power and private property has occurred: wealthy financiers and entrepreneurs have been included in the highest levels of government, and, more insidiously, are able to further their interests by manipulating the levers of political power and corrupt officials.

A rift between society and the state was characteristic of communism, and much of society continues to view the government as its antagonist. While the old state has been destroyed, its backbone, the bureaucracy, has been preserved and revitalized. It now sustains the viability of the new system even as it remains the repository of old habits and traditions. Russia's bureaucracy quickly privatized all the functions of the state. Compared with the corruption of Russia's current bureaucracy, however, the Soviet *apparat* looks innocent.[9] Hasty privatization of state property is taking place, even though most new private businesses cannot function without government support. Russian politics and economics are still defined by government domination—a Russian and Soviet tradition—but the government has been deprived of some of its previous powers. It cannot limit the spread of corruption, and it cannot guarantee order or the security of its citizens. The government has difficulty performing its basic functions, such as collecting revenue, providing social welfare, or reforming its armed forces. Thus in some spheres of Russian life one sees too much state involvement and interference; in others, the state is utterly helpless.

The pre-Soviet roots of current Russian developments are also evident in the personification of power, the succession struggle at the top, the greediness of clans, court politics, nepotism, patrimonialism, and the all-absorbing thirst for power demonstrated by political leaders. The establishment of the superpresidency in Russia follows the country's historic Byzantine model of governance, in which all power is concentrated in a leader—czar, general secretary, president—who becomes the symbol of the nation and its arbiter as well as its main guarantor of stability. In contrast to the Western political tradition, in which power is based on rational ideas and institutions, the Byzantine tradition has always invested power with something sacred, irrational, and personal. The ruler was considered to be simultaneously the father of the nation, omnipotent, and not responsible to any other person or institution. Stalin was the full embodiment of the Byzantine tradition of irrationality, mystery, and contempt for society. In the late communist period, such patrimonialism acquired a collectivist ideological covering and the features of bureaucratic authoritarianism. Yeltsin, with a sense of messianism, seems to have wanted to restore elements of the old patrimonialism as he tried to become a supreme arbiter in the Weberian sense. The past still keeps Russia in its embrace, and it is too early to reach final conclusions as to the ultimate interaction of continuity and change. Yeltsin's attempt to behave like a new Czar Boris while society patiently waits for the state to solve its problems is a legacy of the past. But Russia is gradually understanding the need to finally close the Byzantine chapter of its history.

The Russian transformation has featured revolution, crisis, collapse, stagnation, adaptation, stabilization, revival, reform, and counter-reform, with sometimes astonishing results. The most revolutionary methods, such as the destruction of the old state and liquidation of its mainspring, the Communist Party, became the means of preservation of at least that part of the old ruling class that was able to throw off ideological and institutional limits.[10]

Yet it would be a mistake to view the current Russian ruling class as identical to the old *nomenklatura*. After 1991, it included

281

representatives of other segments of society, notably the intelligent-sia. Paradoxically, this infusion of new blood often strengthened the authoritarian or oligarchic tendencies: the newcomers, who had no *nomenklatura* roots and no social support, tried to survive by relying on a charismatic leader, on bureaucratic connections, or on force. During these years, members of the intelligentsia—Gennady Bur-bulis, Yegor Gaidar, Aleksandr Shokhin, Sergei Shakhrai, Yuri Baturin, Georgy Satarov, Aleksandr Livshits, Sergei Filatov, Anatoly Chubais, and others—surrounded Yeltsin, shaped his rhetoric, and formulated his decisions. They became the new superelite, without giving much evidence of being paragons of democratic principle. And if not even those who call themselves democrats actively follow democratic rules, what can be expected of other members of the political establishment? The Russian establishment pushed the old leaders out of power, concentrated power and property in its own hands, and completely changed the organizing principles of the sys-tem. The members of this new establishment are now becoming conservatives who seek to secure their own hold on power.

Although the term *nomenklatura* is still used as a weapon in inter-clan struggle, the old communist ruling class has long since been dispersed, and fragments of it have acquired new interests. Yesterday's *nomenklatura*—or, more accurately, that part of it able to adapt to the new reality—is the most solid shield against a return to the Soviet past. Even the communist pragmatists have thrown off the fundamental principles of their previous existence, such as respect for hierarchy, party collectivism, and blind adherence to dogma.

The political system passed through a stage of "*nomenklatura* liberalization" in 1991-93, when the transfer of power from Soviet structures to the newly formed Russian central authorities took place, accompanied by fragmentation of the old *nomenklatura*. At that time, Russia had options for its further development; during those years, for the first time, there was a possibility of following the path of democratization.

In 1991-92 Yeltsin and his group had considerable influence, and broad segments of society supported democratic and liberal ideas. The part of the old ruling class that came to power was ready, though reluctant, to follow democratic rules. Revanchist groups had been weakened, and the traditional power structures were dispirited.

Ordinary Russians were ready to make considerable sacrifices in the name of a more prosperous and democratic future. The international environment was generally favorable for the implementation of both market and democratic reforms. Although Russia's historic legacy and its lack of democratic traditions were a hindrance, democracy is rarely built in an environment that is already democratic; more usually it is built by non-democrats and representatives of the old regime.

Unfortunately, however, the chance for steady democratic development in Russia was not seized. A number of obstacles complicated Russian reforms, including the simultaneous needs to establish a new state, to create a new multinational identity, to carry out democratic and economic reforms, to overcome the legacy of seven decades of Soviet communism, and to find a new place in the world. The absence of traditions of private property and of the freedom of the individual slowed the formation of civil society. Russia's position as the successor to the Soviet Union's superpower status, including its powerful military-industrial complex and its hegemonic ambitions—as well as a strand of messianic sentiment among both the elite and the masses—were also obstacles to successful transformation.

There was yet another obstacle to reform, one linked to Russia's vast oil and gas resources. A powerful gas and oil lobby, oriented toward moderate reform and cooperation with the outside world, emerged during Gorbachev's *perestroika* and the first stage of Yeltsin's rule. This group helped to diminish the role of its rival, the military-industrial sector, and to begin the initial stage of market reforms. As early as 1993-94, however, the gas and oil sector, with its huge export-earnings possibilities, began to block further reform. In some senses, the gas and oil sector helped those in power preserve stability[11]; an example is Gazprom's assistance to the government in paying off pension and wage arrears. But stabilization of this sort simply postpones necessary restructuring.

The main blame for the failures of reform lies with the ruling elite of Russia—with the bureaucrats at the top, and even more with the intellectual elite among the politicians, who could have used the confusion in the ranks of the old elite to persuade Yeltsin to move in a democratic direction. Instead, however, they deliberately rejected the building of strong institutions, the adoption of a new constitution, and the creation of checks and balances. The liberals preferred a model of authoritarian transformation through the presidential "pyramid" of power. Having chosen "civilized authoritarianism," they hoped to influence Yeltsin and to push him in the desired directions. They also hoped that, through him, they could preserve their own influence. Thus the reformers themselves were not ready to constrain the activities of the highest executive. Yeltsin, too, bears responsibility for missing great opportunities. He made the final decisions, and he was the person who to a great extent determined the nature of the current regime.

Russia's political elite failed to achieve consensus about the desired course of future development and the country's political structure. Time after time, compromises among the major political players reflected only their own current interests. Moreover, the constitution of 1993 was the result of the victory of, and domination by, a single political force; it could not be considered a social contract between power and society. The absence of any pact among the major political forces in Russia meant that the members of Yeltsin's group were not constrained by the necessity of taking into account numerous interests; they could be more radical in their reform agenda. As subsequent events demonstrated, however, the lack of compromise on the crucial issues of development in Russia was, in the end, a major stumbling block on the way to reform.

The Russian public, however, should not be perceived as totally undemocratic. The majority of the population has shown remarkable receptivity to liberal ideas and democratic processes. Research conducted in 1996 showed that most individuals were "pro-private" rather than "pro-statist"; most were receptive to the idea of a market economy and desirous of a Western standard of living. Most Russians—between 67 percent and 98 percent of all social groups—agreed on the following fundamental principles: that the life of an individual is more important than any other consideration; that the laws should apply to everyone, from the president to the ordinary citizen; that property rights are inviolable; that the main human rights are the right to life, to the defense of one's honor, and to the freedom of the individual; and that freedom is as necessary to Russians as it is to people in the West. Communist or imperial ideology appealed to only about 15-20 percent of the population.[12]

Thus one must ask why no consensus has yet united a significant portion of the population around liberal-democratic values. The answer is that interpretations of these values vary, and there is little agreement on how to implement them. As a result, even among people who support liberal-democratic values, one person in five is ready to sacrifice one or another human right in the name of ensuring order and stability.

Another reason is that it has been traditional in Russian society for people to tie their hopes to those in power; the state has always been the engine of change. But in Russia today, the ruling class is busy using its position and its powers to further its own interests. This is not simply due to the Soviet legacy: elites in the former communist states of Central and Eastern Europe and in some former Soviet republics have proved that they can limit their appetites and ambitions. Vitauskas Brazauskas, the former leader of the Lithuanian Communist Party, for example, has contributed greatly to the strengthening of democracy in his country. It is true that Russia has avoided the worst scenarios and has succeeded in establishing at least a moderate path of reform; the reforms achieved can be compared favorably with developments in some other former Soviet republics. But Russia could have done much better if the ruling group, which was dominated by those who consider themselves democrats and liberals, had not decided to choose for Russia an "enlightened super-presidentialism," giving to one person with rather vague ideas and without strong democratic convictions the entire responsibility for Russia and its reforms.

Although the formation of a liberal economy in Russia is a crucial change, the process is still riddled with problems.[13] Purely formal indicators that measure progress in market reform do not always reflect true qualitative changes in economic relations. An example is privatization. The real scorecard is not the number of enterprises that have been bought up, but who manages them. Most of the privatized enterprises do not yet have responsible owners. The act of privatization alone cannot change unprofitable enterprises into profitable ones. In the majority of cases, the enterprises have been acquired by their former managers, who have become all-powerful owners of the "newly private" enterprise.[14] In most instances, the former directors have made few changes in the way they manage their enterprises.[15] Slowly, however, the role of the

285

investors is becoming stronger; they have a greater stake in the new rules of the game. The new class of entrepreneurs is beginning to understand that profiteering and criminal forms of enrichment are ultimately destructive, as they do not encourage real stabilization, guarantee income, or promote conditions that would forestall calls for a new redistribution of wealth.

PROSPECTS FOR RUSSIAN DEMOCRACY

Russia's progress toward democracy is the issue that most divides optimists and pessimists. The optimists argue that Russia has moved in important ways toward liberal democracy, while the pessimists are convinced that Russia is reverting to its traditional mechanisms of power and that it will always be a threat to democratic civilization. Both sides can find evidence to support their views in today's Russia.

Russian and Western analysts who study Russia's current transformation also differ in their assessments. The Westerners tend to be less pessimistic, while the Russians are usually more skeptical and even bitter, concentrating on the failures and the miscalculations. It is difficult for those who live in Russia to be unbiased and unemotional: they lament the lost opportunities and look for someone to blame for the failures. Pointing out that Europe and America also went through their own difficult historical transformations offers Russians little comfort; it is hard for them to become reconciled to not seeing a civilized and prosperous Russia in their own lifetimes.

Western observers, for their part, have the luxury of looking at Russia from a distance and in a larger context. It is indeed true that, compared with the not-so-distant communist past, Russia has made enormous progress toward democracy since 1991. Many have been surprised at how eagerly the Russian political class has rushed to hold elections, which are characterized by voter turnouts so high that they put Western societies to shame. Electoral politics in Russia is not, however, an outcome of the establishment's democratic convictions but of the fact that the establishment is divided and weak and cannot hold on to power by any other means.[16] It is true that elections provide a society with the possibility of making choices, but Russians have had very limited options—and those not always reassuring ones. Although most Russians vote, they expect nothing from those they elect. Both sides—

the voters and those who are elected—seem to be playing a game, silently agreeing to preserve the status quo and to leave each other in peace. Such elections prompt widespread cynicism, discrediting the concept of democracy.

Compared with the communist period, the Russian people today clearly enjoy far greater freedom of expression and more secure human rights. Yeltsin has not encroached on individual rights and freedoms as he might have done, given the enormous powers he has acquired as president. On the other hand, he has done little to expand or to strengthen the guarantees of these freedoms. Russia's press did experience a relatively short period of real freedom; now, however, the mass media have again become partisan and increasingly dependent on the state or on financial groups. And freedom of expression loses much of its significance if public opinion matters little to those in power. Even more troubling is the fact that basic civil rights established by the Russian constitution—such as the rights to education, work, and compensation for work are constantly violated. Although significant repression is largely absent, Russian citizens are defenseless before the governing structures, especially in the provinces, where semi-authoritarian ruling groups have risen to power. Moreover, the conflict in Chechnya demonstrated that the Russian government is not constrained from resorting to the barbaric destruction of its citizens at will.

After the October 1993 clash between parliament and the presidency, limits were placed on the parliament's independence. Because the political parties no longer influence the formation of the government, their role and power have diminished. Decision making has moved behind the scenes, which increases the role of interest groups at the expense of political parties. The public appears to be disappointed with existing parties, but the government has no interest in establishing mechanisms through which the will of the public can be expressed. Political pluralism in Russia remains weak.[17]

Russia also lacks a system of institutional checks and balances. This has led to the overpersonalization of politics and to a political structure that is far too dependent on the characteristics, capabilities, and physical condition of the leader. The weakness of Russia's judicial system and the fragility of the rule of law are likewise troubling. Many members of the elite appear to have used public service as a vehicle for advancing their own private business interests. That they do not seem to care how their actions are viewed by ordinary citizens is perhaps an indication of how well their escape routes already have been prepared.

One essential characteristic of a mature democracy is the regularity and peacefulness of its political transitions. Although post-communist Russia has yet to experience its first presidential succession, there are some signs that leaders across the political spectrum understand the necessity of what a number of political scientists call a "democratic bargain"—a pact to preclude revenge-seeking after the current leader departs. Nonetheless, there is no guarantee that the next Russian leader will not turn to the typical Soviet model of survival through a new "cleansing" and reversal of the previous leader's legacy. The absence of any guarantee that members of today's ruling class will continue to have "life after power" means that the ruling team may not be willing to give up its place voluntarily.

Most Russians today would be happy to hear their country described as a democracy. In fact, Russia's present regime does not neatly fit any of the familiar categories. It is a regime in which elements of democracy, authoritarianism, post-totalitarianism, delegative democracy, bureaucratic-authoritarianism, oligarchic rule, sultanism, and even monarchy are intertwined in sometimes strange ways. A high degree of decentralization and the asymmetry of the Russian Federation also increase the patchwork character of Russia's political system. The system uses democratic rhetoric, but it often turns to statist and populist ideas. Its leadership is produced by elections, but the leader's rule is highly personal and arbitrary, without legal constraints. The ruling elite is drawn from among family members, friends of the family, or groups that anticipate some reward (as is characteristic of sultanism), and citizen participation in the decision-making process is minimal.

Russia's current political regime likewise resembles what Guillermo O'Donnell (writing about Latin America) calls "delegative democracy": a system that "rest[s] on the premises that whoever wins election to the presidency is thereby entitled to govern as he or she sees fit."[18] The model is also a useful description of the Russian regime, which combines omnipotence and impotence, although it is unlikely that the outcome in Russia will be a Latin American-style military coup. There is also no reason to expect that a Russian delegative democracy, combined with a powerless patrimonialism, will endure once Yeltsin is gone.

Russia's elected presidency has a democratic legitimacy. With its immense powers, however, it is absolutely independent of any political force. In combination with Yeltsin's autocratic style of governance, it thus resembles a monarchy—but an "elected monarchy" is political nonsense.[19] This nonsense, however, reflects the trap in which Russia finds itself. On the one hand, it seems unable to overcome the tradition of personal rule, while on the other hand, the political regime is required to take on some democratic procedures because it has exhausted all other means of retaining power. The incompatibility of the main features of such a regime makes it highly unstable and fragile; its structure is itself a source of major conflicts.

AFTER YELTSIN

Some observers predict that Russia is likely to face upheavals in the future for a variety of reasons. It is not clear how Russia will adapt to Chechen independence. The timing and direction of new economic reforms is uncertain. The old system of social welfare has collapsed, and a new one has yet to be created. Some democratic mechanisms have been discredited. Although deals have been made within the ruling circles, political struggle may become more violent, particularly as there still is no mechanism for a secure transition to the post-Yeltsin period. The limits of the population's patience are another major concern. The political and economic crisis of summer–fall 1998 has demonstrated that many of the alleged successes of the post-communist transformation were illusory.

At the same time, several factors facilitate the survival of the system. The existence of multiple interest groups within the government plays a stabilizing role—both in the center and in the regions. The sheer diversity of these groups gives rise to constant tensions, but it also facilitates the leadership's ability to maneuver and balance among the groups. The same is true of the number of components of the federation: if, instead of eighty-nine, there were only fifteen or twenty powerful players, the center would have a far more difficult time dealing with them. The multiplicity of conflicts—at all levels, both in Moscow and in the provinces—prevents the emergence of a bipolar confrontation either within society or between the population and the regime. The system of under-the-counter deals also acts as a temporary force for stability, since it facilitates the conciliation of interests. In the provinces, the ruling group is armed with both carrots and sticks and can offer

289

bribes to groups (such as the miners) that might cause trouble for the authorities.

Some Russian analysts predict that the regions might attempt to unite against the Moscow elites and to create a new center. Others see a possibility that the weakness of the government might give rise to an extremist scenario, such as the imposition of a dictatorship by a group connected with the upper levels of power.

The present regime, however, already includes representatives of nearly all political orientations: liberals, pragmatists, conservatives, left-wingers, right-wingers, great-power Russia advocates, and others. The "Russian pact" invented by the Yeltsin team drew opposition figures into the ruling structure on a personal basis rather than as representatives of defined political ideologies or forces. This device separated them from obligations to their original constituencies or political parties. Thus the diversity within the ranks of the ruling structure complicates the formation of any serious opposition to the regime.

Ironically, the new Communist Party, with its anti-Yeltsin rhetoric (which helps it preserve influence with a socialism-oriented audience), has become an important factor in generating support for the current regime among the segment of the population that fears that communist rule would be much worse. The Communist Party controls a certain disaffected segment of society, but the fact that it simultaneously bargains with the regime makes it less of a threat to the authorities and prevents the emergence of even more extreme groups.

The current degree of stability in Russia is to a great extent the result of the disillusionment and enormous fatigue of a people who prefer not to risk losing what they have. This type of stability is not, however, grounded in economic growth and trust of democratic institutions; it therefore results in stagnation.

Tensions may arise in Russia in the future from numerous sources, including the ineffectiveness of the system itself and the leadership's attempt to hold power by any means; a further decline in the standard of living of a substantial part of the population; an increase in social differentiation; a broadening of the rift between the authorities and society; or the inability of the establishment to agree on basic questions of further development. The lack of a viable opposition could increase the possibility of spontaneous anti-government actions, or it could push the frustrated masses to support a new charismatic leader. Those who yearn for such a leader gravitate toward General Aleksandr Lebed. The authorities' reliance on the elite military and police units may increase the danger of skirmishes between them and the regular military in the event of social upheaval. But the army and other power institutions thus far have shown no inclination to become an independent political force.

Official corruption and rampant crime have become sources of constant public dissatisfaction with the authorities. The criminalization of regional elites is even more dangerous; generally too weak to stand on their own, these elites may find themselves dominated by criminal organizations. Such developments in several localities where natural gas and petroleum are produced already provide evidence of the serious threat posed by criminal activities in the regions.

An enormous stratum of the population has lost out in the new Russia. Millions of the "forgotten ... at the bottom of the economic pyramid," to use Franklin D. Roosevelt's image,[20] might choose to take protest actions to force changes at the top, but the success of such protests would require a confluence of several factors: a charismatic leader; consolidation of the socially active elements of society, notably the miners or workers in the transportation and energy sectors, with support from others in the industrial areas; support for the protest movement by elements within the government; and the neutrality or sympathy of the army and other power structures. To have an impact on all of Russia, such protest would require some triggering event. It would also have to happen in Moscow or in another big city. The likelihood of such a course of events presently seems rather low, but the possibility of mass protest and destabilization of the system cannot be completely ruled out. Frustration persists in Russian society, creating grounds for constant tension, and no one can tell what spark might set off an explosion.

A number of Russia's characteristics are incompatible with traditional liberalism and democracy. These characteristics include: a legacy of more than seventy years of communism, preceded by absolutism; the absence of a developed middle class and of a tradition of individualism, both of which are necessary for the emergence of a politically responsible electorate; the greediness of the political establishment; and the society's weariness with constant experiments and its disillusionment with Yeltsin's attempts at liberal reform. To this list should be added the existence of ethnic-national and regional conflicts, continuing social and economic stagnation, and Russia's superpower complexes. People are looking for a leader who can create and maintain order until the process

291

of state building is completed. All of these factors impede Russia's progress along a democratic path.

But the rebirth of authoritarianism faces impediments as well: the inability of any political group to gain a monopoly of power for any length of time; the center's lack of effective instruments for establishing authoritarian rule, such as a loyal and capable army and an efficient bureaucracy; the regional divisions of the country and the strengthening of provincial elites who do not wish to see the reestablishment of central control over their affairs; the development of a mixed federal system with elements of confederation; and the evolution of social self-reliance. There is a growing awareness, moreover, that authoritarianism would mean isolation, and that Russia cannot survive if it remains outside the world community. There are signs of oligarchic trends as well, but it is unlikely that any narrow interest group will be able to control Russia or its leader in the near term.

The first several years of the post-Yeltsin era will be a crucial test of the political maturity of the Russian political elite. Sooner or later, the key interest groups must reach a compromise on constitutional changes necessary to restructure the regime. Many forces would prefer to strengthen the role of the government and to eliminate all behind-the-scenes power over the decision-making process; to increase the role of the parliament, making it more responsible; and to strengthen the role of the judiciary. Such an evolution toward a presidential-parliamentary system is feasible, but it would require agreement among the major players.

If the current Russian elite fails to change the rules of the game that have become a source of political instability and national decline, then this will become the task of the next political generation. Will that generation produce aggressive politicians with inferiority complexes and an overwhelming urge to satisfy their own appetites—or will it produce statesmen with a sense of mission, national pride, and the desire to build a new and civilized Russia? Much depends on the next generation's ability to learn from the mistakes of its predecessors in the Yeltsin era.

NOTES

CHAPTER ONE

THE FAREWELL TO COMMUNISM AND THE FIRST REFORMS: 1989-92

1. Juan J. Linz and Alfred Stepan called it "decay-induced post-totalitarianism." Juan J. Linz and Alfred Stepan, *Problems of Democratic Transition and Consolidation: Southern Europe, South America, and Post-Communist Europe* (Baltimore and London: Johns Hopkins University Press, 1996), p. 375.
2. T. H. Rigby, "Reconceptualizing the Soviet System," in *Developments in Soviet and Post-Soviet Politics,* ed. Stephen White, Alex Pravda, and Zvi Gitelman (Durham, N.C.: Duke University Press, 1992), p. 314.
3. Ibid.
4. Linz and Stepan, *Problems of Democratic Transition and Consolidation,* p. 369.
5. A new election law, approved in December 1988, provided for a choice of candidates in local and national-level elections.
6. *Vyedomosti* (Register) of the Congress of People's Deputies of the RSFSR and the Supreme Soviet of the RSFSR, 1990, no. 2, art. 22.
7. Yeltsin himself pushed events in this direction in 1990-91, promising sovereignty to Russia's autonomous republics and calling on them "to take all the sovereignty you can swallow," as he sought their support in his struggle with Gorbachev. Gail W. Lapidus and Edward W. Walker, "Nationalism, Regionalism, and Federalism: Center-Periphery Relations in Post-communist Russia," in *The New Russia,* ed. Gail W. Lapidus (Boulder, Colo.: Westview Press, 1994), p. 81.
8. Boris Yeltsin, *The Struggle for Russia* (New York: Times Books, 1994), p. 17.
9. Ibid., p. 22.
10. Ibid., p. 38.
11. Ibid., p. 39.
12. Ibid., p. 37.
13. Aristotle, *Politics,* Book V.
14. The plotters included KGB Chairman Vladimir Kryuchkov; Interior Minister Boris Pugo; Speaker of the Soviet parliament Anatoly Lukyanov; Soviet Vice President Gennady Yanayev; Oleg Shenin, who was in charge of Communist Party personnel and organizational affairs; Politburo member Oleg Baklanov; and Prime Minister Valentin Pavlov.
15. Yeltsin, *The Struggle for Russia,* p. 106.
16. Leonid Kravchuk played an active role at the meeting. Sergei Shakhrai, a member of the Russian team during the negotiations, said later, "If the Belarussian side was ready to consider the option of a new union,

then the Ukrainian delegation came to say goodbye. I would call the role of Ukraine not decisive, but fateful." Sergei Shakhrai, "Soyuz byl ubit informatsionnym virusom anti-SSSR" (The Union was killed by an anti-USSR information virus), *Nezavisimaya gazeta*, December 10, 1996.

17. Yeltsin, *The Struggle for Russia*, p. 114.

18. Ibid., p. 113.

19. Boris Yeltsin, *Zapiski prezidenta* (Notes of the president) (Moscow: Ogonyok, 1994), p. 152.

20. Alexander Dallin, "Causes of the Collapse of the USSR," *Post-Soviet Affairs*, vol. 8, no. 4 (Fall 1992), p. 296.

21. The first democratic groups that emerged in the Soviet Union in 1988 included Memorial, Democratic *Perestroika*, and *Perestroika*-88. In January 1990, the electoral bloc DemRossiya was formed to prepare for the election of the new Russian legislature. It was turned into a movement in October 1990 and became a major political base for Yeltsin.

22. George Bernard Shaw, *Major Barbara*.

23. Vyacheslav Kostikov, *Roman s prezidentom* (Adventures with the president) (Moscow: Vagrius, 1997), p. 271.

24. Since Gorbachev's first attempts to replace political personnel at various levels in the Soviet power structure, renewal of the elite that both ran and profited from the Soviet system has been limited. Although estimates of elite renewal in the post-communist era vary, it generally appears that 50–60 percent of the Soviet-era political elite in Russia has persisted in leadership positions in the wake of the USSR's collapse. Moreover, more than half of the new holders of elite positions were previously deputies and other influential people who had held positions just below the top rank of the *nomenklatura* in the late Soviet period. At least one-third of the former Party *nomenklatura* continued to occupy leading positions in political affairs, while another third continued to hold high-ranking positions in the economic branches of the Russian government. Only 22 percent of post-communist political officials at the federal level were truly newcomers to political life. See Natalya S. Ershova, "Transformatsiya pravyashchei elity Rossii" (The transformation of the Russian ruling elite), in *Kuda idyot Rossiya* (Whither Russia?), ed. Tatyana Zaslavskaya and Yelena Arutyunian (Moscow: Interpraks, 1994), pp. 154–55.

25. Edward Gonzales, "Up the ladder leading to the market," *Izvestiya*, October 10, 1991.

26. The idea of the presidential pyramid was not new; it had first been presented by Boris Gidaspov, one of the leading representatives of the Communist Party *nomenklatura*, at the 28th party congress in 1990. Gidaspov had suggested sending presidential representatives to the provinces to strengthen the center's control of provincial organs. The idea had then been rejected with considerable indignation by the democratic bloc, and Yeltsin himself strongly condemned it. But after coming to power, he revived it and began to consider the presidential pyramid an

ideal form of power for Russia, or for himself. The ideological justification for this pyramid structure was promulgated by the State Council,
headed by Gennady Burbulis, one of the most active advocates of strong
presidential rule.

27. Linz and Stepan, *Problems of Democratic Transition and Consolidation*,
p. 392.

28. The formal structure of hierarchical relations within the Russian Federation distinguishes among several types of administrative-territorial
units, each with somewhat different rights: it includes twenty-one
republics (all ethnically defined areas), forty-nine oblasts, seven krais,
the federal cities of Moscow and St. Petersburg, the Jewish autonomous
oblast, and ten autonomous okrugs. The oblasts, krais, and okrugs
became known as regions.

29. In the spring of 1991 Yeltsin had already begun his attempts to find
"an intellectual prime minister with his own program." The candidacies
of Mikhail Bocharov, chairman of the Supreme Economic Council, Yuri
Ryzhov, member of the Presidential Council, and economists Stanislav
Shatalin, Yevgeny Yasin, and Grigory Yavlinsky were discussed at the
time. Yeltsin, *The Struggle for Russia*, p. 124.

30. *Komsomolskaya pravda*, August 21, 1992.

31. Yeltsin, *The Struggle for Russia*, p. 125.

32. Ibid., p. 146.

33. Burbulis became first deputy prime minister, and in practice he was
acting prime minister. Shokhin was labor minister before he was elevated to deputy prime minister. Other members of the new government
from Gaidar's team were Anatoly Chubais, privatization minister and
chairman of the State Committee on the Management of State Property;
Pyotr Aven, foreign economic relations minister; Ella Pamfilova, social
affairs minister; Vladimir Lopukhin, fuel and energy minister; and Boris
Saltykov, science minister. Gaidar soon ceded the post of minister of
economics to Andrei Nechayev.

34. Boris Yeltsin, "Faster reforms are Russia's only chance," *Izvestiya*,
November 2, 1991.

35. Ibid.

36. Richard E. Ericson, "The Russian Economy since Independence," in
Lapidus, *The New Russia*, pp. 35–36.

37. Ibid., p. 36.

38. *Nezavisimaya gazeta*, November 20, 1991.

39. Gaidar was criticized for insufficient radicalism as well. The democrat
Leonid Batkin wrote, "Gaidar's program is failing. Not because it is
radical, but because it is not radical enough." Leonid Batkin, "Rossiya
na pereputye" (Russia at the crossroads), *Literaturnaya gazeta*, December
11, 1991.

40. Anders Åslund, *How Russia Became a Market Economy* (Washington, D.C.:
Brookings Institution, 1995), p. 68.

41. *Nezavisimaya gazeta*, February 15, 1992. The situation in the Russian military-industrial complex, which employed about 9 million people, was even more critical. The lack of a well-thought-out program for its transformation threatened to turn the military-industrial complex into a hotbed of opposition to reform. Matters were also complicated by the government's inability to decide whether to issue its own currency, as many at first expected, or rather to try to preserve a unified economic space within the former Soviet Union. The struggle to overcome the budget deficit became senseless in view of the deficits of other former republics, the maintenance of open borders, and unchecked issuances by the other republics' central banks. In these circumstances, opinions about the possibility of successful economic reform in Russia were divided. Yavlinsky, Shatalin, and their supporters warned that the reforms could not succeed without a unified economic space. Academician Vyacheslav Tikhonov and other isolationists felt reform would be possible if the CIS ceased to exist.

42. At the end of 1992 the president and his "gray cardinal" would part ways. Yeltsin wrote in his memoirs, "I won't hide the fact that at a certain point I began to feel an irrational weariness with this man." Yeltsin, *The Struggle for Russia*, p. 159. The president apparently could not forgive Burbulis his attempt to share the limelight and to take public credit as chief strategist; this was an incursion onto the president's own turf. Burbulis refrained for a long time from criticizing his former patron, but in October 1994 he declared, "We need to rid the country of this uncertainty and help the President of Russia to end his presidency in a worthy manner." *Literaturnaya gazeta*, October 12, 1994.

43. Yeltsin first offered the post of vice president to Burbulis, who accepted the offer; one can only imagine how Burbulis felt when the boss then stated that he preferred Rutskoi. This situation may have been the real root of the eventual hatred between Burbulis and Rutskoi.

44. Yeltsin, *The Struggle for Russia*, p. 31.

45. Ibid., p. 32.

CHAPTER TWO

THE NEW POLITICAL SPECTER: 1992

1. Yuri Afanasyev, "Power and society," *Moskovskiye novosti*, March 8, 1992.

2. Gavriil Popov, the democrat and then mayor of Moscow, outlined some of the reasons for the rift between Yeltsin and the democrats: "Yeltsin's attitude toward the democrats is explained by the fact that the democrats themselves did not choose him as their leader and moreover because the democrats were incapable of getting him elected to the post of chairman of the Supreme Soviet of Russia." Gavriil Popov, "August '91," *Izvestiya*, August 21, 1992.

3. *Literaturnaya gazeta*, February 19, 1992.

4. Alexander Dallin, "Where Have All the Flowers Gone?" in *The New Russia*, ed. Gail W. Lapidus (Boulder, Colo.: Westview Press, 1994), p. 247.

5. Yeltsin's ratings in the opinion polls began to fall. In January 1992, 37 percent of those polled said they were disappointed with Yeltsin, while just 8 percent said their feelings toward him had improved. *Literaturnaya gazeta*, January 25, 1992.

6. "From the very beginning," Anders Åslund has written, "many political and institutional problems hampered the implementation of radical reform in Russia. Significant political problems included the problematic relationship between Yeltsin and his government, the weakness of Burbulis, the political isolation and lack of credibility of the government, and the absence of official government programs. Institutional problems proved overwhelming." Anders Åslund, *How Russia Became a Market Economy* (Washington, D.C.: Brookings Institution, 1995), p. 86.

7. The Russian Constitutional Court, however, ruled that these provisions violated the federal constitution.

8. Gail W. Lapidus and Edward W. Walker, "Nationalism, Regionalism, and Federalism: Center-Periphery Relations in Post-Communist Russia," in Lapidus, ed., *The New Russia*, p. 94.

9. The conflict between the two branches of power in Russia was not unique; however, in Poland, for example, neither the widely known animosity of President Lech Walesa toward the parliament (the Sejm) nor his tendency to issue decrees ever resulted in the dissolution of the Sejm. Frances Millard, *The Anatomy of the New Poland* (Cambridge: Cambridge University Press,1994), p. 147.

10. Boris Yeltsin, *The Struggle for Russia* (New York: Times Books, 1994), p. 166.

11. Information provided by the Epicenter research institution, headed by Grigory Yavlinsky, in 1992.

12. Richard Ericson, "The Russian Economy since Independence," in Lapidus, ed., *The New Russia*, p. 56.

13. See the interview with Nikolai Shmelyov in *Literaturnaya gazeta*, October 15, 1992.

14. Gennady Burbulis, "The majority did not understand us," *Nezavisimaya gazeta*, November 6, 1996.

15. Grzegorz W. Kolodko, "Russia Should Put Its People First," *New York Times*, July 7, 1998.

16. Ericson, "The Russian Economy since Independence," p. 56.

17. Ibid., p. 57.

18. Åslund, *How Russia Became a Market Economy*, p. 171.

19. Ibid., p. 297.

20. Aleksandr Nekipelov, "Reformy provotsirovali korruptsiyu" (Reforms provoked corruption), *Nezavisimaya gazeta*, "NG-stsenarii" (NG scenarios), no. 2, February 13, 1997.

21. Aleksandr Nekipelov, *Ocherki po ekonomike postkommunizma* (Notes on post-communist economics) (Moscow: Nauka, 1996). Privatization in other former communist states, however, also ended in the same way: "This is the so-called 'spontaneous privatization' process, with the help of which many *apparatchik* and bureaucrat beneficiaries of the old regime found legal opportunities to establish a solid economic basis for themselves within the framework of the new regime, capitalizing on their control . . . over state property and access to information." Laszlo Urban, "Hungarian Transition from a Public Chosen Perspective," in *Post-communist Transition: Emerging Pluralism in Hungary*, ed. András Bozóki, András Körösényi, and George Schöpflin (London: Pinter Publishers, New York: St. Martin's Press, 1992), p. 93.

22. Georgi Khizha was a former enterprise director and a typical representative of the military-industrial complex; he was a deputy prime minister from May 1992 to May 1993. Viktor Chernomyrdin had begun his career as a member of the provincial communist *apparat* and was appointed director of the Orenburg gas enterprise. In the Soviet period he was a deputy minister, then minister for the gas industry between 1982 and 1989, and a member of the Central Committee of the Communist Party of the Soviet Union. He joined the Russian government from his position as the head of the powerful state gas production industry Gazprom. Yeltsin appointed him deputy prime minister with responsibility for the energy sector. Vladimir Shumeiko had previously been director of an enterprise in Krasnodar. In 1991 he became the deputy chairman of the Supreme Soviet under Khasbulatov.

23. *Izvestiya*, June 5, 1992.

24. *Izvestiya*, June 27, 1992. Valery Zorkin, chairman of the Constitutional Court, did a great deal to ensure that the court would be a genuinely independent institution. In the end, however, he could not avoid partisanship, and in the ensuing struggle for power he took the side of the parliament. Yeltsin dissolved the Constitutional Court in September 1993.

25. *Izvestiya*, June 18, 1992.

26. *Izvestiya*, August 17, 1992.

27. *Literaturnaya gazeta*, May 24, 1992.

28. *Sovietskaya Rossiya*, August 4, 1992.

29. *Nezavisimaya gazeta*, July 29, 1992.

30. *Literaturnaya gazeta*, August 26, 1992.

31. Vyacheslav Kostikov, *Roman s prezidentom* (Adventures with the president) (Moscow: Vagrius, 1997), p. 121.

32. Vladimir Pavlenko, a member of Gaidar's government staff, found that in 1992 the government issued approximately 300 decrees extending various privileges and preferences to certain enterprises and regions. "Over the course of 1992, the government behaved as if it were in a pre-election situation and rushed to enlist the support, not of a large segment of the electorate, but of the bureaucracy, of agrarian and oil

generals, and of regional administrators." Vladimir Pavlenko, "Govern ment of reform at the feeding trough," *Moskovskiye novosti*, April 18, 1993.

33. According to independent observers, Gaidar's government was even more influenced by lobby groups than was Chernomyrdin's cabinet. Yakov Pappe, "The industrial lobby and the government of Russia (1992-1996)," *Pro et Contra*, no. 1, 1996, p. 62.

34. Data provided by the Academy of Sciences Institute of Sociology, 1992.

CHAPTER THREE

A BREWING CONFLICT WITH PARLIAMENT: 1992-93

1. Yeltsin reportedly called Gaidar immediately afterward to tell him not to take this seriously.
2. *Izvestiya*, October 6, 1992.
3. Ibid.
4. Polling data from the Institute of the Sociology of Parliamentarianism, prepared for the November 2, 1993, "Itogi" NTV news program.
5. *Izvestiya*, December 11, 1992.
6. The president personally asked Gaidar not to take part in the contest for the post of prime minister.
7. Not long before this, Yeltsin had firmly said he would not "hand over" Gaidar. But Gaidar himself, understanding the hopelessness of his situation, proposed that the post of prime minister be given to the Russian ambassador to France, Yuri Ryzhov. And when Ryzhov refused, Gaidar proposed the director of AvtoVAZ, one of Russia's industrial giants, Vladimir Kadannikov.
8. Vladimir Kadannikov, director of AvtoVAZ, was a convinced pragmatist. Later on, Yeltsin asked him to join the cabinet as one of the deputy prime ministers, but Kadannikov was not particularly successful in that position. Vladimir Shumeiko, because of his flexibility and pragmatism, enjoyed a dizzying rise to the top, moving from the position of a provincial manager to the post of deputy speaker, and then to that of deputy prime minister. Later, with Yeltsin's help, Shumeiko became speaker of the Federation Council from 1993 to 1995. After that, he remained in the president's circle and worked at organizing a pro-presidential political movement. See Boris Yeltsin, *Zapiski prezidenta* (Notes of the president) (Moscow: Ogonyok, 1994), p. 298.
9. Boris Yeltsin, *The Struggle for Russia* (New York: Times Books, 1994), p. 198.
10. Ibid., p. 199.
11. Ibid., p. 200.
12. Ibid., p. 200.

13. Ibid., p. 201.

14. Ibid., p. 158.

15. Yegor Gaidar, "Dismissal," *Moskovskiye novosti*, November 10-17, 1996.

16. *Obshchaya gazeta*, October 15, 1996.

17. *Nezavisimaya gazeta*, November 6, 1996.

18. See interview with Yegor Gaidar in *Komsomolskaya pravda*, January 22, 1992.

19. *Moskovskiye novosti*, April 26–May 2, 1992.

20. Alexander Dallin, "Causes of Collapse of the USSR, "*Post-Soviet Affairs*, vol. 8, no. 4 (1992), p. 253.

21. Robert Dahl, "Why All Democratic Countries Have Mixed Economies," in *Democratic Community*, ed. John Chapman and Ian Shapiro (New York: New York University Press, 1993), p. 282.

22. John Grey, "Hayek, Spontaneous Order and the Post-Communist Societies in Transition," in *Contending with Hayek: On Liberalism, Spontaneous Order and the Post-Communist Societies in Transition*, ed. Christoph Frei and Robert Nef (Bern: Peter Lang AG, Europaischer Verlag der Wissenschaften, 1994), p. 40. The same conception, together with theories of Milton Friedman, the famous University of Chicago economist, inspired the "Chicago boys"—the team of liberal reformers who performed the "shock therapy" in Chile after General Augusto Pinochet seized power in 1973. "The results of the 'shock' were dramatic," wrote Philip O'Brien. Only gradual change of the economic policy and the softening of authoritarian rule helped to overcome the economic crisis that Chile faced in the 1970s. Philip O'Brien, "Authoritarianism and the New Orthodoxy: The Political Economy of the Chilean Regime, 1973-1982," in *Generals in Retreat: The Crisis of Military Rule in Latin America*, ed. Philip O'Brien and Paul Cammack (Manchester: Manchester University Press, 1985), pp. 157–70.

23. *Nezavisimaya gazeta*, February 19, 1993.

24. "Russian President Boris Yeltsin privately has called on Western leaders for support if he takes 'emergency measures' to preserve his rule in the bitter contests for power in a hostile parliament." *Chicago Tribune*, March 11, 1993. "Mr. Helmut Kohl, the German Chancellor, has written Western leaders urging their support for Yeltsin in his constitutional struggle." *Financial Times*, March 10, 1993.

25. Although Zorkin and Stepankov were nominated to their posts with the support of Yeltsin, they both soon spoke out against his attempts to concentrate power in his hands.

26. One point in the agreement that was especially distasteful to the deputies was that, although the Congress would be dismissed, its members would retain all their privileges until their terms of office expired in 1996. They interpreted this provision as a bribe.

27. Yeltsin had planned to dissolve the parliament in case of an impeachment proceeding. Aleksandr Korzhakov wrote that, "on the balconies

of the parliament building, they decided to place canisters with chloro-picrin 'chemical irritant substances.' The officers who occupied the balconies were ready to release the substance on command." Korzhakov also wrote that "Boris Nikolayevich [Yeltsin] confirmed the plan without hesitation." Aleksandr Korzhakov, *Ot rassveta do zakata* (From dawn to dusk) (Moscow: Interbook, 1997), p. 159.

28. Altai and Kranoyarsk krais, Orenburg, Ulyanovsk, Volgograd, and some other large cities failed to support the president.

29. "If one takes into account the size of the vote on each question, then the electorate voted for the status quo. Yes, it supported the president, but it was against any kind of change, including the proposal for early elections. The president certainly did not receive a mandate to take harsh or otherwise revolutionary measures." *Moskovskiye novosti*, May 2–8, 1993.

30. Oleg Soskovets would soon join the group formed by Aleksandr Korzhakov, chief of Yeltsin's security service, and would become one of the candidates for the position of prime minister, which seriously complicated his relations with Chernomyrdin. Soskovets served as a channel through which some groups from the military-industrial complex and conservative managers could express their interests to the government.

31. *Polityka*, 1993, no. 4, p. 3.

32. *Moskovskiye novosti*, August 14–21, 1993.

33. On March 13, 1993, representatives of eighteen of the then twenty republics initialed a Treaty of Federation with Moscow. A separate agreement was signed by representatives of the oblasts and krais that same week, followed by a third treaty with the autonomous okrugs. Then, on March 31, 1993, the three treaties were signed into law as the Federation Treaty, which eased some of the tensions between Moscow and the Federation subjects but left many critical issues unresolved.

34. *Vyek*, August 16, 1993.

35. The adoption of the new draft constitution took place in the Kremlin Palace, with 4,333 deputies from the regions and social organizations present. Seventy-four percent of them approved the draft, but almost all of the heads of republics abstained from voting. Even those who approved the draft, however, expected to amend it at the sessions of their respective legislative bodies.

CHAPTER FOUR

YELTSIN'S SEPTEMBER "REVOLUTION" AND THE ELECTIONS: 1993-94

1. Yeltsin was forced to suspend Deputy Prime Minister Vladimir Shumeiko and Vice President Aleksandr Rutskoi, who had become the constant "heroes" of corruption scandals. Rutskoi was forbidden to carry out even his ceremonial functions.

2. *Süddeutsche Zeitung*, October 3, 1993.

3. "Is a coup possible?" *Sovietskaya Rossiya*, August 5, 1993.

4. Vyacheslav Kostikov, *Roman s prezidentom* (Adventures with the president) (Moscow: Vagrius, 1997), p. 186.

5. *Izvestiya*, August 13, 1993.

6. *Izvestiya*, August 17, 1993.

7. This was actually Yeltsin's second attempt to establish a council of heads of republics. The first had been part of a midnight deal between Yeltsin and Khasbulatov when the two were nearly forced to resign by the Ninth Extraordinary Congress of People's Deputies in March of 1993. The democrats actively opposed the idea. They feared, not without reason, that such a council would become a "collective Rasputin" and impose its will on Yeltsin. Surprisingly, even the regional leaders did not support the idea of the council.

8. *Nezavisimaya gazeta*, August 13, 1993.

9. Boris Yeltsin, *The Struggle for Russia* (New York: Times Books, 1994), p. 127.

10. According to Shakhrai, the president felt offended by Khasbulatov's speech and gave the order to speed up the decree on dissolving the parliament, which was prepared in two days by Yuri Baturin. Veronika Kutsyllo, *Zapiski iz Bielovo Doma*, (Notes from the White House) (Moscow: Kommersant Publishing House, 1993), p. 83.

11. On September 25, representatives of the moderate forces—including Valery Zorkin, Aleksandr Vladislavlev, Sergei Glazyev, Vladislav Lipitsky, Grigory Yavlinsky, and Yegor Yakovlev—proposed carrying out early simultaneous elections for the parliament and the president of the Russian Federation on December 12, 1993, but neither the president nor the parliament supported this idea.

12. In negotiations under the mediation of Patriarch Aleksii II, with Khasbulatov and deputies Vladlen Sokolov and Ramazan Abdulatipov representing the White House, a protocol was signed on October 2 according to which troops would be withdrawn from the White House while those guarding the parliament would simultaneously be disarmed. The plan was never implemented. Later a zero option was considered that would have returned to the status before Yeltsin's decree dissolving the parliament; at Khasbulatov's insistence, however, the congress rejected this suggestion. Gleb Pavlovsky, ed., *Khronika trevozhnikh dnyei* (Chronicle of turbulent days) (Moscow: Progress Publishers, 1993), p. 108.

13. Ibid., p. 147.

14. V. Zorkaltsev and A. Podberezkin, eds., *Sovremennaya politicheskaya istoriya Rossii* (Modern Russian Political History) (Moscow: Spiritual Heritage, 1997), p. 668.

15. On September 25, asked by the Public Opinion Fund, "Which side in the conflict should the army support?" 62 percent of respondents answered that the army should remain neutral; only 20 percent answered that the army should support the president; and only 5 percent

answered that the army should support the parliament. Pavlovsky, *Khronika trevozhnikh dnyei*, p. 120.

16. Yeltsin, *The Struggle for Russia*, p. 12. Afterward, one of the members of the militia who had taken part in the events recalled: "It was the militia who opened fire near City Hall [on October 2], simply because they couldn't stand the tension. The commanders had given the order not to let anyone through, even our own people. They must really have been scared, if they didn't even trust their own. Even after Yeltsin had read them the riot act, most of the presidential guard 'Alpha' unit did not go on the attack. They had a hard time getting three crews of volunteers for motorized infantry vehicles [to attack the parliament]. The rest of the Alpha force just waited to see what would happen. The talk among the Alpha force went something like this: 'We could turn our guns 180 degrees [on Yeltsin], and everything would change.' In a word, Fortune simply smiled on Yeltsin." *Obshchaya gazeta*, October 28, 1997.

17. Boris Yeltsin, *Zapiski prezidenta* (Notes of the president) (Moscow: Ogonyok, 1994), p. 18.

18. Yeltsin's cohorts thought up a number of fairly inhumane ways of dealing with their opponents. Democrats Sergei Filatov and Gennady Burbulis suggested using a high-frequency radiation device to blind people, who would thus become incapable of participating in demonstrations. Only technical difficulties prevented them from exercising this option. See Aleksandr Korzhakov, *Ot rassveta do zakata* (From dawn to dusk) (Moscow: Interbook, 1997), pp. 164–65.

19. Zorkaltsev and Podberezkin, *Sovremennaya politicheskaya istoria Rossii* (Modern Russian Political History), p. 664.

20. *Literaturnaya gazeta*, September 15, 1993.

21. On October 7, shortly after the storming of the White House, polls asked, "Who is responsible for blood being spilled in Moscow?" The results were: 8 percent, "the president's team"; 40 percent, "both sides"; 12 percent, "the question was too difficult to answer"; the rest refused to give a response. Pavlovsky, *Khronika trevozhnikh dnyei*, p. 130.

22. *Izvestiya*, September 28, 1994.

23. Robert Sharlett, "The Politics of Constitutional Amendment in Russia," *Post-Soviet Affairs*, vol. 13, no. 3 (Spring 1997), p. 198.

24. Arendt Lijphart, "Constitutional Choices for New Democracies," *Journal of Democracy*, vol. 2, no. 1 (Winter 1991), p. 155.

25. See S. E. Finer, "Adversary Politics and Electoral Reform," in *Adversary Politics and Electoral Reforms*, ed. S. E. Finer (London: Anthony Wigram, 1975), pp. 30–31; and Arend Lijphart, "Constitutional Choices," pp. 156–57.

26. Lijphart, "Constitutional Choices."

27. The Party of Russian Unity and Accord (PRES), formed by Yeltsin crony Sergei Shakhrai, had as its purpose the expression of moderate state values. It did not become a mass party. Yabloko, a more successful

movement, was formed by a trio: Grigory Yavlinsky, a reformer who had attained prominence under Gorbachev; Vladimir Lukin, whose orientation was moderate patriotism and who had served for a time as ambassador to the United States; and Yuri Boldyrev, a St. Petersburg democrat who once headed the main accounting department of the presidential administration and was known for his integrity. Yabloko was able to establish a relatively firm social base.

28. Kostikov, *Roman s prezidentom*, p. 125.

29. Rybkin later became chief of Yeltsin's National Security Council, and in March 1997 he was appointed deputy prime minister for CIS (Commonwealth of Independent States) affairs and later a special presidential representative to the CIS.

30. Formal decision-making blocs called "factions" can be formed in the Duma in two ways: (1) by parties or electoral blocs that win more than 5 percent of the popular vote on the proportional representation (or party-list) ballot; or (2) by any thirty-five deputies within the Duma joining together. In addition, fewer than thirty-five deputies can establish a "deputy group."

31. *Izvestiya*, January 20, 1994.

CHAPTER FIVE

MOSCOW'S CHECHEN WAR: 1994-95

1. *Obshchaya gazeta*, January 16–22, 1997.

2. "Our close team," as Korzhakov called it, included Grachev, Barsukov, Pavel Borodin (head of the office that controlled the economic activity of the presidential administration, known as *Upravdelami*), Interior Minister Viktor Jerin, Soskovets, Shamil Tarpishchev (Yeltsin's tennis coach), and Korzhakov himself. Aleksandr Korzhakov, *Ot rassveta do zakata* (From dawn to dusk) (Moscow: Interbook, 1997), p.155.

3. Ibid., p. 170.

4. *Izvestiya*, January 22, 1994.

5. In the summer of 1994, for example, Aleksandr Solzhenitsyn returned to Russia from the United States, but his return did not provoke much interest. He failed to become a moral arbiter and soon found himself on the margins of Russian political life.

6. At this time, Russia witnessed a series of contract murders of journalists, bankers, and politicians; the perpetrators were never found. This signaled the beginning of a fight among criminal gangs for property and political influence.

7. Yeltsin's main associates—Mikhail Poltoranin, Gennady Burbulis, and Ruslan Khasbulatov—had gone to Chechnya in 1991 to show Moscow's support for Dudayev. The Russian political establishment was at that

time trying to replace the local authorities who were loyal to Gorbachev with "their own people."

8. On April 14, 1994, Yeltsin ordered negotiations with Grozny and the preparation of a treaty with Chechnya. Yet the formation of the Russian delegation took more than three months, and its appointed head was Sergei Shakhrai, whom Dudayev had declared "the enemy of the Chechen people." This precluded any possibility of successful negotiations with the separatists.

9. The FSK hired a considerable number of Russian officers, who had not been paid their regular military salaries for months, to form the core support force for the anti-Dudayev opposition. The FSK promised volunteers an easy and rapid victory and substantial remuneration afterward. It is possible that there were more Russians than Chechens in the anti-Dudayev force. The assault detachment, however, was completely Chechen, headed by two leaders with criminal records, Ruslan Labazanov and Beslan Gantemirov—former allies of Dudayev who had fallen out with him.

10. Minister of Justice Yuri Kalmykov was the only one who opposed sending troops to Chechnya, and he later resigned. The future secretary of the National Security Council, Ivan Rybkin, who in 1996-97 would engage in peace negotiations with Grozny, supported the war. It was later revealed that Defense Minister Pavel Grachev arrived at the council's session with a General Staff report that gave a fairly accurate assessment of the situation in Chechnya; it concluded that a small, victorious war against the republic was out of the question. The report stated that Dudayev was well prepared for resistance; that federal forces could suffer severe losses if they tried to storm the republic; and that a successful assault on Grozny would require at least 20,000 men. (The actual attempt was made with a mere 3,000 federal forces.) However, Grachev did not argue against the war at the Security Council meeting; he completely ignored the work of his General Staff. Oleg Vladykin, "The General staff issued a warning that Grachev ignored," *Obshchaya gazeta*, December 11–17, 1997.

11. *Rossiiskaya gazeta*, December 12, 1994.

12. *Literaturnaya gazeta*, December 21, 1994.

13. Lev Ponomaryov, "The Voluntary Foros of president Yeltsin," *Segodnya*, December 31, 1994 ("Foros" was the location of Gorbachev's ill-fated 1991 vacation). Korzhakov described the circle of those responsible for the Chechen war as follows: "As far as the sources of the war in Chechnya are concerned . . . ask the president's advisors, his chief of staff, Yevgeny Savostyanov, the former deputy chief of the FSK [Federal Counterintelligence Service] who spent so much time in that region, and the members of the Security Council whose responsibilities included drafting recommendations on this question." *Argumenty i fakty*, no. 1, 1995, p. 13.

14. Later it was leaked that nearly all of the leaders of the northern Caucasus republics (with the exception of the Ingush leader Ruslan Aushev)

signed a letter to Yeltsin demanding that he implement "constitutional order" in Chechnya. This gave Yeltsin another justification to begin the military operation against the Chechens.

15. Some Russian observers believed that Grachev was simply a scapegoat for the Chechen war in order to clear Yeltsin. Vladimir Dubnov, "The Most symbolic minister," *Novoye vremya*, no. 7, 1995. According to Korzhakov, however, Grachev bears the main blame for the military actions in Chechnya. Korzhakov writes that he said to Yeltsin, just before the military invasion of Chechnya, "Let us wait a bit. Maybe there is sense in talking to them. A Caucasus war would be a nasty thing, and we could be fighting for the rest of our lives. They offer dialogue. Why hurry?" Korzhakov says the president replied, "No; Pavel Sergeyevich [Grachev] said that he will solve everything." Korzhakov, *Ot rassveta do zakata*, p. 371.

16. *Moskovskiye novosti*, January 12-18, 1994. This has been confirmed by Arkady Volsky, the leader of the Russian delegation at the negotiations with the Chechens, who said that Dudayev even ordered a new suit in anticipation of an invitation to meet with Yeltsin. According to Korzhakov, in 1994 alone Dudayev made eight calls to the presidential administration asking that somebody be sent for negotiations. Yeltsin's associates never informed him about these calls. Korzhakov, *Ot rassveta do zakata*, p. 371. Tatarstan President Mintimir Shaimiyev was convinced that Yeltsin was ready for negotiation with Dudayev and was prepared to make a treaty following the Tatar model. The issue of negotiation with Dudayev was controversial, however, and on March 25 the State Duma adopted a decision that excluded the possibility of direct negotiations with Dudayev and demanded new elections in Chechnya as a condition of any further negotiation.

17. According to Aleksandr Kotenkov, one of Yeltsin's advisors and his representative to the State Duma, "none of those who were active in the opposition in Chechnya at the time could match the influence wielded by Ruslan Khasbulatov, who at the final hour was attempting to bring about the normalization of relations between the republic and Moscow." In Kotenkov's opinion, if the president and his advisers had decided to "place their bets on Khasbulatov, they might have taken control of Grozny without any bloodshed." (Meeting with journalists, summer 1995.) Khasbulatov would probably not have opted for a complete split with Moscow, given his pro-Russian orientation.

18. At the start of the Chechen war, everyone sought the culprits responsible for having left arms in the northern Caucasus, and it turned out that both the last chief of the Soviet Army, Marshall Yevgeny Shaposhnikov, and Russia's Defense Minister Pavel Grachev had been directly involved. Grachev and his deputies had conducted negotiations with Dudayev in 1991 and 1992, trying to reclaim the arms, but had left a huge amount of arms where the Chechen separatists could get at them.

19. Andrei Lapik, "Blood—gold—investment," *Moskovskiy komsomolets*, August 12, 1995.

20. Television interview, NTV channel, January 15, 1995.

21. *Izvestiya*, January 12, 1995.

22. Boris Gromov, quoted in "Plans kept from deputy defense minister," *Moskovskiye novosti*, no. 2, 1995.

23. By the beginning of 1995, the war effort had already undermined the state budget. Yegor Gaidar said in January 1995, "A gradual militarization of society is taking place, and this means a rise in military expenditures. If this goes on, it will put an end to the government's economic program." Yegor Gaidar, "Russia at the crossroads," *Izvestiya*, January 10, 1995.

24. *Komsomolskaya pravda*, January 18, 1995.

25. *Moskovskiye novosti*, January 15–22, 1995.

26. Boris Fyodorov, "The Agony of power," *Izvestiya*, January 10, 1995.

27. Vladimir Lukin, "The Last chance," *Nezavisimaya gazeta*, January 24, 1995.

28. Igor Shafarevich, "The Russian state," *Zavtra*, no. 1, 1995.

29. Lev Sedov, "Boris Yeltsin becomes a victim of Boris Yeltsin," *Segodnya*, April 8, 1995.

30. Gail Lapidus, "The War in Chechnya: Opportunities Missed, Lessons to Be Learned," 1998, manuscript.

31. Andrei Bystricky, "What position should Dudayev abandon?" *Literaturnaya gazeta*, July 5, 1995.

32. *Izvestiya*, July 17, 1995.

33. "The Followers of Basayev against the followers of Dudayev," *Izvestiya*, July 15, 1995.

34. Nikolai Gonchar, "Chechnya should be independent of the Russian budget," *Moskovskiy komsomolets*, July 8, 1995.

35. *Izvestiya*, August 20, 1995.

36. Ibid.

CHAPTER SIX

RUSSIA CHOOSES A NEW PARLIAMENT: 1995

1. Aleksandr Gelman, "An Irresponsible prediction," *Moskovskiye novosti*, July 2–9, 1995.

2. Lev Gudkov, "Tension in the country is becoming unbearable," *Izvestiya*, July 29, 1994.

3. Grigory Yavlinsky, "There is no great tragedy in the splits among the democrats," *Izvestiya*, July 13, 1995.

4. Svetlana Gamova, "Lebed—Life itself will force him to take up politics," *Izvestiya*, July 4, 1995; Andrew Nagorski, "The General Waiting in the Wings," *Newsweek*, February 6, 1995, p. 32.

5. All these political leaders of the second and third echelon belonged to the liberal-democratic persuasion, and some of them had support within the Yeltsin team.

6. Albert Plutnik, "The House Russia wants to build," *Izvestiya*, August 15, 1995.

7. *Moskovskiye novosti*, August 19, 1995.

8. *Izvestiya*, September 9, 1995.

9. Anna Ostapchuk and Yevgeny Krasnikov, "A Time of troubles in the Kremlin," *Moskovskiye novosti*, November 5-12, 1995.

10. *Vyek*, October 27-November 2, 1995.

11. Television interview, December 1995.

12. Michael McFaul, *Russia Between Elections: What Do the 1995 Results Really Mean?* (Washington, D.C.: Carnegie Endowment for International Peace, 1996), p. 3.

13. *Elections of Deputies of the State Duma, 1995: Electoral Statistics* (Moscow: Ves Mir, 1996), pp. 243-44.

14. The war in Chechnya was cited as the main event of the year by 54.7 percent of those queried. The murder of the popular journalist Vladislav Listev (the perpetrator still has not been found) was cited by 23.4 percent; the hostage-taking in Budennovsk by 14.4 percent; the series of aviation disasters, 11.6 percent; terrorist acts in Moscow and other cities, 9.7 percent; and the earthquake in Neftegorsk, 4.7 percent. *Moskovskiy komsomolets*, December 30, 1995.

CHAPTER SEVEN

YELTSIN'S STRUGGLE FOR REVIVAL BEGINS: SPRING 1996

1. *Segodnya*, January 23, 1996.

2. This was considered a key appointment: the head of Yeltsin's 1991 presidential campaign, Gennady Burbulis, had subsequently formed the new Russian government.

3. See Boris Berezovsky interview by Chrystia Freeland, John Thornhill, and Andrew Gowers, "Moscow Group of Seven," *Financial Times*, November 1, 1996.

4. Yeltsin's highest trust was still in Korzhakov, to whom he gave oversight of Chubais's accounts in the presidential campaign; it was also rumored in Moscow that Korzhakov's Security Service had gathered compromising and potentially embarrassing evidence about members of Chubais's team.

5. Yegor Stroyev, "People are tired of confrontation," *Pravda*, January 27, 1996.

6. Sergei Kovalyov, "Open letter to Yeltsin," *Izvestiya*, January 24, 1996.

7. According to Korzhakov, however, Chernomyrdin was collecting signatures in preparation for running for the presidency. He reportedly collected 1.5 million signatures, but his people were trying not to attract much attention. Aleksandr Korzhakov, *Ot rassveta do zakata* (From dawn to dusk) (Moscow: Interbook, 1997), p. 361.

8. *Izvestiya*, January 14, 1996.

9. National News Service, April 2, 1996; polls conducted by VTSIOM.

10. The 16.2 trillion rubles allocated to rebuild Chechnya raised serious questions about government priorities. Resources allocated to health care for 1996 were only 5.5 trillion rubles ($1.07 billion), while just 2.4 trillion rubles ($468 million) were directed toward all cultural activities and the arts. The government allocated the generous sum of about 19 trillion rubles ($3.7 billion) for the security services, and 41 trillion rubles ($8 billion) for the army. According to official accounts, the cost of conducting the Chechen war was about 5 trillion rubles ($1.1 billion) in 1995, and about 11 trillion rubles ($2.15 billion) in 1996. Independent experts, however, estimated the overall cost of the war at not less than 25 trillion rubles ($5.16 billion) at this time. In the end the amount spent on "restoring the economy and social services in Chechnya" in 1994-1997 was about 10.3 trillion rubles ($2.33 billion), according to official data. Andrei Illarionov, "The Chechen balance," *Moskovskiye novosti*, January 28-February 4, 1996; Boris Vishnevsky, "Isn't it time to close a black hole?" *Nezavisimaya gazeta*, December 18, 1997. (All U.S. dollar equivalents are calculated at exchange rates then in effect.)

11. Igor Snegirev, "Money to rebuild Chechnya goes to the fighters," *Izvestiya*, January 26, 1996.

12. Yelena Kapustina, "Seven options on ending the war in Chechnya," *Kommersant-Daily*, February 9, 1996.

13. *Kommersant-Daily*, June 6, 1997.

14. Aushev blamed those he thought had pushed Yeltsin further into war, including Sergei Shakhrai, one of the president's close advisors, and Barsukov, Zavgayev, and Interior Minister Anatoly Kulikov. Aushev and others were convinced that if Yeltsin had invited Dudayev to negotiate in 1994 instead of listening to his hirelings, there would have been no war at all. Ruslan Aushev, "Too many are interested in continuation of the war in Chechnya," *Segodnya*, March 15, 1996.

15. Ivan Stolbovoi, "Yeltsin cannot count on the unconditional support of the army," *Nezavisimaya gazeta*, Military Review, February 24, 1996. In my view, however, military protest actions were likely only in the event of a serious crisis in the government and the emergence of several centers of power, and if social unrest led to demands for restoration of order and the direct involvement of the army. In such a case, the army might well have gotten out of control of the civilian authorities, but open military dissent or attempts to usurp power by a military general were very unlikely.

16. Vladimir Borisenko, "Who is flexing his muscles?" *Moskovskiye novosti,* February 11–18, 1996.

17. Vladimir Smirnov, "Bread and salt for the president, but more salt," in *Kommersant-Daily,* February 14, 1996.

18. Irina Savvateyeva, "The Government's promises cost ten trillion," *Izvestiya,* February 14, 1996.

19. *Segodnya,* February 9, 1996.

20. "How the communists will rectify the sins of the democrats," *Izvestiya,* February 15, 1996.

21. Kuptsov was apparently chosen because he kept campaign documentation in his office, and thus the security services hoped to find evidence of illegal communist activity.

22. In his memoirs, Yeltsin bodyguard Aleksandr Korzhakov describes a conversation with Chernomyrdin that he taped, in which the prime minister showed himself to be an active supporter of canceling the vote. Chernomyrdin said: "That's right; we should ban [the elections]." Later he stated: "We must develop a strategy. If we open a dialogue with the communists, then we should postpone the elections. That is the best option." Korzhakov, *Ot rassveta do zakata,* pp. 368–70.

23. Boris Berezovsky discussed this episode in *Kommersant-Daily,* June 17, 1997.

CHAPTER EIGHT

THE OLD-NEW PRESIDENT OF RUSSIA: SUMMER 1996

1. National News Service, VTSIOM press conference, April 17, 1996.

2. In an anecdote from the 1996 electoral campaign that became quite popular, Yeltsin addresses the electoral rally: "Dear Russians, vote for me and you will have a brand new president!" Somebody from the crowd shouts: "And what if we don't vote for you?" and Yeltsin replies, "Well, then you will have the same old president!"

3. Presidential adviser Georgi Satarov accused the communists of making plans to seize power illegitimately. *Nezavisimaya gazeta,* June 1, 1996. Satarov warned that the official count might be falsified and claimed that the communists were even going to conduct their own parallel vote count, potentially leading to a confrontation worse than the October 1993 standoff between the president and the parliament. He alleged that the communists were preparing military units for deployment either before or after the election, but he refused to identify any sources for this information. Interview with Georgi Satarov, OMRI Daily Digest, May 31, 1996.

4. Natalya Konstantinova, "The Kuban greets Yeltsin with ambivalence," *Nezavisimaya gazeta,* April 17, 1996.

5. Leonid Sedov, "Chances for young Russia," *Moskovskiye novosti*, April 14–21, 1996.

6. National News Service, May 15, 1996.

7. The communists began to talk of "slow and gradual takeover through negotiation with the ruling elite." Representatives of the communist think tank headed by Aleksei Podberezkin declared that "the most important step in this process [of takeover] should be the appointment of Zyuganov to the post of prime minister." This scenario was actively discussed, especially during May and June, and it was supported by Zyuganov himself and other leaders of the Communist Party. Valentin Kuptsov and Anatoly Lukyanov, *Sovremennaya politicheskaya istoriya Rossii*, (Current Political History of Russia) (Moscow: The Spiritual Heritage, 1997), p. 843.

8. Anatoly Lukyanov had been head of the Supreme Soviet under Gorbachev, and all three had been active in the August 1991 putsch.

9. Alexander Frolov, "About tactics," *Sovietskaya Rossiya*, April 20, 1996.

10. National News Service reporting the results of Public Opinion Foundation polls, April 16, 1996.

11. The initiator of the bankers' letter was Boris Berezovsky, who soon would become one of the most controversial figures in Russian politics. *Nezavisimaya gazeta*, April 13, 1996.

12. Another reason for the "Letter from the Thirteen" has been suggested: that it was intended to disorient the Communist Party and thereby slow down its activity.

13. Valery Tishkov, "Seven versions for the sake of one thing," *Moskovskiye novosti*, March 31–April 7, 1996.

14. "There are no winners and can be none," *Nezavisimaya gazeta*, April 18, 1996.

15. *Nezavisimaya gazeta*, June 1, 1996.

16. The anonymous report was supposedly based on the work of agents from the federal security service and the president's security service. The report stated that the communists were preparing to destabilize the social and political situation during the elections and were ready to provoke mass demonstrations against the present government in order to seize power. *Nezavisimaya gazeta*, June 8, 1996.

17. *Izvestiya*, June 6, 1996.

18. Yeltsin's press secretary, Vyacheslav Kostikov, discussed this episode. Vyacheslav Kostikov, *Roman s prezidentom* (Adventures with the president) (Moscow: Vagrius, 1997), p. 110.

19. *Segodnya*, June 13, 1996.

20. The newspapers published the transcript of a conversation between Chubais and presidential assistant Viktor Ilyushin that confirmed their participation in illegal financial dealings during the presidential campaign and their attempts to cover up these dealings, but an investigation of these two by the Prosecutor-General's office was quashed under pressure from the top.

21. Tatyana Malkina and Dmitri Volkov, "Aleksandr Lebed's role in history grows," *Segodnya*, June 21, 1996; Vladimir Mukhin, "They were for Lebed: Will they be for Yeltsin?" *Nezavisimaya gazeta*, June 20, 1996.

311

22. One of those close to Yeltsin said, "The country is on the verge of chaos." Stepan Kiselyov, "Yeltsin rules or manages," *Izvestiya*, September 7, 1996. This was an exaggeration: only the president's team was on the verge of chaos.

23. Michael McFaul has written: "Kremlin officials sent clear signals to republican leaders concerning the consequences of not delivering the vote, eliciting quick responses from several key Russian republics. In Tatarstan, President Shaimiyev tacitly instructed state officials to ensure the 'proper' electoral support for Yeltsin in the second round. Those who had not produced the right result in the first round, including the deputy premier for agricultural affairs, were dismissed between rounds. In Dagestan, Yeltsin's representatives tapped so-called 'authorities' (local Mafia bosses) to mobilize the vote for the president." Michael McFaul, *Russia's 1996 Presidential Election* (Stanford, Calif.: Hoover Institution Press, 1996), p. 68. Aleksei Titkov wrote: "There was talk of possible sanctions (mainly financial) against regions that voted the wrong way. If talk was carried out in Moscow, it was in whispers or vague hints, but it seemed much more threatening out in the regions: One example [of its effect] was the desperate plea by Chuvash President Nikolai Fyodorov to his people before the elections." Aleksei Titkov, "The Regional Campaign between the Rounds," *Russia's Presidential Elections*, Bulletin no. 10, Carnegie Moscow Center, 1996, p. 13.

24. Vladimir Musin, "Russian capitalism eliminated the red threat," *Segodnya*, July 6, 1996.

25. "In Tatarstan it seems very likely that the results of the voting in rural regions were sharply skewed toward Zyuganov, and in Kazan, toward Yeltsin. Supporting this conclusion are the sharply increased levels of voter participation and the radical shifts in voter preferences between the rounds. In Tatarstan and Bashkiria, voter turnout rose to 98-99 percent. In some regions of Bashkiria, 98.3 percent of registered voters turned out [in the second round], and 86 percent cast their ballots for Yeltsin, with the number of votes for Zyuganov falling by a factor of four!" Nikolai Petrov and Aleksandr Sobyanin, *Russia's Presidential Elections*, Bulletin no. 10, Carnegie Moscow Center, 1996, pp. 8–9.

26. Even Chubais himself had said on more than one occasion that he would join "neither the government nor the presidential administration." Elmar Murtatzaev, "Chubais drives the government," *Segodnya*, July 6, 1996.

CHAPTER NINE

THE PRESIDENT RETURNS: THE SECOND HALF OF 1996

1. Chrystia Freeland, John Thornhill, and Andrew Gowers, interview with Boris Berezovsky, "Moscow Group of Seven," *Financial Times*, November 1, 1996. Grigory Yavlinsky said: "The closest person to the president for many months past has been his nurse. Of the politicians, it is his daughter Tatyana, who is assuming an ever more active role in the life of the Kremlin." *Komsomolskaya pravda*, February 19, 1997.

2. Chubais himself began to speak of the benefits of resurrecting the Soviet *nomenklatura*. This caused general confusion. "Much of the party system that was developed during the Soviet period should be brought back," said Chubais. *Izvestiya*, September 18, 1996.

3. *Moskovskiye novosti*, August 11–18, 1996.

4. Television coverage, August 31, 1996.

5. Ibid.

6. Altogether, 1.2 million Russian soldiers took part in the Chechen war; 500,000 people were displaced between December 1994 and August 1996, of whom 140,000 lost their homes and all their possessions. At least 60,000 died—Russia's armed forces and interior troops suffered more than 4,500 dead, more than 1,500 missing, and 798 captured. *Obshchaya gazeta*, November 27–December 3, 1997.

7. *Kommersant-Daily*, September 4, 1996.

8. Gleb Pavlovsky, "The Rearguard battles of the fourth estate," *Nezavisimaya gazeta*, August 10, 1996.

9. Anatoly Kulikov, "Russia's black hole," *Moskovskiye novosti*, August 8-15, 1996.

10. Aleksandr Lebed, "I would prefer to deal with . . . ," *Moskovskiy komsomolets*, September 29, 1996.

11. *Nezavisimaya gazeta*, September 9, 1996; September 29, 1996.

12. The mechanism for financing Yeltsin's election campaign was no secret. It was generally known that the president's close advisers had questionable personal links with a few selected banks. The financial structures close to the government had received an enormous amount of money, through large credits (which, it was understood, would not be paid back), tax breaks, and property auctions. In exchange, they gave Yeltsin campaign assistance. After Yeltsin's victory, the banks demanded and got quid pro quo. Banker Aleksandr Smolensky confirmed in an interview that many banks were rewarded for their participation in Yeltsin's election campaign by receiving special status, access to the external debt market, and Eurobonds as compensation for their election expenses: "This is generally true. There was some preferential treatment," he said. *Nezavisimaya gazeta*, January 30, 1997.

13. Yeltsin claimed that his heart disease had been discovered during a routine examination. He clearly did not want to admit that he had had a heart attack before the second round of voting; this would have required admitting that the public had been misled into electing a president who was too ill to carry out his duties.

14. At a press conference on October 16, Kulikov accused Lebed of "an uncontrollable, maniacal struggle for power" and of preparing a coup. *Nezavisimaya gazeta*, October 18, 1996. Chernomyrdin, however, disagreed cautiously, saying that Lebed was "far from thoughts of *putsch* and rebellion," but that "homegrown Bonapartism is clearly much too evident in the country." At the beginning of 1997, a court upheld

313

Lebed's slander suit against Kulikov, saying that there had been no foundation for Kulikov's accusations.

15. Aslan Maskhadov, television interview, October 19, 1996.

16. Polls asked whether respondents thought that Yeltsin was right to fire Lebed. A minority (22.6 percent) thought he had been correct; they were far outweighed by those (39.6 percent) who disagreed. "The General and the civilians," *Moskovskiye novosti*, October 22–27, 1996.

17. "Godfather of the Kremlin?" *Forbes*, December 30, 1996. Berezovsky knew how to make and to change friends at the right moment. Previously a close friend of Korzhakov, he had switched his allegiance for a while to Chubais, then to Lebed. First he gave money to Lebed's election campaign, then masterminded the conspiracy to remove him, then helped him again in the 1998 gubernatorial campaign in Krasnodarskiy krai. Lebed claimed that Berezovsky had said to him, after the Khasavyurt agreement, "You have destroyed such a good business. It was all going so well. Sure, there was some killing, but there has always been killing and there always will be." Berezovsky's failure to sue Lebed for slander suggested that this was an accurate quotation. Berezovsky has been publicly accused at other times of corruption and even of spying on the presidential family.

18. The operation was conducted by a team of Russian doctors under the direction of Renat Akchurin. The famous American cardiologist Michael DeBakey and two German heart-transplant specialists provided consultation. After the operation, Akchurin said that during the summer, Yeltsin had been "seriously ill, as bad as could be." The chances for success of the operation were judged only 50-50. Although it was a success, the surgeon was reluctant to make any predictions about Yeltsin's ability to continue to carry out his duties. Interview with Akchurin on "Vremya" news program, November 7, 1996.

19. Yevgeny Vasilchuk, "Russia is looking into a bottomless pit of general crisis," *Finansovye Izvestiya*, no. 112, 1996.

20. "The Tragic and secret letter from Yasin to Chernomyrdin," *Nezavisimaya gazeta*, November 26, 1996.

21. Aleksandr Minkin, "To Whom am I obligated?" *Novaya gazeta*, September 23-29, 1996.

22. Presentation by Natalya Rimashevskaya, Director of Socio-Economic Problems of Population, Russian Academy of Sciences, at the Carnegie Moscow Center, February 12, 1997.

23. Natalya Rimashevskaya, Aleksei Ovsyannikov, and Andrei Rudin, "The Social floor and the drama of reality and the reality of the drama," *Literaturnaya gazeta*, December 4, 1996.

24. Research by the Institute of Social Analysis, under the direction of Igor Klyamkin, manuscript, Moscow, 1996.

25. Nikolai Shmelyov, "What do we want—to disappear from the face of the earth?" *Literaturnaya gazeta*, December 4, 1996.

26. Igor Korotenko, "Rodionov on the crisis in the army," *Nezavisimaya gazeta*, October 26, 1996.

27. "Russia: The Social Conception of the Transitional Period and the Conception of the Action Program, Natalya Rimashevskaya and Iosif Diskin," eds. (Moscow: Institute of the Social-Economic Problems of the Population, 1996), pp. 59–60.

28. "On the Fulfillment of the Federal Program for the Development of Education," *Moskovskiy komsomolets*, December 2, 1996. The report stated that "no more than 10 percent of the children attending school are healthy, and the number is as low as 2 percent in some areas."

29. Yuri Levada, "The Year of unpaid debts," *Moskovskiye novosti*, December 29-January 5, 1997.

30. *Moskovskiy komsomolets*, December 26, 1996.

31. *Izvestiya*, December 25, 1996.

32. Data from the Independent Russian Institute of Social and Economic Problems, in *Nezavisimaya gazeta*, January 16, 1997.

33. The labor unions announced that 20 million participated, but Interior Ministry data put the figure at 1.8 million. However, polls indicated that 61 percent of Russia's population approved holding the strike; this enormous number showed a rising potential for social protest.

34. Aleksandr Oslon, "Russia's last year," *Nezavisimaya gazeta*, April 10, 1997.

35. Chubais had brought a number of allies into the Finance Ministry, including Aleksei Kudrin and Sergei Ignatyev, who had worked with him in the presidential administration, and former Deputy Economics Minister Sergei Vasilyev, who became deputy to Vladimir Babichev, head of the government staff. Chubais also grasped for himself, in the best Soviet-era tradition, the all-important job of overseeing the media.

36. According to data collected by the Public Opinion Foundation, 55 percent of those questioned approved bringing Nemtsov into the government; 12 percent did not approve; 26 percent could not answer; and 7 percent did not know anything about his appointment. The poll also showed that 16 percent approved of Chubais's appointment; 59 percent disapproved; 21 percent could not answer; and 4 percent did not know about his appointment. Retaining Chernomyrdin as prime minister was approved by 39 percent and disapproved by 36 percent; another 21 percent of those queried could not answer, and 4 percent did not know. The last two categories suggest that there was a large group in the population that did not want to see any changes in the cabinet or did not care much about them. *Moskovskiy komsomolets*, March 25, 1997.

37. At the end of March, a poll of 1,600 people conducted by VTSIOM yielded the following results: only 12 percent of those polled expected the government's performance to improve; 34 percent thought the reorganization was undertaken just to show that the president was doing something; 19 percent anticipated that the new government would only bring new problems and deprivations; 15 percent did not know anything

about the changes; and 19 percent could not answer. *Nezavisimaya gazeta*, April 10, 1997.

38. *Moskovskiye novosti*, June 22–29, 1997.

39. In answer to the question, "Would Nemtsov be a viable candidate for the presidency in 2000?" only 17.6 percent Russians answered "probably yes"; 30.6 percent said "probably no"; 8.7 percent, "not likely"; and 39.7 percent could not answer. *Moskovskiye novosti*, June 22–29, 1997.

40. *Nezavisimaya gazeta*, April 10, 1997.

41. *Moskovskiye novosti*, June 22–29, 1997.

42. Andrei Fadin, "The young performers order the music," *Obshchaya gazeta*, May 29–June 4, 1997.

CHAPTER TEN

1997: NEW REFORMS OR STAGNATION?

1. *Otkrytaya politika*, July-August 1997, pp. 12–13.

2. Ibid., p. 14.

3. Mikhail Berger, "If you're going to cheat, do it honestly," *Segodnya*, November 21, 1997. The funds involved amounted to hundreds of millions of dollars. Chubais repeatedly promised that the funds would be transferred from Oneximbank, but this did not happen in 1997.

4. In this scheme, suggested by Potanin, the banks lent money to the government and got shares of some enterprises in return.

5. On October 1 the Moscow prosecutor-general's office launched a criminal investigation into former privatization chief Alfred Kokh's activity after allegations that he may have done favors for Oneximbank. Kokh received a $100,000 advance from an obscure Swiss firm associated with Oneximbank for a book yet to be published. *Novaya gazeta*, September 26, 1997; *Financial Times*, September 26, 1997. A Duma commission was created in 1997 to investigate major privatization sales. In May of 1998 the prosecutors again charged Kokh with embezzlement and with misappropriation in a complicated real estate deal.

6. *Nezavisimaya gazeta*, September 13, 1997. This article followed publication of an article by Peter Reddaway in the Washington Post, in which Reddaway said of Chubais: "His questionable integrity and authoritarian ways are fostering anti-Western sentiments in the Russian public and compromising the ability of the U.S. government to maintain viable relations with Russia. We should, in my view, stop funding a corrupt government and stop supporting individuals who are not backed by their own people." Peter Reddaway, "Beware the Russian Reformer," *Washington Post*, August 24, 1997. This article was translated and published by all of the anti-Chubais newspapers in Russia.

7. Television appearance, October 1997.

8. Yeltsin also advocated forcing a company's regional branches to pay corporate taxes in the region where they were based, rather than directly to treasury offices in Moscow.

9. Zyuganov's faction lined up 145 votes (communists and some others) of the 226 needed to pass the no-confidence vote. The measure reportedly had the support of some 250 legislators, including 140 communists, 33 agrarians, 39 members of Nikolai Ryzhkov's Power to the People, and 46 deputies of the liberal Yabloko faction.

10. Yavlinsky justified his determination to demand the government's resignation thus: "Income [now] depends on proximity to power; there is no competition; corruption has become widespread throughout the government; the rights of private property have not been developed and they are not defended; there is no resolution of the issue of ownership of land; capital flight is continuing. All of this has led to a situation where 75 percent of the economy depends on barter and promissory notes; enterprises are up to 600 trillion rubles in debt; real unemployment is at least 20 percent; tax collection is less than 50 percent of its target; and there is a crisis in the state's budget." Yabloko demanded an audit of Gazprom and other large monopolies, as well as the introduction of a treasury system, the conduct of public auctions of state property, and support for small and medium-size businesses. *Nezavisimaya gazeta*, October 15, 1997.

11. *Kommersant-Daily*, October 16, 1997.

12. *Kommersant-Daily*, October 18, 1997.

13. During the summer, the Duma and the Federation Council had overridden a presidential veto of the law on government, but Yeltsin refused to sign it. Now the president agreed to discuss a law that would increase the Duma's influence over the government's composition, and in December Yeltsin would sign a draft of that law.

14. VTSIOM survey, *Obshchaya gazeta*, October 16–22, 1997. According to a Moscow survey, in response to the question, "If the Duma votes no confidence in the government, what should the president do?" 6.9 percent of respondents said that he should force the government to resign; 13.5 percent said he should dissolve the Duma; 19.9 percent said the president himself should resign. Other responses accounted for 15.3 percent, with 45.2 percent unable to answer at all. "Sluzhba mneniye" (Opinion survey), *Moskovskiye novosti*, October 19–26, 1997.

15. Mikhail Gorshkov, "Autumn concerns for Russians," *Nezavisimaya gazeta*, October 17, 1997.

16. Gennady Zyuganov, press conference in the State Duma, October 14, 1997.

17. Konstantin Drozdov, "Zyuganov inserts himself into power," *Kommersant-Daily*, November 6, 1997.

18. Dmitri Furman, "Every nation gets the opposition it deserves," *Obshchaya gazeta*, October 23–29, 1997.

19. *Zavtra*, no. 43, 1997.

20. Yeltsin's game did not end here. At the beginning of November, on the birthday of Duma Speaker and opposition leader Gennady Seleznyov, Yeltsin suddenly arrived at the Duma and gave Seleznyov an award and kissed him several times before the television cameras. It was a real "kiss of death" for Seleznyov. At the award ceremony, other opposition leaders could be seen chatting amiably with Yeltsin, and even with the hated Chubais.

21. *Kommersant-Daily*, November 6, 1997.

22. According to newspaper reports, the young reformers, who had just emerged from seeing Yeltsin, got into a skirmish with Tatyana Dyachenko and Valentin Yumashev, who had rushed to the scene. Yumashev allegedly shouted at the deputy prime ministers, "This is your last mistake!" *Kommersant-Daily*, "Transfer to another post," November 6, 1997. See also "The President has only one Chubais," *Obshchaya gazeta*, November 13-19, 1997. This was not, however, the first attempt to remove Berezovsky. The two first deputy prime ministers had gone to Yeltsin with the same request in September. At that time Yeltsin had announced before television cameras that he had no plans to fire Berezovsky. This time he could not hold out. Dmitri Pinsker, "Chubais sneaks in," *Itogi* (magazine), November 11, 1997, pp. 12–13.

23. *Obshchaya gazeta*, October 23–29, 1997.

24. Tatyana Koshkareva and Rustam Narzikulov, "Bureaucrats still lured by the literary life," *Nezavisimaya gazeta*, November 13, 1997.

25. Aleksandr Minkin, "Ekho Moskvy," November 13, 1997.

26. *Itogi* (NTV program), November 25, 1997.

27. *Itogi* (magazine), November 30, 1997, p. 14.

28. Anatoly Kostyukov, "The Rout of the Chubais anti-party group," *Obshchaya gazeta*, November 20–26, 1997.

29. *Nezavisimaya gazeta*, October 16, 1997.

30. *Nezavisimaya gazeta*, October 21, 1997.

31. Ibid.

32. Domestic production of televisions in 1997 was 5 percent of the 1991 levels; washing machines, 10 percent; tractors, 8 percent; knitwear and shoes, 10 percent. Whereas Stalin's experiment in collectivization had led to the loss of 16.2 million head of cattle, Russia's loss in 1992-96 was 19.6 million head. Nikolai Petrakov, "Nice smiles in a bad game," *Obshchaya gazeta*, November 13–19, 1997.

33. *Moskovskiye novosti*, August 12–19, 1997. According to economist Igor Birman, per capita production in Russia was not 6–7 times lower than in the United States, as official data claimed, but 12–13 times lower. If he is correct, then per capita consumption in Russia during this period was on the level of the Congo, Cameroon, and Bolivia. Grigori Khanin's figures show that production assets in Russia had decreased by 20 percent. In 1992-97 they were declining by 5 percent yearly. On the whole, according to Khanin's figures, Russian GDP had declined by 49 percent in 1991-96, while official statistics put the figure at 41 percent. Grigory

Khanin, "Misleading numbers?" *Moskovskiye novosti*, September 28–October 5, 1997.

34. *Kommersant-Daily*, November 29, 1997.

35. Wage arrears in November amounted to 12.8 trillion rubles ($2.15 billion), while nonpayments of pensions and other social funds totaled 13.5 trillion rubles, or $2.25 billion.

36. *Nezavisimaya gazeta*, December 6, 1997.

37. Yavlinsky's position was that the budget was unrealistic. According to Yavlinsky, the world financial crisis was partly responsible for the difficulties, but there were internal reasons as well, including: "the rise in foreign debt; the investment of short-term capital and a drop in tax revenue; and stagnation in production." Yavlinsky quoted in "Half of Russia's enterprises are in a critical situation," *Novaya gazeta*, December 8–14, 1997.

38. *Kommersant-Daily*, December 20, 1997.

39. *Obshchaya gazeta*, December, 11–17, 1997; *Moskovskiye novosti*, December 7–14, 1997.

40. Yuri Levada, "Ten years in the mirror of public opinion," *Moskovskiye novosti*, December 28–January 4, 1998.

CHAPTER 11

YELTSIN STRUGGLES FOR A RESURRECTION: 1998

1. *Itogi* (magazine), March 3, 1998, p. 14.

2. *Izvestiya*, January 24, 1998.

3. *Izvestiya*, January 23, 1998.

4. *Obshchaya gazeta*, February 26–March 4, 1998.

5. *Profil*, no. 2 (1998), p. 13.

6. *Kommersant-Daily*, March 24, 1998.

7. *Kommersant-Vlast*, March 31, 1998, p. 10.

8. Among the possible reasons for Yeltsin's increased dissatisfaction, several analysts noted Chernomyrdin's decision to privatize one of the best morsels of state property, Rosneft, in a way that would benefit Potanin and Oneximbank and be contrary to the interests of Boris Berezovsky, who had much influence on Tatyana Dyachenko. However, the role of Berezovsky in all this was clearly exaggerated by Berezovsky himself, who did not learn about the prime minister's dismissal until after it had taken place.

9. *Moskovskiye novosti*, March 29–April 15, 1998. Aleksei Arbatov wrote, "The president has again demonstrated his proclivity for impulsive, abrupt actions, creating an unforeseen crisis situation, in which decisions are improvised on the basis of Yeltsin's intuition and tendency to push

ahead recklessly, not leaving any moves to spare, not thinking about the consequences of his actions." *Nezavisimaya gazeta*, April 22, 1998.

10. *Itogi* (magazine), March 31, 1998, p. 21.

11. NTV, April 16, 1998.

12. *Ekspert*, April 20, 1998, p. 8.

13. *Moscow Times*, April 30, 1998.

14. *Kommersant-Daily*, May 7, 1998. Unified Energy Systems (UES) appointed Chubais, even though the Audit Chamber had already informed the prosecutor-general that many violations were involved in this nomination.

15. *Izvestiya*, May 12, 1998.

16. *Kommersant-Vlast*, April 28, 1998, p. 10.

17. *The Economist*, May 23, 1998, p. 65.

18. Chubais was restored to the rank of deputy prime minister, but he did not formally join the government, and he retained his job as head of Unified Energy Systems. Yeltsin said Chubais would remain in this role temporarily to help Russia win "certain support." Television interview, *Sevodnya* (NTV news program), June 10, 1997.

19. Federal News Service, June 23, 1998.

20. "The root of the problem is Russia's finances, which have been unhealthy for some time. This has increasingly led investors to withdraw, putting pressure on the ruble and leaving Russia no choice but to raise the interest rates. But they are caught in a vicious circle. Each rise in the interest rate increases their debt service payments and further worsens the public finances." *Financial Times*, May 28, 1998.

21. Among the revenue-raising measures it rejected were a comprehensive 5 percent sales tax, a value-added tax (VAT), a land tax, and increases in the personal income tax.

22. Jeffrey Sachs, director of the Harvard Institute for International Development, was an economic adviser to the Russian government from 1991 to 1994. Jeffrey D. Sachs, "Rule of the Ruble," *New York Times*, June 6, 1998.

23. Ibid. Former Polish Finance Minister Grzegorz Kolodko came to a similar conclusion: "This bailout would only create social dissension without addressing Russia's fundamental problems. Russia needs good advice. But the international financial community is not able to provide it. There is an inherent conflict of interest. Russia and the world must understand that the interests of, say, Siberian miners and short-term portfolio investors are even farther apart than the interests of a fish and a fisherman." *New York Times*, July 7, 1998.

24. *Nezavisimaya gazeta*, July 14, 1998.

25. *Financial Times*, July 23, 1998.

26. Pyotr Rushailo, "Fear has big eyes," *Vlast*, August 25, 1998, pp. 12–13.

27. Interfax, August 18, 1998.

28. Igor Klochkov, "Abdication of Boris," *Vlast,* September 1, 1998.

29. *Izvestiya,* August 25, 1998.

30. *Moscow Times,* August 25, 1998.

31. *Izvestiya,* August 25, 1998.

32. *Kommersant-Daily,* August 25, 1998.

33. *Ekspert,* August 31, 1998, p. 11; *Financial Times,* August 26, 1998.

34. But not everyone thought Yeltsin was ready to bow out or to take a back seat. A majority of ordinary Russians, when asked whether they believed Yeltsin was going to retire, were skeptical: 85 percent said no; 8 percent, yes; and 7 percent were not sure. As reported in *Obshchaya Gazeta,* in a poll conducted by VTSIOM, September 10-16, 1998.

35. *Segodnya,* August 28, 1998; *Kommersant-Daily,* August 27, 1998.

36. *Komsomolskaya pravda,* August 27, 1998.

37. *Kommersant-Daily,* August 29, 1998.

38. *Washington Post,* August 30, 1998.

39. *Itogi* (television program), August 30, 1998.

40. RTR News, September 1, 1998.

41. According to some observers, Zyuganov and Luzhkov on August 30 reached a bargain, and this was one more explanation for the sudden refusal of the communists to sign the agreement and to support Chernomyrdin. Igor Malashenko, "The line of defense in case of attack," *Obshchaya gazeta,* September 17–23, 1998.

42. *Kommersant-Daily,* October 6, 1998.

CHAPTER 12

BORIS YELTSIN AND THE FUTURE OF DEMOCRACY IN RUSSIA

1. Vladimir Lenin, "Iz dnyevnika publitsista" (From the diary of a journalist), *Collected Works* (Moscow: Politizdat, 1949), vol. 25, p. 271.

2. Boris Yeltsin, *Zapiski prezidenta* (Notes of the president) (Moscow: Ogonyok, 1994), p. 347.

3. Ibid., p. 14.

4. Boris Yeltsin, *The Struggle for Russia* (New York: Times Books, 1994), pp. 205, 288.

5. "Boris Yeltsin is not always good in the process of governance. . . . He often is too straightforward and impatient precisely when patience, detailed analysis of all arguments, and a gradual approach are necessary. His character often turned out to be harmful for the national interests. Foreign leaders who knew Boris Nikolayevich well used his weaknesses, forcing him to make one-sided concessions . . . often . . . during receptions." Yegor Gaidar, "Days of Defeat and Victories," *Itogi* (magazine), November 5, 1996.

6. Yeltsin, *Zapiski prezidenta*, p. 14.

7. Ibid., p. 153.

8. Ralph Waldo Emerson, "History," *Essays: First Series* (1841).

9. Former dissident Lev Timofeyev writes: "Corruption in Russia has everywhere become the norm in social behavior. That is, one no longer speaks of violation of the standards, but the emergence of a shadowy set of norms—not just corruption, but mega-corruption!" Lev Timofeyev, "A New theory of socialism," *Moskovskiye novosti*, December 8–15, 1996. The experience of other countries—Latin America, for example—demonstrates that corruption is not a uniquely Russian invention or tradition.

10. In fact, in every post-communist state, the old political establishment has been preserved at least partially. This succession, according to Polish analyst Jacek Wasilewski, "facilitated the relatively peaceful transition from communism to a post-communist regime," since democracy "did not represent a direct threat to the previous elite." Wasilewski's analysis of the arrangement of personnel in 1988 and 1993 in Hungary, Poland, and Russia led him to conclude that one-third of those who were in leadership positions in 1988 remained in approximately the same positions in 1993. In several sectors the continuity was even higher: in Russia, 50.7 percent of the economic elite, 48.2 percent of the political elite, and 40.8 percent of the cultural elite remained the same. A significant part of the new elite in 1993 had previously held other, lower-ranking *nomenklatura* positions: 49 percent in Russia, 34.4 percent in Hungary, and 26 percent in Poland. The ratio of "victors" (those who entered the new elite) and "defeated" (those who lost their positions by 1993) was 86:10 in Russia, 23:10 in Poland, and 22:10 in Hungary. In Poland and Hungary, continuity was greater than in Russia because a considerable number of representatives of the previous elite groups returned to power after the parliamentary elections in Poland in 1993 and in Hungary in 1994, and after Poland's 1995 presidential elections. See Jacek Wasilewski, "Communist Nomenklatura in Post-Communist Eastern Europe: Winners or Losers of Transformation?," Polish Academy of Sciences, 1995. In the Czech Republic and Slovakia, half of the current parliamentary and governmental elites are people who had *nomenklatura* positions during the communist period. John Higley, Judith Rullberg, and Jan Pakulski, "The Persistence of Post-Communist Elites," *Journal of Democracy*, vol. 7, no. 2 (April 1996), p. 136.

11. "Exploitation of oil eventually encourages a type of oil-based social contract among organized interests, but it does so at high cost. The advantages of this arrangement lie in the prolonged periods of regime stability that oil exploitation can foster . . . but this regime stability is based on a predatory relationship with the state and the perpetuation of oil dependency." Terry Lynn Karl, *The Paradox of Plenty* (Berkeley, Los Angeles, and London: University of California Press, 1998), pp. 57–58. The same may be said of gas dependency.

12. Tatyana Kutkovets and Igor Klyamkin, "Russian Ideas," *Nezavisimaya gazeta*, January 16, 1997.

13. Simon Kordonsky has written that the "Russian economy may be called a market economy only in a very narrow sense, if one compares it to world markets. The corruption of the apparatus, widespread theft by entrepreneurs and by ordinary people, barter and money substitutes: these are not temporary phenomena, but systemic features of the Russian administrative market that replaced the Soviet administrative market." Simon Kordonsky, "How Russia is built," *Pushkin*, vol. 3, no. 9 (June 1, 1998), p. 14.

14. Around four-fifths of Russian privatized companies are owned by insiders, mainly directors. A mere 11 percent are majority-owned by outside investors. Only a quarter of privatized enterprises have restructured enough to achieve a significant impact on their sales and output. *The Economist*, July 12, 1997, p. 12.

15. In the words of Yevgeny Saburov, first deputy prime minister of the first Russian cabinet: "Our faith in privatization by the *nomenklatura* has not been justified. In the majority of cases, those managers could not fulfill their responsibility for the property. In essence, it was their function to be supervisors rather than real managers. Being a manager in a market economy is an entirely different thing." Yevgeny Saburov, "The Face of Russian capitalism," *Segodnya*, January 26, 1996.

16. Elections in Russia are to some extent an expression of "electoralism," merely the attempt to produce the surface manifestations of a democratic polity such as parties, electoral laws, contested campaigns, and the like. "Elections in themselves do not constitute democracy," writes Terry Karl; they can also impede democratization, as, for instance, when they simply "rectify existing power arrangements." Terry Karl, "Imposing Consent? Electoralism vs. Democratization in El Salvador," in *Elections and Democratization in Latin America, 1980-1985*, ed. Paul W. Drake and Eduardo Silva (San Diego: University of California Press, 1986), p. 34. Michael McFaul identifies the Russian political system as an "electoral democracy" and notes that "electoral democracies are not liberal democracies; elections are only one component of a fully consolidated democracy." Michael McFaul, "Democracy Unfolds in Russia," *Current History*, vol. 96, no. 612 (October 1997), p. 319. Fareed Zakaria introduces the term "illiberal democracy" for cases where the political system is marked by elections but lacks constitutional liberalism. Fareed Zakaria, "The Rise of Illiberal Democracy," *Foreign Affairs*, vol. 76, no. 6 (November–December 1997), pp. 22–23.

17. Russia's political pluralism is consistent with "state corporatism" but not with "societal corporatism," in the terms of Juan J. Linz and Alfred Stepan, *Problems of Democratic Transition: Southern Europe, South America, Post-Communist Europe* (Baltimore and London: Johns Hopkins University Press, 1996), p. 45.

18. Guillermo O'Donnell, "Delegative Democracy," *Journal of Democracy*, vol. 5, no. 1 (January 1994), pp. 59–62.

19. This term was used to explain the peculiarities of Russia's current regime by Igor Klyamkin and Lilia Shevtsova, "This powerful powerless power," *Nezavisimaya gazeta*, June 24–25, 1998.
20. Franklin D. Roosevelt, radio address, April 7, 1932.

INDEX

Abdulatipov, Ramazan, 302 n12
Administration for Territorial
    Affairs, 68
Afanasyev, Yuri, 10, 15, 32, 33, 90
Agrarian Party of Russia, 92, 145,
    147, 149
Agrarian Union, 83, 88
Agreement on Social Accord, 106
Aksiuchits, Viktor, 35, 40
Alfa Bank, 219
All-Russian Union of Industrialists
    and Entrepreneurs, 16
Andropov, Yuri, 6
Anpilov, Viktor, 35, 103, 149, 188
Åslund, Anders, 46, 297 n6
Astafyev, Mikhail, 35, 40
Aushev, Ruslan, 166, 309 n14
Aven, Pyotr, 57, 161, 295 n33
AvtoVAZ, 299 n7–8
Avturkhanov, Umar, 111, 145

Baburin, Sergei, 34, 35, 40, 119,
    147, 173
Baklanov, Oleg, 293 n14
Baltic republics, 9, 12
Barkashov, Aleksandr, 119
Barsukov, Mikhail, 99, 107, 158,
    304 n2, 309 n14
    Chechen war and, 112
    dismissal of, 187
    in presidential elections (1996),
        159, 187
Basayev, Shamil, 123, 209–10
Bashkortostan, 56, 77
Batkin, Leonid, 32
Baturin, Yuri, 121, 282, 302 n7
Belarus, 12, 173
Belovezhskiy Forest agreement,
    12–13, 171–72, 173
Belyaev, Sergei, 147
Berezovsky, Boris, 220, 311 n7,
    314 n17, 318 n22, 319 n8
    Chernomyrdin and, 259
    CIS appointment, 242, 244

    conflict with "young reformers,"
        218, 219, 255
    political significance, 161,
        202–03
    removal from office, 227–28
    Security Council appointment,
        202
    Yeltsin and, 249, 255
Berger, Mikhail, 217–18
Black Tuesday (1994), 110
Bocharov, Mikhail, 295 n29
Bogomolov, Oleg, 26, 46
Boiko, Maksim, 228
Boldyrev, Yuri, 303–04 n27
book-publishing scandal, 228–29
Borodin, Pavel, 241
Bovin, Aleksandr, 243
Brazauskas, Vitauskas, 285
Brezhnev, Leonid, 6
Bryntsalov, Vladimir, 175
Buddenovsk hostage crisis,
    123–24, 125
Bulgak, Vladimir, 244
Bunich, Pavel, 26
Burbulis, Gennady, 19, 20, 24,
    42–44, 51, 57, 81–82, 90, 282,
    294–95 n26, 295 n33, 297 n6,
    303 n18, 308 n2
    Gaidar and, 23
    Rutskoi and, 296 n43
    Yeltsin and, 17, 27–28, 296 n42
bureaucrats
    after elections of 1993, 103
    influence in Yeltsin presidency,
        82
Burtin, Yuri, 32, 117

Camdessus, Michel, 171
Charitonov, Nikolai, 147
Chechen war
    after presidential elections
        (1996), 197
    casualties, 116–17, 152, 313 n6
    economic burden, 307 n23,
        309 n10

Russian economic crisis of 1998
and, 247, 250
Commonwealth of Independent
States, 12, 13
Berezovsky appointment, 242
communist-nationalist alliance,
34–35, 47–49
Communist Party of the Russian
Federation (KPFR), 68, 124,
125, 209
after presidential elections
(1996), 196
Chernomyrdin no-confidence
vote (1998), 222, 223
in Chernomyrdin nomination as
prime minister (1998), 258,
259, 261
in Congress of Civil and Patriotic
Forces, 34–35
current status, 2, 290
Duma politics, 161–62
in first reform period, 8, 24
ideological differences within,
177–78
in Kiriyenko confirmation, 241
in October compromise (1998),
225, 226–27
in parliamentary elections
(1993), 103
in parliamentary elections
(1995), 134–36, 145, 147,
149, 150, 151, 188, 191–92
planning for Yeltsin succession,
221–22
in presidential elections (1996),
163–64, 169–70, 171, 177–80,
310 n3, 311 n16
presidential elections (2000)
and, 267
renunciation of Belovezhskiy
Forest agreement, 171–72
in September "revolution"
(1993), 83
Yeltsin and, 276
Communist Party of the Soviet
Union
dissolution of, 11

in dissolution of Soviet state,
5–6
Congress of Civil and Patriotic
Forces, 34–35
Congress of Left Democratic
Forces, 68
Congress of People's Deputies, 9,
15, 22, 40
executive branch power and, 22,
58, 59–60
political significance, 40
see also parliament, before 1993
elections
Congress of Russian Communities
(KRO)
ideological basis, 133–34
parliamentary elections (1995),
133, 134, 150
constitution
Duma power structure, 93, 151
electoral law, 144–45
executive branch appointments,
59–60
on incapacitation of president,
208
individual civil rights, 287
referendum (April, 1993),
59–60, 66, 67–69, 71, 73–74
referendum (December, 1993),
92, 93–95, 96, 98–99
reform (1997), 208–09
Constitutional Conference (1993),
76–78, 98
Constitutional Court, 37, 95,
298 n24
on Yeltsin's special regime
decree, 71–72
corruption, 36, 52–53, 291,
316 n6, 322 n9
book-publishing scandal,
228–29, 316 n3, 316 n5
power structure of Duma and, 93
Council of Heads of Republics, 81,
122
coup attempt (1991), 139
amnesty, 104
democrats in, 16
political outcomes, 11–12, 14

327

ABOUT THE AUTHOR

LILIA SHEVTSOVA is a senior associate in the Carnegie Endowment's Russian and Eurasian Program, dividing her time between the Endowment's Washington offices and its Carnegie Moscow Center. She is one of Russia's best known and most respected political analysts and writers and is a frequent commentator for both Russian and Western media.

Before joining the Carnegie Endowment, where she co-chairs the project on Russian domestic politics and political institutions, Dr. Shevtsova was deputy director of the Moscow Institute of International Economic and Political Studies of the Russian Academy of Sciences, a guest scholar at the Woodrow Wilson International Center for Scholars, and a visiting professor at Cornell University and at the University of California at Berkeley. She is a recipient of the Russian Union of Journalists' award for best political commentary and is the author of numerous books and articles on the problems of communism, the role of the church in Eastern Europe, and the paradoxes of the Russian transformation.

ABOUT THE CARNEGIE ENDOWMENT

The Carnegie Endowment for International Peace was established in 1910 in Washington, D.C., with a gift from Andrew Carnegie. As a tax-exempt operating (not grant-making) foundation, the Endowment conducts programs of research, discussion, publication, and education in international affairs and U.S. foreign policy. The Endowment publishes the quarterly magazine, *Foreign Policy*.

Carnegie's senior associates—whose backgrounds include government, journalism, law, academia, and public affairs—bring to their work substantial first-hand experience in foreign policy. Through writing, public and media appearances, study groups, and conferences, Carnegie associates seek to invigorate and extend both expert and public discussion on a wide range of international issues, including worldwide migration, nuclear nonproliferation, regional conflicts, multilateralism, democracy-building, and the use of force. The Endowment also engages in and encourages projects designed to foster innovative contributions in international affairs.

In 1993, the Carnegie Endowment committed its resources to the establishment of a public policy research center in Moscow designed to promote intellectual collaboration among scholars and specialists in the United States, Russia, and other post-Soviet states. Together with the Endowment's associates in Washington, the center's staff of Russian and American specialists conducts programs on a broad range of major policy issues ranging from economic reform to civil-military relations. The Carnegie Moscow Center holds seminars, workshops, and study groups at which international participants from academia, government, journalism, the private sector, and nongovernmental institutions gather to exchange views. It also provides a forum for prominent international figures to present their views to informed Moscow audiences. Associates of the center also host seminars in Kiev, Ukraine, on an equally broad set of topics.

The Endowment normally does not take institutional positions on public policy issues. It supports its activities primarily from its own resources, supplemented by nongovernmental, philanthropic grants.

Carnegie Endowment
for International Peace
1779 Massachusetts Ave., N.W.
Washington, D.C. 20036
Tel: 202-483-7600
Fax: 202-483-1840
E-mail: carnegie@ceip.org
Web Page: www.ceip.org

Carnegie Moscow Center
Ul. Tverskaya 16/2
7th Floor
Moscow 103009
Tel: 7-095-935-8904
Fax: 7-095-935-8906
E-mail: info@carnegie.ru
Web Page: www.carnegie.ru

345